SCANDAL AT BIZARRE
RUMOR AND REPUTATION IN JEFFERSON'S AMERICA

CYNTHIA A. KIERNER

For the shore kids

Zachary, Anders,
Danielle,
Brett, and Alison

SCANDAL AT BIZARRE
© Cynthia Kierner, 2004.

First published in 2004 by
PALGRAVE MACMILLAN®
175 Fifth Avenue, New York, N.Y. 10010 and
Houndmills, Basingstoke, Hampshire, England RG21 6XS
Companies and representatives throughout the world

PALGRAVE MACMILLAN is the global academic imprint of the Palgrave Macmillan division of St. Martin's Press, LLC and of Palgrave Macmillan Ltd. Macmillan® is a registered trademark in the United States, United Kingdom and other countries. Palgrave is a registered trademark in the European Union and other countries.

ISBN 1–4039–6115–8 hardback

Library of Congress Cataloging-in-Publication Data

Kierner, Cynthia A., 1958–
    Scandal at Bizarre: rumor and reputation in Jefferson's America / Cynthia A. Kierner.
        p. cm.
    Includes bibliographical references and index
    ISBN 1–4039–6115–8 (alk. paper)
        1. Randolph family. 2. Morris, Anne Cary Randolph, 1774–1837.
3. Randolph, Richard, 1770–1796. 4. Scandals—Virginia—Farmville Region—History—18th century. 5. Gentry—Virginia—Farmville Region—Biography. 6. Farmville Region (Va.)—Biography. 7. Jefferson, Thomas, 1743–1826—Family. 8. Virginia—Social life and customs—18th century. 9. Virginia—Social life and customs—19th century. 10. United States—Social life and customs—1783–1865. I. Title.

F234.F1854 2004
975.5'63202—dc22   2004044735

A catalogue record for this book is available from the British Library.

Design by Newgen Imaging Systems (P) Ltd, Chennai, India

First edition: December 2004

10 9 8 7 6 5 4 3 2 1

Printed in the United States of America.

CONTENTS

Maps and Figures

Maps

Figures

PREFACE

In 1991, I found some arresting letters in the collections of the Virginia Historical Society. While many letters that plantation mistresses addressed to their female confidantes exuded fatigue and loneliness born of domestic drudgery and rural isolation, these letters were particularly poignant. For more than a decade, from 1793 until at least 1806, Judith Randolph corresponded regularly with her friend and cousin Mary Harrison. In her letters, Judith repeatedly bemoaned her wretched health, unending toil, money problems, and, above all, her utter and complete desolation and loneliness. By 1798, at the age of twenty-six, Judith was convinced that she would never again be happy—and apparently she never was. What, I wondered, was the story behind this seemingly immutable and debilitating sadness that was still, two centuries later, so strikingly palpable?

I soon learned that Judith Randolph was the wife of Richard Randolph of Bizarre, who was widely believed to have had sexual relations with his sister-in-law Nancy—Judith's sister—which resulted in her pregnancy. Rumor had it that Richard either helped Nancy to conceal her condition or, worse still, to terminate her pregnancy. In April 1793, Richard Randolph of Bizarre appeared in court to defend himself against the charge of "feloniously murdering a child delivered of the body of Nancy Randolph or [being] accessory to the same." Known then and now as the "Bizarre scandal," this episode left a surprisingly scant paper trail: a few ambiguous or oblique references in private letters, some lawyer's notes, a brief entry in the order books of the local county court. Nevertheless, as Judith Randolph's letters suggest, the scandal cast a long shadow over the lives of its principals.

A defining moment in the lives of the Randolphs, the Bizarre scandal was also a revealing episode in the public and private worlds of their contemporaries. This book situates the Bizarre scandal within the wider social and cultural context of "Jefferson's" America. Thomas Jefferson was, in fact, related to the Randolphs—his mother was a Randolph and his favorite daughter, Martha, married Judith's oldest brother—and he himself played an important supporting role in the story that follows. More important still, Jefferson's lifetime coincided with and in some ways was emblematic of the transformation of Virginia and America in the late eighteenth and early nineteenth centuries. Born in 1743 and dying in 1826, Jefferson's life spanned the heyday of gentry dominance in colonial Virginia, the political and economic changes of the revolutionary years, and the partisan and sectional tensions of the early republican era. These changes, in turn, provided the context in which the Bizarre scandal unfolded in 1792–93, as well as that in which Virginians and others subsequently retold the Bizarre story and reinterpreted its significance.

Debt pervaded the world of Virginia planters, as it does that of authors. My own greatest debt is to Deborah Gershenowitz, who was enthusiastic about this project from the start. Her insights, both as an editor and a historian, helped me to refine my ideas about the historical significance of the Bizarre scandal while telling the Randolphs' story in a way that would be accessible to general readers. Debbie's comments on early drafts of my chapters vastly improved the final product. Brendan O'Malley took on this project as editor in midstream. His keen attention to detail and probing questions clarified my text, while his encouragement to be more "cinematic" enlivened my prose.

Several scholars have commented on my manuscript as it evolved, for which I am truly grateful. Jon Kukla offered good advice about writing the book proposal. Peter Bardaglio and Michele Gillespie read the proposal and some early chapters. Their comments and suggestions, which guided my revisions, were extremely helpful. My colleagues at the University of North Carolina at Charlotte have discussed pieces of this book at History Department brown bag seminars for the past four years at least, always asking incisive questions and offering constructive criticism. Thomas E. Buckley, S.J., read some chapters and shared his knowledge of marriage, divorce, and politics in post-revolutionary Virginia.

Others have generously shared insights and information from their own work, for which I am most appreciative. In the project's early stages, Diane Miller Sommerville and J. Jefferson Looney alerted me to the existence of a previously neglected cache of Randolph papers at the American Philosophical Society. Brent Tarter offered helpful advice on using eighteenth-century Virginia court records, provided me with some old Virginia maps, and, best of all, sent me copies of some recently discovered papers pertaining to the case of *Commonwealth v. Randolph*. Sara Bearss shared her vast knowledge of Virginia history on demand, responding promptly to my frequent, frantic emails. Lee Shepard answered many questions about courts and law in early Virginia. Sharla Fett, John Riddle, and Marie Jenkins Schwartz supplied information on herbal remedies and abortifacients. Anne Boylan, Alan Pell Crawford, Melvin Ely, Joanne Freeman, Mary Hackett, Sarah Hand Meacham, Holly Cowan Shulman, Herbert Sloan, and Mariam Touba all responded graciously to my queries, which, in every case, were entirely unsolicited.

In the course of researching this book, I also benefited from the assistance of present-day residents of the Randolphs' erstwhile homes. Addison Baker Thompson and Sue Thompson, the current residents of Tuckahoe, have preserved this eighteenth-century Randolph mansion and opened it to visitors. Beth Roane gave my Virginia friends—Howson, Betsy, and Mary Hill Cole—and me a superb tour of the house and grounds at Tuckahoe. Sue W. Seawell of the Cumberland County Historical Society answered my questions about Bizarre and its environs. At the Cumberland County Circuit Court Office, Carol Blanchetti, Kate Spry, and Ruby Stout were welcoming and helpful. At the Earl Gregg Swem Library of the College of William and Mary, Margaret Cook efficiently filled my Inter-Library Loan requests for countless reels of Tucker-Coleman Papers and kindly informed me that the library's collections also included a separate collection of Nancy Randolph letters. The Reverend Martha Overall, pastor of St. Ann's Episcopal Church of Morrisania, New York, helped me to obtain photographs of her church, which was named for Nancy Randolph, and of Nancy's grave, which is located inside.

This project received financial support from the University of North Carolina at Charlotte and from the Virginia Historical Society. A faculty grant from UNC Charlotte funded a portion of my research, as did a Mellon Grant from the Virginia Historical Society. A semester's leave from the College of Arts and Sciences and a Cotlow Fellowship from the Department of History gave me two semesters away from teaching, during which I completed the first draft of the manuscript. The Graduate School at UNC Charlotte paid for most of the book's illustrations, for which I am thankful.

Authors traditionally save the last paragraph of their acknowledgments to list the family and friends who helped—or sometimes hindered—their book's completion. While neither my husband, Tom Bright, nor my parents, Bob and Bea Kierner, answered history questions or read successive drafts of my manuscript, they have always shown interest in my writing, which I think is even better. My sons Zachary and Anders Bright, my niece Danielle Kierner, and Brett and Alison Durant—heroic kids of special parents—are just a lot of fun. To them, I dedicate this book with appreciation and with love.

Cynthia A. Kierner
Charlotte, North Carolina

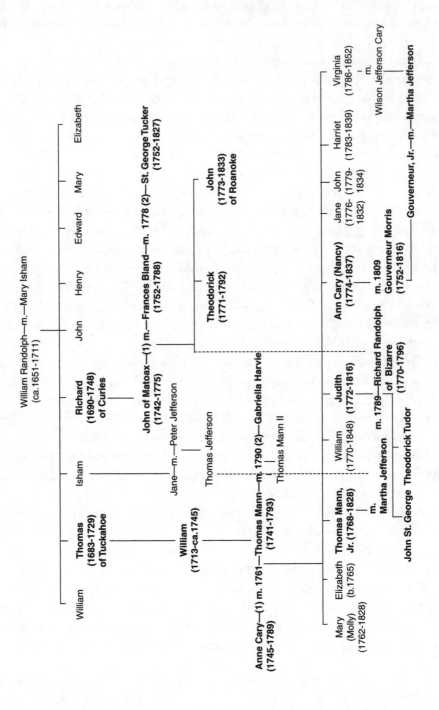

Prologue

Scandal at Bizarre

On Monday, the first day of October, in 1792, five young people traversed the sparsely populated county of Cumberland in central Virginia. The two women, Judith Randolph and her sister Ann Cary Randolph—known as Nancy—squeezed their copious skirts into a smallish horse-drawn carriage. Judith's husband Richard, Richard's brother John—or Jack—and cousin Archibald Randolph accompanied the carriage on horseback. Richard Randolph's plantation, Bizarre, was located at the county's southern edge, on the Appomattox River. The travelers' destination was Glentivar, the plantation home of Mary and Randolph Harrison, about thirty miles away in the northern part of Cumberland County. This visit was one of many exchanged between the Randolphs and the Harrisons, young couples whose close friendship was rooted in their families' shared membership in Virginia's gentry elite. Yet this would be no ordinary visit. What happened after the party arrived at Glentivar caused a scandal that reverberated for decades among the Randolphs, their extended family, the wider community, and far beyond.[1]

On this journey to Glentivar, the travelers may have passed the hours pondering their varied concerns and problems. Like many Virginia planters of his generation, Richard Randolph was plagued by debts, and knowledge of his mounting financial obligations may have weighed heavily on him as he rode through the seemingly endless expanse of tobacco fields that separated his own plantation from that of the Harrisons. His wife, Judith, who shared Richard's financial worries, also must have fretted about leaving her only child behind at Bizarre. Perhaps the four-month-old John St. George Randolph had already exhibited signs of the deafness that would afflict him from infancy, compounding the anxiety of his doting mother. Nancy, Judith's younger sister, felt ill that day, and she, like the other members of the party, may have still mourned the death of Richard's brother Theodorick, whom she professed to love. Only twenty years old, Theo had died nearly seven months earlier, probably of tuberculosis, or what contemporaries called "consumption." Richard's other brother, nineteen-year-old Jack, who may have pined for Nancy, was himself recovering from an unidentified illness that left him, in his biographer's words, "beardless, with a soprano voice, and, it is generally presumed, without sexual capability."[2] Archie Randolph, a brother of Mary Harrison and the final member of the group that day, courted Nancy without her encouragement but with the approval of her recently widowed father.

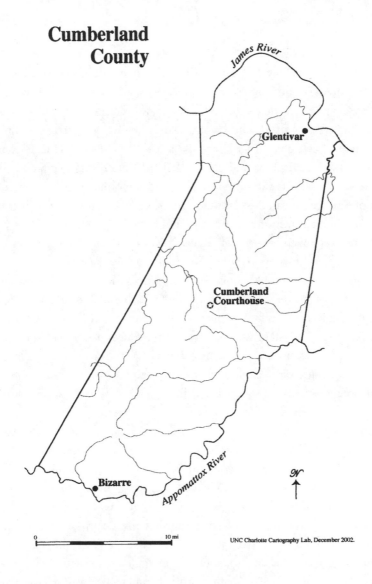

UNC Charlotte Cartography Lab, December 2002.

After a long day's journey, the travelers neared the county's northern end and turned left off the main road onto the narrow lane that took them to the Harrisons' home. There they found a still-unfinished wooden house with two stories, each of which had two rooms, separated by a center hallway to facilitate the circulation of air and diffusion of light inside the house. Although it was spacious compared to the two-room cottages of most Virginia farmers, the Harrisons' house was nonetheless small by gentry standards. Its name, "Glentivar," was vaguely Scottish and purposefully romantic, calling to mind Gothic images of rural borderlands which American gentlefolk found increasingly appealing in the post-revolutionary era.[3]

Randolph and Mary Harrison, whose marriage had produced two children in as many years, lived frugally at Glentivar. Although the Harrisons employed a white housekeeper named Mrs. Wood and claimed ownership of ten slaves as well, they dined simply. "A piece of middling [pork] and greens," one of their descendants recalled, was a typical supper at Glentivar. On 1 October 1792, the Randolph party arrived at the Harrisons' home before nightfall, whereupon they exchanged greetings with their hosts and with Judith and Nancy's youngest sister, seven-year-old Virginia, who was staying with the Harrisons. Soon they all had supper and retired for the night. Randolph and Mary Harrison and their two children slept downstairs, giving their guests the two rooms on the second floor. Nancy occupied a room, which she perhaps shared with her sister Virginia, on one side of the narrow staircase, while Judith and Richard lodged in the room on the other side. According to Randolph Harrison, the two upstairs rooms were in close proximity to each other, separated only "by the width of the stair-case." Archibald Randolph and Richard's brother Jack slept elsewhere that night, perhaps at Clifton, the nearby home of Randolph Harrison's parents, or at a local tavern.[4]

What happened that night at Glentivar remains a matter of some controversy. The best contemporary accounts came from the master and mistress of the house, Randolph and Mary Harrison, who either saw or overheard much of the drama that unfolded upstairs on that otherwise quiet country night. Neither of the Harrisons could have imagined that inviting the Randolphs to visit would lead to their being star witnesses in a murder investigation, but that is exactly what happened. Although years later both Nancy and Jack would add important, if sometimes dubious, details to the story, the Harrisons' sworn depositions, taken several months after the Randolphs' visit, provide the fullest account of what transpired that Monday night and in the days that followed.[5]

Both Randolph and Mary Harrison would later recall that Nancy, who suffered from abdominal pains or cramping, which contemporaries referred to generically as "colic," was the first to go to bed that evening. Husband and wife also agreed that Nancy took some medication to ease her pain, though they disagreed about what exactly she had used. Some time late that night, after everyone had retired, the Harrisons "were waked by loud screams which they supposed to proceed from Mrs. [Judith] Randolph," who was prone to illness and hypochondria. Mary went upstairs, where she found Judith alone in bed and learned that Nancy was the one who had screamed out in pain. When Mary inquired about Nancy's condition, Judith cryptically "conjectured [Nancy] had the hysterics as she had been subject to them; and [that] she did not think that the cholic would make her scream so."[6]

After speaking with Judith, Mary crossed the hall to Nancy's room to look in on her ailing guest. She found the door "fastened by a Bolt, but this she supposed to be because the spring-latch was broken & the door could only be kept shut by being bolted." When Mary knocked, however, the door "was opened instantly" to reveal Richard, young Virginia Randolph, and "a negroe girl of about fifteen" attending to Nancy, who said she had taken laudanum—a mixture of alcohol and opium derivatives—to ease her pain. Nancy asked Mary to leave her candle outside the room because the laudanum made her eyes sensitive to light. Mary stayed with the patient and her attendants in the darkened room for a while. She went back downstairs only when Nancy was "easier," explaining apologetically that "she had a sick child who would not rest well without her."[7]

Not long afterward, as they tried to get back to sleep, the Harrisons heard footsteps coming down the stairs and proceeding out of the house. Randolph Harrison later averred that he and his wife "supposed . . . from the weight of the step on the stairs" that the footsteps belonged to Richard; they later heard the same footsteps re-enter the house and continue back upstairs. At the time, the Harrisons concluded that Richard had sent for a doctor for Nancy, who they now believed to be suffering from "an hysteric fit." On later learning that no physician had been summoned, the Harrisons decided that the footsteps had been those of servants, who, they claimed, "frequently passed up and down stairs during the night."[8]

The next day, Tuesday, Nancy remained in bed while the rest of the Harrisons' guests continued their visit. That morning, when Randolph Harrison went upstairs to build a fire in Nancy's room, he noticed that she was extremely pale. Mary Harrison also remembered that Nancy was "very pale" and that "the Blankets were drawn close around her" as she lay in bed. The mistress of Glentivar also found bloodstains on the stairs, as well as on Nancy's pillowcase and on the other bedclothes, too. When she examined the bedding, Mary later explained, "it appeared as if an attempt had been made to wash it," though the stains were still visible. Later that day, Susanna Randolph Harrison, Randolph's mother, on hearing that Nancy "was unwell," came to Glentivar, though it was another three days before the patient felt fit enough to receive visitors.[9]

On either Wednesday or Thursday, an unnamed "negroe-woman" informed the Harrisons that on Monday night Nancy had miscarried or delivered a child whose discarded body had been found by slaves in some obscure spot on the plantation. The Harrisons later claimed that they did not believe the enslaved woman's story, and if the Randolphs knew of this rumor, they simply ignored it and acted as if nothing had happened. At least when they were in the presence of their hosts, Nancy, Judith, and Richard appeared to be on good terms with each other. Mary Harrison later recalled that she "did not discover in Mrs. [Judith] Randolph that allarm or confusion, which might be expected if she supposed her sister was about to be delivered of a child, or that resentment which would arise from suspecting" that her own husband may have been somehow complicit in the affair. Instead, Mary maintained, "there appeared to be entire harmony between Mr. Randolph & his lady." Randolph Harrison declared that Judith's and Nancy's behavior toward each other was "the same as usual" during the remainder of their stay in his house.[10]

The Randolphs' decision to stay at Glentivar until Saturday, rather than fleeing homeward, tacitly invited others to scrutinize their conduct and to conclude that whatever had happened on Monday night was not serious enough to cause discord among them. Richard, Judith, and Nancy also maintained their composure for the most part in the coming months when they received visitors at Bizarre, though Randolph Harrison detected some tension when he and Mary visited there in late October, about three weeks after the incident at Glentivar. Although Mary stubbornly insisted that harmony prevailed at Bizarre, her husband observed that Richard "seemed somewhat crusty" toward his wife.[11]

The news that Randolph Harrison brought the Randolphs during that late October visit must have either caused or aggravated the friction he sensed between husband and wife. As it turned out, the slaves at Glentivar, who had initiated the rumors about Nancy's pregnancy and its termination, did not let the matter drop after the Randolphs left. "Some time after" Randolph Harrison's bondwoman had informed him of the slaves' suspicions about Nancy, he "heard a Report among the negroes that the Birth had been deposited on a pile of shingles between two Logs." Harrison shared this information about the slaves' continuing gossip and the increased specificity of the rumors they promulgated with Randolphs when he went to Bizarre in late October. Perhaps still hoping that the rumors would subside, Harrison put off investigating the slaves' new allegations. Only in December, after it became obvious to him that the gossip would not abate, did Harrison finally inspect "such a place, where there was a shingle which appeared to have been stained." As he later testified, however, he found there no conclusive evidence of foul play—no stained bedclothes, no tiny corpse—only a shingle with a nondescript sort of stain. By then, more than two months had passed since the alleged crime.[12]

Although Nancy's reputation was the most obvious potential casualty of the continuing rumors, gossip about the alleged incident at Glentivar posed dangers for Richard and Judith, too. If the unmarried Nancy indeed had been pregnant, she had flouted social conventions that equated feminine virtue with chastity and afforded male protection only to those who remained sexually pure.[13] But who was the father of Nancy's child? Randolph Harrison never said whether or not the enslaved people of Glentivar had accused Richard Randolph of complicity in the affair, but their interpretation of the night's events presupposed that someone had aided Nancy by disposing of the infant's body. Given the Harrisons' recollection of the incident, Richard would have been the prime suspect. But what, if any, crimes had he committed in his capacity as Nancy's alleged accomplice? At worst, Richard was party to the murder of a living infant; perhaps he was also the father of the aborted child. At best, he had only helped his sister-in-law to conceal the stillborn or miscarried product of an illicit pregnancy. Either way, however, Richard appeared culpable. In this patriarchal society, both scenarios also raised questions about both Richard's marriage to Judith and the overall moral environment at Bizarre. Was Richard a wanton rogue or a man of virtue? Was Judith a loving and beloved wife? Did she promote virtue and morality within her household, as women were enjoined to do?[14]

In the coming months, Richard came to assume a more prominent role in the gossip, which spread from the Harrisons' slaves to the black and white population of Cumberland and beyond. Enslaved people spread gossip as they worked or visited kin at neighboring plantations or mingled at markets, taverns, or churches with local whites, who, in turn, shared the story with their friends and relatives. Increasingly, the most common rumors cast Richard not only as Nancy's accomplice in committing infanticide, but also as the father of her illegitimate child. This interpretation made him a possible murderer as well as a particularly vile kind of fornicator, since sexual relations with a spouse's sibling were defined as incestuous under Virginia law. By December 1792, when Randolph Harrison finally felt obliged to examine the "stained" shingle at Glentivar, local criticism of Richard specifically prompted the Randolphs to consider leaving Cumberland County. In January, Nancy, Richard, and Judith sought refuge with their relations, first in Williamsburg and then in Albemarle County, only to find that the gossip had preceded them to both locales. In fact, the story soon spread as far as Philadelphia, where that April Secretary of State Thomas Jefferson, who was kin to the Randolphs, encountered the "rumor" even before he received a letter about it from his daughter in Virginia.[15]

The gossip persisted as fall became winter and winter spring, leading Richard to a Cumberland County courtroom to defend himself against a murder charge in the naïve hope of recouping his damaged honor. In 1792–93, Richard Randolph, Bizarre's nominal patriarch and a member of one of Virginia's oldest and most honored families, found himself vulnerable to the gossip of enslaved blacks, plebeian whites, and members of Virginia's gentry elite. Nancy, whose social rank and gender should have rendered her virtue beyond reproach, was widely assumed to have borne—and perhaps murdered—an illegitimate child. Judith, who had been taught to regard her husband as patriarch and protector, instead would be forced to assume the role of his stoic defender.

The chapters that follow tell the story of the Bizarre scandal and the long shadow it cast over the lives of its principals. Other historians have told this story in whole or in part. Indeed, the Bizarre scandal has received substantial coverage in more than a dozen historical or biographical works; the episode also has been the subject of at least three historical novels and even a recent opera.[16] Portrayals of Nancy Randolph vary widely: she has been described as a fiercely courageous "tigress," an irretrievably "condemned" woman, and a "first-class bitch"—none of which strike me as entirely accurate. Richard Randolph has been depicted, seemingly contradictorily but with some justification, as both a debauched wastrel and a man of honor.[17] Most accounts characterize Judith Randolph as austere and morose, but authors disagree about the causes and consequences of her profound unhappiness. Although most previous chroniclers have assumed that Nancy was pregnant when she visited the Harrisons—which she herself admitted in later years—none has solved the mystery of who fathered Nancy's child; nor has any proven conclusively what happened that fateful night at Glentivar.[18]

My book, too, will leave these issues unresolved, instead approaching the scandal from the perspective of microhistory.[19] My rendering of this specific and seemingly small episode—hence the prefix "micro"—aims not only to tell the Randolphs' story but also to provide a glimpse into the world that they inhabited. On the surface at least, the Bizarre scandal was simply about illicit sex and its consequences for families and communities. Close examination of how contemporaries interpreted the episode and its significance, however, illuminates an array of wider concerns and issues and, more important still, helps us to distinguish between cultural prescription—what law, religion, moral treatises, and social conventions deemed proper behavior—and social reality. Virginia law, for instance, defined slaves as chattel, yet the enslaved people of Glentivar initiated rumors that wreaked havoc on the reputation and well-being of one of the state's leading families. Although advice books and sentimental novels sternly warned female readers that death and destruction awaited the unchaste, Nancy Randolph survived the scandal, prospered, and ultimately even had a church built in her honor.

The Randolphs' world was one in which the printed word proliferated to mold the opinions and shape the manners of an increasingly literate public. Newspapers, which had existed in Virginia since 1736, became more numerous and more widely read after the Revolution, but their largely political fare competed with that of the enormously popular sentimental novel.[20] The simultaneous influence of partisan newspapers and sentimental novels reflected the tensions between public and private, reason and emotion, in post-revolutionary America. The Randolphs and other interested parties sought to use both genres to interpret and explain the Bizarre scandal and its significance. At a time when educated Virginians especially appreciated the power of the written word, however, they and their less privileged contemporaries nonetheless continued to spread and credit gossip about the Randolphs and, more generally, about both public and private life.

Doing microhistory, as one practitioner has observed recently, is like "holding our eye up to a peephole . . . [that] reveals a wide expanse of culture and society, not a tiny chamber."[21] The Bizarre scandal, though an exceptional story in its own right, is also a point of entry into the wider world of Jefferson's America. Our story begins in colonial Virginia, where the Randolphs and their gentry peers dominated a seemingly orderly and hierarchical society. It ends in the 1830s, a decade characterized in the United States by an increasingly vigorous democratic ethos (at least among white men) and an emerging sectional consciousness. In the intervening decades, in Virginia and elsewhere, Americans pondered and in some instances reformulated their political values, class identities, gender conventions, and attitudes towards slavery, work, and family life.[22] Though a uniquely dismal chapter in the Randolph family history, the Bizarre scandal also signaled a more general malaise that engulfed Virginia's gentry elite during the post-revolutionary era. While the sensationally dysfunctional Randolphs were by no means typical of Virginia's post-revolutionary gentry, their story can be understood, and was, indeed, understood by their contemporaries, as symptomatic of broader problems and issues Americans faced in this crucial transitional era.

1

ONE OF THE FIRST FAMILIES OF
THE COUNTRY

"When traveling in Virginia, you must be prepared to hear the name of Randolph frequently mentioned," observed the Marquis de Chastellux in 1782. "This was one of the first families of the country, since a Randolph was among the first settlers," the Frenchman noted, "but it is also one of the most numerous and wealthiest." Indeed, by 1782, descendants of the earliest colonial Randolphs numbered in the hundreds, and Randolph family lands stretched from the older tidewater counties through the richly productive piedmont and on into the west. Hundreds of enslaved people worked the Randolph land, producing the tobacco that they and other colonial Virginians had exported to Britain in vast quantities. Tobacco profits had enabled great planters and their families to live genteelly. Chastellux, who enjoyed the hospitality of the Randolphs and some other leading planters, found much to admire in the great houses of the Old Dominion.[1]

Nevertheless, the Randolphs' circumstances were in a state of flux by 1782, as were those of many other prominent Virginia planter families. In the decade or so before the Revolution, Virginians had amassed debts to British merchants, which they found themselves hard pressed to repay when the costly and disruptive war was over. Politics, a source of profit and prestige for Virginia gentlemen before 1776, seemed both less lucrative and less honorable a calling to many with the rise of revolutionary republicanism. From the 1760s through the 1790s, economic and political malaise slowly engulfed many gentry families. Among the Randolphs, the revolutionary generation—the parents of Richard, Judith, and Nancy—were the first to grapple with the consequences of their family's inexorable fall from the pinnacle of wealth and power.

The Randolphs enjoyed more than a century of prosperity in the colony of Virginia. William Randolph, the family's progenitor in America, left England for Virginia in the early 1670s. Within a few years, he had made the contacts that would give him access to patronage—in the form of political appointments and land titles—which was essential to the success of aspiring planters in the colony. For example, in 1674 William succeeded his childless uncle as clerk of the Henrico County court, a post that would be instrumental in making him a leading landowner in Virginia. The Henrico court oversaw much of the confiscation and resale of land in the wake of the major uprising, which occurred in 1676, known as Bacon's Rebellion. William Randolph, who appears not to have supported either side in the rebellion, nonetheless got first pick of the confiscated properties. After 1676, he purchased prime plantation lands at modest prices from the estates of James Crews and rebel leader Nathaniel Bacon. Some time before 1680, William also enhanced his prospects by marrying Mary Isham, the only child of wealthy planter Henry Isham and the principle heir to his estate.[2]

In the early 1680s, William and Mary Isham Randolph settled at Turkey Island, a James River plantation that had once belonged to the rebel James Crews. At Turkey Island, they built one of the colony's early mansions, a "goodly house, with a portico on three sides, surmounted by a dome visible a great way off to the navigators of the James River" who came to William's wharves to buy his tobacco. William and Mary had nine children—seven sons and two daughters—who lived to adulthood. While the daughters presumably acquired the sorts of practical and ornamental accomplishments that would make them appealing wives to Virginia's striving gentlemen, the Randolphs, like most elite parents, took a more purposeful approach to their sons' education. Six of the Randolph boys attended William and Mary, the fledgling college in Williamsburg; one, John, continued his education in England. In a world in which attaining political office, land, and even credit depended on patronage and personal connections, time spent in Williamsburg, the provincial capital, was an opportunity for young men to acquire contacts and social graces as well as book learning. Like most of the college's colonial alumni, the four Randolph brothers who remained in Virginia—three settled in England—later attained prominence both as planters and as officeholders at the county and provincial levels.[3]

This first generation of Virginia-born Randolphs also benefited handsomely from their parents' economic success, which derived in large part from William's extensive political contacts in the colony. While planters typically gave their daughters slaves or other moveable assets as bequests or marriage settlements, most aspired to endow their sons with sizeable landed estates. Like many ambitious and well-connected planters, William Randolph used his political influence to acquire land from a succession of Virginia governors, who wielded exclusive power to distribute land not previously granted to white claimants in the colony. As the king's representative in Virginia, the governor could recommend that the Crown issue a document—known formally as royal letters patent, but more commonly called a patent—that conferred title to a specific tract on the grantee and his heirs in perpetuity. Like other great planters, William Randolph prevailed on the governors to use their influence in London on their behalf, speculating extensively in both improved and unimproved land throughout Virginia.[4]

By any standard, William Randolph succeeded in providing amply for his seven sons. By the time he died in 1711, besides his more remote speculative holdings, he owned some 10,000 acres in Henrico, the large county that embraced much of central Virginia until its western portion became the separate county of Goochland in 1727. Six of William Randolph's sons became known by the names of the family seats they established in Henrico or Goochland on the banks of the James River: William of Chatsworth; Thomas of Tuckahoe; Isham of Dungeness; Richard of Curles; Henry of Longfield; and Edward of Bremo. The other son, John, inherited land in Williamsburg, where he resided, along with acreage in York County.[5]

Four of the Randolph brothers followed their father's footsteps, acquiring large speculative landholdings, especially in the counties of Henrico, Goochland, Amelia, and Brunswick, to provide for their own sons. Those who had the best political connections in the colony and who survived to enjoy the land-grabbing frenzy of the 1730s and 1740s netted the most acreage. Thomas of Tuckahoe—the great-grandfather of Judith and Nancy Randolph—amassed an additional 6,874 acres in Henrico and Goochland before he died in 1729. Isham of Dungeness, who returned to Virginia after living for decades in England, received patents for 9,035 acres in Goochland and Amelia in the 1730s. The more politically active brothers attained even bigger prizes. Between 1703 and 1733, William of Chatsworth, who succeeded his father as clerk of the Henrico County court and also became clerk to and later a member of Virginia's colonial assembly, the House of Burgesses, received land patents for more than 13,000 acres. Finally, Richard of Curles, a longtime member of the House of Burgesses who outlived all his brothers, accumulated some 40,000 acres.[6]

Richard Randolph of Curles died in 1748, dividing his vast landholdings in Goochland, Amelia, Brunswick, and Prince George counties among his four sons. Included among the tracts that went to his youngest son, John, were two on the Appomattox River, Matoax and Bizarre. In 1749, these tracts would become part of the new counties of Chesterfield and Cumberland, respectively. In early 1770, John Randolph and his bride, Frances Bland, took up residence at Matoax, where later that year their eldest son, Richard, was born. Richard Randolph, along with his brothers Theodorick and John, spent his childhood at this 1,305-acre plantation that bore the Powhatan name used by Pocahontas, an ancestor of their paternal grandmother, Jane Bolling Randolph, wife of Richard Randolph of Curles. Young Richard, in turn, would later settle his own family upriver at Bizarre.[7]

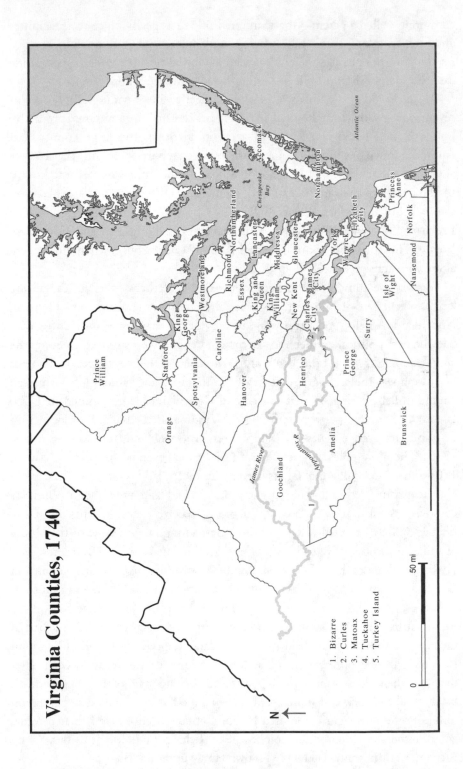

Virginia Counties, 1740

1. Bizarre
2. Curles
3. Matoax
4. Tuckahoe
5. Turkey Island

50 mi

0

N

Prince
William

Stafford

King
George

Spotsylvania

Orange

Caroline

Westmoreland

Richmond

Northumberland

Essex

King and
Queen

King
William

Hanover

Goochland

James River

Appomattox R.

Amelia

Henrico

New Kent

Charles
City

James
City

Lancaster

Middlesex

Gloucester

York

Warwick

Elizabeth
City

Prince
George

Surry

Brunswick

Isle of
Wight

Nansemond

Norfolk

Princess
Anne

Accomack

Northampton

Chesapeake
Bay

Atlantic Ocean

The last generation of colonial Randolphs, which included the parents of Richard, Judith, and Nancy, exemplified the gentry ideal of refinement, benevolence, and authoritative leadership in the wider community. Prodigious landowners and mansion-builders, the various branches of the Randolph family boasted an array of grand houses and family seats in the provincial capital of Williamsburg and in the tidewater and piedmont counties. They wielded power and influence as suppliers of credit and other commercial services to small and middling planters in their local communities. As members of their parish vestries, the local governing bodies of the established Church of England in the colony, they oversaw and regulated church affairs. As justices of the peace, chosen by the king through his governor because of their "substance and ability of body and estate," they presided over the local courts to "preserve the peace and good government of their county." In addition, between 1750 and 1775 eighteen men who bore the Randolph name represented their counties in the House of Burgesses.[8]

Thomas Mann Randolph, father of Judith and Nancy and head of the Tuckahoe branch of the Randolph family at the time of the Revolution, was an exemplary member of the family's revolutionary generation. He had a head start in life, at least financially speaking. Born at Tuckahoe in 1741, Thomas Mann

Figure 1.1 Tuckahoe. Thomas Mann and Anne Cary Randolph lived, with their ten children, in this elegant riverfront mansion. Like other Virginia colonial great houses, this imposing structure was designed to convey a sense of the wealth and solidity of the gentleman who possessed it. Photograph by the author.

Randolph was the third child and only son of William Randolph and Maria Judith Page, whose marriage in 1735 had united two wealthy and powerful Virginia gentry families. By 1745, however, both had died, leaving the four-year-old Thomas in possession of some five thousand acres, including Tuckahoe, the elegant family seat on the James River in Goochland County. In his will, William Randolph requested that his "dear and loving" friend Peter Jefferson, who had married a daughter of Isham Randolph of Dungeness, move to Tuckahoe with his family and act as guardian for young Thomas and his sisters. Jefferson acceded to his friend's wishes, moving his wife and daughters and his own two-year-old son, also named Thomas, into the Randolph home. Thomas Jefferson, Thomas Mann Randolph, and their siblings received their earliest education in a small building designed by Peter Jefferson and situated adjacent to the great house at Tuckahoe. The Jeffersons remained at Tuckahoe until 1752, when both boys began their formal schooling elsewhere.[9]

Unlike Thomas Jefferson and most of his own male Randolph relations, Thomas Mann Randolph did not receive the customary gentleman's education at the college in Williamsburg, but his adult life was in most other ways representative of those of the last generation of Virginia's colonial elite. In 1761, Randolph's marriage to Anne Cary, the eldest daughter of Archibald Cary of Ampthill, connected him with another affluent and influential planter family. Befitting his status as one of his county's leading landowners, in the 1760s Thomas Mann Randolph of Tuckahoe became a justice of the peace, a vestryman in his local parish church, and an elected member of the House of Burgesses. Like most local magnates in late colonial Virginia, he sold his tobacco to British merchants, and, in turn, provided credit and other resources to smaller planters in his neighborhood. All in all, his family connections, property holdings, and local and provincial offices marked him as a man of consequence both in Goochland and throughout the colony. Thomas Mann Randolph remained on friendly terms with his childhood companion, Thomas Jefferson, who described him as an "excellent good man."[10]

At the same time, however, the Randolphs, like many gentry families, experienced mounting financial difficulties as the colonial period drew to a close, and those difficulties became even more pronounced during and after the War of Independence. Although the Randolphs and their sort kept up appearances, the luxuriant hospitality that the Marquis de Chastellux and other visitors received from them belied their growing financial problems. Colonial debts to British merchants, followed by high wartime taxes, and coupled with soil exhaustion and continuing instability in the tobacco market, compounded their financial difficulties in the coming decades.[11]

As befitting their social status, Thomas Mann and Anne Cary Randolph had been avid participants in the genteel culture of public balls, polite manners, and conspicuous consumption that complemented and reinforced the authority of the gentry before the Revolution. They journeyed to Williamsburg to partake of the fancy balls and other social amenities and obligations that coincided with the meetings of the House of Burgesses. At Tuckahoe, they received guests in the H-shaped mansion Thomas's father had built between 1733 and 1745, embellishing the interior with an ornately carved staircase and rich walnut carving in the public, ceremonial rooms on the ground floor. The spacious house, according to one impressed visitor, had been built "solely to answer the purposes of hospitality." Another European guest praised a "delicious supper, served with all possible elegance" at Tuckahoe in 1782. He described the chamber in which he slept as "worthy of a Prince's Palace . . . every piece of furniture was exquisitely beautiful, of mahogany or rosewood, with very beautiful mirrors." Thomas Mann Randolph's own "apartment" was "all done in velvet and gold" and his bed was richly decorated "like a Feast Day."[12]

Like many of his contemporaries, Thomas Mann Randolph spent lavishly before the Revolution, and he and his circle figured prominently among the burgeoning ranks of deeply indebted Virginia gentry when the war was over. The root of the problem was that planters, many of whom already owed money to British merchants who marketed their produce, continued and even increased their consumption of imported goods despite a dramatic fall in tobacco prices in the 1760s and 1770s. Then, the conflict with Britain effectively ended tobacco exports, while the war forced Virginians to pay increasingly higher taxes. When the war ended and trade resumed, the planters still depended on British firms to ship and market their tobacco, but they now had to pay increased customs duties as a result of their separation from the British Empire. One historian has estimated that planters' shipping costs roughly doubled and that duties absorbed nearly four-fifths of the sale price of their tobacco after 1783. Small wonder that so many sought to evade or at least delay payment of their prewar accounts. Debt, like wealth, moreover, passed from one generation to the next. When Archibald Cary died in 1787, his son-in-law, Thomas Mann Randolph, inherited more than £20,000 (the 1990s equivalent of nearly $900,000) in unpaid debts.[13]

Uncertainty pervaded the financial outlook of the Randolphs and their peers in the 1780s. On the one hand, most retained enormous assets in both land and slaves. Tax records for 1787 indicate that Thomas Mann Randolph of Tuckahoe owned some 14,000 acres in four Virginia counties; he also paid taxes on 366 slaves, making him the state's seventh largest slaveholder. On the other hand, appearances were deceiving because debt deeply encumbered Randolph's seemingly immense estate. Planters resisted repaying what they owed to British merchants until the U.S. Supreme Court finally ruled in the creditors' favor in

1796. The subsequent settlement of these accounts sometimes took decades and, as we shall see, often resulted in the loss or liquidation of family estates.[14]

The political visibility and influence of Thomas Mann Randolph and many of his gentry peers also waned during and after the War of Independence, despite the fact that revolutionary republicanism brought few formal changes to Virginia's political institutions and none that directly threatened the gentry's access to political power. After 1776, for instance, Virginia law still required ownership of either twenty-five acres "with a house and a plantation" or one hundred acres of unimproved land to qualify to vote, thereby effectively limiting the electorate to roughly sixty percent of the state's white adult men. Voice-voting, another holdover from the colonial period, ensured that elections would continue to be social dramas in which each voter, by publicly declaring his choice of candidate before the assembled electorate, averred his trust in and admiration for a powerful gentry neighbor.[15]

Nevertheless, certain changes made officeholding both less exclusive and less prestigious than it had been during the colonial era. After 1776, men who attained prominence by their service to the Revolution sought and received county-level judicial appointments that once had been accessible only to gentlemen. The number of elected legislators also grew after 1776, when Virginia's first state constitution replaced the governor's council—the colony's appointive upper house—with a twenty-four–member senate, and the creation of additional counties encouraged an infusion of still more new men into the lower house. Gentlemen who wielded power before 1776 now found themselves working alongside newcomers at both the state and county levels. Another change mandated by the state constitution limited the governor and his chief advisors to a maximum of three years in office. Although republican fears of executive tyranny inspired this provision, some contemporaries believed that enforced "rotation" in the state's highest offices was an effective tool for, in one historian's words, "compelling mobility in a deferential society where men too often felt obliged to reelect their rulers for fear of dishonoring them." In 1779, the movement of Virginia's capital from Williamsburg to Richmond further symbolized the break from an earlier era of gentry political dominance.[16]

Many gentlemen did not look favorably on these changes that, along with their pressing financial concerns, led them to withdraw from public life. The first decades of republican government saw decreasing political activity among many of the Old Dominion's foremost gentry families of the colonial era. Only one of the seventeen men who served on the governor's council between 1765 and 1776 had a significant political career after independence, and none of the sons of these colonial officeholders ever achieved a position of prominence in Virginia's state government. Of the eighteen most powerful members of the pre-revolutionary House of Burgesses, only six held a legislative seat or some other elective post after 1778. In the 1780s, the overwhelming majority of the members of Virginia's bicameral legislature had not been lawmakers during the colonial period. In 1787, only two of Virginia's one hundred wealthiest men—based on their holdings in land and slaves prior to the settlement of their debts—were members of the state senate, and only sixteen held seats in the lower house. So wealthy and powerful during the colonial period, members of these elite families now accounted for less than one-tenth of the total membership of each legislative house.[17]

Thomas Mann Randolph, who completed his last legislative term in 1776, acknowledged that his Goochland County neighbors, who had deferred to him routinely during the colonial period, were increasingly likely to scrutinize his conduct and question his authority. During the war, some criticized the master of Tuckahoe for offering hospitality and "liberality" to British army officers, despite Randolph's clear political and financial commitment to the revolutionary cause. After the war, the farmers of Goochland approached Randolph as an equal, rather than a superior, at least on some occasions. In 1782, for instance, an English visitor reported that three local "peasants" came to Tuckahoe and unceremoniously "entered the room where the Colonel [Randolph] and his company were sitting, took themselves chairs, drew near the fire, began spitting, pulling off their country boots all over mud, and then opened their business," which concerned flour to be ground at the mill at Tuckahoe. After they left, Randolph bemoaned the "unavoidable" social consequences of the Revolution. The "spirit of independency," he explained, "was converted into equality, and every one who bore arms, esteemed himself upon an [equal] footing with his neighbor."[18]

In the midst of the gentry's political and economic malaise, Thomas Mann and Anne Cary Randolph had to rear, educate, and provide for the ten of their thirteen children who survived infancy. Born between 1762 and 1786, these three sons and seven daughters—Mary, Elizabeth, Thomas, William, Judith, Nancy, Jane, John, Harriet, and Virginia—were educated in keeping with the genteel ideals of the colonial era, although they were destined to come of age in a vastly different world. Lessons with a private tutor at Tuckahoe constituted the first phase of the youngsters' schooling, as was customary among Virginia's colonial planter elite. Then, in 1784, Thomas Mann Randolph sent sixteen-year-old Thomas Mann, Jr. and fourteen-year-old William to study in Edinburgh. The elder Randolph advised his sons to dress well, and he approved their plan to tour France, despite what he called "the low state of my finances." Financial considerations precluded travel abroad for Randolph's youngest son, John, who was born in 1779; the least promising intellectually of the Tuckahoe Randolph boys, he trained with a local physician but eventually took up farming.[19]

Straitened finances along with their parents' conservative tastes in education prevented the seven Randolph sisters from attending one of the female academies that were becoming increasingly popular after the Revolution, as reformers sought to educate young women to promote virtue and industry within their families to safeguard the future of the infant American republic. In the early 1780s, Thomas Mann Randolph gave his older daughters two hogsheads of tobacco each year to purchase the "dresses and ornaments" that he thought essential accoutrements of feminine gentility, and he ensured that they received a respectably genteel education to prepare them for domesticity, motherhood, and polite sociability. The Randolph sisters learned sewing, knitting, and other domestic skills from their mother or other female relations, besides receiving academic instruction from private tutors whom they shared with their brothers. In 1788, Thomas Mann Randolph charged his eldest son with recruiting a Scottish tutor to teach his younger children: sixteen-year-old Judith, fourteen-year-old Nancy, and their younger siblings Jane, John, and Harriet. Presumably reflecting the opinion of the father whose commission he sought to fill, Thomas Mann Randolph, Jr., viewed women's education primarily as preparation for genteel courtship and marriage, a means by which to "insure their pleasing . . . the greater part of the other sex."[20]

This preference for a largely ornamental education assumed that young ladies would move safely and directly from the protective custody of one male to another. Fathers ideally would provide financially for their daughters to enable them to choose husbands that were both personally appealing and financially sound. Husbands, in turn, ideally would have the economic resources to give their wives the houses, servants, clothing, and other accoutrements necessary for genteel domestic life. Women, for their part, most contemporaries assumed, would happily submit to a regimen in which they enjoyed some leisured luxury and cultural influence in return for their dependence. As it turned out, in the case of the Randolph sisters, all of these assumptions were ill-founded.

The surviving letters of Judith and Nancy show that they matured into literate women with lively intellects, who to varying degrees resented the deficiencies of their education. Judith was twelve in 1784 when her brothers left for Scotland and when she herself began corresponding with her cousin and future sister-in-law, Martha Jefferson, who attended a French convent school while her father represented the United States as a diplomat in Paris. Judith envied Martha's opportunity to become "mistress of French" and experience life firsthand in "the Beau Monde," and she bemoaned her own bleak prospects for securing a "tolerable education" in Virginia. Less studious than Judith as a youngster, Nancy nonetheless became a lifelong reader. While Judith gravitated toward devotional reading, Nancy's favorite texts were sentimental novels, the most popular literary genre among Americans, especially women, in the post-revolutionary era. These novels typically told tales of seduction and lost innocence, which their authors, significantly, tended to attribute to the neglected state of women's education.[21]

Judith Randolph of Tuckahoe nevertheless fulfilled her parents' expectations, becoming a lovely and accomplished young woman who attracted at least three serious suitors before her sixteenth birthday. In 1787, her kinsman Peter Randolph visited Tuckahoe "if possible to storm the citadel in which was contained Miss Jud[it]h's virtues and accomplishments." The smitten youth praised the fifteen-year-old Judith's "incomparable musick" and her ability to perform "the honors of the table with the most ineffable sweetness and modesty." Peter Randolph characterized the object of his affections as "the most perfect of her sex . . . beautiful, sensible, polite, good-tempered, agreeable, and . . . truly calculated by both her virtues and accomplishments to render any man happy." John Leslie, the Randolphs' Scottish tutor, also fell in love with Judith, whom he continued to remember fondly long after he left Virginia in 1789. "In her society I could have forgotten Europe and consented to become a lawyer or a backwoodsman," he mused in 1822. Instead, Leslie left Tuckahoe broken-hearted because his "sweet little girl" had rejected him in favor of her kinsman Richard Randolph.[22]

Judith's favored suitor was the grandson of Richard Randolph of Curles and son of John and Frances Bland Randolph of Matoax. The Blands, like the Randolphs, were a wealthy and well-established planter family who would play an important role in the Revolution in Virginia. John Randolph of Matoax and his brother-in-law, Theodorick Bland, advanced funding to the patriot cause, and Bland later served both in the Continental Congress and as a colonel in Washington's army. John Randolph, however, died in 1775, at the age of thirty-eight, leaving his twenty-three-year-old widow with several plantations, substantial debts to British merchants, and three sons between the ages of five and three, of whom Richard was the eldest. Three years later, Frances Bland Randolph married St. George Tucker, a well-connected Williamsburg attorney, who assumed responsibility for both the Randolph boys' education and the management of their father's estate. Tucker developed close relationships with his Randolph stepsons, and he continued to act as their guardian after their beloved mother died in 1788.[23]

Although Richard Randolph and his brothers shared the declining economic fortunes of their Tuckahoe kin, their education was potentially better suited to the economic and social challenges of the post-revolutionary world. Like the elder Thomas Mann Randolph, St. George Tucker had hired private tutors for his boys and then sent them elsewhere to complete their formal education. Tucker's stepsons attended Walker Maury's peripatetic grammar school, first in Orange County and then later in Williamsburg. After completing his studies with Maury, Richard began his college career at William and Mary, studied law briefly in Williamsburg in 1786, and in 1787 attended Princeton with his younger brothers, Theodorick and Jack. In 1789, Theo and Jack transferred to Columbia College in New York, where their uncles Thomas Tudor Tucker and Theodorick Bland, both members of the first federal Congress under the new Constitution, could monitor their progress. At Tucker's urging, Richard returned to Williamsburg to resume his legal studies.[24]

Unlike Thomas Mann Randolph, Tucker insisted that his stepsons—and later his sons—eschew planting to train for specific learned professions. Richard read law in Williamsburg with the eminent George Wythe, who had trained Tucker, Jefferson, and most of the best attorneys in Virginia, and he later studied with Tucker himself. In 1789–90, Jack studied law with his kinsman Edmund Randolph, who was then serving as attorney general of the United States. Tucker planned to send Theo, his middle stepson, to Edinburgh to study medicine. Although he believed that law was the most promising and prestigious of the learned professions, Tucker accepted medicine as a viable alternative that might spare Theo "the frowns of fortune" in an unsettled post-revolutionary world.[25]

A native of Bermuda who came to Virginia in 1771, St. George Tucker enjoyed a sympathetic detachment from the entrenched hierarchy of the colony's planter elite. The astute and assiduous Tucker quickly became one of Virginia's leading lawyers, rising through the ranks of provincial society through the patronage of his gentry friends. But during and after the Revolution, perhaps because of his marriage into the debt-ridden Randolph and Bland families, Tucker saw that most great planters were losing ground, and he concluded that only education and professional training could ensure the prosperity of the rising generation. In his letters, Tucker repeatedly urged his stepsons to study hard, behave well, and strive to be useful and productive. "The boy who diligently attends to his studies, who is dutiful in his conduct to those under whose care he is placed," he advised, would grow to be a man who is "careful and attentive in his Business [and] . . . discharge all the duties of a good Citizen" to merit the "esteem and Confidence of his Acquaintances & Countrymen."[26]

The Matoax Randolph boys, however, shared neither their stepfather's enthusiasm for hard work nor his respect for formal educational training. Like many young men in this revolutionary age, the Randolphs rejected the authority of their elders, running afoul of both Tucker and their schoolmasters from time to time. Although Richard and Jack were bookish and clearly intelligent, a combination of arrogance, laziness, and dissipation sometimes got them, as well as their less studious brother Theo, into trouble. Tucker reprimanded each of his stepsons on occasion for neglecting their studies, showing disrespect toward their teachers, and partaking of various unnamed vices. In the end, none of the Randolph boys either earned a college degree or entered the profession that

Tucker had chosen for them. Theo, the least promising of the three, acquired a reputation for debauchery at Columbia before developing what would become a fatal illness, probably tuberculosis, in 1790. Stubborn pride in their planter lineage led both Richard and Jack to choose the agricultural life that their ancestors had pursued for generations. Richard saw himself as too genteel to follow in Tucker's footsteps by practicing law.[27]

Dashing, passionate, and self-indulgent, Richard Randolph seems to have charmed most who knew him. No portrait of Richard has survived, but his admiring brother Jack remembered him as "the most manly youth and elegant gentleman that I ever saw." Richard often wrote his mother and stepfather during his student days, always dutifully expressing his love and gratitude, but invariably adding a request for more money to meet his mounting expenses. "I wish very often that I could spend the Evening with you at Matoax, and the next morning here [studying law] with Mr. Wythe," he wrote ingratiatingly to his mother in 1786, adding, "I should thank you very much . . . if you would send the Shirts I wrote for . . . together with some Stockings, & some money to pay the Hair Dresser." Richard was profoundly affected by the revolutionary environment of his formative years. In the 1790s, he addressed his correspondents as "Citizen" to show his support for the French Revolution, but he went much further than most of Virginia's genteel democrats by unequivocally condemning slavery as a "violation of . . . the inherent, unalienable and imprescriptible rights of man." A free-thinker or deist in religion, Richard also exercised his libertarian bent in a series of amorous affairs. He admitted having sexual relationships with at least two white women before he married Judith. Fragmentary evidence suggests that there may have been others.[28]

Yet those who knew Richard well always stressed his better qualities. His half-brother, Henry Tucker, remembered his "generous and noble and affectionate temper . . . and extraordinary talents." His sister-in-law, Nancy Randolph, believed that "Nature made him of her best materials," citing his "native feelings of Honor" and other "noble qualities." Jack Randolph, who envisioned his brother as the ideal Virginia gentleman—"neither debauched nor dissipated . . . regular, studious, and above low company of any sort"—cherished his memory long after his death in 1796. "Our poor brother, Richard . . . would have been fifty-six years old on the 9th of this month," John wrote to a Tucker half-sibling in 1826. Choked with grief, he ended, "I can [write] no more."[29]

In June 1788, Richard met Judith in Richmond, where both participated in the social whirl surrounding the convention charged with deciding whether Virginia would ratify the Constitution that had been drafted in Philadelphia the preceding fall. Richard's stepfather, St. George Tucker, and his uncle, Theodorick Bland, were present as delegates, as was Judith's father,

Thomas Mann Randolph of Tuckahoe. Tucker probably brought eighteen-year-old Richard to the state capital both to circulate socially and to further his education in law and politics. At sixteen, Judith was several years younger than the typical Virginia bride, but her parents recognized experience and grace in social situations as an important part of her education and perhaps an essential precondition for her future happiness.

Although Judith's parents did not anticipate her finding a prospective husband in 1788, her subsequent attachment to her kinsman Richard was typical of gentry courtships of the time. The youngsters selected each other from among a gathering of elite Virginia families on the basis of romantic attraction. In other words, young romance had free reign, but only within a relatively controlled social environment. Post-revolutionary gentry parents continued the colonial practice of orchestrating balls, visits, and other social occasions to monitor the company their children, especially their daughters, kept, though the departure of royal officials, loyalists, and British merchants after independence considerably attenuated the social networks of Virginia elites. Judith and Richard were distant cousins, but marriage between kin was increasingly common among the state's financially ailing gentry families, who not only moved in narrower social circles than their colonial forebears but now also strove to maintain control of family land and other resources in economically troubled times. The initial attraction between Richard and Judith led to negotiations between their parents, who debated the youngsters' compatibility, their financial prospects, and the timing of their expected nuptials.[30]

Judith's mother was the main obstacle to the proposed match. Anne Cary Randolph worried that Judith and Richard were too young to marry. Teenagers, she believed, were prone to infatuation and therefore liable "to be sour when the delirium of love is over, and Reason is allowed to reascend her Throne." As she explained in a letter to St. George Tucker, Anne Cary Randolph hoped to delay Judith's marriage and to keep all of her daughters single "till they were old enough to form a proper judgment of Mankind, well knowing that a woman's happiness depends entirely on the Husband she is united to." Judith's mother spoke from experience, since she herself had married at sixteen and borne thirteen children by the time she was forty-one. Her oldest daughters, Mary (or Molly) and Elizabeth, had married at eighteen and twenty, respectively, ages that were roughly typical for elite southern brides at this time.[31]

But Anne Cary Randolph's caution gave way to her daughter's infatuation and her husband's willingness to accept the match, though he professed to be "well acquainted" with the troubled "Circumstances" of the estate of Richard's deceased father. Accordingly, the Randolphs of Tuckahoe gave Richard's letters to Judith and allowed her to respond to them, thereby beginning the process that helped genteel young lovers to become better acquainted before making a final and irrevocable commitment to each other. St. George Tucker, who, since his wife's death the preceding year, was acting as Richard's sole guardian, reluctantly supported this decision, which amounted to an endorsement of the courtship and intended marriage. But Tucker nonetheless hoped to delay the wedding, concerned that Richard had not completed his legal training and that the youngsters lacked the financial resources necessary to sustain an independent household.[32]

In March 1789, however, the death of Anne Cary Randolph at the age of forty-four removed the main impediment to the speedy union of Judith and Richard. Left with eight unmarried children, five of whom were daughters, the master of Tuckahoe began to consider their futures in earnest. The girls must have recognized that their mother's death would forever change life at Tuckahoe: Judith, Nancy, and their youngest sister, three-year-old Virginia, etched their names in one of the house's upstairs windows above an inscription reading "March 16th 1789," the date their mother died. Soon thereafter Thomas Mann Randolph clearly did begin to reconsider the future of his unmarried daughters, and he apparently decided that it would be good to have Judith, the eldest, settled in her own household. St. George Tucker nevertheless resisted pressure to move up the wedding date, urging Randolph to fix a financial settlement on his daughter before the marriage took place. While Tucker hoped that Richard's education "would have qualified him for the immediate pursuit of his intended profession," he worried about the debts that encumbered his father's estate. In November 1789, Tucker therefore wrote to Thomas Mann Randolph, pressing him to consider the "material Interest" of the young couple and put them on a "proper footing," financially speaking, to help ensure their future "Happiness."[33]

Although Thomas Mann Randolph never appears to have responded directly to Tucker's concerns, Judith and Richard, both of whom were eager to wed, probably took matters into their own hands to get what they wanted. Despite a rising torrent of prescriptive literature that emphasized the importance of chastity for white women, it was not uncommon for young people to engage in sexual relations before marriage. In fact, the incidence of premarital sex and pregnancy was on the rise in post-revolutionary America. Aside from whatever ungovernable sexual urges they might have experienced, youngsters from respectable families knew that pregnancy could be a potent weapon in persuading reluctant parents both to hasten the arrival of their wedding day and to acquiesce in their choice of a prospective spouse. Circumstantial evidence suggests that Judith Randolph had become pregnant by late 1789. Some time in 1790, Judith traveled to her sister Mary's house "to be confined," or to endure the final stages of what both she and Richard believed to be a full-term pregnancy. Years later, Nancy, recalling the eve of her own fateful visit to Glentivar in 1792, wrote that Richard then had believed her own "state of health was exactly what Judy's had been when she, in 1790, went to [Mary's house] to be confined." If Judith's first, unhappy experience in childbirth, which the infant did not survive, occurred during the first half of 1790, conception must have preceded and expedited her nuptials.[34]

On the last day of 1789, Richard and Judith were wed at her father's house, as was customary in Virginia. The ceremony and subsequent festivities probably followed the format of other genteel nuptials held in eighteenth- and early nineteenth-century Virginia. The bride and her attendants—one of whom was likely Nancy, Judith's eldest unmarried sister—would have descended from Tuckahoe's ornately carved north staircase, joining Richard and his groomsmen, including his brothers, Theo and Jack, in the great hall, where the ceremony would occur. After a brief but solemn liturgy and recitation of vows from the Episcopal Book of Common Prayer, the bridal party, hosts, and guests proceeded to their celebration, which typically included dancing, singing, and a bountiful wedding feast. The celebration usually lasted for several days, with guests sleeping wherever they could find space in the crowded house.[35]

Judging from a satirical verse St. George Tucker penned on the day after Richard's and Judith's wedding, Thomas Mann Randolph spent extravagantly—and, in Tucker's view, unwisely—on his daughter's wedding feast. Tucker wrote:

> The guests were numerous and the board
> With dainties plentifully stored.
> There mutton, beef, and vermicelli
> Here venison stewed with currant jelly,
> Here turkeys robbed of bones and lungs
> Are crammed with oysters and with tongues.
> There pickled lobsters, prawn, and salmon
> And there a stuffed Virginia gammon.
> Here custards, tarts, and apple pies
> There syllabubs and jellies rise,
> Ice creams, and ripe and candied fruits
> With comfits and eryngo roots.
> Now entered every hungry guest
> And all prepared to take the feast.
> Our cynic cries—"how damned absurd
> To take such pains to make a ___!"[36]

In February 1790, after the customary round of post-wedding visits to various family members, the newlyweds set up housekeeping at Matoax, the 1,305-acre plantation on the Appomattox River that constituted a portion of Richard's inheritance from his father's estate. Matoax was about twenty-five miles from Judith's family at Tuckahoe, in Chesterfield County near Petersburg, the site of horse races and theatrical performances and third-largest town in the state, after Richmond and Williamsburg. The white frame house at Matoax, where Richard and his brothers had spent their childhood years, was commodious and relatively accessible to society. Judith's oldest sister, Mary, and her husband, David Meade Randolph, lived nearby, as did Richard's Bland relations and some of his and Judith's Randolph cousins.[37]

Richard's self-indulgence as a college student presaged his behavior as master of this plantation household. Although the Tucker family had resided at Matoax as recently as 1788, he and Judith felt compelled to add to the house's furnishings. Within months of their arrival, they bought several carpets, a table, and a chest of drawers—all of which Richard imported from Britain, on credit, and charged against the small income he received from his father's estate. At Matoax, the young Randolphs also entertained extravagantly, going through prodigious amounts of meat, flour, and other provisions to feed their numerous guests. By June 1790, they were in such bad financial straits that Richard tried to sell his horses in order to pay his creditors. Three months later, however, he made yet another major purchase, a phaeton or carriage, which he also charged to his father's estate. Reckless spending exhausted Richard's money and his credit, too. By early 1791, Virginia merchants were refusing to honor his bills of exchange.[38]

St. George Tucker, who worried about his stepson's lavish spending, was apparently instrumental in persuading him to settle permanently on his landholdings in Cumberland County, some ninety miles northwest of Matoax. For at least a generation, the Cumberland County plantation had been known as "Bizarre," a name that probably referred to the irregular dimensions of its house, which contrasted markedly with the symmetrical Georgian style of architecture favored by Virginia's colonial elites. Judith agreed that moving to Cumberland, where the house was smaller and society less plentiful, would enable Richard and her to support themselves more readily on what she called his "small patrimony." In November 1790, after less than a year of marriage, Judith and Richard moved to Bizarre. Tucker and the Randolph family's hired managers in Chesterfield continued to oversee business at Matoax plantation. A few years later, however, the insolvent Richard was forced to sell his ancestral home.[39]

The Randolph family's association with Bizarre and its environs dated to the 1720s, when five sons of William and Mary Isham Randolph received some of the earliest royal patents for land in the Virginia piedmont, the area west of the tidewater but east of the Blue Ridge. The Randolph brothers secured nearly

30,000 acres in the piedmont counties of Goochland and Amelia. When part of Goochland became the separate county of Cumberland in 1749, the heirs of the recently deceased Richard Randolph of Curles owned a total of nearly 15,000 acres in the new county. One of the legatees was John Randolph, the father of Judith's insolvent husband. One of the tracts he inherited was a plantation called Bizarre. Situated along the Appomattox River, Bizarre was prime acreage in the fastest-growing tobacco-producing region in Virginia.[40]

Before the Revolution, the Randolphs participated in the piedmont tobacco boom mainly as absentee owners of large tracts, known as "quarters," cultivated by growing numbers of enslaved workers and overseen by resident plantation managers. In 1759, the county's first complete surviving tax list included two Randolphs, Peter and Ryland, who had begun to improve their landholdings. Each was part of a tiny elite of nine taxpayers (out of a total of 547 in the county) who claimed twenty or more "tithables," which the law defined as white males and blacks of both sexes, aged sixteen and above. In the next decade, Cumberland's elite got richer while their neighbors' access to bonded labor remained unchanged, at least in absolute terms. In 1768, five Randolph cousins, none of whose primary residence was in Cumberland, were assessed for a total of 131 tithables, 51 of whom were chargeable to the estate of the deceased Richard Randolph of Curles. Primarily as a result of the expansion of the holdings of a few leading planters like the Randolphs, enslaved people now constituted a majority of the county's population. By 1790, the county's population had risen to some 8,153 souls, of whom 4,434 were slaves. Young Richard Randolph, who had forty bondpeople to work his 779-acre plantation, became one of Cumberland's largest slaveholders on his arrival at Bizarre.[41]

The house at Bizarre, which is no longer standing, had been built decades earlier to accommodate the Randolphs on their occasional trips to Cumberland. Frances Bland Randolph Tucker and her children had lived there after fleeing Matoax to escape the advancing British army in 1780. The two-story house sat atop a huge stone foundation cut by slaves from a nearby vein of rock. Though small and rustic by gentry standards, at least one notable visitor commented favorably on it. When Benjamin Henry Latrobe, future architect of the national Capitol in Washington, passed through Cumberland in 1796, he observed that the name "Bizarre" was "not quite applicable" because "there is nothing *bizarre* about" the Randolphs' house.[42]

Still, Richard and Judith's new home was far removed from the social life of Tuckahoe or even that of Matoax. Although the county's population had grown significantly since its founding, the inhabitants of Cumberland resided in rural seclusion on widely dispersed tobacco plantations. The county seat, Cumberland Courthouse, was a mere crossroads located approximately fifty miles southwest of Richmond and twenty miles from Bizarre. A few small and scattered churches

Virginia Piedmont Counties, 1790

Fredericksburg

Richmond

Williamsburg

Petersburg

Chesterfield

Orange

Louisa

Goochland

Powhatan

Amelia

Nottoway

Fluvanna

Cumberland

Lunenburg

Albemarle

Buckingham

Prince Edward

Mecklenburg

Amherst

Campbell

Charlotte

Halifax

Pittsylvania

Henry

N

0   100 mi

UNC Charlotte Cartography Lab, December 2002.

served the spiritual needs of the populace. Old Briery Church, a Presbyterian congregation across the Appomattox River in Prince Edward County, was the one nearest to Bizarre. Reflecting on his rural isolation, one of Cumberland's more cosmopolitan planters gave his home a French name—Hors du Monde—which means "outside the world." The name was "very appropriate" in the eyes of Benjamin Latrobe, who found "no possibility of communication by letter or visit, but by riding half a dozen miles *into* the world."[43]

Either a desire for companionship or a sense of family obligation led Richard and Judith to open their home to two of their siblings not long after they set up housekeeping at Bizarre. Judith's sister, seventeen-year-old Nancy Randolph, came to Bizarre some time in 1791. Richard's sickly twenty-year-old brother Theo, who had spent the past few years drinking and debauching at Princeton and Columbia before going to Bermuda for his health, arrived around the same time. The pair had known each other for at least two years. Indeed, Nancy later claimed that she had fallen in love with Theo in 1789, exchanging clandestine letters with him in defiance of her father's wish that she remain aloof from Richard's dissipated brother. Although there is no contemporary evidence of Nancy's romantic involvement with Theo—their relationship, after all, was supposed to be secret—Nancy later asserted that she had regarded herself as "engaged" to Richard's younger brother. According to Nancy, only Richard knew of their romance, though the brothers' aunt Martha Bland had heard rumors of Theo's impending marriage to an unspecified woman, possibly Nancy herself, by September 1790.[44]

Nancy's alleged paramour, Theodorick Randolph, shared all the vices and few of the virtues of his elder brother. As a student, Theo had been more troublesome than Richard, having been dismissed from Walker Maury's establishment for having "too little thought either of study, or conformity to the discipline of the school." Jack Randolph later claimed that Theo had "set a bad example" for him during their college days, when he neglected his studies and devoted himself entirely to "pleasure and fun." Theo's vices, Jack maintained, "undermined his constitution and destroyed his health forever." Yet others besides Nancy were fond of the young man. Martha Bland wrote affectionately of him to St. George Tucker in 1790, as did Tucker's sister Eliza, who came to know Theo during his visit to Bermuda in 1791. John Holcombe, a friend of the Randolphs and the Tuckers, admired the young man's "great flow of Spirits," as he lay mortally ill in Cumberland in 1792. On 9 February, Holcombe, who reported to St. George Tucker that Theo "cannot walk or stand without assistance," averred that he "never was so desirous for any young man to recover in my life." Less than a week later, Theo, whose body had become a "mere skeleton," died at Bizarre.[45]

While Theo had gone to Bizarre to convalesce, Nancy sought refuge there from the unhappiness she experienced at Tuckhoe following the loss of her beloved mother. The death of Anne Cary Randolph in March 1789, which hastened the marriage of Judith and Richard, also led Thomas Mann Randolph to explore the marital prospects of Nancy, the eldest of his remaining unmarried daughters. According to Nancy, her father persistently pressed her to marry a wealthy man. Archibald Randolph, brother of Mary Randolph Harrison of Glentivar, was one of his approved suitors. Middle-aged widowers General Henry Lee and Benjamin Harrison were others.[46]

Then, in September 1790, the forty-nine-year-old Thomas Mann Randolph decided to wed the teenaged, but well-connected, Gabriella Harvie. Although Harvie was much younger than the master of Tuckahoe, middle-aged widowers typically remarried, and they often chose young and previously unmarried women to be their second wives. Thomas Jefferson's reaction to his old friend's marriage to Harvie may have been typical. "Colo[nel] Randolph's marriage was to be expected," he noted, without commenting on the age gap between him and his new wife. "All his amusements depending on society," Jefferson observed, Randolph "cannot be expected to live alone" at Tuckahoe.[47]

Even as a widower, however, Thomas Mann Randolph had never lived "alone," and the fact that he did share his house with five children, ranging in age from three to fifteen, probably provided him added incentive to take a second wife. As Randolph's eldest unmarried daughter, Nancy had acted as mistress of Tuckahoe following her mother's death and Judith's departure. Gabriella's arrival thus diminished Nancy's status in her father's house, as her young stepmother eagerly assumed her position as mistress of the household. Within months of the wedding, Gabriella began redecorating, painting the black walnut walls in the first-floor parlor white—a change that in Nancy's eyes must have amounted to a purposeful attempt to expunge both the memory and the influence of her own mother. Tensions mounted, and Gabriella urged her husband to redouble his efforts to get Nancy suitably married and away from Tuckahoe. Nancy later claimed that she left her father's house "to avoid a Marriage hateful to me," one that Gabriella Harvie Randolph appears to have promoted.[48]

Even more than their mother's death the preceding year, the decision of forty-nine-year-old Thomas Mann Randolph, Sr., to take an eighteen-year-old bride threatened the comfort and security of his children, especially his daughters. Martha Jefferson, who recently had wed Thomas Mann Randolph, Jr., Nancy and Judith's eldest brother and the presumed heir to Tuckahoe, worried that his father's remarriage would adversely affect the financial settlements destined for her husband and his siblings. As it turned out, Martha had good reason to worry, because her father-in-law's second marriage would produce one son, another Thomas Mann Randolph, who would supplant his older half-brother as heir to the family's ancestral home. Nevertheless, in 1790, Thomas Jefferson advised his daughter to be conciliatory and look on the marriage as "a bad stop on your harpsichord" that she should "not touch," instead making herself "happy with the good ones." Nancy and at least one of her sisters, however, could not view the situation with such philosophical detachment. Virginia, the youngest, seems to have spent as much time as possible with her brother Tom's family in Albemarle County. Nancy fled Tuckahoe shortly after her father's remarriage, staying first with her "father's excellent Sisters" and then with her brother Tom and sister-in-law Martha. Then, some time in 1791, Nancy joined Judith and Richard (and soon Theo, too) at Bizarre.[49]

Although subsequent events would cast doubt on the wisdom of this decision, as a young single woman Nancy had few options. Safeguarding feminine virtue was widely held to be a prerequisite for making a respectable marriage and thus the surest means for a woman to ensure her own security and prevent herself from becoming an economic and social liability to her family. Because contemporaries assumed that fathers, husbands, and brothers were the best protectors of feminine virtue, young single women risked damaging their reputations if they sought to live independently. By leaving her father's house for that of her brother-in-law, Nancy Randolph seemed to comply with the gender conventions of her time and place, exchanging one male-headed domestic environment for another. Indeed,

Figure 1.2 Nancy Randolph in 1796. Nancy was twenty-two years old when Benjamin Henry Latrobe visited Bizarre and sketched her "from Memory" in his journal. Latrobe's drawing reveals more about the style of women's clothes in the period than about his subject's physical appearance or personality. The Maryland Historical Society, Baltimore, Maryland.

Nancy came to Bizarre precisely because she believed that she no longer enjoyed the care and protection of her father, Thomas Mann Randolph of Tuckahoe.

What kind of a life did Nancy anticipate on her arrival in Cumberland County? Did she believe that Theo was or would be living there, too, or did she merely suppose that living with Richard and Judith might give her an opportunity to see him occasionally without her father's interference? Or was Richard, for whom she always professed affection, her true romantic interest, as some would later charge? Who invited Nancy to join the Bizarre household? Perhaps Richard issued the invitation, seeking to promote the romance between her and Theo, to seduce Nancy himself, or merely to protect her from the designs of a mercenary and insensitive father and stepmother. Or maybe Judith, who lived in relative seclusion in rural Cumberland, simply desired her sister's companionship. Whatever the intent of the principals, Nancy would spend most of the next thirteen years at Bizarre.

Born in September 1774, Nancy Randolph was almost two years younger than her sister Judith and in her seventeenth year when she arrived at Bizarre. Lively and attractive, she was appealing to suitors despite her father's financial woes and her own apparent stubbornness, curious about the world and eager to shine in its society. Benjamin Latrobe found Nancy sufficiently engaging to sketch her "from Memory" following a brief meeting with her in 1796. A family friend described her as having "rare genius and personal accomplishments," while Nancy herself equated "Existence without Genius and Taste" to a "World without a Sun." In retrospect it should be obvious that such a lively young woman would be unhappy in her sister's remote and frugal household, even if she was enamored of Richard's ailing brother.[50]

Although subsequent events would jaundice recollections of life at Bizarre after the arrival of Nancy and Theo, at least one guest recalled never having seen "any Marks of ill will or discontent between Mr. [Richard] Randolph & his Lady" or among the others. Another, who "visited the family without ceremony" some time in 1792, also professed to see "the most perfect harmony" at Bizarre.[51] Still, at a time when most white Virginians lived in families composed of a father, mother, and children, the Randolphs' living arrangements were highly unorthodox. The residents of Bizarre, the oldest of whom was Richard, who turned twenty-one in 1791, were in effect children without parents. Death had robbed the Randolph brothers of both father and mother, while Judith and Nancy had lost their mother to death and their father to indifference. Moreover, until mid-1792, when Judith gave birth to her first son, the Bizarre household was unusual in lacking both parents and offspring. Contemporary moralists and social critics valued marriage, parenthood, and family life generally as sources of order and virtue in an unsettled and potentially disorderly post-revolutionary republican society—a view that later would be in some respects vindicated by the scandal at Bizarre.[52]

Members of the Bizarre ménage did not reject family ties, but rather embraced and adapted them in ways that accentuated the growing preference for affection over authority as the chief basis of family life in eighteenth-century America. Lacking fathers of their own, the residents of Bizarre looked to St. George Tucker as a surrogate, despite the fact that Tucker, who lived in distant Williamsburg and had only temporary custodial power over the Randolphs' property, possessed none of the carrots and sticks traditionally associated with fatherhood. Richard called Tucker his "beloved father," expressing an affection that the older man reciprocated.[53] After marrying Richard in 1789, Judith also adopted Tucker as her "dear father," and, though he had a daughter of his own, Tucker referred to Judith as his "dear daughter," too. Richard and Judith had two sons, whose names reflected both their formal Randolph heritage and the informal, affective bonds to Tucker and his family. Following Virginia custom, their sons, John St. George Randolph and Theodorick Tudor Randolph, bore names that commemorated Richard's father and grandfather, but they took their middle names from St. George Tucker and his brother, Thomas Tudor Tucker, whom Richard regarded as his uncle and benefactor. Significantly, Richard and Judith's boys were invariably known as "Saint" and "Tudor," another sign that their parents highly valued their connection to the Tuckers.[54]

Even more striking was the relationship that blossomed between Tucker and Nancy Randolph. After moving to Bizarre, Nancy initiated a correspondence with Tucker that lasted until his death in 1827. Like Judith, Nancy referred to Tucker as her beloved "father" and solicited his advice on personal and financial matters. The fact that both sisters occasionally appealed to Tucker as their "more than Father" suggests that they turned to him to fill a void left by the seeming desertion and subsequent death in 1793 of Thomas Mann Randolph. Tucker reciprocated, continuing to play the paternal role for the Randolph women long after the deaths of his stepsons.[55]

Visiting, mostly among family, was the chief form of sociability for the Randolphs of Bizarre. They journeyed to Williamsburg—about one hundred miles away—once a year to visit St. George Tucker and his new wife, Lelia Skipwith Carter, who in turn made the long trip to Cumberland from time to time. Otherwise, Judith and Richard exchanged visits mainly with their siblings and other young married couples within the extended Randolph family. Judith and Richard spent their wedding night at Presqu'ile, the James River plantation of Judith's oldest sister, Mary, and her husband, David Meade Randolph; some months later, a pregnant Judith returned to Presqu'ile for her first "confinement." Judith and Richard, along with Nancy, also exchanged visits with Thomas Mann Randolph, Jr., and his wife Martha Jefferson, who during these years made at least three extended visits to Bizarre, on one occasion accompanied by another Randolph sister. Cousins Anne and Brett Randolph of nearby Powhatan County were also frequent guests at Bizarre, as were Carter Page and his wife, Mary Cary, who, though a near-contemporary of Judith and Nancy, was a younger sister of their deceased mother.[56]

Mary Randolph and Randolph Harrison, who married in 1790, completed the social circle of young couples that included the Randolphs of Bizarre. Born in 1773, Mary Randolph was a first cousin to Judith, Nancy, and their siblings, among whom she had spent most of her childhood years. As an adult, Mary kept in touch with most of the Tuckahoe sisters, but she was particularly close to the middle sisters—Judith, Nancy, and Jane—who were nearest to her in age. In the years immediately following her marriage to her cousin Randolph Harrison, Mary's ties to Judith become especially strong as a result of their shared experiences. Both cousins were seventeen years old when, within months of each other, they married young men of prominent families but limited means; within a year, the young Randolphs had moved to Cumberland County, where they joined the Harrisons as members of the local planter elite. Both Mary and Judith also experienced pregnancy soon after marrying and in more or less alternating years thereafter, as was typical among elite southern women of their generation. Judith had her first unhappy experience with childbirth in 1790; she gave birth to a son in 1792, miscarried the following year, and bore a second son in 1795. Mary gave birth to three children during this same period, and she would endure another thirteen pregnancies in the next twenty-five years.[57]

Mary's husband, Randolph Harrison, came from a family as prominent and highly-placed as her own. Randolph Harrison was descended from Benjamin Harrison, who settled in Virginia some time before 1634, when he became clerk of the governor's council. Like the early generations of Virginia Randolphs, Benjamin Harrison and his sons and grandsons used both political connections and strategic marriages to accumulate vast acreage in the colony. Carter Henry Harrison, a member of the fourth generation of Virginia-born Harrisons and the father of Randolph Harrison, inherited some three thousand acres in Cumberland County from his maternal grandfather, Robert "King" Carter, the wealthiest Virginian of his generation. In 1754, shortly after completing his studies at the College of William and Mary and London's Inns of Court, Carter Henry Harrison became a fulltime resident of Cumberland.[58]

Carter Henry Harrison settled at Clifton, where he built a fine white clapboard house and established both a thriving family and a commanding presence in Cumberland County. Harrison married Susanna Randolph in 1763, and with her raised a family of six children. Carter Henry Harrison was a colonel in the Cumberland County militia and one of the justices of the county court. A leader of the patriot movement in his locale, in April 1776, Carter Henry

Figure 1.3 Randolph Harrison. The master of Glentivar was a member of one of Cumberland County's leading families. Unlike many of his contemporaries, he prospered as a planter in post-revolutionary Virginia. Virginia Historical Society, Richmond, Virginia.

Figure 1.4 Mary Randolph Harrison. First cousin to Judith and Nancy Randolph, with whom she shared a sisterly intimacy, Mary Randolph married Randolph Harrison and moved with him to Glentivar in 1790. Virginia Historical Society, Richmond, Virginia.

Harrison penned the resolutions of the Cumberland County committee, which called on Virginians to assert their independence from Great Britain.[59]

The third of four sons of Carter Henry Harrison and Susanna Randolph of Clifton, Randolph Harrison was thus born into one of Cumberland's wealthiest and most prominent planter families. Like the Randolphs, however, the Harrisons suffered serious financial reverses during and after the War of Independence. The same tax records that so vastly over-estimated the true value of the estate of Thomas Mann Randolph of Tuckahoe in 1787 similarly exaggerated the prosperity of Carter Henry Harrison. In 1787, Harrison paid taxes on 4,670 acres and 129 slaves, though he was in danger of being forced to liquidate his estate to discharge his debts. At that point, his eighteen-year-old son Randolph stepped in, determined to preserve both his father's standing in the county and his own future prospects.[60]

By the time Randolph Harrison married Mary Randolph in 1790, he had proven himself to be as ambitious, competent, and hard-working as any Virginia planter of his generation. In two years, Randolph Harrison put his father's estate in order, selling some land to pay his debts and improving the management and productivity of the rest. Carter Henry Harrison rewarded his son's efforts with a gift of some eight hundred acres within a mile or so of Clifton, along with ten slaves to work his new plantation.[61] Here he and his young wife built their modest house, Glentivar, which was still unfinished when the Randolphs made their fateful visit on 1 October 1792.

As the Randolphs approached Glentivar on that autumn day, they could not have anticipated the events of the coming days and months. Nancy's screams, Richard's footsteps, and a few stained shingles caused the slaves to gossip. The stories they told, in time, spread to the wider community. The resulting scandal would divide the Randolph family and elicit their neighbors' outrage, leaving Richard Randolph, the improvident scion of a prestigious family, little choice but to defend his reputation as Bizarre's putative patriarch and as a man of honor.

2

Honor and the Court

In Richard Randolph's Virginia, honor was a precious commodity that men defended with their lives. Reputation was everything in this relatively homogeneous planter society where personal contacts were still essential to secure credit, marry well, and obtain posts of public influence and trust. Noting its pervasiveness in the Old South, one historian has defined honor as a "cluster of ethical rules, most readily found in societies of small communities, by which judgments are ratified by community consensus." In other words, an honor culture, as another southern historian has observed, is one that subscribes to a "system of values within which you have exactly as much worth as others confer upon you."[1] In 1792–93, as it became clear to Richard Randolph that his neighbors now questioned his worth as a gentleman and a patriarch, he acted to restore his tainted honor.

In eighteenth-century Virginia, as in most other honor-bound cultures, what constituted honorable conduct in the eyes of the community varied according to an individual's gender, race, and social rank. Contemporaries generally equated white women's honor with sexual purity, while white southerners regarded African Americans as inherently incapable of honor. By contrast, Richard's neighbors expected him, as an elite white male, to exercise mastery over his family and his slaves and to wield authority in his local community. But they also expected an honorable man to protect his dependents and show benevolence toward those whom he—and his neighbors—deemed his deserving inferiors. If the rumors about Richard having had sexual relations with his dependent sister-in-law were true, his claim to honor was forfeit. And so, too, was his standing as a gentleman and a patriarch, both in his own household and in the wider community.[2]

Accordingly, once Richard concluded that the gossip about him would not die down, he was determined to defend his honor. First, he confronted his accusers, challenging them to retract their statements or defend them publicly, either verbally or on the field of honor. When these efforts failed, Richard next turned to the courts for vindication. Legal proceedings, he hoped, could provide him with

official certification that he was not guilty of any crime. More important still, the
courtroom, like a dueling ground, would be a public forum in which he might
confront his foes and, by doing so, regain his reputation as a man of honor.

Because gossip is typically ephemeral, it is difficult to recover precisely who said
what about the Randolphs and when they said it. In late October 1792,
Randolph Harrison reported to the family that the slaves were still talking about
Nancy's recent misadventures at Glentivar. More ominously, however, new
rumors soon were spreading among white Virginians in Cumberland and far
beyond. Richard's brother Jack, who resumed his studies at the College of
William and Mary shortly after his visit to Glentivar, had heard gossip about
what allegedly had happened in Chesterfield County, as well as in Williamsburg.
The story Jack heard, though damaging to Nancy, was far more critical of
Richard, whom gossips now portrayed as the father of her child and its murderer
as well. Lawyer James Monroe—the future president—informed Thomas
Jefferson that public opinion in Cumberland was "deeply fixed" against Richard.
Jefferson's young kinsman and future son-in-law John Wayles Eppes concurred,
noting that the gossip had elicited a strong "prejudice" against Richard among
the "people of Cumberland." Clearly, blacks and whites, elites and plebeians,
were talking about the Randolphs. The gossips' diverse and always implicit
motives will be explored in more detail in the next chapter.[3]

By January 1793, three months after the incident at Glentivar, Richard, Judith,
and Nancy had fled Cumberland, perhaps hoping the gossip would abate in their
absence. They traveled first to Williamsburg, where Richard sought the advice of
his stepfather, St. George Tucker, who counseled him to stay calm and remain in
Williamsburg, at least for the time being. By mid-March, however, Judith, whom
Richard now knew to be pregnant (she would later miscarry), accompanied him to
Tuckahoe. Richard may have anticipated the unfriendly reception he received
there from his in-laws. Years later, Nancy claimed that before her sister and
brother-in-law left Williamsburg she had prepared Richard for the encounter with
the Tuckahoe Randolphs by giving him a written statement in which she named
Theo as the father of her child, absolving Richard of all culpability.[4]

When he arrived at Tuckahoe, Richard found that Judith and Nancy's male
relations were his most hostile critics. He informed St. George Tucker that
Judith and Nancy's brother William was the chief source of the "horrid and
malicious lie" that he had seduced Nancy, a story that had been circulating "for
some time too freely" throughout Virginia. Around the same time, moreover,
William's older brother, Thomas Mann Randolph, Jr., sent Richard a letter in
which he threatened reprisals should Richard attempt to escape guilt by naming

his dead brother Theodorick as Nancy's seducer. If Richard attempted to "transfer the stigma" to Theo, Tom warned Richard that he would "wash out with your blood the stain on my family."[5]

Nancy's brothers clearly regarded the rumors about what had happened at Glentivar as real or potential threats to both their interests and their honor.[6] Tom and William knew that maintaining their sister's innocence was essential if she hoped to marry into a respectable gentry family; because single women were often financially dependent on their kin, the brothers had more than an emotional stake in her defense. Not only was Nancy's reputation for sexual purity compromised, but so, too, was the honor of her male kin, who should have shielded her from defilement. To preserve their own honor as gentlemen, Nancy's brothers had to show that they were in no way responsible for her disgrace. Only an admission of guilt from Richard—in other words, from someone whom they could have regarded as another presumably worthy protector of their sister's virtue—could absolve the Tuckahoe Randolphs from the taint of dishonor.

Richard, however, proved uncooperative, repeatedly insisting that nothing sordid had transpired at Glentivar or Bizarre. At Tuckahoe, he refused to use Nancy's statement to defend himself. Even if Richard could have persuaded others that Theo had been her lover, conceding Nancy's pregnancy would have been tantamount to admitting that he was unable to protect and govern his dependents at Bizarre. Richard therefore maintained that any rumors about Nancy's pregnancy or his own alleged relationship with her were baseless, and that the allegations against him, in particular, were so specious that ignoring them would result in his utter and complete disgrace. Once he came to believe that William Randolph was primarily responsible for those rumors, Richard confronted his brother-in-law, seeking to avenge his insults on the field of honor.

Dueling became increasingly popular in the uncertain cultural climate of post-revolutionary America, as insecure gentlemen jealously defended their reputations as possessors of manly qualities—such as honesty, courage, and benevolence—that in colonial times had justified their membership in the ruling elite. In the southern states, where most communities remained small and homogeneous and where white men's need to show mastery over slaves informed their relationships with others, too, interactions between elite white men could be especially volatile. A real or imagined insult, according to one historian, "immediately evoked images of mastery and slavery" because it "involved the imputation of 'slavelike' behavior—of being a coward, thief, liar, or something similar." So, when the Randolph brothers accused Richard of defiling their sister and then being too cowardly to own up to his transgression, the code of honor dictated that he challenge them either to prove or withdraw these allegations which, in Richard's telling words, had "blackened" his "character."[7]

In March 1793, Richard challenged his brother-in-law, William Randolph, to account for his conduct. In doing so, Richard risked the possibility of having to fight a duel with William, though he probably expected the affair to be resolved, as were most affairs of honor between gentlemen, without an exchange of gunfire. Typically, the prospect of a duel resulted in negotiations that elicited a carefully worded statement from the offending party, who withdrew his original insult without admitting that he himself had acted dishonorably by being purposefully dishonest. A statement of this sort, like an actual duel, would have afforded Richard a measure of public vindication, but William proved intractable. An exasperated Richard informed his stepfather that he had "endeavored, by every method I could devise, to bring William Randolph to personal explanation of his conduct, and to give me personal satisfaction for his aspersions of my character." William, however, did not accept Richard's challenge, deeming none of his brother-in-law's complaints or insults "sufficient to rise his feelings." By not engaging Richard in either verbal or physical combat, William further demeaned him, refusing to recognize him as either his equal or a man of honor.[8]

When William did not respond to his overtures, Richard began to explore the possibility of taking legal action against him. While most eighteenth-century Virginians assumed that family quarrels and affairs of honor were best resolved by extralegal means, they sometimes sought the intervention of the courts as a last resort, especially when such disputes affected the wider community. In March 1793, Richard urged his father-in-law, Thomas Mann Randolph, Sr., to initiate a slander suit against William to defend Nancy's honor—and, by extension, Richard's, too—by denying that anything either criminal or unseemly had transpired at Glentivar. Richard hoped that he, Judith, and Nancy might spend the summer in the northern states while the courts exposed "the circumstances, from beginning to end, of the persons accusing and accused . . . and the villainy of the traducers." But the master of Tuckahoe, who had been estranged from Nancy since remarrying and was now in declining health, spurned litigation that would likely reflect badly on both himself and his sons.[9]

Thomas Mann Randolph's refusal to undertake legal action against his son William changed Richard's travel plans and left him alone to pursue the public hearing he now deemed essential to defend his honor. Despite his earlier promise to Judith "not to say anything more, or make any further enquiry into the abominable story," by late March Richard felt compelled to act. St. George Tucker supported his stepson, averring that "nothing short of a *fair, open,* and *judicial enquiry* into the truth of the charges . . . could effectively wipe them off" and dispel the "aspersions" that had been cast on his good name. Acting on the advice of his stepfather, on 29 March, Richard penned a public notice denouncing his accusers, whom he challenged to confront him openly. His notice appeared in the state's leading newspaper, the *Virginia Gazette, and General Advertiser,* on 3 April 1793. Addressed "To the Public," Richard's public notice appeared on the paper's third page, immediately following an account of the French revolutionaries' beheading of King Louis XVI in Paris.[10]

Richard's notice was an open letter to the readers of the *Gazette,* whom he called on to witness his efforts to disprove "the imputation of crimes at which humanity revolts" that had "daily acquired strength in the minds of my fellow citizens." Specifically, Richard announced that he would surrender himself to the Cumberland County court at the beginning of its April session so that he might "answer in due course of law, any charge or crime which any person or persons whatsoever shall then and there think proper to alledge against me." Although he did not mention his accusers by name, clearly he sought to spark a public confrontation with his in-laws at Tuckahoe.[11]

At least superficially, Richard's letter "To the Public" was a continuation of the affair of honor he had tried to initiate at Tuckahoe a few weeks earlier. In the 1790s, politically prominent men increasingly enlisted the partisan press to issue or rebut insults that eventually resulted in confrontations, even duels, in defense of personal honor. Richard appears to have had no political ambitions, but, he, too, brought his concerns about personal honor into the public sphere by attempting to defend himself in print in 1793. Richard knew that duels waged over intimate matters often became public spectacles that variously enhanced or damaged the personal reputations of combatants in the wider community. Because the allegations against him had spread so *"far and wide,"* Richard concluded that the community he needed to address extended far beyond his own neighborhood. He accordingly took the very unusual step—for a nonpolitical man—of publicizing his case in print. Writing to newspapers, for Richard, as for the politicians, demonstrated a concern for "public opinion" that had been unknown among the more secure and self-confident gentry of the pre-revolutionary era.[12]

Like the duelist who believes that his own conduct is beyond reproach, Richard imputed dishonor to his accusers, whom he challenged in print to present evidence against him, asserting that he would put his life "in hazard" to avenge his honor. "Calumny to be *obviated* must be *confronted,*" he asserted, and he offered his accusers the option of confronting him either in court, where he would face conviction for a capital offense, or in the public press, where he risked even greater "public odium" than he had experienced thus far. Richard challenged his detractors to state "with *precision* and *clearness* the *facts* which they lay to my charge and the *evidence* whether *direct* or *circumstantial* by which I am to be proved guilty," leaving the court and the community to "judge between me and them." He even informed his readers that he would subject Nancy to public scrutiny in order to remove "the stigma which has been imposed upon me." "Let not a pretended tenderness towards the supposed accomplice in the imputed guilt shelter me," Richard wrote, predicting that Nancy would "meet the accusation with a fortitude *of which innocence alone is capable*."[13]

Richard's new willingness to expose Nancy to public curiosity and opprobrium betokened the desperation arising from his increasingly perilous situation in Cumberland. By presenting himself as a wrongly accused man who confidently and voluntarily confronted those who would impugn his honor, Richard aptly played the role of a self-possessed gentleman, but his performance belied reality. By April 1793, local authorities were considering arresting him and submitting his case to the county court, not on his invitation but rather in response to the mounting popular outrage against him. Courts, after all, were supposed to enforce community values and preserve the public peace. In Cumberland, condemnation of Richard was so pervasive that, writing from Matoax, Judith confided to Mary Harrison that she had "very little thought of ever returning to Bizarre."[14]

On Thursday 18 April, at least partly in response to popular pressure, justices Joseph Michaux and Anderson Cocke ordered the county sheriff to apprehend Richard, and Nancy, too, so that they might appear "on the fourth Monday in this Month, at the Courthouse of [Cumberland]." Although the sheriff reported that Nancy, who remained at Matoax with Judith, was "not found in my bailiwick," Richard surrendered himself to the inevitable and was taken into custody. Four days later, on Monday 22 April, three justices convened at the Cumberland County courthouse and charged Richard Randolph of Bizarre with "feloniously murdering a child delivered of the body of Nancy Randolph or [being] accessory to the same." The justices committed the accused to the county jail, where he was held without bail "until he shall be thence discharged by due course of law." The authorities did not pursue their investigation of Nancy at this point, knowing that they could charge her, if necessary, after resolving Richard's case. After Richard's arrest, Judith, Nancy, and the rest of the family summarily returned to Bizarre. Richard spent the next week in the jail in the village of Cumberland Courthouse, some twenty miles away from his family. Then, on Monday 29 April, Richard Randolph took his place in the courtroom as a defendant charged with a capital crime before all sixteen of the county's justices and a crowd of curious onlookers.[15]

In eighteenth-century Virginia, law and hierarchy promoted social order, but by the 1790s both were in a state of flux. On the one hand, many Virginians increasingly complained that the county courts, which had been their most visible and effective sources of law and governance in the colonial period, had become uninformed, inefficient, and incapable of serving their judicial needs in the post-revolutionary era. On the other hand, the political and economic changes of the revolutionary era weakened Virginians' habitual deference toward their society's traditional elites. Those elites, who typically had deep roots in their communities, were the same men who generally presided as justices of the peace over the proceedings of the county courts.

George Carrington epitomized the patriarchal ideal of gentry governance in colonial Cumberland. In 1746, the voters of Goochland County selected him as one of their representatives to the colonial House of Burgesses. When Carrington's legislative district became the separate county of Cumberland in 1749, the governor appointed him as one of the new county's first justices of the peace, a post he retained until his death in 1785. The 1752 elections, the first in which the voters of Cumberland chose their own legislators, resulted in Carrington's reelection to the House of Burgesses, where he represented his county until 1761, returning to the legislature in 1765 and again during the revolutionary era. Carrington was also the county's first coroner, a colonel in its militia, and a member of the parish vestry of his local Church of England congregation. By the 1760s, his sons were following in his footsteps, becoming justices, vestrymen, and militia officers. In April 1793, four of George Carrington's six sons would be among the county justices presiding when Richard Randolph appeared before the Cumberland County court.[16]

The Carringtons and other county justices personified law and governance for most Virginians, who welcomed the opportunity to attend the court's sessions to socialize, conduct business, and resolve local conflicts. The justices convened monthly for civil cases, which constituted the bulk of their business, and quarterly for criminal matters, in which the county courts had final jurisdiction only in cases in which the conviction of the defendant did not result in the loss of "life or limb." In these more serious felony cases, the county court remanded indicted defendants for trial in a higher court. At the county level, the courts and the men who ran them aimed to promote social order and the rule of law. The rituals of court day—the solemn entry of the justices, their elevation on the bench, the maintenance of order and decorum—showcased the authority, wisdom, and benevolence of the gentlemen-justices, reaffirming their status and influence, both individually and collectively.[17]

By enlisting the participation of freeholders as jurymen and witnesses and in other capacities, the courts also taught ordinary citizens how the law worked in their community. By involving a broad cross-section of the white male population in judicial determinations and law enforcement, the courts enhanced the legitimacy of those processes. Finally, by providing a forum in which Virginians could defend their most cherished assets—their property and their reputations— with words instead of violence, the courts also offered a peaceable and rational alternative to the physical confrontations that nonetheless remained common in most Virginia communities.[18]

Criticisms of the county courts mounted after the Revolution, however, when the justices were overwhelmed by a deluge of civil cases in the economic chaos of the postwar years. Most county justices were planters with no formal legal training who owed their places on the bench to their political contacts and high standing in their county communities. By the 1780s, Richard Randolph's stepfather, St. George Tucker, was one of the prominent and learned attorneys who led the assault on the county magistrates, arguing that only a judiciary of highly educated and salaried professionals could restore the efficiency and efficacy of Virginia justice. Tucker and his associates spearheaded an effort which, in 1787, resulted in the enactment of a law dividing the state into eighteen judicial districts, each having a new court that could hear civil cases—thereby decreasing the volume of business on the county dockets—and that could serve as appellate courts for cases initially adjudicated at the county level. The new district courts, which commenced operation in 1789, also had jurisdiction in felony cases, supplanting the old General Court, which previously had adjudicated serious felony cases for all Virginia. Consequently, if the Cumberland County court found sufficient evidence to issue a formal indictment against Richard Randolph in 1793, the justices would remand his case not to a tribunal in Richmond which had jurisdiction throughout the state but rather to the nearby Prince Edward District Court.[19]

When Richard appeared before the Cumberland justices in April 1793, his objectives and those of the court were at least potentially complementary. The justices sought to restore order and stability in the county, either by punishing or clearing an elite defendant against whom resentment was so high that he required a "strong guard" for protection as he made his way from the jail to the court-house.[20] Richard hoped that the growing scandal surrounding him and his family would dissipate when he challenged his detractors to present their evidence against him in open court. Both justices and defendant, then, sought to resolve the matter and to restore peace and order in the county. In pursuit of that objective, however, both Richard and the justices had several legal options. Richard could have initiated a civil suit against William Randolph or some other of his accusers to refute their allegations and quash the rumors, but he instead waited for the local authorities to act and faced a criminal charge instead. For their part, the county justices could have charged Richard or Nancy—or both of them—with a variety of crimes ranging from fornication to murder and infanticide.

Only a thorough understanding of the county's legal culture can explain the choices made by both the justices and their defendant. In eighteenth-century Virginia counties, as much as ninety percent of the courts' business was in civil cases, the vast majority of which pertained to debt. Suits for trespass were the second most common type of litigation to come before the courts, both before and after the Revolution. Although trespass often involved physical violence, criminal prosecutions for violent offenses of any sort were comparatively uncommon, at least among the county's white inhabitants. So, too, were prosecutions for the statutory crimes of fornication, adultery, and other sexual offenses.[21]

Because there was no concrete evidence—no body, no weapon—that a murder had occurred at Glentivar, civil litigation might have put the matter to rest, but Virginia's legal culture discouraged Richard from initiating a slander suit to defend himself against William Randolph or others who vilified him as Nancy's seducer. Although the law of slander entitled Richard to seek satisfaction in the courts, slander was a deeply gendered offense in eighteenth-century America. Under the common law, an individual could sue for slander if he or she were wrongly said to have committed a criminal act, transmitted a heinous disease or condition, or engaged in dishonest or incompetent business dealings, or if he or she sustained pecuniary losses—known as "special damages"—as a result of malicious speech. In practice, however, the law of slander worked differently for men and women. Men typically initiated slander suits to defend their reputation for honesty and trustworthiness, assets that were essential for conducting business in a face-to-face credit-based local economy. By contrast, women (sometimes represented by male guardians) went to court to protect their sexual reputations, which determined their prospects for marriage, the financial security it could confer, and harmonious domestic life.[22] This gendered understanding of both reputation and slander undoubtedly deterred Richard from initiating legal proceedings against William Randolph in 1793. In Virginia's patriarchal and honor-bound culture, women—not men—went to court to certify their sexual propriety.

At the same time, sexual innuendo and misconduct, though clearly facts of life in eighteenth-century Virginia, were increasingly less likely to make their way into the legal culture of its county communities. Most legal historians agree that cases involving sexual slander, though common during the seventeenth century, became less so after 1700. Such cases were rare in post-revolutionary Cumberland. Between 1780 and 1800, the Cumberland County court appears to have heard at most two cases involving a woman's sexual reputation, while only one female plaintiff sued for slander during this period in the newly established district court.[23]

Criminal prosecutions for the sexual offenses of fornication and adultery, though relatively common in the seventeenth and early eighteenth centuries, also declined precipitously by mid-century and thereafter. Because local authorities most commonly enforced statutes prohibiting fornication and adultery to discipline unruly servants, the gradual displacement of white indentured servants by African slaves in Virginia's labor force after 1700 was an important cause of the decline in prosecution of these offenses. While the courts had imposed additional years of service on white indentured servants convicted of adultery, fornication, or bastardy, such penalties would have been meaningless to African laborers who were enslaved for life. Although the criminal statutes pertaining to various sexual offenses remained unchanged through the revolutionary era, the authorities rarely enforced them. Indeed, one recent study has shown that even the enforcement of laws prohibiting sexual relations between blacks and whites was remarkably lax in many Virginia communities.[24]

Consequently, though the statutes would have authorized the county justices to charge both Richard and Nancy with fornication in 1793, doing so would have been contrary to prevailing legal customs. In the half-century following the creation of Cumberland County in 1749, its courts heard only three criminal cases concerning illicit sexual relationships between consenting women and men, all of whom were white. Two cases involved charges of adultery, which the law defined as a sexual relationship between a man and a married woman, who was deemed the exclusive sexual property of her husband. One of these cases never came to trial, and the court dismissed the charges against the defendant in the other. Because Nancy Randolph was an unmarried woman, any sexual relationship in which she engaged would have met the legal definition for fornication, not adultery. Between 1749 and 1800, the Cumberland County court heard only one grand jury presentment for fornication, but that case never came to trial. Clearly, even if Richard and Nancy—or, for that matter, Nancy and Theo—had been guilty of fornication, it would have been extremely unlikely for the local authorities to have prosecuted them for that offense.[25]

Although Nancy could have been legally liable for prosecution for bastardy—giving birth to a child out-of-wedlock—if the authorities could prove that she had, in fact, given birth, bastardy was another statutory offense that never resulted in a court verdict in eighteenth-century Cumberland. Although studies of colonial grand jury presentments suggest that women presented for bastardy constituted one of the largest groups of offenders in most Virginia counties, presentments for bastardy dropped off significantly after mid-century, as communities became less involved in policing the sexual behavior of their members. Between 1749 and 1800, the Cumberland County court handled twenty-five cases concerning out-of-wedlock births, but of these only five cases originated in grand jury presentments against the unwed mothers. The rest came to the court's attention as the result of complaints lodged by the mothers or on their behalf in an attempt to force the fathers of children conceived outside of marriage to accept financial responsibility for their "maintenance." Court records therefore suggest strongly that local authorities were likely to intervene in cases of out-of-wedlock births only to prevent children from becoming economically dependent on the county community.[26]

The general preference for filing complaints against reputed fathers shows that economic, not moral, considerations were foremost in eyes of the court and its constituents. Although most white Virginians subscribed to conventional Anglo-American sexual mores, public acknowledgment of an out-of-wedlock birth did not necessarily result in social ostracism in eighteenth-century Cumberland. In 1755, a pregnant but unwed Elizabeth Bandy successfully sued her lover when he failed to marry her; within six years, Bandy, however, had found herself a husband. Patty Sammons, who bore a child by James Durham, Jr., in 1789, wed him three years later. Agnes Dickerson, who bore children by two different men, married a third in 1804.[27] Similarly, men who had been implicated in bastardy cases continued to be active in the public life of their community. For instance, John Holt, who in April 1787 posted bond for "raising and for Maintaining" an illegitimate child, was appointed as a surveyor of the roads by the county justices just three months later.[28]

Elite white women like Nancy Randolph had little chance of being hauled into court on a bastardy charge, but, unlike Patty Sammons or Agnes Dickerson, they would almost certainly suffer harsh social penalties as a consequence of their offense. Propertied families stood to lose both financially and socially as a result of an out-of-wedlock birth. On the one hand, although the common law did not provide for inheritance by illegitimate children, a father or grandfather could make special provision during his lifetime or by his will for such offspring, thereby diminishing the patrimony of his legitimate heirs. On the other hand, and more important still, the sexual impurity of an elite white woman had significance that reached beyond the family unit as Americans increasingly looked to such women as the custodians and promoters of the virtues essential to the preservation of a polite and moral society. Virtuous women could use their influence as wives and mothers, many believed, to promote sensibility, piety, and patriotism among men who, in turn, would shape the politics and society of the American republic. As a result, the private indiscretions of one such woman had a wider public significance.[29]

The sad story of Rachel Warrenton of Yorktown illustrates both points. In 1782, Warrenton, who came from a well-heeled family, bore a child out-of-wedlock. The child's father was the commander of the French military forces in America, Viscount Rochambeau, who returned home after the war, refusing either to marry Warrenton or to support their son. As a result of her "departure from female rectitude," Warrenton's family disowned and disinherited her, though they eventually accepted and provided for her illegitimate son. The willingness of her family to support the boy, as well as Rochambeau's flight, prevented the courts from becoming involved in Warrenton's case. Nevertheless, her transgression was widely known and her eventual marriage to a poor laborer was striking evidence of its economic and social consequences. Warrenton's girlhood friends told and retold her story, less as gossip than as a cautionary tale for their daughters and other young women.[30]

Wealth and class privilege likewise would have shielded Nancy Randolph, had her child lived, from facing bastardy charges in a Cumberland County courtroom, and the justices would not have summoned the reputed father to post bond for the child's support. But doubtless Nancy knew that she, like Rachel Warrenton, would suffer the informal censure of her family and her community if her illicit pregnancy were ascertained. And doubtless she and Richard also knew that, in her case, the death of the infant—interpreted variously as murder or miscarriage—and the subsequent loss or destruction of its body could either doubly damn her or permit her, however implausibly, to deny her lapse from chastity and the resulting pregnancy.

If the Cumberland County authorities wanted to initiate criminal proceedings against one or more of the Randolphs, they could have charged Nancy with infanticide, perhaps citing Richard as her accessory or charging him with murder in his own right. The legal distinction between murder and infanticide was significant, and knowledge of that distinction must have contributed to the decision—probably made by Richard in consultation with his stepfather— to have only Richard surrender to the local authorities. In the case of murder and every other crime except infanticide, the burden of proof was on the prosecution to persuade the justices and juries of the defendant's guilt. By contrast, Virginia statute, which followed English precedent, defined infanticide specifically as a mother's murder of her bastard child and stipulated that "the mother so offending, shall suffer death, as in the case of murder, except such mother can make proof, by one witness at least, that the child . . . was born dead." Both statute and custom rendered infanticide a crime peculiar to unwed mothers, and it was the only crime in which the accused was presumed guilty instead of innocent.[31]

Although poor women who lacked access to protective female networks were most vulnerable to infanticide charges, one recent case from Cumberland County showed that sometimes the authorities also prosecuted women from respectable families of long standing in the community. The Beacham family had resided in Cumberland and owned property there since at least 1758. In 1785, six Cumberland County justices remanded Sarah Beacham to the General Court for "Feloniously Murdering" her infant son. The court also indicted Susanna Beacham, who was probably Sarah's mother, as an accessory. The women were confined to the county jail until they were tried in Richmond by the General Court. Although their fate is unknown because the court's records have not survived, the General Court handed down at least twelve death sentences to free white women who were found guilty of infanticide between 1736 and 1774.[32]

In the spring of 1793, knowledge of the law of infanticide and of the Beacham case especially must have influenced the legal strategy of Richard Randolph and his stepfather. Because St. George Tucker practiced law in Richmond, where the General Court convened, he must have known about the Beacham case and its origins in Cumberland, where four of the six men who remanded the women for trial still served as county justices eight years later. Both Richard and his stepfather also were aware of the different standards of evidence for murder and infanticide cases, and they knew that murder was by far the more difficult crime to prosecute. Finally, both men were familiar with the common law of marriage, which rendered husband and wife one in the eyes of the law. One consequence of that legal construction of the marital relationship was to prevent wives from giving testimony against their husbands. If Richard, rather than Nancy, were the defendant, the common law would bar the testimony of Judith, the only white adult who could have witnessed what happened upstairs in Nancy's bedroom at Glentivar on that fateful night. Virginia law barred slaves from testifying in any case involving a white defendant.

Richard Randolph's privileged status as a member of the gentry afforded him certain advantages, but it did not free him entirely from the strictures of community censure or the authority of the county court. Richard's social position probably led county authorities to delay his arrest until public outcry demanded it. His own knowledge of the law and, more important still, the advice of his learned and influential stepfather undoubtedly helped him to choose his most promising legal option. Richard brought those advantages to court with him on 29 April 1793, when he stood before his family and his neighbors accused of a capital crime, hoping to preserve his life and avenge his honor.

Richard Randolph's day in court was a big event in Cumberland County, where, as in most Virginia communities, legal proceedings concerning violent crimes of any sort were uncommon. Between 1749 and 1790, the Cumberland County court handled fifty-three cases of criminal assault, two of rape, two of infanticide, and eighteen murders.[33] Twelve of the alleged murderers were slaves, whose cases were heard, in accordance with a 1692 statute, by the Court of Oyer and Terminer, which was a special tribunal of county justices who tried and sentenced defendants "without the solemnitie of the jury." The six white defendants, by contrast, appeared before an examining court (also known as a "called" court) of county justices, who determined whether the evidence was sufficient to remand them for trial in a higher court.[34] Of the six white men the Cumberland justices examined on murder charges before 1790, the three accused of murdering slaves were released from custody, as was one who had been accused of killing a white man. The justices remanded only John Griffin and John Chiswell, both of whom were charged with killing white men, for trial in the General Court.[35]

The Chiswell case, which involved a defendant as prominent and well-connected as the Randolphs, suggested the limits of the gentry's control of the county courts even during the colonial era. In 1766, the wealthy and powerful John Chiswell, whose son-in-law was the speaker of Virginia's House of Burgesses, killed merchant Robert Routledge in a Cumberland County tavern. Chiswell's status did not shield him from prosecution. The Cumberland justices convened as an examining court, charged him with murder, and remanded him to the General Court in Williamsburg for trial. Once he arrived there, Chiswell's powerful friends and connections among the eastern tidewater gentry gave him special treatment, though the resulting outcry among piedmont and upcountry planters compelled the authorities in Williamsburg to take the charge against him seriously. The case ended dramatically with John Chiswell's suicide as he awaited trial in Williamsburg in the fall of 1766.[36] *King v. Chiswell* was the most spectacular case that the Cumberland court handled during the colonial period. A generation later, *Commonwealth v. Randolph* would be its most notorious case of the post-revolutionary era.

Commonwealth v. Randolph was the dramatic final act of a court session that had begun on Monday 22 April with the usual round of debt-related business. On the last day of the six-day session, the court convened—probably at nine o'clock, as usual—with all sixteen county justices in attendance. According to the official written record of the Cumberland County court, defendant Richard Randolph appeared before the justices, who sat as an examining court and heard the testimony of several witnesses. Because the court proceedings marked the official climax of the Bizarre scandal and because the court's ruling amounted to the official resolution of the mystery of Glentivar, the written record of *Commonwealth v. Randolph* is worth quoting in full:

> At a court held for Cumberland county the twenty ninth day of April one thousand seven hundred and ninety three for the examination of Richard Randolph who stands committed and charged with feloniously murdering a child said to be born of Nancy Randolph. Present—
>
> > Mayo Carrington, Thomas Nash, William Ma[c]on, Nelson Patte[r]son, John Holman, Ben Allen, Joseph Carrington, Henry Skipwith, Joseph Michaux, Anderson Co[c]k, Cary Harrison, Walter Warfield, Benjamin Wilson, Coddrington Carrington, Archer Allen, Nathl. Carrington, Gentlemen Justices.
>
> The Court being thus constituted the prisoner was led to the bar in custody of the sheriff to whose custody he was committed for the aforesaid and being charged

with the same denied the fact, Whereupon, Sundry witness were sworn examined touching the premises and the prisoner heard in his defence.[37]

As told in the Cumberland County order books, the story of *Commonwealth v. Randolph* is brief, and in this instance as in so many others, few additional court documents survive to help recapture the details of the case. Court records, which can be so revealing as sources of social history in the aggregate, tell us little about the particulars of the legal case against Richard Randolph of Bizarre.

Who were the justices who assembled that day to assess the evidence against Richard? Unlike the defendant, the justices were men with deep roots in Cumberland, even if some were relative newcomers to the county magistracy. Benjamin Allen, whose Presbyterianism had precluded his appointment to the bench in the days when Virginia had an established church, and Benjamin Wilson, who rose to prominence by his involvement in the local committees of the revolutionary era, were among the court's recent appointees. They served, however, alongside four members of the Carrington family—Cumberland's great judicial dynasty—and others representing the similarly long-serving Patterson and Harrison families. The Carringtons may have borne a grudge against Richard, whose father, John Randolph of Matoax, once accused their kinsman, Judge Paul Carrington, of "vilany" in his land dealings, but justice Henry Skipwith, whose niece Lelia had wed St. George Tucker in 1791, was probably well-disposed toward the defendant. In terms of wealth, the landholdings of seven of the sixteen justices exceeded Richard's 779 acres—three owned more than twice that amount of land in the county—but nine had less. The fact that Richard owned more slaves than all but two of the justices, however, suggests that Bizarre was more thoroughly cultivated, and thus more valuable, than the plantations of most of the justices.[38]

Although the court's records do not list the "Sundry witnesses" who testified before the justices that day, the authorities had issued summonses to a total of eleven individuals whom they believed might shed light on the alleged wrongdoings at Glentivar and Bizarre. On 19 April 1793, one day after they issued the order to arrest both Richard and Nancy, justices Joseph Michaux and Anderson Cocke summoned eight "material witnesses" to "come before us to give such evidence as they know concerning the . . . [alleged] offense." Three of these persons—Randolph and Mary Harrison and Randolph's mother Susanna Randolph Harrison—had been present at Glentivar during all or part of the Randolphs' visit. Three others—Judith and Nancy's aunt Mary Cary Page, her husband Carter, and Martha Jefferson Randolph—were frequent guests at Bizarre. The remaining two, William Randolph and his wife, Lucy, were known to be prominent among the ranks of Richard's accusers. On 24 April, the authorities also summoned three Cumberland County residents who were not kin to the Randolphs—Thomas Ferguson, James Holman, and Peter Johnson—"to testify and say the truth" before the examining court that was scheduled to convene five days later. Based on these documents and on the notes of John Marshall, one of three attorneys who represented the defendant, it seems reasonable to assume that most of these witnesses testified either for or against Richard before the assembled justices. John Wayles Eppes, who attended the day's proceedings, observed that Richard's "own relations were his prosecutors and particularly active."[39]

Eighteenth-century Virginia court records usually included neither transcripts nor summaries of witnesses' testimony, nor did they recount the spectators' reaction to the courts' judgments. But the spoken pronouncement of rules and decisions were nonetheless essential to asserting and legitimating the authority of the courts in a society where literacy was far from universal. Likewise, oral testimony provided the basis not only for the court's decision in any given case but also for shaping community perceptions of general social norms as well as of specific cases and their protagonists. Richard Randolph and St. George Tucker appreciated both the official and unofficial power of the court. On 29 April 1793, their objective was to secure not only formal legal certification of Richard's innocence but also informal vindication or even approval in the eyes of his "fellow-citizens."[40]

Well aware that evidence could be elicited and especially interpreted in a variety of ways, Richard and his stepfather engaged a first-rate team of lawyers to present his case to an audience unaccustomed to such courtroom virtuosity. After the creation of the district courts in 1789, most of Virginia's ablest attorneys abandoned county practice for the bigger fees, more complex cases, and more professional atmosphere of the higher courts. As a result, county-level proceedings, in which the employment of attorneys had never been universal even in capital cases, were less and less likely to feature the state's best legal talent. A judge since 1785 and one of the first appointees to the district bench, St. George Tucker was keenly aware of the growing gap in legal standards between the county and district levels, and he enlisted a galaxy of legal stars to dazzle the amateur gentlemen-justices and their neighbors.[41]

As professor of law at William and Mary between 1790 and 1803, Tucker trained a generation of Virginia lawyers and produced a standard reference work for practicing attorneys. He knew that the most gifted courtroom lawyers interpreted bodies of evidence in a way that put their clients in the best possible light and in so doing molded their audience's understanding of the cases they tried. He also knew that a carefully constructed and sympathetically presented story could sway judges and juries alike, especially when they lacked training and based their decisions less on law than on sentiment or prejudice.[42] Drawing on these insights, Tucker helped his stepson to assemble a team of lawyers whose collective fame and ability was without precedent in any criminal case heard at the county level. The talents and tactics of defense lawyers John Marshall, Alexander Campbell, and Patrick Henry would orchestrate the telling of Richard's story to the justices and to the wider community.

Marshall and Campbell, both prominent Richmond attorneys, would have been obvious choices, at least from Tucker's perspective. Marshall was a close friend of Tucker's, distant kin to the Randolphs, and connected by birth or marriage to other Virginia gentry families. In 1793, he was thirty-eight years old and an established star of the Richmond bar. His reputation for logic and learning would soon help him win appointment as chief justice of the United States, a post from which he would profoundly influence the development of U.S. law until his death in 1835. Campbell, the Richmond-based U.S. attorney for Virginia, was related to Tucker, and he was an "esteemed" friend of Richard Randolph, who later named him as one of nine executors of his estate in the event of Judith's death. Like most Virginia lawyers, both Marshall and Campbell did the overwhelming majority of their work in civil litigation. Campbell divided his time between his government duties and private civil practice, while Marshall took on only three or four criminal cases in his entire career as a practicing attorney. Both men, nevertheless, agreed to represent Richard Randolph in the Cumberland County court.[43]

They were joined as co-counsel by Patrick Henry, a hero of the Revolution and one of the most successful criminal attorneys in the state. By 1793, the fifty-seven-year-old Henry had moved from his farm in Prince Edward County to a larger plantation in Campbell County, on the Staunton River, where he lived in semi-retirement. Henry, who had more than thirty years experience in county litigation, won acclaim in the 1760s as an eloquent critic of British imperial policies, most famously for his patriotic ultimatum "Give me liberty or give me death!" His oratorical talents contributed to his enviable reputation as a courtroom lawyer, especially in criminal cases as counsel for the defense. They also made him a local hero in the piedmont counties, where his popularity helped him win election as Virginia's first governor in 1776 and re-election to that office in 1784. Although St. George Tucker disliked Henry personally, he acknowledged his accomplishments as an orator and courtroom lawyer.[44]

Despite Richard's financial woes, both Tucker and his stepson clearly believed that Henry's services were worth the hefty fee it took to lure him out of retirement to serve as defense co-counsel in *Commonwealth v. Randolph*. Henry's grandson and biographer reported that Richard wrote to the great man in April 1793, offering the handsome sum of £250 to secure his services. Henry demurred, claiming that he was "too unwell" to make the two- or three-day journey from Campbell to Cumberland. A few days later, however, Richard's messenger returned, this time with a letter in which he doubled his original offer. Where did Richard intend to get this vast sum? Apparently, he and Tucker decided to negotiate a deal with Henry first and to figure out how to pay his price later. This time, Henry conferred with his wife, and the two agreed that £500 was sufficient incentive to travel to Cumberland and to take the case of the desperate but well-paying defendant.[45]

Wealth, along with personal and professional connections, afforded Richard Randolph access to Virginia's finest legal talent, but in choosing attorneys of such vastly different styles and temperaments, he and Tucker revealed their sensitivity to the diverse world views of the court's prospective audience. Marshall and Henry were probably the state's most successful lawyers in 1793. The two had worked together often, most recently on opposite sides of a lurid divorce case and on the same side, with Campbell, as co-counsel for local planters who were being sued by British merchants for unpaid debts.[46] Marshall's and Henry's approaches to the practice of law differed dramatically. In the courtroom, Marshall was succinct, plain-spoken, and rigorously logical. "So perfect is his analysis that he extracts the . . . kernel of inquiry, unbroken, undivided, clean, and entire," one admirer observed, adding, "His arguments are remarkable for their separate and independent strength, and for the solid, compact, impenetrable order in which they are arrayed." By contrast, Henry used his great eloquence to appeal to the "recesses of the human heart." According to one contemporary, the great "charm" of Henry's voice "consisted in the easiness of its inflexions, the fullness of its notes, the distinctness of its articulation, the variety of its cadences, the felicity with which it adapted itself to every emotion and the vast compass which enabled it to range with irresistible effect through the whole empire of human passion, from the deep and tragic half-whisper of horror, to the wildest exclamation of overwhelming rage."[47]

While Marshall's approach appealed to St. George Tucker and many other well-educated Virginians, Henry's eloquence—which Thomas Jefferson regarded as "impressive and sublime" but without intellectual merit—clearly swayed those who lacked both legal training and the Enlightenment preference for empiricism and logic. Like evangelical preachers, Henry and other popular politicians used their eloquence both to ignite emotions and evoke the primal authority of the people and the nonhierarchical spoken word. Henry's eloquence—and its challenge to the authority of learned elites—therefore struck a responsive chord among ordinary Virginians and even among some county justices. St. George Tucker acknowledged Henry's ability to use both his voice and his body language to convey his skepticism or distrust of authority while eluding the baneful consequences of open disrespect or rebellion. Tucker recalled that Henry "had a half sort of smile, in which the want of conviction was perhaps more expressed, than that cynical or satyrical emotion which probably prompted it. His manner & address to the court, and jury, might be deemed the excess of diffidence & modesty . . . [and] in his reply to Counsel, his remarks on the Evidence, and on the conduct of the parties, he preserved the same distinguish'd deference and politeness, still accompanied by the never failing index of this Sceptical smile, where the Occasion promised."[48]

Still, most rural citizens were likely to identify with Henry, the upwardly mobile planter who shared their economic ambitions, unpolished manners, and localist outlook. Although he had learned how to play the part of the gentleman, Henry preferred to be in the country, where he "delighted to be free from [the] restraints" of "polite society." According to one of his legal colleagues, Henry was an accomplished planter, a "man of business . . . [who] could buy or sell a horse or a negro as well as anybody, and was peculiarly a judge of the value and quality of lands." In other words, he possessed all the manners and the abilities that Virginia farmers respected. At least partly for that reason, Henry and his courtroom tactics were much-admired in Cumberland and neighboring Prince Edward County. The young lawyer Richard Venable "heard much of Patrick Henry's Eloquence" when he traversed the area in 1791, and he personally witnessed Henry's "ingeneous defense for one Barrett charged with rape," which won the defendant a hung jury in the Prince Edward district court.[49]

Together, the pair of Henry and Marshall was admirably equipped to address an audience whose members could be moved alternately by reason or sentiment or, as Jefferson so famously put it, by "head" or by "heart." Although Enlightenment rationalism and improved legal training may have made elite Virginians prone to evaluating arguments and evidence according to strict empirical standards, they also increasingly embraced a culture of sensibility. Stimulating the sentiments or emotions of individuals, many believed, inspired them to act morally and benevolently both at home and in society. Proponents of sentimental novels, for instance, defended them on the grounds that readers who keenly felt the pain and despair of a victim of seduction would remain chaste and virtuous themselves. Post-revolutionary Virginians purposefully cultivated sentiment in their reading, religion, and family relationships. Reason and emotion thus intermingled in the culture and world view of many gentle-folk, who could admire the rigorous logic of a Marshall and yet be susceptible, as were both Tucker and Jefferson, to Henry's remarkable eloquence.[50]

Although there is no way to know for sure who testified before the court that day, Marshall's notes on *Commonwealth v. Randolph* suggest that the lawyers interviewed and took depositions from seventeen prospective witnesses. Four—Beverly Loyd, William Bradley, John Ker, and Chandler Skruggs—simply deposed "that they knew nothing of the matter." Archibald Randolph, who had accompanied the Randolphs on their visit to Glentivar, noted that though Richard and Nancy were fond of each other, he had no reason to believe she had been pregnant. Archie's friend, Peyton Harrison, stated that he "had been informed by a servant" that Nancy "had miscarried" while visiting his brother Randolph at Glentivar. Richard's younger brother, Jack, claimed that Nancy had been engaged to his brother, Theodorick, whose death still weighed heavily on her when she visited the Harrisons. Jack "never suspected" Nancy of being pregnant, though he thought "from her pallid & emaciated appearance [and] from her complection" that she suffered from an "obstruction" of the menses, a common uterine disorder often accompanied by severe anemia.[51]

Others, however, provided more detailed descriptions of the relationship between Richard and Nancy, as well as of Nancy's physical condition before and during her visit to Glentivar. Carter Page, Martha Jefferson Randolph, and Anne Randolph, all of whom where kin to the Randolphs and frequent guests at Bizarre, claimed to have suspected that Nancy had been pregnant, though Anne Randolph would add that her cousin's change in size also could have been the result of "ill Health." Carter Page, Anne Randolph, and Randolph Harrison also asserted that Richard and Nancy had an unusually close relationship. Page claimed to have seen them "kissing and fond of each other." Harrison, too, noted that he had "observed imprudent familiarities be[tween] Mr. [Richard] Randolph and Miss Nancy," though he "observed no mark of pregnancy" and had "too high an opinion of them both to entertain any suspicion of a criminal correspondence," the polite legal term for an illicit sexual relationship. Both Randolph and Mary Harrison maintained that they did not believe that Nancy was pregnant when she came to visit. Mary averred that she had "entertained no suspicion which was unfavorable to Miss Nancy, untill she was told by a negroe-woman that she had miscarried." Brett Randolph, Anne's husband, agreed, noting that "perfect harmony" prevailed among the Randolphs and that he "saw no cause to suspect a pregnancy or criminal conversation" at Bizarre.[52]

Marshall's deponents also disagreed about the medicine Nancy used to ease her pain during her first night at Glentivar. Randolph Harrison believed that Nancy took "essence of peppermint, which she had been accustomed to take for cholic." Mary Randolph, however, reported that Nancy used gum guaiacum. In a society in which plantation mistresses generally attended to the medical needs of their families, Mary Randolph's statement probably carried more weight than her husband's.[53] Mary's testimony was strengthened, moreover, by Martha Jefferson Randolph's assertion that she herself had supplied Nancy with gum guaiacum a few weeks before her visit to Glentivar. In her deposition, Martha described this medicinal herb as "an excellent medicine for the cholic, but . . . at the same time . . . a dangerous medicine, as it would produce an abortion." In fact, gum guaiacum was most commonly used as an effective treatment for rheumatism, and some authorities explicitly stated that it could either cause or aggravate stomach and intestinal ailments, such as cholic.[54] Was Martha simply ill-informed or did she purposefully seek to give her sister-in-law a plausible excuse for ingesting a tincture of gum guaiacum? This herb probably was not a particularly effective abortifacient, but it was one of the plants used to stimulate menstruation and thus possibly to terminate a pregnancy. Although eighteenth-century physicians tended to be vague and evasive on the subjects of abortion and birth control, one reported that, "several physicians have apprehended mischief from the use of the guaiacum in a spiritous tincture," adding, "I am certain that it sometimes happens."[55]

Three other prospective witnesses, all of whom were present at Glentivar during Nancy's travail, offered evidence that was at worst ambiguous and at best extremely useful to the defense. Mrs. Wood, the Harrisons' white housekeeper, deposed that she had examined Nancy's bed and found it stained with blood. In his notes, Marshall wrote that, though the housekeeper stated that the stains "would justify the suspicion of a Birth or abortion," she "thinks another cause might have produced the same effect." Randolph Harrison's mother, Susanna Randolph Harrison, who visited Nancy later that week, "saw no mark (either by milk, fever, or otherwise) of her having been delivered of a child, nor did she discover any reason to suspect it." Finally, Marshall also took a deposition from Judith, who might be called to testify if the authorities decided to file criminal charges against her sister. The implacably stoic Judith insisted that she had been awake all night and that "a child could not have been born or carried out of the Room without her knowledge." Moreover, she was certain that Richard had been upstairs all night and "did not go downstairs untill after day."[56]

For the defense, the day's most dangerous witness was probably Mary Cary Page, wife of Carter Page and the younger sister of Judith and Nancy's deceased mother. Both oral tradition and John Marshall's notes suggest that Henry's eloquence and courtroom tactics were especially essential in discrediting Page's potentially damaging testimony. Marshall's notes indicate that Page offered circumstantial evidence that a crime may have occurred at Glentivar and that Nancy, at least, was involved in it. Although she had not been present at Glentivar at the time of the alleged murder, Page asserted that when she visited Bizarre shortly before then, "she could see through a crack" in a closed door that Nancy "was in her underdress and appeared . . . to be pregnant." The fact that Page herself was both a woman and a mother made her an expert witness in the eyes of an audience that still for the most part regarded pregnancy and childbirth as the domain of midwives and other women. The fact that she was Judith and Nancy's aunt may have given her the added authority of a surrogate mother. Henry, however, used his rhetorical talents to undermine Page's credibility. As his grandson, William Wirt Henry, drawing on personal interviews and oral tradition, recounted the aging patriot's legendary performance: "Mr. Henry at once resorted to his inimitable power of exciting ridicule by the tones of his voice, and in a manner which convulsed the audience asked [Mary Cary Page], 'Which eye did you peep with?' The laughter in the court-room aroused the anger of the witness, which was excited to the highest pitch when Mr. Henry turned to the Court, and exclaimed in his most effective manner: 'Great God, deliver us from eavesdroppers!' " Henry's kindly but earnest manner toward the witness made him appear fair and reasonable, while his silent skepticism effectively discredited her by conjuring conventional stereotypes of nosy and malevolent women.[57]

So, too, could Marshall deploy his terse logic to shape both the justices' and the audience's understanding of the story behind *Commonwealth v. Randolph*. Marshall concluded his notes on the case by listing five circumstances that, in his view, "would excite suspicion": the close relationship between Richard and Nancy; the latter's apparent pregnancy; her use of the gum guaiacum; her illness at Glentivar; and her prior refusal to let her aunt, Mary Cary Page, see her undressed. In logical, empirical, common-sense fashion, Marshall argued that none of these circumstances in truth proved the guilt of the defendant. "I believe there is no man in whose house a young Lady lives, who does not occasionally pay her attentions," he contended, "which a person prone to suspicion may consider as denoting guilt." Although several witnesses believed that Nancy was pregnant, others did not; surely, Marshall declared, the Harrisons would have noticed if she were "near a delivery" when she arrived at Glentivar. Gum guaiacum, Marshall averred, was used for purposes other than inducing abortions. Surely, if Nancy had wanted to use it to terminate a pregnancy, she would have done so sooner and "at home, where the whole would have been concealed, and not abroad where discovery was inevitable." Nancy was, indeed, ill at Glentivar, Marshall conceded, but the notion that she had a miscarriage was a rumor begun and spread by "servants" for whom "any suspicious appearance would be considered . . . as full proof" of foul play. Finally, though he regretted Nancy's refusal to submit to her aunt's scrutiny, Marshall asserted that "the most innocent person on earth might have acted in the same manner . . . [because] purity resents suspicion; the resentment is still stronger when we are suspected by a friend."[58]

As Marshall's notes show, Richard's attorneys ably exploited the cultural assumptions of white Virginians to neutralize testimony that reflected badly on the defendant and on Nancy, his presumed co-conspirator. While the law prohibited slaves from testifying against white defendants, Marshall could also use pejorative attitudes toward African Americans—whom he dismissed as simple-minded "servants"—to discredit evidence from blacks when white witnesses introduced it indirectly. Similarly, Marshall could invoke popular ideals of feminine modesty and virtue to justify or even to applaud Nancy's unwillingness to disrobe in her aunt's presence, just as Henry had exploited more venerable images of feminine vice in his handling of Mary Cary Page. In sum, cultural stereotypes that cast both African Americans and white women irrational, untrustworthy, and even vengeful enabled Richard's attorneys to exclude or discredit the best evidence against him. In the end, both the law and the cultural context in which it operated shaped the story that the lawyers presented both to the court and to the assembled populace.

Still, both the particulars of *Commonwealth v. Randolph* and its manner of presentation made Richard's day in court spectacular by the standards of rural Cumberland. This case was one of only four in the county's forty-four-year history in which both the alleged murderer and his victim both were white. Because the most recent of the three previous cases had occurred twenty-one years earlier, in 1772, *Commonwealth v. Randolph* may have been the first murder case witnessed by many of those who gathered at the courthouse. And because it involved both sex and violence it was arguably the most sensational case ever heard by the Cumberland justices. Marshall's notes indicate that the justices and their audience heard detailed testimony about a flirtation—or more—between Richard and his sister-in-law. They also heard testimony about Nancy's intimate physical attributes, her bloody bedclothes, and the use of abortion-inducing elixirs. A court that tread lightly in the area of sexual offenses, especially those perpetrated by elite white men, in this instance entertained a story of alleged fornication and incest as part of its examination of a murder suspect.

In addition, the courtroom drama featured a wealth of noteworthy performers. The examining court included all sixteen of the county's justices, which was unusual in itself. Spectators flocked to the courthouse to see Henry, the popular revolutionary hero and former governor of the commonwealth, and Marshall, the champion of Virginia's legions of tobacco-growing debtors. Other participants included men and women from the county's leading families, as well as celebrity guests from farther afield. Most notably, spectators saw Martha Jefferson Randolph, daughter of Washington's secretary of state, take the stand as a key witness in the affair.

In the end, the justices heard plenty of sordid gossip and innuendo, but no firm evidence that Richard had committed murder during his visit to Glentivar. "On consideration whereof and of the circumstances relating to the fact," the court's clerk wrote, "it is the opinion of the Court that the said Richard is not guilty of the felony wherewith he stands changed and that he be discharged out of custody and go hence thereof without delay." The defendant got the official vindication he sought—the court declared him "not guilty"—and he was free to return to his family at Bizarre.

Richard's carefully choreographed defense therefore attained its legal objective, but to what extent did the court's decision serve the larger purpose of redeeming the tarnished reputations of the Randolphs of Bizarre? To what extent, in other words, did the lawyers' stories and the justices' ruling allow Richard to recoup his honor?

Observers disagreed, but lawyers, who had great faith in the cultural authority of the judicial system, were most likely to believe that people would accept the court's finding as proof of Richard's innocence. "The people of Cumberland who carried their prejudices so far that a strong guard was necessary to protect Mr. Randolph on his way from the prison to the court house," attorney John Wayles Eppes optimistically reported, "unanimously cried out in shame on the accusers after the evidence was heard." James Monroe, who practiced law in Fredericksburg, claimed that public opinion was "universally" in Richard's favor after the court proceedings "removed impressions that were before deeply fixed." In contrast, Martha Jefferson Randolph did not share the lawyers' faith in the persuasive powers of the lawyers and the justices. Richard and Nancy, she informed her father, were "*tried* and acquited tho I am sorry to say his Lawers gained more honour by it than they did as but a small part of the world and those most inconsiderable people in it were influenced in there opinion by the dicision of the court."[59]

In a rare reference to Richard's legal and personal difficulties, eight days after the court's ruling St. George Tucker informed a friend that his "poor son . . . has been acquitted, as I understand, with Honor."[60] Tucker's statement was knowingly ambiguous. Undoubtedly relieved by Richard's acquittal, Tucker, who was more aware than either Monroe or Eppes of the continuing slights to his stepson's reputation, was less convinced than they of the ameliorative effects of the court's judgment. Tucker's statement was significantly equivocal on the issue of whose honor or reputation the outcome of *Commonwealth v. Randolph* truly had vindicated. Was it that of the justices, who, despite their lack of legal training and their possible resentment toward the traditionally absentee Randolphs, had ruled according to the laws of evidence? Or that of the lawyers, who gave the people of Cumberland County a demonstration of legal talent and professionalism of the highest rank? Or did the court's decision truly vindicate the honor and reputation of Richard, the defendant?

Cumberland County's court effectively articulated social norms and expectations and in so doing fostered order in its surrounding community. John Wayles

Eppes had believed that the county's inhabitants, outraged by Richard's alleged crime or perhaps fearing that his elite status would afford him preferential treatment, appeared to be on the verge of riot before the court convened. The seriousness with which both court and defendant approached the case defused a potentially violent situation. When the court adjourned, the crowds dispersed and Richard returned safely to Bizarre. From Eppes's perspective, justice had been served, the expectations of the community satisfied, and violence averted. The whole sordid episode, it seemed, was over.

But while a court's decision might restore a defendant's legal rights and freedom, legalism alone could not reinstate his honor. While its practitioners increasingly regarded the law as a science in which conclusions emerged from analysis of impersonal empirical evidence, honor was derived from the subjective and extremely personal opinions of other community members. Paradoxically, by going to court to clear his name Richard Randolph had enhanced the authority of the gossip and innuendo that he sought to discredit. His submission to the county authorities was tantamount to an admission that his honor had been impaired by that gossip. The court proceedings, far from silencing the rumors about him and Nancy, facilitated their circulation among a wider audience, many of whom continued to believe that something unseemly and dishonorable, if not criminal, had transpired at Glentivar and Bizarre.

3

SPREADING THE WORD

On 5 May 1793, a week after the Cumberland justices had decided the case of *Commonwealth v. Randolph,* St. George Tucker published a full-page notice in the *Virginia Gazette, and General Advertiser.* In his notice, which also was reprinted separately as a broadside, he informed the "Public" of his stepson Richard's acquittal, which, he asserted, was "sufficient for every *legal* purpose." Nevertheless, Tucker worried that "the public mind is not always convinced by the decisions of *a court of law.*" When "the characters of individuals are called into question," he continued, "there lies an appeal to a *higher tribunal;* A COURT OF HONOUR! The *community* at large are the *judges* THERE." Tucker thus penned a long statement, to which he appended new documentary "evidence" to affirm his stepson's innocence. In so doing, he told the Randolphs' story in a way that might vindicate Richard in the eyes of "that *solemn,* and *awful tribunal*" of Virginians at-large, or at least those who constituted the state's growing newspaper readership in the post-revolutionary era.[1]

Tucker's version of the Bizarre scandal, however, was destined to remain but one of several competing narratives, as Virginians and other interested parties used both the oral and printed word to interpret, explain, and draw lessons from the Randolph family story. The courtroom drama of *Commonwealth v. Randolph* itself had showcased several interpretations of that story via the oral testimony of a range of witnesses and commentary by the counsel for the defense. Yet oral testimony in the form of gossip persisted long after the court ruled, though the stories that gossips over the years would tell changed in some important respects. At the same time, the printed word could convey both the specific tale of Richard Randolph and his family—as in the case of Tucker's public notice—or a more general parable about seduction and its consequences. The learned and legalistic St. George Tucker enlisted the newspapers to present what he believed to be compelling evidence that could shape public opinion in the aftermath of *Commonwealth v. Randolph.* But other literate Virginians turned to an even more popular literary genre, the sentimental novel, for a more plausible and more emotionally satisfying interpretation.

The Randolphs' contemporaries thus used both the oral and the printed word to exchange information and opinions about the Bizarre scandal from the first revelations about Nancy's pregnancy until the time of Richard's unexpected death in 1796. Talk about the Bizarre scandal was always more common than writing about it. In the early republic, newspapers existed primarily to spread political information and promote partisan allegiance among the voting public. Though Richard's ancestry and connections may have afforded him a certain celebrity status, in 1793 the legal troubles of a member of a famous family were not fodder for the public press unless he had or sought political power. At this time, many people also refrained from discussing sensitive or controversial subjects in their private correspondence. Although postal service was improving, in this era before trains and steamboats most letters traveled slowly by horse or horse-drawn coaches. A long and difficult journey increased the likelihood of letters getting lost or delivered into the wrong hands: misplaced or opened letters sometimes ended up being shared or even published.[2] Talk, unlike writing, involved none of these risks—and anyone could do it. Enslaved people, middling men, women, and others who lacked the literacy, leisure, or public stature to write about the Randolphs could talk about them to a variety of audiences. As a result, gossip about the Bizarre scandal was common even for decades after 1793. In the 1830s, according to one commentator, the episode was still a "*cause celebre*" that remained "well known in that part of the country."[3]

Why did the enslaved people of Glentivar begin telling the story of Nancy Randolph's alleged miscarriage or infanticide? How did the slaves' gossip spread across Cumberland County and beyond? Why did many white Virginians, who generally held African Americans in low esteem, nonetheless find some aspects of their gossip credible? How and why did white gossips alter the slaves' story? Why did the gentry, who might have tried to protect Richard as one of their own, instead became leading purveyors of gossip and accusations about the Randolphs of Bizarre?

The answers to these questions lie in the particular social context in which gossip unfolded in 1792 and after. Gossip in the post-revolutionary era was not just idle talk, but a way either to jockey for social position or to undermine the authority of the mighty (or those aspiring to mightiness) in a relatively small, homogeneous, and face-to-face society. Communities with weakened or unstable social hierarchies in particular were vulnerable to gossip.[4] In Virginia, the Revolution had undermined the ideological and economic bases of both slavery and gentry dominance, at least in the short term. The resulting uncertainty and instability made Virginia communities potential paradises for gossips, as elite and plebeian whites jockeyed for position and as African Americans sought freedom, either absolute or by degrees.

The Revolution had a profoundly unsettling effect on slavery in Virginia. Beginning in 1775, when the province's last royal governor, Lord Dunmore, issued a proclamation offering emancipation to able-bodied male slaves who deserted rebel masters to join the king's forces, thousands of enslaved Virginians exploited wartime opportunities to assert their freedom. Some performed military service and others left with the invading British; many simply escaped bondage and began new lives as free people. At the same time, the ideals of the Revolution led increasing numbers of white Americans, including some Virginians, to condemn slavery as inimical to republican political values. While Virginia, unlike the northern states, did not attempt to end slavery statewide, a 1784 statute made it easier for individual slaveholders to free their bondpeople. Many did so, especially in the state's northern counties, where planters increasingly turned to wheat production in preference to the more labor-intensive tobacco.[5]

The cumulative effect of wartime escapes, emancipations, and natural population increase was a tenfold increase in the state's free black population between 1776 and 1800. At the dawn of the new century, Virginia's twenty thousand free black inhabitants constituted a palpable, if mostly tacit, challenge to the institution of slavery. White Virginians believed, with some justification, that plantation discipline was jeopardized by the presence of free blacks, who were actively discouraged from settling in areas with large slave populations for fear that they might incite or encourage slave insurrections. As a result, Virginia's free black population was unevenly distributed across the state, with proportionately the fewest free African Americans in the piedmont's prime tobacco-producing counties, such as Cumberland. In 1800, Cumberland County had 9,839 inhabitants, of whom only 183 were free blacks.[6]

The enslaved population of the piedmont counties, by contrast, grew significantly in the decades following 1776. During the war, tidewater families who owned land in Cumberland and other piedmont counties moved slaves westward in hopes of preventing them from meeting British forces who might lure them into service or incite them to rebellion. Many of these slaves remained to work in the tobacco fields of the piedmont after the war ended in 1783, while others were relocated westward to the piedmont with decline of tobacco cultivation in Virginia's tidewater and northern counties in the postwar era. One historian estimates that approximately one out of every twelve slaves in Virginia and Maryland moved west during the 1790s. In Cumberland, the slave population grew at a faster rate than the county's overall population, reaching 5,711— 58 percent of the county's total—by 1800.[7]

As a result of these changes, enslaved people at Glentivar and throughout the Virginia piedmont developed strong local community and family ties, but they also retained family networks that connected them to African Americans elsewhere. After the Revolution, Virginia's enslaved population grew mainly by new births—rather than by new importations—and slaves were increasingly concentrated on large plantations. Both of these circumstances also encouraged the emergence in the piedmont of multigenerational kinship networks and a stable African American community. Newcomers to the piedmont kept in touch with those they had left behind, creating in the process bonds of affinity and identity that reached far beyond their neighborhoods. Such personal ties facilitated the flow of information among enslaved people, many of whom, in turn, had contacts among whites and free African Americans.[8]

While piedmont slaves developed extensive family and community networks, the economic challenges of the post-revolutionary era led some area slaveowners to adopt strategies that threatened to undermine slave living conditions and to disrupt those personal connections they valued so highly. So-called improving planters tried to augment the efficiency of their plantations by diversifying crops and by monitoring laborers' work more closely. Their attempts to improve plantation management and productivity resulted in more work for slaves, who, consequently, had less time to spend with their spouses, children, and other near connections, who often resided on other plantations. Because most big slaveholders held more than one tract of land, a planter's drive for efficiency also sometimes led him to shift slaves from one plantation to another without regard for the personal ties of his bondpeople. Planters' efforts to economize or to escape debt could also result in the break-up of slave families by the sale of individual members. Slaves bitterly resented such threats to their families and communities and, as historians have shown, they resisted such threats by whatever means possible.[9]

As it turns out, Randolph Harrison, the master of Glentivar, was one such improving planter. On assuming the management of the estate of his financially troubled father in 1787, Randolph Harrison began buying, selling, or redistributing laborers among the family's scattered properties. In 1790, Randolph's father, Carter Henry Harrison, paid taxes on sixty-three slaves in Cumberland; the following year the elder Harrison was assessed for seventy-two slaves in the county. In 1792, however, the Harrisons, father and son, had a combined total of only fifty-one slaves; they were assessed for a total of sixty slaves in 1793. Clearly, Randolph Harrison was juggling his father's slave labor force to maximize their efficiency. His managerial decisions, which would have disrupted or even severed family and community ties, must have elicited anger and resentment on the part of his bondpeople.[10]

Randolph Harrison was an ambitious and hard-driving man of affairs who devoted much time and energy first to saving his family's property and then to ensuring the prosperity of his own progeny. Unlike most Virginia planters of his generation, including most of his own kin, Randolph Harrison prospered and enlarged his estate continually over the course of his long life. Although Carter

Henry Harrison had bequeathed only a fraction of his land to young Randolph on his death in 1793, within a decade Randolph had purchased the land of his less solvent brothers and moved from Glentivar to nearby Clifton, with its greater acreage and more genteel and spacious house. By 1809, Randolph Harrison was the county's largest slaveowner, commanding the labor of forty mature bondpeople over the age of twelve; his slaveholdings continued to grow, nearly doubling in the coming decades. When he died in 1839 at the age of seventy, Harrison stipulated that all but two of his slaves be sold and that each of his twelve surviving children should receive a cash bequest of $5,000 from the proceeds his estate.[11]

As a young planter, Harrison sold or moved slaves to improve efficiency and sought to maximize his control of his labor force by acting as his own overseer at Glentivar. Later in life he sold slaves, on occasion, in Richmond, where the prices were better, though a slave sold in this commercial center had a greater chance of being removed far from their kin and community in Cumberland. On at least two occasions, Harrison also vigorously pursued slave runaways, one of whom got as far as Fredericksburg, nearly seventy miles to the north and close to freedom. Although there is no evidence that Randolph Harrison was a particularly cruel or malevolent master, his efforts to manage and control his slave labor force to ensure his family's continuing prosperity clearly sometimes had dire consequences for the enslaved people who performed most of the physical labor on his plantations.[12]

The enslaved people at Glentivar therefore had cause for resentment, but they also existed in a wider social environment in which some Virginians, to an unprecedented degree, were questioning slavery or at least its uglier aspects. Perhaps Harrison's slaves knew that his kinsman, Ryland Randolph, had emancipated nine bondpeople when he died in 1784, or that St. George Tucker was an outspoken critic of slavery.[13] More likely, they were aware of the strong antislavery feelings of Richard Randolph, who often visited the Harrisons' house, where he may have spoken freely about his plans to emancipate his own enslaved workers.[14] At the same time, Cumberland's free black population, despite its small size, provided important role models for enslaved people who aspired to freedom or even to just a greater degree of self-governance. Historians have found that enslaved people employed an array of stratagems to resist the authority of their masters and assert a degree of autonomy within slavery. Slaves could use gossip—much as they stole, feigned illness, or ran away—to their master's detriment and thereby hope to influence his future conduct.[15]

Often characterized as a "weapon of the weak," gossip has been a common feature of slave societies. Enslaved people in the southern states, who faced whipping, maiming, or death for disobedience, theft, or other overt acts, could gossip about their masters and other whites with comparatively little risk. After all, both law and culture deemed the word of slaves untrustworthy and undeserving of recognition and, hence, not worth punishing. A white victim of slave gossip would not seek redress via either physical or legal means because doing so would constitute an admission of the power of slaves' words to inflict injury and dishonor.[16] Of course, slave gossip, especially when spread among and accepted by whites, could be powerful nonetheless. Such was the case in 1792, when the Harrisons' slaves began spreading the story of Nancy Randolph's misadventures at Glentivar.

But why would the enslaved people of Glentivar propagate rumors about Nancy, a young and unmarried cousin of the Harrisons who was simply visiting their household? Why was no gossip, by contrast, spread by Richard Randolph's own slaves, despite the fact that a clandestine sexual liaison between Nancy and either him or his brother Theo had taken place at Bizarre? Because the rumor and the unfolding scandal discredited Nancy and brought Richard to the brink of ruin, it is tempting to conclude that slave gossip intentionally targeted the entire gentry class at a time when Virginia's elite was already both politically and economically vulnerable.[17] But the circumstantial evidence of Randolph Harrison's aggressive plantation management—and his frequent buying, selling, and moving of slaves, in particular—suggests that he, not the Randolphs, was gossips' prime target. Resentful of an ambitious master, and perhaps emboldened by the Revolution and its consequences, some of Harrison's slaves seized the opportunity that Nancy's visit presented to cast doubt upon his ability to govern and protect his household. If the slaves' stories of Nancy's miscarriage or infanticide were true, Harrison, far from being a benevolent governor and protector to his family, had instead exposed them to debauchery and dishonor.

Like all gossips, the enslaved people of Glentivar exploited real or imagined breaches of widely accepted social norms, in this case to advance their own interests by denigrating and discrediting the alleged offender. The story they told became a parable about the fatherly responsibilities of patriarchs and a warning about what might happen if masters shirked those responsibilities. From the slaves' perspective, Harrison's willingness to open his house to unruly and dissipated guests, like his willingness to destroy slave families, suggested that he was either unwilling or unable to show the benevolent paternalism that late-eighteenth-century Virginians increasingly expected. Masters, in one historian's words, "created the fiction of the contented and happy slave" and the humane and fatherly slaveholder to justify the perpetuation of slavery in a revolutionary age and to counter the real and imagined threat of slave rebellion. Randolph Harrison's slaves deployed their gossip (as it turned out, unsuccessfully) to goad him into taking more seriously his responsibility to act benevolently and protectively toward both his black and white dependents.[18]

Although little is known about the movements of the Harrison slaves in 1792–93, historians have shown that enslaved people had ample opportunity to spread gossip and other types of information among themselves and to others. House servants, who were privy to the most intimate details of the daily lives of the white people they served, were important conduits of gossip and information to the wider slave community. Those who labored outside the plantation house, in turn, were surprisingly mobile. Some acted as boatmen or messengers for their masters. Many, with or without their masters' permission, visited family and friends on neighboring plantations, attended church services, and engaged in casual social relations with free and enslaved blacks and with poor whites. Enslaved people developed economic relationships with free blacks and whites beyond their plantations, selling both their free time and the goods that they produced in their gardens and quarters or those acquired by trade or theft. As one historian has observed, black and white Virginians "paid close attention to the lives of their friends, neighbors, families, and owners and shared all sorts of information about them" whenever they got the opportunity.[19]

Although slaves and other lesser folk commonly deployed gossip against the mighty, all sorts of people were in fact producers, consumers, and subjects of gossip in eighteenth-century Virginia. The diary of Landon Carter, a great tidewater planter, shows how elite Virginians also exchanged information with people across the social spectrum in the decades preceding the Revolution. As a planter, justice of the peace, churchgoer, guest, and host, Carter both received and shared gossip on a regular basis. His diary reveals that he got most of his information about his neighbors, his business, and even the imperial crisis and ensuing revolution, from oral communications, despite his wide reading in colonial and British periodicals.[20]

Although Carter's informants were usually white men, they ranged in status from gentry, merchants, and the local parson, on the one hand, to middling planters and agricultural laborers on the other. Merchants and ships' captains, who resided in port towns but traveled inland to trade with Virginia planters, played an important role in spreading gossip and other news, as did dancing masters and music teachers who made the circuit of the great planters' houses to instruct their sons and daughters.[21]

But Carter also occasionally received information from slaves—indeed, he probably did so more frequently than he reported in his diary—and as a justice of the peace, he facilitated the spread of slave gossip at least on one occasion. In 1772 an altercation arose between Edward Pridham and his neighbor Parson Giberne. Pridham complained that the parson's horse had gotten into his corn-field, but Giberne defended himself, noting that "the night before's wind had blown down everyone's fences . . . but as to his horses . . . they had been kept up for a Particular purpose." According to Giberne, some slaves later overheard Pridham threaten to kill the offending horses; the parson cited the slaves' gossip as evidence against Pridham when he subsequently found "one of his horses shot in his own pasture." Giberne approached Carter, in his capacity as a county justice, seeking to have Pridham jailed but settling for swearing out a complaint to seek damages against him in the county court. Carter, however, recounted the parson's story in his diary and, since the diary was above all a record of his social interactions, it seems likely that he passed on the tale to others he encountered. In so doing, he repeated not only Giberne's unflattering characterization of Pridham but also the testimony of enslaved people, whose observations might influence public opinion, despite their inadmissibility as direct evidence in court.[22]

Although Virginians in Carter's time clearly gossiped about their neighbors' sexual transgressions, men more commonly scrutinized their peers' performance as plantation managers. In colonial Virginia, a man's public reputation derived in part from the quality of his crops—especially his tobacco crop—and his ability to manage effectively his labor force, livestock, and other resources. Substandard crops and ineffectual management betokened poor judgment and a lack of mastery over the natural world and over his supposed inferiors. Accordingly, in 1770, the supercilious Carter bristled when Parson Giberne informed him, in the presence of several other men, that "the general town talk" noted the "worthlessness" of the overseer at Carter's Rippon Hall plantation. Carter attributed rumors of "indifferent" crops and "bad management" at Rippon Hall to the vanity and envy of his neighbors, but he clearly viewed such criticism as a challenge to his prestige.[23]

By the 1790s, the social context within which Virginians gossiped had changed dramatically. Political revolution and the spread of religious denominationalism had fractured the traditional organic society of the colonial era, undermining the gentry's power and influence in their communities. The deterioration of Virginia's tobacco economy and the ruin of many indebted planter families eroded the economic basis of the gentry's social authority and led to quarrels within gentry families over the division of diminished estates. Finally, a relatively united colonial ruling class gave way in public life to an elite divided along ideological and party lines, first between supporters and opponents of the Constitution, and later between Hamiltonian Federalists and Jeffersonian Republicans. As we have seen, many Virginia gentlemen reacted to these changes by retreating to the emotional security of their own households. Renouncing public acclaim in favor of heartfelt affection, they pursued happiness in the emotional fulfillment that many increasingly associated with domesticity and family life.[24]

The Randolphs' experience suggests that the gossip of post-revolutionary Virginians reflected these wider social changes in at least three respects. First, although slaves and plebeian whites continued to snipe at those above them on the social ladder, elites, motivated by dynastic, economic, or partisan concerns, were now more likely to gossip viciously about their peers, including their own relatives. In 1792–93, Richard's and Nancy's close kin were their leading detractors; decades later, Thomas Jefferson's grandchildren similarly implicated their cousins, Peter and Samuel Carr, in an affair with Sally Hemings, hoping to derail persistent rumors about Jefferson's own long-term liaison with this Monticello bondwoman.[25] Second, the instability of Virginia's tobacco economy and the economic devastation of so many leading planters undermined the utility of crops and other artifacts of plantation management as social markers. Accordingly, neither Richard Randolph's precarious financial circumstances nor those of his kinsmen became fodder for local gossip. Third, gossip about unfaithful spouses, predatory parents, and promiscuous maidens blossomed into scandal in this culture of heightened sensibility, which idealized companionate marriage and domestic tranquility. Although colonial Virginia had its share of fornicators and adulterers, as well as an occasional infanticide, no episode from the colonial period resulted in a scandal comparable to the one that followed the Randolphs of Bizarre.

Although Randolph Harrison's slaves initiated the rumors about the Randolphs, gossip about their visit to Glentivar soon spread among the area's white inhabitants. And while Nancy had been the protagonist of the slaves' story, Richard became the focus of the gossip of white Virginians. Before the Revolution, in all but the most extreme instances plebeian criticism of elite men was too tentative to provoke public confrontation. Richard, however, eventually found himself compelled to submit himself to local authorities in part because of the outcry against him from plebeian whites in Cumberland. Landon Carter, who irritably recorded plebeian slights in his diary in the 1770s, was still secure enough to believe that he could ignore them in public. Two decades later, Richard Randolph of Bizarre enjoyed no such real or imagined security.

Richard was fair game for plebeian gossip—and he took such gossip seriously—because the diminished circumstances of the post-revolutionary gentry placed him on a more equal footing with his neighbors than the gentry of Landon Carter's generation. Under ordinary circumstances, social competition occurs mainly between those whose status is roughly comparable, because large gaps in power and status usually make real competition impossible. But the extraordinary circumstances of political revolution and economic turmoil disrupted the social bonds between elites and their dependents and accordingly narrowed, or at least destabilized, the gap between them. After the Revolution, the gentry's inability or unwillingness to provide financial credit and acceptable political leadership to their erstwhile followers undermined their authority. When common whites attacked Richard Randolph, they took on not a man who was economically secure and politically influential, but rather one who was financially troubled and seemingly divorced from public life. In some respects, Richard may have even epitomized the image of aristocratic arrogance and profligacy that was common among post-revolutionary republicans, who were less likely than their colonial forebears to defer to men from famous families without considering their other attributes.[26]

The most vicious gossip about the Randolphs' domestic concerns, however, came from within the gentry and especially from members of their own extended family. Their outrage and animosity, as we have seen, was aimed nearly exclusively at Richard, who, in their view, was a failed patriarch, whose malevolence and irresponsibility toward his dependents reflected badly on the entire gentry elite. In the words of Martha Jefferson Randolph, Richard's actions exposed the Randolph family to the gossip of "inconsiderable people," thereby further eroding the gentry's prestige and social authority.[27]

Richard's antislavery proclivities, moreover, probably made him doubly offensive in the eyes of his slaveholding relations, most of whom, like Thomas Jefferson, professed to abhor slavery without doing anything about it. As a young man, Richard reportedly had insisted that he would assume ownership of "not a single negro for any other purpose than his immediate liberation." Richard planned to free his share of his father's slaves when he came into his inheritance in 1791, but found that emancipation would be possible only after settling the estate's outstanding debts. A few years later, when he wrote his will, Richard angrily denounced his ancestors, who "usurped and exercised the most ... monstrous tyranny" over blacks, who he deemed "equally entitled with ourselves to the enjoyment of liberty and happiness." His condemnation of slavery for its injustice to blacks—rather than, as was far more typical, for its deleterious effects on whites—would have been especially unpopular among white Virginians, many of whom had soured on the idea of emancipation by the 1790s.[28]

By assailing his ancestors and rejecting slavery and its patriarchal trappings, Richard made himself a pariah among a large segment of the Virginia gentry. By reviling him as an unscrupulous seducer and failed patriarch, those who had reason to despise Richard sought to reaffirm patriarchal values and thereby vindicate themselves. With so much at stake, it should come as no surprise that few were swayed by the court's decision in *Commonwealth v. Randolph*. Perhaps that is why when Richard left the court's custody he went not to Bizarre, but to Williamsburg, to consult with St. George Tucker, who seems to have discerned that his "poor son Richard's persecutions" were not over.[29]

The same people who shared gossip about Richard Randolph and the Bizarre scandal inhabited a world in which the written word was increasingly authoritative and one in which more Virginians than ever before were both reading and writing. The most notable artifacts of these remarkable developments were the growing numbers of newspapers and the seemingly ubiquitous sentimental novel. Both played a role in how Virginians' imagined and interpreted what allegedly happened at Glentivar and Bizarre. Sentimental novels, with their central themes of seduction and its consequences, provided a framework within which literate Virginians could imagine the scandal and gauge its significance. Richard and his stepfather used the newspapers to present an alternative version of the story, one that they believed was real and particular, as compared to the fictional and generic tales of the sentimental novels. By presenting evidence to support his story, Tucker also hoped to assert an exclusive right to interpret for others what had happened at Glentivar and Bizarre.

Several overlapping factors accounted for the impressive expansion of print culture in the post-revolutionary decades. Perhaps most important was the ideal of an informed, independent, and self-improving citizenry that took shape during and after the Revolution, generating an unprecedented demand for information, particularly among those who aspired to upward mobility. In 1792, the Post Office Act, responding to this demand, provided that all newspapers be sent by mail at cheaper subsidized rates, making them accessible to a wider audience. Like etiquette books, novels, and political oratory, newspapers helped satisfy demands for information, and, more generally, for practical education, among citizens of the American republic. Literacy rates, which had begun to improve before the Revolution, continued to do so in the post-revolutionary era, as a result of both the desire for social mobility and the resurgence of scripture-based Protestantism. Rising literacy rates for white Americans of both sexes created a growing market for prospective editors and authors, and thus a greater potential source of profits. By the 1790s, newspapers also played a critical role in the increasingly bitter partisan battles between Federalists and Republicans. As disseminators and interpreters of political information, newspapers helped to legitimate party politics and thereby shape political debate in the early republican era.[30]

The contents of Virginia's newspapers evolved to meet the new political and cultural demands of a post-revolutionary republican world. Colonial gentlefolk had cultivated and exhibited their personal virtues in the public forum of the press to strengthen their collective claim to political and social authority. To that end, the colonial *Virginia Gazette* had featured social news from England, poetry, and polite essays, all of which attested to the benevolence, sensibility, and cosmopolitan outlook of its gentry readers. On the eve of the Revolution,

Virginia gentlemen also used newspapers to address a broadening readership in the guise of the universal public interest, thereby buttressing their claims to leadership in the province. By comparison, the post-revolutionary press adopted partisan rhetoric to sway an increasingly divided audience of prospective voters. The contents of post-revolutionary newspapers were more thoroughly political, reflecting both the growing ardor of party conflict and the republican preference for separating the affairs of the public sphere from those of private life.[31]

Post-revolutionary newspapers therefore reported scandalous sexual affairs only when they seemed politically significant, as, indeed, was sometimes the case in the late eighteenth century when the political legitimacy of new and untried American institutions seemed to hinge on the perceived honor and trustworthiness of the men who ran them. In this unsettled political climate, leaders became obsessed with both protecting their own reputations and scrutinizing the conduct of others. The well-known fragility of republican governments justified Americans' seemingly outrageous attacks on the private behavior of public men. Although the insulted parties often initiated duels to defend their reputations, as we have seen, they also turned to the press, both to attack their foes and to defend themselves. Both Alexander Hamilton and Thomas Jefferson, the leading partisans of the age, became targets of scandalous allegations of a sexual nature, which appeared in newspapers associated with their political opponents. In 1797, the Republican press revealed that Hamilton had an affair with Maria Reynolds, a married woman. In 1802, a Federalist newspaper in Richmond reported that Thomas Jefferson had a long-term sexual relationship with Sally Hemings, an enslaved woman at Monticello.[32]

The notoriety of Jefferson's offense, in his own time if not later, was more a function of his public stature as president and party leader than of the fact that Sally Hemings was an enslaved African American. In Jefferson's time, white Virginians deemed the seduction of presumably innocent and virtuous white women far more morally repugnant than discreet liaisons with black women, whom they self-servingly imagined as inherently promiscuous and corrupt. Moreover, when a white man had illicit sexual relations with a white woman, he challenged the patriarchal authority of her father or her husband—hence, Richard Randolph's expectation that Thomas Mann Randolph would come to the defense of his unmarried daughter. When a white man engaged in sexual relations with his own bondwoman, by contrast, he reaffirmed his own patriarchal right to control and rule over her in the most basic sense. In addition, because interracial sexual liaisons of any sort had no legal standing, they could not result in any inconvenient financial claims against either the white family or the wider community.[33]

A sex scandal with very different social implications surrounded Henry Lee of Stratford Hall, the elder half-brother of Robert E. Lee, in the 1820s. In 1817,

Lee married Anne McCarty and became the legal guardian of Anne's seventeen-year-old sister, Elizabeth, posting a $60,000 bond for performance of his duties as guardian. Three years later, after the death of the Lees' young daughter plunged Anne into depression and opium addiction, Henry initiated sexual relations with Elizabeth, who soon reported that she was pregnant. In a manner reminiscent of the earlier Randolph scandal, rumors implicating Henry in fornication, incest, and infanticide—Elizabeth's pregnancy also ended prematurely—circulated widely. Henry Lee, who admitted his liaison with his sister-in-law, had to sell Stratford Hall, his family's ancestral home, in order to pay the bond for his failed guardianship. Perhaps his admission of guilt and the high financial cost of his transgression prevented the initiation of criminal proceedings against him. For the next few years, Henry and Anne attempted to live quietly in Fredericksburg. A new nickname, "Black-Horse Harry," juxtaposed Henry's unmanly misdeeds with the bravery of his father, "Light-Horse Harry," a hero of the revolutionary War of Independence.[34]

Despite important and obvious differences, Jefferson's relationship with Sally Hemings resembled both the Lee and Randolph scandals in several notable respects. All three cases involved members of prominent Virginia gentry families. As was typical of such affairs, all three also involved older and more experienced men (Randolph and Lee were married; Jefferson was a widower) and younger unmarried women, and in each instance, both parties were members of the same household. Even more striking is the fact that Jefferson, Lee, and Randolph all were implicated in liaisons with their wives' sisters: both Lee and Randolph were currently married to sisters of the women with whom they were sexually linked, while Sally Hemings was the daughter of planter John Wayles and an enslaved woman and thus half-sister to Jefferson's wife, Martha Wayles Skelton, who had died in 1780. In terms of the ages of the men and women involved, their blood relationships, and their domestic arrangements, each of these cases represented a malfunctioning of domestic patriarchy, albeit with vastly different social consequences.[35]

The emergence of the Randolph, Lee, and Jefferson scandals within a few decades of each other suggests that elite Virginians may have been unusually susceptible to scandal in the post-revolutionary era. The rural isolation in which most planter families lived provided the seclusion in which illicit liaisons might occur without detection. Once discovered, however, illicit behavior could either be ignored or censured; while Virginians rarely appear to have chosen the latter course during the colonial period, many more had incentive to do so in the post-revolutionary years. For one thing, gentry families were more vulnerable to criticism and to challenges to their authority as a result of their diminished wealth and stature. At the same time, many Virginians had reason to resent or distrust the gentry, or at least those who most egregiously violated social norms and values. Enslaved Virginians, perhaps sensing the possibility of freedom, resented those who kept them enslaved. Poor and middling whites resented the loss of gentry patronage and perhaps also the fact that the Revolution and its gentry leaders had not done more to democratize politics and society in Virginia.[36] Finally, financial problems, political differences, and sensitivity about their new vulnerability caused divisions among the gentry themselves. All of these conditions helped make the Old Dominion a hotbed of gossip and scandal in the post-revolutionary era.

Because Jefferson was a widower and because his sexual partner was neither elite nor white, his affair was less threatening to the values and interests of his Virginia contemporaries, but his prominence as a public man made his sexual exploits—unlike those of Henry Lee and Richard Randolph—appropriate fare for the newspapers of the era. While Lee's neighbors in Westmoreland County and Randolph's in Cumberland gossiped for years about their illicit affairs, only Jefferson's Albemarle County neighbors became press informants.[37] Significantly, newspapers alluded to Henry Lee's sexual escapades only when it appeared that he might obtain a position of public trust. In 1829, eight years after his offense became widely known, President Andrew Jackson named Lee consul to Algiers. In early 1830, Jackson submitted Lee's appointment to the Senate for confirmation, and both the Washington-based *National Intelligencer* and the *Richmond Enquirer* reported cryptically that the Senate's "principal subject of deliberation . . . [has] been the nomination of Henry Lee, as Consul General for the States of Barbary; and it is said the nomination was rejected." Indeed, as a result of Lee's scandalous past the senators voted unanimously against him. Three years later, Lee explicitly compared his case to Jefferson's, complaining that his own offense was the less serious because it was "the crime of a private man." In fact, because he had been implicated in an illicit relationship with a white woman, Lee's transgression was more damning than Jefferson's, and it became a public issue when he, like Jefferson, sought political office. Because the office Lee sought was appointive, not elective, attaining it was even more difficult insofar as any senator who voted in Lee's favor would appear to condone or at least excuse his behavior, which violated some of the most basic social and religious values of early nineteenth-century Americans.[38]

Despite the parallels between Richard Randolph's alleged relationship with Nancy and the Jefferson and Lee cases, no Virginia editors deemed the Bizarre story worth reporting in their columns. Because Richard was politically inactive, his private vices had no political consequences and, thus, no place in the newspapers of the early republic, at least from the editors' perspective. Nevertheless, Richard and his stepfather wanted the newspapers to publicize the story, though they insisted on their own exclusive right to present and to interpret the facts of what allegedly occurred at Glentivar and Bizarre.

In the 1790s, sex scandals involving politically insignificant Virginians appeared in newspapers only in the form of public notices or advertisements placed by the principals at their own expense. Virginians used newspaper notices to announce the de jure or de facto termination of a marriage by divorce, separation agreement—what one historian has called a "do-it-yourself divorce"— or desertion. In some cases, the spouse who placed the notice included sordid details about the illicit sexual activities of the other to help justify the dissolution of the marriage in the eyes of the wider community—salacious stories that the editors of the era would not have deemed newsworthy. For instance, one cuckolded husband announced that his wife had "totally alienated her affections from me, by the vile and insidious machinations of an execrable Monster of Baseness and Depravity, with whom . . . she has for some time past indulged a criminal intercourse." As a result, he declared himself not liable "for any debts which she may contract" after her abandonment of his "bed and board for the protection of her seducer." Just as this husband's notice was the sole press coverage of the particulars of what would become a sensational divorce case, Richard Randolph's letter in Richmond's *Virginia Gazette, and General Advertiser* had been the only coverage of the Bizarre scandal before the case came before the Cumberland County court.[39]

Shortly after Richard's attorneys had secured the dismissal of the charge against him, the Bizarre scandal made its second appearance in the Richmond press. This time, the author of the newspaper notice was St. George Tucker, who may have prepared it in consultation with Richard, who arrived in Williamsburg just days before the notice appeared, on 5 May 1793, in the *Virginia Gazette, and General Advertiser.* In this full-page piece, Tucker deployed his considerable prestige and talents on behalf of his troubled stepson. Worried that the court's acquittal was insufficient to persuade the "public mind" of Richard's innocence, Tucker sought to use his legal expertise, literary skills, and status as a father figure to accomplish what the justices and lawyers apparently could not. Tucker's notice told a story in which he and Judith Randolph were the main characters. He presented his readers with an array of both personal family stories and purportedly new evidence in an attempt to sway both their heads and hearts.[40]

While Richard had placed his earlier newspaper notice to discredit his enemies and seek redress for an honor offense, Tucker now used the press to continue the process that Henry and Marshall had begun so brilliantly in the courtroom, enlisting both sentiment and rational argumentation to prove his stepson's innocence. In the notice's opening section, Tucker posed as a character witness for the accused. Richard Randolph, he declared using the third person,

TO THE PUBLIC.

MY connexion with Mr. Richard Randolph, junior,[†] might perhaps have justified me to the world, had I long since undertaken the task of vindicating his character from the aspersion which it has suffered for some time past.—A conviction that nothing short of a *fair, open*, and *judicial enquiry* into the truth of the charges rumoured against him, could effectually wipe them off; a determination to promote, rather than to stifle such an enquiry, as far as my advice to him could operate to produce one; and a resolution not to attempt, by any act of mine, to anticipate the public adjudication, imposed on me a rigid silence, except to a few most intimate and confidential friends, from whom I sought to be informed of the extent of the charges against him.

The public has seen his notification: It only remains to inform them of the result.—He appeared at Cumberland court, pursuant thereto—was arrested by a warrant from a magistrate; was committed to prison, without bail, tried before an examining court, at which *fourteen* magistrates presided, and *acquitted*.

A letter from a gentleman *present* at the trial, to a very respectable friend of mine now at this place, contains the following short, but emphatical account of the result of it. "*The charge against* Mr. Randolph, *with all its circumstances turned out to be the darkest, and most unfounded calumny that ever disgraced a country.*"

This acquittal is sufficient for every *legal* purpose; but the public mind is not always convinced by the decisions of *a court of law*. In cases where the characters of individuals are drawn in question, there lies an appeal to a *higher tribunal*; a COURT OF HONOUR! The *community* at large are the *judges* THERE. To that *solemn*, and *awful* tribunal I now submit the *character* of one, for whose conduct through life, I have held myself responsible, if not to the world, at least, to my own heart.—The evidence which I shall beg leave to produce, is that of a person who neither was, nor could have been admitted to testify in his behalf, at his trial; and consists shortly in a couple of letters now in my possession. The *first*, to Mrs. *Pleasants*, was communicated to me by that lady about four weeks ago.—A letter from herself to Mrs. *Judith Randolph*, which was brought to me from the post-office whilst the latter was at my house, in Williamsburg, prompted me to hope that in the correspondence between the *sisters*, something on this subject might be mentioned. To satisfy myself, and at a proper time, the world safe, I called on Mrs. *Pleasants* in my journey to Charlottesville, and obtained from her the satisfaction I expected. It is but justice to that lady to mention, that she was perfectly satisfied by its contents, and that Mr. *Pleasants* appeared no less so.—The *second* letter is to myself. It was written in answer to one from me to Mrs. *Randolph*, on the 9th of April, communicating to her in the fullest manner *all* that I had heard alledged against her husband. My letter was enclosed to my son-in-law *John Randolph*, with injunctions to deliver it *privately* to his sister: that he complied with those injunctions will appear by the extract of a letter from him to me.

[†] Mr. Randolph *is the son-in-law of the writer; was educated by him from a very tender infancy, and remained under his guardianship during his whole minority.*

No. I.

A copy of a letter from Mrs. Judith *Randolph, dated Tuckahoe, March* 15, 1793.—*Directed to Mrs. Eliza* Pleasants—*Four Mile Creek—to the care of Mr. Mewburn.*

I WAS grieved beyond measure to find by my dear sister's letter which I received last night, that she, too, had been induced to listen to the infamous report which I have been acquainted with from its first being publickly circulated, with all the aggravated circumstances which malice could invent.—That it is as false as the vile wretch in whom it originated, and that I have ever believed, and positively known it to be so, my conduct sufficiently proves—it is true I shall not return to Bizarre, for some time, but not as it is supposed, through fear of being made unhappy; no, but by continuing down the county to give my husband an opportunity of proving to the world the falsity of such an accusation, which the purity of his heart, renders the idea of, horrible to the last degree. We return to Williamsburg in a day or two, not without feeling great regret at not seeing my dear sister, to whom I feel myself unalterably attached: before long I hope to have the pleasure of being with you.—My dear little boy sends you a kiss, he stands very well, and I hope with soon walk—don't let the little girls forget me, and assure Mr. Pleasants of my esteem.

Believe me my dear sister,
sincerely your friend,
JUDITH RANDOLPH.

Papa, and all the family here, are well.

No. II.

A copy of a letter from Mrs. Judith *Randolph, dated Marmce, April* 21, 1793.—*Directed to the Honourable St. George Tucker, Esq. Fredericksburg.*

MY DEAR SIR,

I RECEIVED your very affectionate letter two days ago, and thank you most sincerely for it, since it gives me an opportunity of writing to you, what I in vain endeavour to speak of, during my stay in Williamsburg; could I but convince the world of my poor husband's innocence, as perfectly as I can myself convinced of it, I should be the happiest of human beings, for until this vile report destroyed his peace, I never knew what it was to be otherwise.—You judge rightly in supposing me acquainted with every circumstance relative to this horrid tale, as it is industriously circulated by those, whose malice disgraces human nature.

Mr. *Randolph* has informed me of it, from his first hearing of it, with all its aggravations. I have endeavoured to recall to my mind, every circumstance which happened during our visit to Mrs. *Harrison* last October, which, as they made no impression on me at the time, had entirely escaped my memory. I perfectly recollect Nancy's complaining one night of being ill, and went into the room to see, immediately before I went to bed, whether it was necessary for her to take any medicine; but I did not think any thing of her indisposition, which appeared to be only a trifling complaint in the stomach.—A very sudden change in the weather prevented my getting up during the night, as I was apprehensive of taking cold, and it was not until I had repeatedly urged Mr. *Randolph* to go into her room, that he went, as it was with difficulty I could waken him sufficiently to get up—there was a candle burning all night, in the room where I slept, and there was no way of going out of Nancy's room, without passing immediately by my bed. I am *positive* that the circumstance which is said to have happened at that time, could not possibly have taken place, without my knowledge, as our rooms were so situated, that the most trifling noise could be distinctly heard from one to the other, and I was kept awake the *whole* night by Nancy's complaints—in addition to this it is also said, that my husband left my sister's room and went down stairs instantly, in the night; this I assert to be a falsehood, as I recollect perfectly, his going down sometime after day and not before, and then he had been in bed several hours.

With regard to any dispute which happened between us, during her stay at Bizarre, I assure you my dear sir, that nothing disagreeable ever passed between us, in our whole lives, the remembrance of which ever lasted more than a few moments—on the contrary the most perfect cordiality has ever subsisted between us. I do not recollect that Nancy ever kept her room, more than four or five days in all the time she was with us, although her health was very bad; and I visited her constantly every day during that time, and I declare most solemnly that nothing ever passed between her and her brother-in-law, that could have created suspicions in the most jealous mind.

I have now answered all your questions, as fully as my memory will permit me; and will conclude with assuring you, that my husband knows nothing of what I have written, neither has he seen your letter, as he is gone up to Cumberland court.

Believe me, my dear sir, my heart feels most gratefully yours, and Mrs. *Tucker's* affectionate conduct to us all, and I shall ever think myself happy in being permitted to call myself, Your sincerely affectionate daughter,
JUDITH RANDOLPH.

No. III.

Extract of a letter from John H. *Randolph, dated Marmce, April* 21, 1793.—*Directed to the Honourable St. George Tucker, now at Fredericksburg.*

MY DEAR SIR,

A GREEABLE to the request of your letter of the 9th instant, I delivered your enclosed to Judy—her answer accompanies this—I pledge my word that my brother is entirely ignorant of her having received my letter from you—he set off for Cumberland court this morning, and the enclosed answer was written since dinner.

(Signed) JOHN H. RANDOLPH.

TO these letters I may be permitted to add, that Mrs. *Randolph's* conduct to her *sister* and her *husband*, during *eight weeks spent together* under my roof, in the months of *January, February* and *March, last*, was sufficient to have convinced the most hardened sceptic in the universe that these letters contain the *truth*, the *whole truth*, and, *nothing but the truth*.

To a candid mind any remarks upon the contents of them are unnecessary; on one of a different stamp they can make no impression.

I am, the Public's most respectful
and obedient servant,
S. G. TUCKER.

Fredericksburg, May 5, 1793.

Figure 3.1 "To the Public." St. George Tucker published this broadside, along with a similar newspaper notice, just days after the Cumberland County court dismissed the charge against his stepson. Tucker worried that the court's decision would be insufficient to vindicate Richard in the "COURT OF HONOUR." Virginia Historical Society, Richmond, Virginia.

"was educated by [the author] from a very tender infancy, and remained under his guardianship during his whole minority," thereby implying that Tucker's own well-known integrity and wisdom marked the character of his stepson. Next, Tucker played the role of an attorney, using the first person to review dispassionately what he claimed to be compelling evidence of Richard's innocence. First, he recounted the court's verdict. Next, he quoted a spectator, who, on hearing the evidence against Richard, deemed the charges against him "*the darkest, and most unfounded a calumny that ever disgraced a country.*" Then, finally, Tucker produced his new evidence, which consisted chiefly of two letters from Judith, "a person who neither *was,* nor *could have been* admitted to testify" either for or against Richard in court. A third letter, from Richard's brother, Jack, attested to the authenticity of Judith's missives. Tucker himself concluded the notice with a brief note adding that the conduct of Judith and Richard during the months before his court appearance "was sufficient to have convinced the most hardened sceptic in the universe that these letters contain *the truth, the whole truth, and nothing but the truth.*"[41]

In Judith's first letter, addressed to her older sister, Elizabeth Randolph Pleasants, on 15 March 1793, she presented herself as an unwavering defender of Richard and an innocent casualty of the gossip against him. "I was grieved beyond measure to find by my dear sister's letter . . . that she, too, had been induced to listen to the infamous report" of Richard's alleged seduction of Nancy, Judith wrote. "It is as false as the vile wretch in whom it originated," she asserted, "and that I have ever believed, and positively known it to be so, my conduct sufficiently proves." From Tuckahoe, after their unpleasant meeting with her brother William, Judith reported that she and Richard were "continuing down the county to give [him] an opportunity of proving to the world the falsity of such an accusation, which the purity of his heart, renders the idea of, horrible to the last degree." Judith closed by lamenting that Richard's need to contest the vicious gossip, which she supported and understood, prevented her from visiting her sister and other kin, whose company she dearly missed.[42]

The second letter Tucker presented was written by Judith, but addressed to him, supposedly in response to a series of "questions" he posed to her around the time Richard surrendered himself to the Cumberland County authorities. There is no evidence that Judith had ever written to Tucker prior to this occasion, and this letter appears to have been carefully scripted for public consumption. To give her account an added air of authenticity, perhaps on Tucker's advice, Judith claimed that Richard knew nothing about either Tucker's questions or her response to them. She portrayed herself as a loving and loyal wife wronged not by her husband's alleged indiscretions but by his enemies' malice. "Could I but convince the world of my poor husband's innocence, as perfectly as I am myself satisfied of it," she declared, "I should be the happiest of human beings, for until this vile report disturbed his peace, I never knew what it was to be otherwise."[43]

In this forum that afforded her freedom from solemn oaths and from the prospect of a skeptical or even hostile cross-examination, Judith then went on to provide the testimony she might have given in court if she had been allowed to testify on Richard's behalf. She categorically denied that the alleged birth and subsequent infanticide occurred at Glentivar. "I am *positive* that the circumstance which is said to have happened at that time, could not *possibly* have taken place without my knowledge," she averred, because the guest rooms "were so situated, that the most trifling noise could be distinctly heard from one to the other, and I was kept awake the whole night by Nancy's complaints." Judith also insisted that Richard never went downstairs that night, and therefore that he could not have disposed of a corpse, a fetus, or anything else. In addition, she firmly stated that "nothing ever passed between [Nancy and him], that could have created suspicions in the most jealous mind."[44]

In an age when newspapers increasingly focused exclusively on public— especially political—matters, notices like Tucker's purposefully blurred the boundaries between public and private. Tucker placed family letters that discussed the most intimate issues and emotions in an explicitly public forum, even going so far as to address his notice boldly "TO THE PUBLIC." In addition, because he published the notice as both a newspaper advertisement and a separate broadside, Tucker was able to circulate the piece both impersonally and via his own personal networks. The notice appeared in the newspaper only once, on 5 May 1793, but Tucker enclosed copies of the broadside in letters to his friends both then and from time to time thereafter.[45]

Tucker's tenacity showed his faith in the authority of the written word, but other forms of written testimony, which he could not control, ultimately were more influential in shaping how people interpreted and imagined the stories of the Randolphs of Bizarre. Tucker's version of the Bizarre story challenged conventional wisdom about relations between the sexes in post-revolutionary America. In Tucker's tale, Richard Randolph, a twenty-three-year-old white man, the master of a large plantation and its corps of slaves, was the pitiable victim of gossip and intrigue, while his young wife Judith was his foremost protector. As Tucker told the story, at least for public consumption, Nancy was at best a secondary character. In most respects, Tucker's narrative was the exact opposite of the one most familiar to literate Virginians: the story of the dashing but lascivious man who seduces and ruins an innocent young woman, a story at the heart of the era's most popular literary genre, the sentimental novel.

Although most contemporary social critics condemned reading novels as frivolous or worse, sentimental novels became increasingly popular among readers of both sexes in the post-revolutionary era. The predominantly female authors of sentimental fiction wrote tales that engaged their readers' emotions and ideally served a didactic purpose, especially for their primarily female readership. Sentimental novels typically recounted stories of virtuous young women who become infatuated with, and eventually seduced by, seemingly honorable and virtuous men. But appearances were deceiving: in novel after novel, the young heroine becomes pregnant and, abandoned by her lover, dies alone and in shame. Sentimental heroines became prey to unscrupulous men because they lacked paternal protection or maternal guidance, and usually both. These tales, which were wildly popular among female readers throughout the United States, eclipsed more traditional advice books as practical guides for living in post-revolutionary America.[46]

Female novelists, in turn, saw themselves as providers of the sort of education in the ways of the world, especially the rules of conduct and courtship, that readers needed to find their way in such a perilous and changing world. Susanna Haswell Rowson, author of the enormously popular *Charlotte Temple* (1791), saw her protagonist—seduced, impregnated, and abandoned by a British soldier—as a negative role model for her readers. Charlotte's story was a cautionary tale that Rowson addressed to "the many daughters of Misfortune who, deprived of natural friends, or spoilt by a mistaken education, are thrown on an unfeeling world without the least power to defend themselves from the snares not only of the other sex, but from the more dangerous arts of the profligate of their own." Similarly, Hannah Webster Foster, author of *The Coquette* (1797), professed to use the sad story of her seduced and ruined heroine to teach the "American fair . . . to reject with disdain every insinuation derogatory to their true dignity and honor . . . and for ever banish the man, who can glory in the seduction of innocence and the ruin of reputation."[47]

Incest was a common subplot in these early seduction novels, many of which purported to be based on true stories. In the most general sense, American novelists were warning their readers of the dangers resulting from social disorder in a world in which the old social distinctions were increasingly untenable. In theory at least, white Americans could choose their mates from anywhere across the social spectrum, a worrisome prospect that for many was emblematic of cultural decay and social chaos. Beginning with William Hill Brown, whose *The Power of Sympathy* (1789) is generally considered the first American novel, some American writers used incest to symbolize the extreme social disorder they feared might result from the democratizing impulse of revolutionary republicanism. *The Power of Sympathy*, in fact, presents readers with four intertwined seduction stories, all of which end in death or dementia for their principals. Two concern the theme of brother-sister incest. One features young people who fall in love and plan to marry, only to learn at the last minute that they were fathered—one legitimately and the other out-of-wedlock—by the same man. The other is the story of Ophelia, who commits suicide after being seduced by her sister's husband.[48]

Whether or not the Randolphs and their neighbors read *The Power of Sympathy*, Ophelia's story is representative of the powerful cultural paradigm within which they would have interpreted allegations about what happened at Glentivar and Bizarre. Ophelia visited her sister—known to the reader only as "Mrs. Martin"—and her husband in Rhode Island, on returning from a trip to Europe. Mr. Martin received his sister-in-law politely, but he soon "conceived a passion" for her and offered her "an elegant apartment at his house in town" so that she would remain nearby. Then, "by a series of the most artful attentions, suggested by a diabolical appetite," Martin "prevailed upon the heart of the unsuspicious Ophelia, and triumphed over her innocence and virtue." By this "incestuous connexion" Ophelia became pregnant, which resulted in alienation from her father and her own eventual suicide. Ophelia's sister exchanged "her former gaiety of heart . . . for sad, serious thoughtfulness"; though she "put on a face of vivacity . . . her cheerfulness was foreign to the feelings of the heart."[49]

Although the liaison between Ophelia and Martin differed in some important respects from the alleged relationship between Nancy Randolph and her brother-in-law, the two roughly contemporary stories also exhibited some striking parallels. The most important differences between the two stories are that Nancy, unlike Ophelia, did not kill herself, and that her pregnancy, unlike that of Brown's tragic heroine, did not result in the birth of a living child. While Ophelia's father tried to convince her to confront and expose her seducer to protect the honor of his family, there is no evidence that Nancy's father reacted in any way to the gossip about his daughter, though the Randolph brothers, as we have seen, pressed Richard to admit his culpability. Nevertheless, Judith Randolph bore the scandal with the sad resignation of her fictional counterpart, and Nancy's education, much like Ophelia's, had focused disproportionately on "the vain parade of . . . manners" and social graces instead of moral instruction. Ophelia's haughty father and her seemingly absent mother, whose protection and guidance might have saved her, were also reminiscent of Nancy's virtual orphanhood after her mother's death and father's remarriage to Gabriella Harvie, which resulted in Nancy's exile from Tuckahoe.[50]

The pervasive themes and ideals of literary sentimentalism clearly predisposed contemporaries to cast Nancy as the victim and Richard as the villain in the Randolph family drama. In so doing, the purpose was not to praise or vindicate Nancy, who, according to the morality of the sentimental novelists, would have been deemed beyond redemption and at least partly responsible for her

The STORY of OPHELIA.

"*O Fatal! Fatal Poison!*"

Figure 3.2 Frontispiece from William Hill Brown, *The Power of Sympathy*. Ophelia, the tragic heroine of this 1789 novel, committed suicide by taking poison after being seduced and made pregnant by her sister's husband. The corruption of feminine virtue and its consequences were the main themes of the era's popular sentimental novels. From the copy in the Rare Book Collection, the University of North Carolina at Chapel Hill.

own tragedy. Instead, the point was to revile Richard, the deceiver and sexual predator, whose depravity, that of like his fictional counterparts, threatened feminine virtue, domestic harmony, and social order.

An exchange between Thomas Jefferson and his daughter, Martha Jefferson Randolph, illustrates how literary sentimentalism and contemporary gender ideals gave rise to assumptions and prejudices that shaped popular interpretations of Nancy's and Richard's respective roles in the Bizarre scandal as it unfolded. On 28 April 1793, Jefferson, who was then secretary of state, informed his daughter that a copy of Richard's newspaper notice had made its way to Philadelphia, thus confirming the rumors he previously had heard about the incident at Glentivar. In this letter, written the day before Richard appeared before the Cumberland County court, Jefferson pronounced the summary judgment that Nancy was "the pitiable victim, whether it be of error or slander," adding, "In either case I see guilt in but one person, and not in her." Martha Jefferson Randolph, too, cast Nancy as the injured party and Richard as the predator, when she responded to her father on 16 May, about two weeks after she most likely stated in open court that she believed Nancy had been pregnant when she visited the Harrisons at Glentivar. Despite her conviction that Nancy had erred gravely by engaging in illicit sex, Martha characterized her as "the poor deluded victim" and described Richard as "her vile seducer," a "villain" who had been "no less sucessful in corrupting her mind than he has in destroying her reputation."[51]

This interpretation, which coincided perfectly with the tales of so many sentimental novels, clearly prevailed over Tucker's version of what had happened at Glentivar and Bizarre. Indeed, even some who understood and supported Tucker's efforts to redeem his stepson were nonetheless reluctant to view Richard as an innocent victim of the scandal. Take, for instance, the case of Margaret Page, the wife of John Page, a close friend of St. George Tucker and his family. When Tucker sent the Pages a copy of his newspaper notice, its contents inspired Margaret to pen a poem which, in her husband's words, sought to "baffle the Efforts of envious Slanderers" of Richard and Nancy alike. In fact, Margaret Page wrote nothing either negative or positive about Richard. Like so many others, she believed that Nancy was the more injured party in the wake of *Commonwealth v. Randolph*. Page portrayed Nancy, whose name she romanticized as "Anna," as an innocent victim of either gossip or seduction. "Each candid female hears with tears thy moan," Page wrote, "And views thy Cause, Oh Anna as her own." John Page suggested that with Tucker's "correcting Touches" his wife's verses "may well deserve a Place in the public View." Tucker did not pursue the matter at least in part because he, unlike the Pages, regarded Richard, not Nancy, as the scandal's chief casualty.[52]

And what of Judith? Tucker's newspaper notice had thrust Judith Randolph into the public spotlight, where she played a carefully scripted role. In Tucker's version of the story, she was a faithful wife whose life had been rendered miserable by the slanderous attacks against her husband. That part of Tucker's story was undeniably true. Judith remained loyal to Richard, out of love or more likely out of a combination of pride and profound awareness that as a woman with little property in a society that assumed that marriage was forever—at least among respectable people—she had no real options. The grief Judith suffered as a result of the scandal was equal to and possibly greater than Richard's own. Yet neither Margaret Page nor Martha Jefferson Randolph—indeed, no one, aside from Tucker—acknowledged Judith's suffering or her loyalty. Nor did anyone see her as a significant character in the drama that unfolded at Glentivar and Bizarre. In the cultural paradigm of the sentimental novel of seduction, the character of the wronged wife was either minor, as in the case of *The Power of Sympathy*, or nonexistent, because her suffering served no didactic purpose. One wonders whether Judith thought that her suffering served a purpose as she resumed her life with Richard and Nancy at Bizarre.

Perhaps Judith hoped that her sister might live elsewhere, which could help diffuse the scandal, while affording her and Richard the opportunity to establish a more conventional household. If so, she must have been disappointed when, either at Richard's urging or because she had nowhere else to go, Nancy returned to Bizarre with her after the court delivered its ruling and Richard left for Williamsburg. The sisters rode together in Richard's phaeton, while Jack Randolph accompanied them on horseback. No one knows exactly what Judith and Nancy said to each other during their twenty-mile journey, but Jack noted in his diary that they quarreled. When Richard rejoined them, the unhappy trio embarked on the next phase of their life together at Bizarre.[53]

Judith became increasingly estranged from both Richard and Nancy in the coming months. Perhaps influenced by the courtroom testimony against her husband, Judith appears to have had second thoughts about his innocence. Two weeks after the court's ruling, Judith described her state of mind in a letter to her friend Mary Harrison. Virtually admitting that she had lied to protect Richard, she mused, "I scarce know whether I should have suffered so much had I doubted my husband's innocence, for then, I confess my esteem for him would have been so diminished, that I should not have felt *what I did on his account,* but perfectly conscious of *that,* . . . & still dreading the diabolical machinations of his, & Nancy's . . . enemies, words are inadequate to express what my weak mind endured." In other words, Judith had lied on Richard's behalf out of concern for his and Nancy's reputations, but she now used the past tense to describe her certainty of Richard's innocence. Judith never asserted that Richard was either a fornicator or an accessory to infanticide, and she still occasionally called him "the best of husbands." Nevertheless, this ambiguous private statement to Mary Harrison differed dramatically from her confident declaration of his innocence, which had appeared both in John Marshall's notes and in Tucker's broadside and public notice in the *Virginia Gazette, and General Advertiser.*[54]

Whether or not Richard was guilty of any crime, he clearly had put his own honor—and even the reputations of Theo and Nancy—ahead of the feelings of his wife. Years later, when Nancy would tacitly admit that she, indeed, had been pregnant when she visited Glentivar, she insisted that Theo, not Richard, was the father of her child. After Theo died in February 1792, however, Nancy confided in Richard, who helped her to hide her pregnancy, which would have been difficult, but not impossible, given the dimensions and weight of women's clothing at this time. Richard also took charge of the affair once the gossip started. "Dick directed all I did on that subject," Nancy later explained to St. George Tucker, noting "he at first could scarcely keep me sile[nt]." In March 1793, Judith had elicited Richard's promise to cease his quest for vindication, which embarrassed and divided the Randolph family and reflected badly on the entire Bizarre household. As we have seen, Richard promptly broke this promise. The deepening scandal dishonored him while inverting conventional gender roles by forcing Judith to protect her embattled husband.[55]

Richard's conduct also forced the twenty-one-year-old Judith to play the pathetic role of the rejected wife, which had a chilling effect on their marriage once they returned to Bizarre. After 1793, Judith and Richard continued to have sexual relations—she bore a second son in 1795—but, unlike most wives, Judith rarely mentioned her husband in her letters to friends and relatives. Like many of her contemporaries, Judith turned to religion, seeking solace in divine providence while at the same time asserting her sense of self by repudiating Richard's cherished secular rationalist views. "Nothing but Religion, which *I but too feintly* possess," she observed in December 1793, "enables us to bear the heavy hand of affliction." By then, Judith's afflictions included the public disgrace of her family, the deterioration of her marriage, and conclusive proof of the deafness of her young son.[56]

As Richard and Judith became increasingly estranged, he turned to Nancy for companionship. After the crisis of *Commonwealth v. Randolph,* Nancy remained fiercely loyal to her brother-in-law. Close companions before the scandal, the pair's friendship blossomed in its aftermath. Although the relationship between Richard and Nancy probably did not include physical intimacy, their continuing closeness fed persistent rumors of impropriety. Nancy later recalled that she was a "best friend" and confidante to Richard, who gave her "several little presents" as tokens of his affection. Judith resented these presents, which she claimed "*she never* cou'd afford to have." She reproached her sister for "too great fondness for Dick" and often referred to her as "the blaster of my happiness." At some point, Richard may have contemplated divorce, a radical step that most of his friends and relatives would have deemed both morally objectionable and socially irresponsible. Nancy believed that Richard considered taking "a journey to Connecticut to obtain a divorce" to take advantage of that state's more liberal laws. In Virginia, an individual could petition the state legislature to obtain a divorce, but success was rare. As of 1795, the legislators had granted only three such petitions.[57]

In the years following the scandal, the Randolphs' social isolation compounded the bleakness of their lives at Bizarre. After 1793, Richard pointedly severed relations with his Tuckahoe in-laws. Judith followed suit in deference to her "husband's command," while Nancy did so out of loyalty to her brother-in-law. The Harrisons visited Bizarre much less often than before, perhaps because their presence evoked memories of that dreadful night at Glentivar. Neighbors Creed Taylor and his wife, Sally, were more frequent guests. Although Judith never criticized the Taylors, Creed and Sally were on especially cordial terms with Richard and Nancy.[58]

At the same time, economic woes heightened tensions in the Bizarre household. In July 1794, Richard's deepening indebtedness brought him back to the Cumberland County court, where Patrick Henry successfully sued him to recover the cost of his legal defense. Around the same time, Richard took on the added expense of housing his cousin, Anna Dudley, who had fled a bad marriage in North Carolina, along with her two children. Jack Randolph, who previously had been a frequent guest, now also became a permanent member of the Bizarre household. Richard's money problems may have led him to reconsider his stepfather's admonition that he enter the legal profession. In 1795, perhaps at Tucker's urging, Richard successfully applied for certification to practice law in nearby Prince Edward County. Richard's change of heart, if sincere, was nonetheless short-lived. He never took a case and claimed to be repulsed by the chicanery and baseness of the law and its practitioners.[59]

Despite the tensions and travails of their daily lives, for the benefit of outsiders at least, the Randolphs strove to maintain a facade of domestic harmony and comfort. On 12 June 1796, for example, Benjamin Henry Latrobe found himself lost in Cumberland County, where he was supposed to meet "the Superintendants of the river" to consider ways to make the Appomattox more navigable. The frustrated engineer stumbled upon "Mr. Richard Randolph's house," where he found the inhabitants both welcoming and sociable. The members of the Randolph family, he reported, "have shown me every attention and kindness in their power."

Even Richard, who was "very dangerously ill, with an inflammatory fever," was thoroughly hospitable. Despite the Randolphs' concerns about Richard's physical state, Latrobe noticed no signs of discord or tension at Bizarre.[60]

By the time of Latrobe's visit, Richard had been ailing for a week and a physician finally had been summoned to examine him. Since his brother Jack was away in Petersburg at the time, Judith must have called for Dr. Smith, who Latrobe described as "a medical practitioner in the neighborhood" and "a man of good sense." Although Smith could not name the specific malady that afflicted Richard, his opinion, according to Latrobe, was "against the probability of Mr. Randolph's recovery, though masqued by a long string of hopes and technical phrases." Latrobe reported that the family was "melancholy" on hearing the doctor's prognosis. Nancy informed St. George Tucker that Richard was delirious—"a perfect bedlamite with a most violent serious fever"—and that he "did not know a creature." Judith, she wrote, was "quite overwhelmed." Nancy also tried in vain to reach Richard's younger brother. "My dear Jack in perfect madness I write," she scrawled in anguish, "Come oh God come or it will be too late."[61]

On 14 June 1796, Richard Randolph died at the age of twenty-six. His closest companions mourned him profusely in keeping with the sentimental temper of the times, which regarded death as an occasion for the tearful lamentation of the loss of a loved one and earnest meditation on the evanescence of earthly life. For Nancy, Richard's death meant the loss of a friend and protector. At his deathbed, she "felt more than it was possible for [her] to conceal," and for years afterward she defended his memory. As for Judith, she mourned not only the loss of a husband but also the promise of an idealized domestic life. Judith memorialized Richard as the "best of husbands," but she seems to have mourned him less as a lover and companion than as an essential piece of the domestic ideal she coveted. "If my heart does not deceive me in its emotions, every chord of it was meant by nature to vibrate to such sweet affections," Judith lamented a year after Richard's death, adding that the word "Husband . . . once comprehended my *all*, & now, even that *All* is lost to me forever." In 1799, she attributed her seemingly constant "gloominess" to "a total disappointment in domestic life, by a loss irretrievable and irremediable."[62]

In some ways, however, Richard's death affected his brother Jack the most profoundly. Jack's unexpected loss of a beloved and much admired elder brother capped a succession of crises that, according to his half-brother and confidant, Nathaniel Beverley Tucker, shaped his future life. In 1792, Jack had suffered from an unidentified affliction that left him frail and probably sterile. His condition and Theodorick's death left Richard alone to ensure the family's survival and continuing stature in future generations. But Richard's status as the family standard bearer became problematic as a result of his public disgrace and revelations that his son and heir, St. George Randolph, had been born deaf. Richard and Judith had a second son, Tudor, in 1795. A year later, however, Richard's sudden death gave Jack the added responsibility of attending to his brother's family and financial obligations, while depriving Richard of the opportunity to augment the next generation of Randolphs and restore his personal and family honor.[63]

People of all social ranks talked about, and, in some cases, wrote about, the Randolphs of Bizarre. Those who told the Randolphs' story, however, interpreted it differently in light of their own interests and cultural contexts. For the enslaved people of Glentivar, the fact that something sordid happened in their master's house was more important than which of its white inmates actually perpetrated the alleged crime. St. George Tucker, by contrast, told a tale in which no crime occurred at all, though few Virginians found his account persuasive. Steeped in assumptions about masculine vice and feminine weakness—ideas promoted but not invented by sentimental novelists—most contemporaries, including many of the Randolphs' kin, concluded that an illicit liaison had occurred and that Richard was at fault. After Richard's death, his brother Jack would strive mightily to displace this prevailing view, blaming Nancy instead for the ruin of his brother and his family, and by extension for the malaise of decay and dishonor that afflicted Virginia's gentry in the post-revolutionary era.

4

DECAYED GENTRY

The years following Richard's death were difficult for the Randolphs of Bizarre. While mourning Richard, Judith and Nancy also suffered the interrelated trials of economic distress and social isolation. Jack Randolph inherited his older brother's economic woes and assumed nominal leadership of the Bizarre household. Relations between the three were often stormy. In time, Jack's hostility toward Nancy and his efforts to alienate Judith from her sister would lead Nancy to leave Bizarre.

The Bizarre scandal influenced relationships within the Randolph family while also subtly shaping the Randolphs' responses to their continuing political and economic troubles. Most of the Randolph men faced financial debility and political decline with silent resignation, sinking increasingly deeper into penury and obscurity after 1800. Only Jack, driven in part by the scandal that engulfed his nearest relations, acted on a driving ambition to recover what he idealized as the colonial golden age of the gentry and their world. Most of the Randolph women, by contrast, sought to mitigate the effects of their husbands' misfortunes by becoming models of resourcefulness, contributing in varied and unprecedented ways to their family economies. For Judith Randolph, the economic and social stakes were especially high as she aspired to allay talk about her troubled marriage and assume the role of loyal wife, mother, and steward of Richard's legacy to their sons. As if to compensate for the sordid stories about her family's recent past, Judith made herself, in her own words, "the heroine of my own tale" of domestic fortitude and competence, while at the same time taking advantage of the opportunities for independence that her widowhood occasionally afforded.[1]

After 1796, Nancy looked to her widowed sister for board and shelter, though she was painfully aware that Judith could revoke her hospitality at any moment and turn her out-of-doors. As an unmarried woman with little property, Nancy was both financially and emotionally dependent on her family. Accordingly, she sought to reconcile with her Tuckahoe siblings and to nurture connections with others to whom she might turn if she found herself homeless or otherwise distressed. Beginning in 1805, Nancy's troubled search for alternative living arrangements demonstrated both her dependence and the extent to which she was a liability to her already financially straitened relatives. From Nancy's perspective, her kin were variously neglectful or malevolent. "I supposed myself, at length, about to sail gently down the current of life," she mused metaphorically in 1807, "however, the breath of some Randolph, with pretended regard, or avowed enmity, is ever ready to blow me into a whirlpool."[2] A few months later, Nancy Randolph became the first of her siblings to leave the Old Dominion, fleeing poverty and scandal in search of a better life.

On Richard's death in 1796, twenty-three-year-old Jack Randolph became an important figure in the Bizarre household. Although Richard had bequeathed all of his property to Judith, whom he also named as executrix of his estate, in practice Jack assumed responsibility for managing the plantation on which the family based its livelihood. In addition, he took seriously his new and largely self-imposed role as surrogate father to his nephews, St. George and Tudor, aged four and one, respectively. Having secured his new status as nominal head of Judith's household, Jack also determined to enter and excel in public life. Unlike most of the Randolph men, who withdrew from political life after the Revolution, Jack aggressively pursued public acclaim and honor.

By all accounts, John Randolph was intelligent, sharp-tongued, and haughtily aristocratic. Tall, thin, and sickly even in youth, in adulthood Jack was marked by the debilitating illness of 1792, which "left him without palpable signs of manhood"—a circumstance that must have complicated his relations with women. Jack's patrician demeanor, rapier wit, and strong opinions invariably made him the center of attention; people either loathed him or admired him profusely. He had a keen sense of honor and was fiercely loyal to his friends. Conversely, he was known to hold a grudge and to be remarkably vicious to those whom he regarded as his foes.[3]

An 1804 portrait by Gilbert Stuart shows a self-assured figure, whose boyish looks belied his thirty years. Posed against an equestrian backdrop, Jack surrounded himself with accoutrements of class privilege and gentility. Acutely conscious of the image he presented to others, his most perceptive biographer has observed that Randolph "always dressed to please himself and his clothes reflected his sense of himself as Virginian, patriot, horseman—gentleman. . . . His was the dandyism of a young man who wanted to be taken for nothing other than what he was. . . ."[4] Nevertheless, John Randolph had inherited the problems of his father and other colonial grandees, who had faced losing their self-mastery and their mastery over others as a result of mounting debts.

Because mastery and independence were characteristics that elite Virginians associated with honor and manhood, planters struggled to understand and to

Figure 4.1 John Randolph in 1804. This portrait shows the boyish-looking Randolph, at the height of his congressional career, elegantly attired and posed in a fashionable armchair. In the background, a horse signals his aristocratic taste for horseracing and breeding. Gilbert Stuart, *John Randolph*, 1804/1805, Andrew W. Mellon Collection, Photograph © Board of Trustees, National Gallery of Art, Washington.

rationalize the psychic implications of their financial problems.[5] John Page, a close friend of St. George Tucker and the Randolphs, chronicled his own descent into debt and debility in his letters to the London merchant John Norton, one of his many creditors. In 1771, Page worried that Norton thought him dishonorable and protested that he would "endeavour to remove as soon as in my Power all Possibility of Suspicion," though he would need to sell his own slaves—and thus abdicate his position as master and patriarch—to raise the needed funds. As his financial prospects worsened, Page tried to evade both shame and culpability by finding a scientific explanation for his problems. In 1772, he designed an instrument to measure rainfall and kept "an exact Journal of the Weather" for thirteen months to show Norton that unusually heavy rains, which had hurt tobacco crops, were the real source of the planters' woes. In so doing, however, Page tacitly admitted that he and other gentlemen planters were subject to ungovernable natural forces and thus lacked the mastery and independence that they so ardently valued.[6]

Twenty years later, with no financial relief in sight, Page, like many other Virginia planters, scrambled to evade or to delay their increasingly impatient creditors. In 1792, Page weakly restated his promise to pay what he owed, giving a series of feeble excuses for ignoring the "Proposition of Payment" Norton had sent. "Nothing but the incessant Round of Business both public & private in which I have been engaged & in which at one Time I mislaid your Letter . . . prevented my answering it," he asserted. Page also claimed that the illness of first his wife and then "of several of my Children" prevented him from "attempting a Settlement." In the space of a few decades, John Page had gone from being a gentry patriarch, who governed and protected his family and his slaves, to a man who sold his slaves and invoked the problems of his wife and children to placate his creditors.[7]

This progression from debt to dependence to dissembling was replicated among the Randolphs and most other gentry families. Members of the younger generation, however, were probably slow to appreciate the extent to which their families' fortunes had declined because of the mixed messages they received from their elders. The three sons of Thomas Mann and Anne Cary Randolph of Tuckahoe, for example, two of whom had received a gentleman's education in Europe, inherited land, slaves, and livestock, along with some $64,000 in unpaid debts.[8] The grandeur of their family connections, bolstered by their mother's injunctions to honor and emulate their illustrious Bland and Randolph forebears, similarly diluted the impact of St. George Tucker's repeated recommendation that his stepsons explore occupational possibilities other than planting in the post-revolutionary era. Although Richard, Theo, and Jack each inherited a plantation and slaves from their father, much of their patrimony eventually would be sold to pay his sizeable debts.[9]

Although Jack, like his brothers, spent lavishly in his youth, after Richard's death he strove to regain the real or imagined independence and mastery that his ancestors had enjoyed in their heyday. Beginning in 1796, Jack spent years settling both his father's and his brother's debts, thereby "sav[ing] much of the estate that might otherwise have been sacrificed" to their creditors. He also

Figure 4.2 Roanoke Plantation. Jack Randolph moved to Roanoke from Bizarre in 1810. He lived in the clapboard house on the right in the summer; the log house on the left served as his winter residence. The smaller buildings in the background housed his slaves. Roanoke's simple structures, scattered in the dense forest, stood in marked contrast to the ordered gentility of the plantation homes of Jack's colonial forebears. From Henry Howe, comp., *Historical Collections of Virginia* (Charleston, S.C.: Babcock & Co., 1845).

purchased additional acreage, nearly doubling his landholdings in and around Charlotte County, where his own plantation, Roanoke, was located. John Randolph of Roanoke, as he eventually came to be known, became Charlotte County's leading slaveholder, eventually claiming ownership of nearly 400 bondpeople. Randolph's passion for horse-breeding and racing, his well-stocked table, English coach, and extensive library signaled his affinity with the values of the old colonial gentry, though his rustic house at Roanoke, to which he moved in 1810, stood in marked contrast to the Georgian mansions of Virginia's old colonial elites.[10]

John Randolph's failure to build a new house may have reflected his self-conscious "devotion to old things" and his sense that no new house could replace his ancestral seat at Matoax, which Richard had sold for some £ 3,000 to help meet his most pressing financial obligations back in 1794. Jack viewed landed estates as emblems of the planter elite and the colonial social hierarchy over which they had presided. During the Revolution, Thomas Jefferson had successfully championed changes in the law of inheritance to encourage the division of great landed estates and thus promote democracy and equality of opportunity among propertied white men in Virginia. Jack, by contrast, vehemently opposed the abolition of primogeniture and entail, inheritance customs that together had ensured the preservation of landed estates intact to be passed from generation to generation, from eldest son to eldest son. Randolph condemned Jefferson's reforms and scorned men who alienated the "graves of their forefathers," but he especially lamented the loss of his own patrimony. While traveling between Richmond and Petersburg, he once noted bitterly that "my forefathers . . . once owned all the country hereabouts, that was worth having." But, now, he observed ruefully, "Their possessions are in the hands of strangers. The mansion Houses dismantled—the Churches profaned & rifled . . . Everything bears the marks of decay."[11]

Compounding Jack's sense of impending doom and degeneration was the recognition that he himself would not sire and rear a new generation of Virginia gentlemen. Randolph considered marrying only one woman, Maria Ward, whom he professed to love "better than my own soul or Him who created it!" Some time around 1799, the two became engaged, though their engagement soon was broken. While some of Randolph's biographers have attributed the break-up to his "physical condition"—specifically, his impotence—another has argued that when Maria learned of Jack's previous sexual relationship with a Philadelphia woman she changed her mind about marrying him. In 1805, marriage between the two was again rumored, but it was not to be. Maria wed Peyton Randolph the following year, and Jack would never marry. The loss of Maria Ward, whatever the cause, devastated Jack, who, years later, called the dissolution of their engagement an "event which . . . prostrated all my faculties and made a mere child of me," adding, "I am the very same child still."[12]

Lacking children of his own, Jack nonetheless sought to reprise the patriarchal role of his colonial forebears. At Bizarre he acted as a surrogate father, advising Judith on how best to educate her sons and developing close relationships with his nephews and some other young relatives. After Jack moved to Roanoke in 1810, at least five young male relatives or protégés, besides his nephews, resided there with him for extended periods, during which he monitored their education and upbringing. These relationships continued through an exchange of letters after the young men left his household. At the same time, Jack also cultivated paternalistic relations with his nieces and with women in general, envisioning himself as a benevolent mentor to and monitor of the female sex. He also saw himself as a patriarchal master to his slaves, seeking to inculcate loyalty and obedience by avoiding both "perpetually scolding and correcting, or . . . the other extreme of leaving them to themselves and spoiling them by false indulgence."[13]

Just as he sought to replicate the idealized world of colonial patriarchs in his family and on his plantation, Jack also tried to revive older ideals of gentry leadership and the deferential political culture of the colonial era. Despite the maintenance of relatively high property qualifications for voting, Virginia politics changed significantly as a result of the Revolution. Many members of old established gentry families withdrew voluntarily from public life, resentful of the greater inclusiveness of republican politics or perhaps fearful of the economic costs of continued public service and neglect of their estates. Political culture in general and election campaigns in particular changed to reflect the voters' increasing sense that representatives ought to be accountable to their constituents. Thomas Jefferson, whose own family had been among the second rank of the colonial gentry, believed that many of Virginia's most important and powerful old families bore an aristocratic stigma that significantly diminished their political influence among their less privileged neighbors after the Revolution. "A Randolph, a Carter, or a Burwell," he declared, "must have greater personal superiority over a competitor to be elected by the people. . . ."[14]

For the Randolphs, Jefferson's assertion was especially apt. During the last quarter-century of the colonial period, eighteen men bearing the Randolph surname had served a total of seventy-eight legislative terms, some of which lasted as long as seven years, the maximum period between elections under the imperial regime. Between 1776 and 1800, by contrast, only seven men bearing the Randolph name served a total of twenty-seven one-year terms in Virginia's state legislature. The Randolphs were even less visible in state politics after 1800. Between 1801 and 1825, six Randolph men served a total of only fifteen one-year terms in either house of the Virginia legislature.[15]

Of the first post-revolutionary generation of Virginia Randolphs, only Thomas Mann Randolph, Jr., had a significant political career at the state level. This eldest brother of Judith and Nancy seemed to continue his family's tradition of political leadership when he was elected to the state senate in 1793 at the age of twenty-five. Between 1803 and 1807, Tom also represented his district in the U. S. House of Representatives. Between 1819 and 1825, he won a total of five one-year terms in the state assembly, and from 1819 through 1822, the legislators, in turn, elected him to the maximum of three one-year terms as governor. But Tom's political success was more the result of his strong association with his father-in-law, Thomas Jefferson, than with his own family's continuing public influence. Neither of his brothers ever held public office. Only one of his brothers-in-law, Wilson Jefferson Cary, another Jefferson protégé, was politically active, serving in the state assembly from 1821 until his death in 1823.[16]

Unlike his cousin at Monticello, Jack Randolph looked not to Jefferson but rather to his colonial ancestors as exemplars, even as he accommodated and sometimes exploited certain aspects of the new republican political order. Jack's early political impulses had been liberal and democratic. Like his brother Richard and like Jefferson himself, he had admired the French Revolution. In 1799, moreover, he entered politics under Jeffersonian auspices, running for a congressional seat with the approval and sponsorship of Creed Taylor, a Republican state senator and a key leader among Jefferson's piedmont partisans. Jack Randolph's politics, however, became increasingly elitist and reactionary. While Jefferson supported universal suffrage for white men, whom he trusted to govern themselves, Randolph believed that only men of education and wealth should wield political power. Jack decried democracy as the tyranny of "King Numbers" and backed the maintenance of strict property qualifications for voting. Moreover, he contended that once white male freeholders had expressed their preference at the polls, they should thereafter defer to the authority and judgment of the gentlemen they chose to be their governors. Like a typical colonial grandee, Jack Randolph was certain of his superiority over the bulk of his neighbors and resented having to solicit their directions or approval.[17]

Despite his unrepentantly aristocratic outlook, Jack proved to be a remarkably successful campaigner among the farmers of the Virginia piedmont. Oratory, his preferred method of campaigning, allowed him to maintain physical distance between himself and his constituents while affording ample opportunity to showcase his gentlemanly attributes. Randolph's first attempt at public speaking occurred during his first congressional campaign. In March 1799, he shared an audience at Charlotte Court House with his brother Richard's erstwhile defense counsel, Patrick Henry, who was running as a Federalist for a seat in the state senate. Jack had the unenviable task of following Henry, the foremost orator of the age. Although no detailed accounts of his performance have survived, fragmentary evidence suggests that he acquitted himself admirably. The Reverend John Holt Rice, who witnessed Randolph's debut, years later recalled the "clear, silver tones and spirit-stirring accents of the youthful orator," noting the impression he made on the crowd of skeptical onlookers. "I tell you what," remarked one "countryman" with homely appreciation, "the young man is no bug-eater neither"—meaning that he was not a trifling fellow, notwithstanding his frail, youthful, and effeminate demeanor.[18] In 1799, both Randolph and Henry won their elections. Although Henry died before taking office, John Randolph, aged twenty-six, left Bizarre that November to take his seat in Congress.

John Randolph developed into one of the most accomplished orators of the Jeffersonian era. His style of speaking featured simple arguments punctuated with satire and biting sarcasm to devastate his adversaries. Randolph attracted and entertained large audiences whenever he spoke in his home district, which embraced the piedmont counties of Cumberland, Prince Edward, Charlotte, and Buckingham. His constituents clearly admired and respected his talents, which reflected well on their community when he represented them in Washington. According to one Charlotte County resident, local voters felt a "country pride" in Randolph and his importance—first as a Jeffersonian party leader and later as a fiery opposition figure—in national politics. In a congressional career that ultimately spanned more than three decades, Randolph lost only one election. Only in the midst of the crisis of the War of 1812, which he opposed, did his constituents choose another man to represent them in Washington.[19]

By most measures, then, John Randolph was unusually successful. Unlike his parents and brothers, who died young, he lived a long, if sickly, life. Unlike the majority of his surviving kin, he prospered financially and became politically influential both locally and at the national level. He had close relationships with his sister-in-law, Judith, and her sons, with his Tucker step-siblings, and with an array of friends and political associates in Virginia and beyond. Nevertheless, these advantages and achievements did not compensate for the pain and resentment Jack felt as a result of what he believed to be the unwarranted demise of the Virginia gentry and, more particularly, the decline of his own illustrious family.

After Richard's death, Jack blamed a succession of scapegoats for the decline of the Old Dominion from its colonial grandeur, epitomized in his mind by the marked deterioration of the status of the Randolph family. In public life, he saw the Revolution as the main culprit, with its most objectionable consequence being the abolition of primogeniture and entail in Virginia. In Randolph's mind, Thomas Jefferson personified these changes both because of his embrace of democratic politics and because of his leadership in promoting inheritance reform to undermine "aristocracy" in Virginia. Jack bitterly concluded that the demise of the Randolphs and the ruin of Virginia's other great families was the "inevitable conclusion to which Mr. Jefferson and his leveling system has brought us." Although he broke politically with Jefferson in 1805 over more timely issues, the Republican leader's earlier role in reforming Virginia's inheritance laws made his subsequent political success epitomize, in Randolph's mind, what went wrong with America's revolution.[20]

In his private life, Jack made Nancy Randolph, and to a lesser extent St. George Tucker, the prime scapegoats for his family's downfall. Despite his previously cordial relationship with his stepfather, he eventually blamed Tucker for his financial problems, preferring to accuse him of corruption and incompetence during his tenure as guardian of the Randolph property rather than admit that his own father had left behind an indebted and poorly managed estate.[21] At the same time, Jack held Nancy responsible for Richard's disgrace and, by extension, for the humiliation and unhappiness of the entire Bizarre household.

For nearly a decade after Richard's death, Jack skirmished with Nancy who, in turn, confided in Tucker. Meanwhile, Jack's relationship with his sister-in-law, Judith, was also occasionally embittered and contentious.

Jack's presence at Bizarre was both a blessing and an irritant to Judith, who in widowhood confronted a series of opportunities and challenges. As a widow, Judith was free from the strictures of coverture, the common law doctrine that vested control of all property belonging to a married couple in the hands of the husband. Richard's will gave Judith title to and control of all his property, but she soon found that managing hundreds of acres and a large corps of slaves—all of whom Richard's will had destined for eventual freedom—was a daunting task, rendered more complicated by the debts encumbering the estate. As a result, Judith sometimes was grateful for the guidance of her brother-in-law.[22] At the same time, Richard's death altered the dynamics of personal relationships in the Bizarre household. While Richard had encouraged both Judith and Nancy to coexist more or less peacefully with each other, Jack, whose hatred for Nancy blossomed during these years, promoted rancor between the sisters.

Like growing numbers of widows, Judith never seriously considered remarrying, though Jack encouraged or approved relationships between her and at least three different men during her twenty-year widowhood, perhaps hoping to find another man to take his place in looking after the family at Bizarre. In 1799, Jack brought his friend, William Thompson, to Bizarre to live and urged him to "cultivate a familiarity" with Judith. Thompson found in her "a gentleness of manners, an uniformity of conduct, and a majesty of virtue," and the pair enjoyed each other's company until 1800, when he left Bizarre to allay rumors that he hoped to profit materially by wooing its mistress. Ten years later, Jack declared that he would "not be disappointed" if Judith "should give her hand" to an unidentified Presbyterian minister with whom she had developed a close relationship, but she never did. Finally, in 1816, Jack unsuccessfully predicted and promoted a match between his sister-in-law and widower John Coalter. Preferring either to retain her autonomy or to avoid a recurrence of her first unhappy marriage, Judith remained a widow and focused primarily on her maternal role.[23]

Although contemporaries increasingly lauded mothers for cultivating the moral, as well as the physical, well-being of their offspring, widowed mothers typically had the additional responsibility of promoting their children's material welfare.[24] In widowhood, Judith traded her previous identity as an embittered wife for that of a devoted and self-sacrificing mother. Judith certainly loved her sons, but she also enjoyed the authority and independence that her status as a sole parent could bring. In widowhood, she sometimes invoked her perceived maternal obligations to justify financial and other choices she made for herself, her children, and the Bizarre household.

When Richard died in 1796, Judith was already aware of her family's financial problems. A month after her husband's death, as she awaited St. George Tucker's assessment of Richard's estate and her own future prospects, Judith intimated that she expected bad news. "You need not fear my dear Sir, to tell me the worst, when I assure you I am prepared for any event that may deprive [her sons], *even* of the little property their dear Father *could* ever call his own," she wrote. "Our *wants* in this world are very few, [and] my wishes have ever been . . . as moderate as those of any human being," she continued, noting that her sole wish now was "for a bare subsistence for myself, my poor Sister, & my darlings, who are now the universe to me."[25]

In spite of their straitened circumstances, Judith, Nancy, and Jack lived together more or less amicably for more than a year after Richard's death. Judith welcomed her brother-in-law into her home, declaring that "by his affectionate conduct [he] is every day dearer to my heart." Jack got along well enough with Nancy, too, at least initially. When Henry Tucker, Jack's half-brother, visited Bizarre in the fall of 1796, he reported to his father that "Sisters Judy & Nancy are well" and the family was generally happy. During this period, Judith's letters to St. George Tucker expressed her constant desire for his company and that of his family. In 1797, Judith also seemed genuinely sorry to report to her father-in-law that Nancy was ill with a "Gouty" complaint. Nancy's letters to Tucker, which constitute the only surviving documentation of her life at Bizarre during these years, likewise reflected sisterly empathy for Judith's efforts to cope with her "irreparable loss." Judith took an occasional jaunt to Petersburg or to Amelia County to see friends, leaving her sons in Nancy's care, and Nancy visited her cousin Brett Randolph and sister Jane, thus beginning to repair her relations with her estranged siblings. Although Nancy was criticized—probably by Jack—for leaving Bizarre to visit her sister, in most other respects frugal tranquility seemed ascendant at Bizarre.[26]

The first signs of serious problems between the sisters came in 1798, after they returned from a winter visit to the Tuckers' Williamsburg home. Judith and Nancy spent most of January and February in Williamsburg, taking advantage of what would become a standing invitation from St. George Tucker to enjoy a family visit in the midst of the relatively lively winter society of Virginia's former capital. Clearly, Tucker believed that both Judith and Nancy should be out in society, attending balls, and meeting prospective suitors, and Nancy at least enjoyed the respite from the dreary isolation of Bizarre. Indeed, dressed in her "Elegant Book Muslin dress, with Balloon sleeves, little Pearl colored Sattin Hat, stuck on one side the head" to go to a ball in Williamsburg, Nancy was scarcely recognizable, Judith reported to Mary Harrison. Judith herself, however, rejected out of hand the prospect of being "metamorphosed into a fine Lady" during her stay with the Tuckers. As she explained to her friend, "no my dear girl, full many a joyous dance have we led up together, with hearts as light as air, but the keen dart of misfortune has blunted all those feelings in my breast. . . ." A year and a half after Richard's death, Judith refused to go to balls and continued to dress in black. Secure in her virtuous widowhood, she may have feared that her public image as Richard's rejected wife would make her an object of pity or ridicule if she chose to re-enter Virginia society. Perhaps in part to counteract that image, Judith also continued to wear her wedding ring, claiming that "it had never been off since the first day it was put on."[27]

Although what happened between the sisters in Williamsburg is unclear, the visit proved to be a turning point both in their association with the Tuckers and their relationship with each other. Judith did not write to St. George Tucker for roughly a year after returning from Williamsburg. Her letters to Mary Harrison during this period were unusually bleak, dwelling on her financial problems, domestic drudgery, and loneliness, though they did not mention Nancy explicitly. In May, however, Judith's description of her sons, St. George and Tudor, now aged six and three, as her "chief society" implied that she and Nancy were estranged. By July, Judith claimed to be desperately lonely and without hope that her situation would improve, either financially or emotionally. Though at twenty-six she was "at an age when most people are eager in pursuit of that phantom, happiness," she confided, she saw herself as one who, having "arrived at the last stage of a journey, . . . endeavours to sit down contentedly with having lost that end, which they have striven to attain."[28]

Meanwhile, Nancy wrote often to St. George Tucker, whom she now addressed as her "more than Father." Such an extravagant declaration of affection and dependence, unusual even in this sentimental age, suggests that Nancy saw herself as increasingly isolated and imperiled at Bizarre. In her letters to Tucker, Nancy intimated that Judith was trying to turn both Jack and Tucker's own daughter, Fanny, against her, and that her sister's ultimate goal was to force her to leave Bizarre. Partly in response to her increasingly uncomfortable position in her sister's household, Nancy stepped up her efforts to repair her relations with her other siblings. In May she met her brother William on "amiable" terms at the home of Creed Taylor. "I dined with him once, and promised to continue the intercourse, when he returns from Alexandria," she explained to Tucker, adding defensively that William, who Richard had believed to have been one of his foremost enemies, "vows he never injured me." That summer, Nancy made another visit to her sister Jane, after which she planned to stay with her brother Tom at Monticello. "I have partly promised to visit my Brother before my return to Bizarre," she informed Tucker. Nancy alluded to her strained relationship with Judith, noting that someday "I shall rejoice to recollect having strenuously endeavor'd to cast a veil of oblivion over the chasm made by several members of my Father's family, in the bonds by which nature united me with them."[29]

In 1798, John Randolph's relations with both sisters were strained, though he eventually joined forces with Judith against Nancy and helped solidify the sisters' estrangement from each other. According to Nancy, Judith had begun to question her brother-in-law's management of her property and to worry that "her interest [was] endanger'd by his uncommon attention to his own." Nancy listened sympathetically to her sister's concerns and to Judith's account of Jack's efforts to "slight" Nancy on some unspecified grounds. Nancy responded by showing Judith a letter that Jack had written to Nancy herself, which she had previously kept secret. Although Nancy's explanation of this exchange between her and her sister was extremely cryptic, it seems clear that Jack's letter concerned love, not money, and that Nancy shared its contents—with Judith and perhaps with Jack's beloved Maria Ward?—to ridicule Jack. But Nancy's effort to make common cause with Judith against Jack was doomed to failure. Already antagonistic toward Nancy for her real or imagined role in Richard's downfall, Jack encouraged Judith to regard her sister with hostility and suspicion. Perhaps resenting her sister's enjoyment of the balls of Williamsburg, Judith soon accused Nancy of "having transgressed the bonds of decorum in [her] behaviour to Jack." Shortly after that, Nancy began to ponder the possibility of having to leave Bizarre.[30]

Despite her sometimes contentious relationship with Judith, Nancy came to believe that Jack was chiefly responsible for her growing unhappiness. In early 1799, when Jack left Bizarre for Philadelphia, the sisters got on relatively well, despite continued money problems and Judith's "complaints of ill health." In March, Nancy reported to St. George Tucker that she and Judith had "spent a fortnight entirely *alone,* during which time her conduct has compensated for every former harsh expression . . . Heaven knows how dearly I love Judy, who possesses some most inestimable qualities." While Nancy exaggerated the extent of her reconciliation with Judith for Tucker's benefit, the next major crisis in the sisters' relationship did not occur until Jack returned to Bizarre and Nancy found herself again under pressure to leave the house. Although Nancy initially blamed Judith for her impending exile, she soon concluded that Jack was the real problem. Nancy spent August and September 1799 at Monticello. She does not appear to have returned to Bizarre until early December, by which time Jack was back in Philadelphia beginning his first congressional term.[31]

Although Nancy's presence at Bizarre was a constant reminder of the scandal that had befallen her family, Judith allowed her sister to remain there at least in part because of St. George Tucker's sympathy for Nancy and her own desire to avoid a major altercation with the Tuckers. Given the death of her own parents and her cool relations with her Tuckahoe siblings, Judith regarded the Tuckers as her closest kin, aside from Jack. Indeed, Richard and Jack's half-siblings— St. George Tucker's daughter, Fanny, and his sons, Henry and Beverley—were among Judith's most frequent and cherished visitors at Bizarre. Henry and Beverley Tucker each lived briefly at Judith's house while studying law in the vicinity, presumably helping out with expenses during their stays. After Richard's death, Judith cultivated a more intimate and emotionally satisfying relationship with Fanny, who eased her suffering during the early years of her widowhood, when she was a frequent guest at Bizarre. "To her lively & agreeable humour, I am indebted for all the cheerful moments I have known for 6 months past," Judith observed in 1797. "Few indeed they have been, but without her uninterrupted flow of spirits to enliven me, they would all have past, (as I fear my future ones will) in gloomy melancholy." The relationship between Fanny and Judith became more reciprocal after Fanny married John Coalter in 1802 and became mistress of her own household. By extending frequent invitations to the lonely and unhappy Judith, Fanny provided companionship "so congenial in its kind to my temper & sentiments, [it] diffuses its influence over my unquiet spirit." Judith, for her part, nursed Fanny through several serious illnesses, most of which resulted from pregnancy or childbirth, and was with her when she died in 1813 at the age of thirty-four.[32]

Judith also received some direct benefits from Nancy's continued presence in the form of the labor and other resources she contributed to the household. Like Judith and the other Randolph sisters, Nancy had inherited $6,000 from her father's estate. Since she was virtually penniless when she finally left Bizarre for good, it seems reasonable to assume that she contributed at least a portion of that money to the household's funds or that she paid all or part of her own expenses while she resided at Bizarre. More important still, like most dependent single women Nancy was expected to be part of the household's labor force. Historians have shown that plantations mistresses at this time did an enormous amount of work. Their chores ranged from the relatively genteel sorts of needlework and childrearing to physically demanding tasks like making cloth, tending gardens, and even processing slaugh- tered animals. In 1803, Nancy complained that her "employments" in her sister's house "generally consist of some species of drudgery, or needlework," but she also frequently cared for Judith's young sons.[33]

As Judith adjusted to penurious widowhood, she performed her maternal and domestic tasks with self-conscious competence and efficiency that became essen- tial parts of her identity. With some justification, Judith imagined herself as heroically persevering for the benefit of her family. In 1798, as her relationship with Nancy deteriorated, she reported to Mary Harrison with a mixture of pride and regret that she had left Bizarre only three times in the past three months and "had company about as often" because of her grueling domestic work schedule. With neither house slaves nor children to assist her, Judith found needlework especially demanding. "I must rely on my own fingers to keep my children, my Brother [Jack Randolph], & myself whole," she mused, on the verge of completing "the third of seven shirts for [Jack] . . . & I have not even the assistance of having the tails hemmed for me." A year later, Judith confided that though she found herself adrift on a "sea of misery" and had suffered "total disappointment in domestic life," she nonetheless endeavored to "fulfil the duties of my station with cheerfulness, & by a continual round of domestic occupations" distract herself from the "gloominess" that would otherwise lead her to "sink almost into a state of apathy."[34]

Although Judith was unlikely to acknowledge Nancy's assistance, her sister's presence nonetheless afforded her not only another set of working hands but also an occasional respite from the dreary isolation of Bizarre. While rural men often attended courts, markets, and political events, plantation women generally found themselves isolated and with few opportunities for sociability outside their households, in part because they could not take time away from either their children or their domestic responsibilities. Nevertheless, at least twice each year Judith was able to leave her sons in Nancy's care and make extended visits to friends or relatives in other counties or, better still, to the popular Virginia springs.[35] These visits gave Judith an occasional independence enjoyed by few mothers of young children at this time—an independence she never acknowledged because it conflicted with both prevailing gender ideals and her own identity as a frugal housewife and selfless mother.

Similarly, while Judith's financial problems were both genuine and debilitating, they also provided a convenient justification for her to assert control of her own social life both at home and beyond. Richard's death enabled her to alter dramatically the tone and style of living at Bizarre. While he had offered generous, even excessive, hospitality to a parade of guests, Judith ushered in a regime based on frugality. Before Richard was even in his grave, she saw to it that his cousin, Anna Dudley, left Bizarre. Judith apparently had never gotten along well with this long-term houseguest, who, with her two children, she regarded as an economic liability. After Richard's death, Judith also professed her reluctance to leave home or to entertain guests at Bizarre as a result of her "pecuniary embarrassments." In an oblique reference to Richard's extravagance and lack of business skills, she bemoaned the consequences of the "possession of a considerable & expensive property illy managed" and avowed "the necessity of pursuing a plan of the most limited expense until I am extricated from so disagreeable a dilemma." Judith resolved to deny herself "everything but absolute necessaries" until she felt she had "a *right* to gratify myself."[36]

By invoking debt and debility, Judith quietly asserted her independence. In fact, only a month before she renounced "everything but absolute necessaries," she had been at Sweet Springs, a popular gathering place for well-heeled Virginians seeking health, relaxation, and sociability. Judith visited the springs in 1799, 1801, and again in 1802, ostensibly to attend to her own chronic ill health or that of Richard's half-sister, Fanny Tucker Coalter.[37] Although visiting the spas of western Virginia was clearly more costly than receiving guests at home, Judith could justify her visits to the springs on health grounds, which was part of the spas' appeal to normally housebound women. Isolated rural women especially craved female companionship and, in the absence of balls or other social engagements, they might use health or sickness to create other occasions for sociability.[38]

In widowhood, Judith also invoked penury and maternal duty to maintain a polite independence from St. George Tucker and his family. After Richard's death, Tucker continued to offer fatherly advice to both Judith and Nancy. While Nancy maintained close ties to Richard's stepfather, Judith became more distant, either because of Tucker's continuing sympathy for Nancy or because she, unlike Nancy, had other male advisors and enough property to get along without his help. Beginning around 1800, Judith used her maternal obligations and financial woes as excuses to avoid her customary annual visits to the Tucker home in Williamsburg. Affecting the role of the dutiful daughter, she repeatedly averred her desire to visit, but claimed that extended absences from Bizarre would be detrimental to her family's economic welfare. Given Judith's willingness to visit the Virginia springs without her sons for extended periods, the Tuckers might have questioned her sincerity, but they would have found it difficult to criticize her determination to forgo pleasure for the benefit of her sons. Judith knew that self-sacrifice was a key maternal virtue, and she played that card when it suited her. Indeed, on at least one occasion she went so far as to claim that her responsibilities at Bizarre precluded her even from writing to the Tuckers. "If I do write, it must be of my children," she informed St. George Tucker in 1803, adding, "every exertion I make is for their benefit, every pain I feel originates in my anxious solicitude for their welfare."[39]

As Judith's evasiveness toward the Tuckers suggests, the Bizarre scandal and Richard's subsequent death had a dramatic impact on visiting patterns and sociability in the Randolphs' extended family circle. Before the scandal, Judith exchanged visits mainly with her married sisters, her brother and sister-in-law at Monticello, Mary Harrison, a cousin with whom she shared a sisterly intimacy, and Richard's stepfather, St. George Tucker. For years after the scandal, by contrast, she rarely saw her siblings; visits to or from the Harrisons were also infrequent, despite her continuing reliance on Mary's letters for "distant imaginary converse." Although Judith repeatedly expressed a desire to visit the Harrisons—and especially to attend Mary in her many confinements—she does not appear to have done so.[40] Instead, Judith exchanged visits mainly with two women who had not figured prominently in her painful past. Born in 1779, Fanny Tucker had been too young to know much about the Bizarre scandal and she had not been involved at all in Richard's defense. Maria Ward, John Randolph's one-time fiancée, was Judith's other close companion. By 1804, Nancy complained of the "lover-like attentions" exchanged by her sister and Maria Ward, to whose enmity she at least partly attributed her own increasingly untenable position at Bizarre.[41]

Despite these sustaining female friendships, Judith had a deeply unsatisfying life. An admitted "egotist" and "hypochondriac" who suffered from an array of chronic complaints, she nonetheless had good reason to fear for the future of her sons. St. George, who was deaf, evidently had learned to read and write, but in 1805 Judith concluded that further instruction would not "improve" her elder son. While Judith reveled in the promise of her younger son, Tudor, she worried frantically about his physical well-being. A protracted illness in 1805 left her especially distraught and convinced that he would never completely regain his health.[42]

The needs of Judith's growing sons, moreover, posed new financial problems. Although Judith had always worried about the general likelihood of her being able to preserve the boys' patrimony, she now had more specific concerns about how to pay for their education. Jack had persuaded her that St. George would benefit from special treatment and education that he could obtain only from the Englishman Thomas Braidwood, who had a school for the deaf at Hackney near London. In 1806, Saint, as he was known to the family, was slated to travel to England with James Monroe, a friend and political associate of John Randolph who was to represent the United States at the Court of St. James. Around the same time, ten-year-old Tudor would begin attending school in Richmond. Just months before the boys' departure, Judith confided to Mary Harrison that she did not expect her plantation's proceeds to cover her sons' expenses. She would also experience even greater loneliness and a desire to have "somebody in their place" once the boys left Bizarre.[43]

Meanwhile, the imminent departure of Saint and Tudor rendered Nancy's position in her sister's household even more tenuous. As early as 1803, Nancy had described herself somewhat melodramatically as "cast on a merciless world without a home." She spent much of the next year living with her brother Tom's family in Albemarle County. In November 1804, however, she returned to Bizarre and stayed with her nephews while Judith, finally acceding to the Tuckers' wishes, spent the winter in Williamsburg. In May, Nancy nursed Tudor through a relapse of his recent illness while Judith visited Maria Ward in Amelia. For "a whole week, my clothes were not off, except for the purpose of changing them," Nancy informed St. George Tucker, adding with satisfaction, "the dear boy is now nearly well."[44]

In these years, to St. George Tucker at least, Nancy repeatedly professed her desire to remain at Bizarre. In 1804, as she contemplated leaving her sister's house perhaps for good, Nancy lamented that Judith had "finally dismissed me from this spot (to which I am inexpressibly attached)." Two months later, in exile in Albemarle, she wrote, "Oh God! if I cou'd only be allowed to remain [at Bizarre] in peace—my whole soul is devoted to the spot," adding, "with joy, wou'd I conform to any rules by which I cou'd *possibly* please the family."[45]

For Nancy, Bizarre's attractions included her nephews, on whom she doted, material security, and perhaps cherished memories of a youthful romance, too. Although she may have thought of Theo, whom she claimed as her betrothed, Nancy wrote only of Richard when she admitted her fondness for Bizarre. Judith clearly thought that Nancy remembered Richard much too affectionately, and by 1804 she was routinely upbraiding her younger sister for several unspecified "little presents" she had received from Richard. Nancy complained that Judith was "always mentioning the separate articles, [and] the *price* of *each*."[46] In 1805 and 1806, as Judith and Nancy's relationship deteriorated, Jack would join with Judith to drive Nancy from Bizarre.

Nancy had begun to plan for her impending exile as early as March 1804, after a particularly bitter row in which Judith taunted her about Richard's "little presents," accused her of "the most dishonorable conduct against Jack," and complained that she was an economic liability in the Bizarre household. Around the same time, Jack upbraided Nancy for, in her words, "acting as if I were in a Tavern." In this era, such an accusation embraced an array of unladylike possibilities, from general coarseness to sexual promiscuity; the vehemence with which Nancy disputed the charge suggests that Jack implied the latter. Soon Nancy concluded that her situation at Bizarre was hopeless. "I expect to Board in this neighborhood, in a very obscure and humble family," she informed St. George Tucker. "The law of necessity," she declared ominously, "is inflexible." Nancy hoped to receive "enough barely to support me" from her brother Tom in Albemarle.[47]

In 1804, Nancy informed St. George Tucker "I am on friendly terms with my brothers and sisters," adding, "it is impossible they can respect [Judith] because she has involved them in such painful situations."[48] The Tuckahoe Randolphs apparently still regarded Nancy, not Richard, as the victim of the Bizarre scandal and blamed Judith for the continuing unpleasantness the scandal caused.

In 1804 and 1805, Nancy's inability to find lodgings with some "quiet retired family" in Cumberland or neighboring Prince Edward County led her to seek refuge in the homes of her siblings and other family and friends. Nancy and Judith spent most of these two years avoiding each other: Nancy visited relatives or friends when her sister was at home and Judith returned the favor when Nancy was at Bizarre. In 1804, Nancy spent nearly six months with her brother Tom, during which she also visited her sister Jane, who lived nearby. In April 1805, Nancy stayed with family friends, the Dillons of Sandy Ford, in Prince Edward County. That summer, when Judith returned from visiting Maria Ward, Nancy went to Rocky Mills, near Tuckahoe, stayed with her brother William and his wife, and enjoyed the "genuine delights of social intercourse" for two months, including a visit with William Thompson, Judith's former suitor, and his new wife. That winter, Nancy may have spent some time with the Tuckers, whom she had not seen since she had danced at the balls of Williamsburg in 1798.[49]

During these troubled years, Nancy especially cherished the time she spent with Thomas Jefferson's extended family at Edgehill and Monticello. Nancy's first lengthy stay with Tom and Martha Jefferson Randolph was in 1799, when Judith first threatened to make Nancy leave Bizarre. She returned to Monticello in 1801 and again in 1804, after spending several months at Edgehill, the Albemarle estate that the elder Thomas Mann Randolph had settled on his son Tom shortly after he married Martha Jefferson. For six months, from May through October, Nancy marveled at tranquility and cheer of the Randolph-Jefferson household, which stood in marked contrast to the gloominess of Bizarre. From Monticello she wrote to St. George Tucker that "The Harmony in this house is never interrupted, and I regret that we are so soon to separate. Never did there exist a more excellent woman than the one to whom my brother has the good fortune to be married . . . It is not uncommon for twenty grown persons and a dozen children to assemble here—the house is full at present." Besides the Randolphs' growing family—they would have twelve children in all—Nancy's sister Harriet was among the current guests and another sister, Virginia, the youngest, resided more or less permanently in the Randolph-Jefferson household.[50]

In 1806, when Nancy left Bizarre for good, accompanied by her maid Phebe, she hoped to return to Monticello. That spring, not long after Judith returned home from a three-month stay with Fanny Coalter and around the time Saint departed for England, Nancy wrote to her brother Tom, asking him to come to Bizarre to take her to the Jefferson home. Nancy had parted with Tom and his wife, Martha, on good terms, exchanging "affectionate letters and messages frequently" since 1804, when Nancy last stayed at Monticello. Nevertheless, in 1806, according to Nancy, Martha Jefferson Randolph "wou'd not permit" her husband to bring her to their home "nor will she assign any reason for her conduct." Nancy believed that her sister-in-law's position was both mean-spirited and groundless. As she explained to St. George Tucker, "I have known her to imbibe strong prejudices in two other instances toward absent persons."[51]

In fact, however much they might have sympathized with her plight, Nancy's brothers must have regarded her as a financial burden that they could ill afford. John, the youngest of the brothers, who had trained as a physician, had "little skill or capacity" for medicine, and instead became a planter—an occupation in which his lack of success left him destitute and dependent largely on the goodwill of his relatives. William Randolph, the middle brother, was likewise financially ruined. Meanwhile, Thomas Mann Randolph, Jr., who became solely responsible for his father's obligations by virtue of his younger brothers' insolvency, fell deeper into debt. As early as 1802, Tom contemplated moving to the Mississippi Territory to become a cotton planter, but the objections of his wife and father-in-law, along with the difficulty of transporting his slaves, led him to reconsider. In Virginia, his financial situation worsened, eventually leading him to mortgage all his properties. Although Tom still lived comfortably at Monticello in 1806, neither he nor Martha looked confidently toward the future. As

Figure 4.3 *The Plantation*, ca. 1825. This nostalgic painting by an unknown American artist aptly captures the eighteenth-century Virginia plantation ideal. A hill-top mansion sits above smaller houses, just as the colonial gentry had presided over lesser folk in the social hierarchy. Grape vines and lush foliage signify rural plenty, while the ship betokens commercial prosperity. The wealth and influence of many gentry families declined precipitously in the post-revolutionary era. All rights reserved, The Metropolitan Museum of Art.

Martha Jefferson Randolph reported to her own deeply indebted father in 1808, "The ruin of the family is still extending itself daily."[52]

Nancy's sisters and their spouses also had severe financial problems. The eldest sister, Mary (or Molly) had married David Meade Randolph, who succeeded as a planter, inventor, and Federalist political appointee before suffering a series of political and financial reversals that left him destitute. By 1806, the couple had sold their plantation and moved into their Richmond mansion, Moldavia, where Molly was soon taking in boarders to make ends meet. The youngest sisters, Harriet and Virginia, were both recently married to men whose financial circumstances were equally precarious. The financial troubles of Jane—who stood between Nancy and Harriet in the family birth order—and her husband, Thomas Eston Randolph, would eventually lead to the sale of Dungeness, his ancestral home, as well as all his slaves. "The situation of, what are called, 'decayed gentry' is surely the most uncomfortable that can be," Jane Randolph observed knowingly. "With all the habits & inclinations of the wealthy, we feel the necessity of practising the same self denial with the poor—good sense & prudence tells us tis folly, tis madness to do otherwise, habit, inclination, *pride,* (that fruitful source of error) drags us on,' till the last piece of property is gone & we are left beggars."[53]

Without aid forthcoming from her troubled siblings, in the spring of 1806 Nancy headed toward Richmond, where she hoped to take advantage of the clustering of Randolph homes in and around the state capital. First, she stayed at Moldavia, the Richmond home of Molly and David Meade Randolph. Then, she went to Curles, the ancestral seat of Richard and Theo's branch of the Randolph family, located in nearby Henrico County. Then, Nancy sought refuge at Benlomond, the Goochland County estate of Archibald Randolph. Archie, who had hoped to woo Nancy in back in 1792 when he accompanied Richard, Judith, and her on their visit to Glentivar, had married Lucy Burwell in 1797. After "two wretched months" in and around Benlomond, Nancy decided to move on.[54]

Nancy's dependence on penurious kin made her a social outcast. Two of her neighbors at Benlomond had been "perfectly amiable," she explained to St. George Tucker, but the others "have attacked my forlorn situation, saying I am on object of *charity* cast on them to support and that they do not believe my brothers have promised to take me away." Nancy concluded that, "Those who are amiable in this part of the world, have their small houses as full as they can hold." As a result, in November 1806, she asked Tucker to send a carriage to take her "to the little town of Jefferson in Powhatan [County]," where she hoped to find new lodgings. Before he could respond to her entreaty, however, Nancy persuaded her brother John to take her to Tuckahoe, where she arranged to meet with Tom to discuss her future prospects. Despite his own pressing obligations,

Tom eventually settled a small sum on his sister, enabling her to move to Richmond in January 1807.[55]

Richmond, Virginia's capital, was a thriving town with an expansive commercial economy. Canals, the first of which opened in 1800, along with ongoing work to improve the navigation of the James River, facilitated Richmond's emergence as an important commercial center. In 1804, the founding of Virginia's first bank, with its headquarters in Richmond, also encouraged commercial development. Although flour milling and tobacco processing were Richmond's main industries, the city's white and black labor force also produced iron, textiles, paper, ceramics, soap, and other items. A mere hamlet at the time of the Revolution, Richmond boasted 5,737 inhabitants in 1800 and 9,735 by 1810. European immigrants accounted for much of the increased population, but so, too, did members of planter families who, like Nancy Randolph and her sister Molly, moved to the capital in search of economic opportunity.[56]

City life had certain advantages for women without fortunes, especially if they were single, in nineteenth-century America. In rural areas, most unmarried women lived with kin, just as Nancy had resided at Bizarre. A single white woman might work for pay as housekeeper for another family or perhaps as a governess. In the city, employment opportunities, though still limited, were more varied. In Petersburg, Virginia, for example, white women ran boardinghouses and taverns and worked as shopkeepers, milliners, midwives, prostitutes, seamstresses, and domestics—and they did factory work, too, beginning in the 1820s. If she were educated and genteel, a woman might earn a meager living by teaching in one of the many academies for girls that were established during the post-revolutionary decades, when educating the mothers of the republic's future citizens was for some a high priority. Richmond was home to several of these schools, including the Richmond Academy for Female Education, which received its charter of incorporation in January 1807.[57]

Despite the involvement of urban women in various types of paid employment, Nancy's genteel past and sordid present in different ways undermined her ability to find paid work in Richmond. Her social status as a Randolph precluded her from working for wages in a shop or tavern or in any sort of manufacturing position. Milliners were the elite of female artisans and one Randolph woman had been a milliner in the 1770s, but Nancy lacked the capital required to buy the inventory necessary to start a millinery business. Nor did she have a house which, like her sister Molly, she might use for commercial purposes.[58] Nancy's chief assets were the Randolph name, her genteel manners, and a reasonably good education. These attributes ordinarily would have made her an appealing candidate for the classroom, but the lingering aura of scandal had the opposite effect. Proprietors of schools and academies, who insisted that their young charges would be educated in a strictly moral environment, could not risk hiring a woman whose moral reputation was at best questionable. Indeed, the stated purpose of the Richmond Academy was to promote feminine virtue as a means to "national reform." "Enlighten and exalt the female mind," one of the school's promoters intoned, "and you forthwith banish from the world, baseness, vice, villainy, and ignorance."[59]

Nancy's time in Richmond began with a disastrous and sobering introduction to the city's market economy. Lodging was scarce in the growing town, and Nancy, who lacked experience with such matters, gratefully accepted the help of her brother-in-law, David Meade Randolph, in finding a "comfortable apartment." She regretted accepting her brother-in-law's help when he advanced three months' rent to an unscrupulous landlady for a room that proved to be filthy, damp, and unexpectedly unfurnished. Years later, Nancy recalled sleeping "on a blanket, spread over the sacking" without a proper mattress. Though she and her maid stayed in that room for only four days because the dampness made them ill, the landlady refused to refund a even a portion of the money she had received. Nancy concluded that David Meade Randolph, who was teetering on the edge of financial ruin, had conspired with the woman to defraud her of her money.[60]

Nancy's subsequent living arrangements, though less dreary, suggest that her tainted reputation may have barred her from most of the more respectable lodgings in Richmond. By late February, she had taken a room in the home of John and Anne Whiting Pryor, proprietors of Haymarket Gardens, the leading pleasure park in town. Although John Pryor's wealth and service in the Continental Army brought him both connections and respect, many Richmonders regarded Haymarket's public balls, cockfights, gaming, drinking, and other forms of entertainment as "dangerous to virtue." Nevertheless, Nancy insisted that "Mr. Prior's dwelling and the enclosure round it were wholly distinct from [Haymarket] garden." She characterized Anne Whiting Pryor as a woman of "good birth" and "correct principles."[61]

Nancy and her new landlady, in fact, had much in common. Born in 1779 and thus five years younger than Nancy Randolph, Anne Whiting was also a younger daughter in a prestigious but economically troubled planter family. She, too, had her childhood disrupted by the death of one parent and subsequent remarriage of the other and had thereafter resided in the home of a married older sister. Nancy's residence in Judith's house had brought unhappiness in the form of scandal. Anne Whiting's residence in her sister's home ended with her marriage to John Pryor in 1796—an arrangement that would bring unhappiness as well. When Nancy arrived in the Pryor home in 1807, Anne cared for her husband, but she was not in love. Three years later, she would fall in love with her French teacher, Charles Fremon, and John would order her to leave his house. In 1811, John Pryor petitioned the state legislature for a divorce and, though unsuccessful, his widely publicized case popularized the image of Anne as an adulteress who, with her lover, unsuccessfully plotted the murder of her respectable and trusting husband.[62]

At Haymarket, Nancy rented an unfurnished room and a smaller, more private "closet" at a cost of twenty dollars, plus "work for the house," for three months. She later described her position in the Pryor household as "differing from that of a servant only in this: I received no wages, but was permitted to sit at table, where I did not presume to enter into conversation or taste of wine, and very seldom of tea or coffee." She did some of the cooking, becoming "proficient . . . in the culinary art." Yet Nancy still kept her maid, the enslaved woman Phebe, who was both a companion and a financial asset. "My wants have long been comprised within a very narrow compass," she wrote with resignation to St. George Tucker in February 1807, shortly after her arrival at Haymarket. "Never shall discontent establish its empire in any place which I have a right to call my home."[63]

At Haymarket, Nancy's complaints mostly concerned the mistreatment and neglect she believed she suffered at the hands of her relations. She reported to St. George Tucker that her brother Tom was "among the only ten Randolphs who possess Sincerity—the others give Judas Iscariot's kisses and rest on their long exercised caution for security." The penniless William, she admitted, also sympathized with her plight. Judith, perhaps experiencing guilt or loneliness at Nancy's departure, "offers the utmost sympathy in my distresses and laments her inability to alleviate them." Others ignored her calls for help or, worse still, tried to profit by her misfortune. David Meade Randolph, she explained, came to Haymarket and urged her to "rent the whole wing promising to pay me for one half, in which he wou'd put a bed for his own occasional accommodation," an arrangement she wisely rejected. Bemoaning her situation, Nancy described herself as "a helpless woman, on the wide world with three hundred dollars a year, to rent a room, hire a servant, furnish raiment for herself, together with food for the servant and herself," while fending off predatory relatives.[64]

Nancy's prospects for a simple, happy life in Richmond were further diminished by the proximity of three people whom she considered her most inveterate foes: Maria Ward, Gabriella Harvie Randolph, and Jack. By 1807, Maria Ward had married Peyton Randolph and moved from Amelia County to Richmond. Nancy believed that Maria spread malicious gossip about her and that she was primarily responsible for turning her sister-in-law, Martha Jefferson Randolph, against her. Nancy's stepmother, Gabriella Harvie Randolph, came to Richmond on marrying Dr. John Brockenbrough after the death of Nancy's father. In 1807, Brockenbrough served as a juror in the treason trial of former vice president Aaron Burr, who had been indicted for conspiring to create a western confederacy, separate from the United States, in the Louisiana Territory. Fortuitously, Jack was Brockenbrough's fellow-juror at the trial, and the two men became close friends. Jack also struck up a friendship with Brockenbrough's wife, Gabriella, with whom he shared a love of literature and a hatred for the Pryors' newest lodger.[65]

Nasty gossip about Nancy's past, which she attributed chiefly to Jack, made her position in Richmond increasingly untenable, especially if she hoped to work there as a teacher, governess, or genteel companion to supplement her dwindling resources. In 1805, Jack Randolph had deployed sexual innuendo when he joined with Judith to drive Nancy from Bizarre. According to Nancy, on that occasion, she was "dismissed, with matchless rudeness, by Jack, [who] among other things said I behaved as if I were in a Tavern." Now, he was spreading rumors that Nancy was living as a prostitute in Richmond—a tale rendered more plausible by the Bizarre scandal and by her residence in a neighborhood known for unseemly activities.[66]

Jack Randolph's rising rage against Nancy coincided with a series of setbacks and controversies he experienced in public life. In 1799, Jack's auspicious entry into politics offered the prospect of reversing his family's disgrace, caused by what he saw as Nancy's corrosive influence over his older brother. In national politics, Jack had risen meteorically to become a leader of the Republican party in Congress during Jefferson's first term as president. Beginning in 1804, however, a succession of issues gradually transformed Jack into an outspoken opponent of the Jefferson administration. Along with other conservatives, who worried that the president increasingly compromised the ideals of limited government he previously espoused, Jack excoriated the administration's support for the Yazoo compromise, which compensated land speculators who had been defrauded by the Georgia legislature, and for its clandestine efforts to purchase West Florida. By 1806, Jack had emerged as leading spokesmen for a small group of dissident Republicans known as the *Tertium Quid*, or "third something." Jack was significantly more isolated in his opposition to the administration's pursuit of commercial retaliation against Britain for violating the rights of American shippers on the high seas in 1806–7, an issue on which his extreme rhetoric alienated even most conservative Republicans and Quids who were his potential allies. By the time he arrived in Richmond to serve on the Burr jury in 1807, Jack was a political outcast in Washington.[67]

Jack Randolph's animus against Jefferson was both personal and political. On the one hand, Jack was ideologically committed to the principles of limited government and states' rights, and he truly feared that Jefferson's enormous popularity was creating a dangerously expansive executive power. On the other hand, he also felt personally slighted by Jefferson, who enlisted others—including his own sons-in-law—as his congressional spokesmen, and he especially resented being passed over in 1806 for a diplomatic post in London. Randolph detested

Secretary of State James Madison, Jefferson's hand-picked successor to the presidency, and his outspoken preference for James Monroe to succeed Jefferson also poisoned his relationship with the administration. Finally, the fact the Jefferson sympathized with Nancy, welcoming her to Monticello in 1799 and again in 1804, imparted an even more personal dimension to Jack's animosity toward the president. In a striking example of the overlap of family and partisan concerns, in 1806 Jack nearly fought a duel with Thomas Mann Randolph, Jr., whom, as Jefferson's son-in-law, a loyal political supporter of the president, and Nancy's brother and financial benefactor, he found triply offensive.[68]

Around the same time, Jack also turned bitterly on St. George Tucker. In this case, too, the sources of his outrage were both political and personal, and at least indirectly linked to Nancy and the scandal at Bizarre. Jack's previously cordial relations with his stepfather began to cool in 1805, around the time Nancy left Bizarre, perhaps because he anticipated criticism from Tucker, who had always sympathized with Nancy and encouraged amicable relations among the residents of Bizarre. Soon Jack severed his social and familial relations with Tucker ostensibly over the latter's support for presidential candidacy of James Madison over his own choice, James Monroe. By 1810, Jack's feelings toward his stepfather were so acrimonious that he accused him of embezzling from the Randolph brothers' inheritance—a charge that, though clearly unfounded, brought the younger man to the verge of initiating a lawsuit against him.[69]

Nancy used the language of contemporary partisan political culture to describe her relations with Jack around this time. In 1805, as Jack Randolph sought to redefine himself politically by distancing himself from Jefferson's administration, Nancy attempted to discern and then to navigate what she called the "party" divisions within her family. As she explained to her friend, Mary Johnston of Prince Edward County, she had made "indefatiguable efforts to heal those wounds" and divisions in her family, though her own "circumspection provides no remedy for [the] party-rage" of others. Nancy described herself as "a victim of party spirit," though she herself also acted in a partisan manner when she vigorously championed her own defenders. "I do not silently hear either Mr. Tucker, or Mr. Jefferson traduced," she declared, "nor can I permit the ashes of the Dead [Richard and Theo] to be disturbed with impunity." Such behavior, which challenged Jack's political judgment as well as his personal authority within the family, Nancy believed, had resulted in her expulsion from Bizarre. While Jack believed that Nancy's departure would rid the house of an unchaste and corrupting influence, Nancy described her banishment as "the last paroxism of tyrannic power."[70]

Politics probably also influenced the treatment Nancy received from her sister Molly and her husband, David Meade Randolph. In the 1790s, David's strong Federalism chilled previously cordial relations with his brother-in-law, Thomas

Mann Randolph, an avid supporter of Jefferson's emerging Republican party. The Jeffersonians' victory in 1800 led to David's loss of his lucrative post as Virginia's collector of the federal excise, while a severe downturn in the tobacco market compounded his financial problems. By 1802, David sought revenge by allying with James Callendar, the partisan journalist who first published the allegations about Jefferson and Sally Hemings. Molly followed suit, making her house a center of Federalist gossip and sociability in Richmond. "Fr[om] this lady," one visitor reported in 1807, "I heard more pungent strictures upon Jefferson's head and heart . . . than any I had ever heard before." Around the same time, David apparently was defrauding Nancy of precious funds provided by her brother, Tom, son-in-law and political beneficiary of the man David chiefly blamed for his own dramatic downfall.[71]

Some time in 1807, Nancy confided to St. George Tucker that she was "so weary . . . of every species of persecution that I shall go as soon as possible with an irrevocable vow never to impart my distresses to any person in existence." Gossip from various quarters, she claimed, hastened her determination to "quit this state forever." On leaving Virginia, she added melodramatically, "I care very little what becomes of me, but shall endeavor to board in some decent house."[72] Judith professed to be surprised by the news of Nancy's departure and weakly protested St. George Tucker's "unjust accusations" that Judith herself had been the source of her sister's problems. "Since poor Nancy left Bizarre," she maintained, "I have vainly endeavored to conciliate her by every means in my power." There is no evidence, however, that Judith had met with or even written to Nancy, or that she ever considered inviting her to return to Bizarre.[73]

Nancy Randolph's experience in the decade following Richard's death illustrates both the economic and social dependence of single women on their kin and their vulnerability as a result of that dependence. While she resided in Judith's house, Nancy had subsistence and social position—as a sister, a spinster aunt, a Randolph—albeit on Judith's sufferance. Leaving Bizarre, in turn, jeopardized both her social identity and her material security. Expecting support from family in the form of shelter, funds, or even good advice, Nancy found herself repeatedly disappointed in part because most of her relations, despite their sympathy, were themselves in bad financial straits and thus in no position to help. Nancy's dependence and her lack of funds, in particular, made her even more vulnerable to gossip. When Jack Randolph and others spread rumors about her past and present promiscuity, their stories impeded her search for respectable work or lodging in Richmond and thereby prevented her from refashioning a new, more independent identity for herself.

5

"Happiness Such as Mine"

Nancy Randolph and her sisters had been raised to believe that virtue was the surest road to security and happiness for women. Contemporary moralists taught that piety, sensibility, and, above all, sexual purity were essential virtues for women, whether or not they married. "If you have hearts disposed by nature for love and friendship, and possess those feelings which enable you to enter into all the refinements and delicacies of these attachments," cautioned the author of one popular advice book, "consider well, for Heaven's sake, and as you value your future happiness, before you give them any indulgence." Exposure to sentimental novels and the real-life drama of the Bizarre scandal probably heightened the credibility of such ominous pronouncements for the Randolph sisters. Perhaps speaking from experience, Judith Randolph declared in a letter to Mary Harrison that older women, especially mothers, should shield "guileless" young females from the "danger of evil counsellors" whose influence might result in "unexampled calumny" and sadness. Years later, her youngest sister, Virginia Randolph Cary, would write a book explaining and extolling feminine virtue, *Letters on Female Character.*[1]

Because many Virginians believed that Nancy Randolph lacked virtue, both material security and contentment eluded her while she remained in the Old Dominion. Indeed, her unpleasant experience in Richmond seemingly proved the conventional wisdom that an untarnished reputation for virtue was a prerequisite for, though no guarantee of, marriage or genteel employment, which for a woman of Nancy's social status were the only paths to respectability and comfort. Accordingly, in 1807, at the age of thirty-three, Nancy Randolph ventured northward in hopes of escaping the scandal that for fifteen years had so profoundly shaped her life. "In quitting Virginia every chord of my heart burst asunder," she recalled shortly after her departure.[2] Though she had never before traveled beyond the borders of her native state, Nancy saw her journey, which took her first to New England and then to New York, not as an adventure but rather as a last resort in her quest for respectability.

In leaving Virginia, Nancy Randolph did not set out to escape the conventions of feminine virtue but rather to embrace them more fully. When

LETTERS

ON

FEMALE CHARACTER,

ADDRESSED TO

A YOUNG LADY,

ON THE

DEATH OF HER MOTHER.

BY

MRS. VIRGINIA CARY.

Let others fly to pleasure's distant dome;
Be mine the dearer task to please at home.
HALEY'S *Triumphs of Temper.*

" Thy husband shall have rule over thee." Gen. iii. 16.
" The price of a virtuous woman is far above rubies." Prov. xxxi. 10.
" Favour is deceitful, and beauty is vain: but a woman that feareth the Lord,
she shall be praised." Prov. xxxi. 30.

RICHMOND, Va.
PUBLISHED BY A. WORKS.
1828.

Figure 5.1 Title page from Virginia Randolph Cary, *Letters on Female Character*. In 1828, Judith and Nancy's youngest sister, Virginia Randolph Cary, published this advice book for young women. Cary sentimentalized relations between men and women—especially husbands and wives—but she cited Scripture and other authorities to assert the importance of feminine purity and virtue and the necessity of women's submission to male authority. Photograph from a copy in the Women's Collection, Special Collections and University Archives, Walter Clinton Jackson Library, The University of North Carolina at Greensboro.

she married in 1809 and bore a son in 1813, she gloried in her new roles as wife and mother and basked in the unaccustomed admiration and protection of an unabashedly loving husband. Despite having seemingly found a safe haven in New York, however, she remained vulnerable. Within a few years, old and new enemies would attempt to exploit the Bizarre scandal to ennoble or enrich themselves at Nancy's expense and to sabotage her efforts to lead a conventionally virtuous domestic life.

Nancy left Tuckahoe, accompanied by her brother John and her maid Phebe, some time in the autumn of 1807. Her journey took her some 500 miles to Newport, Rhode Island, a declining seaport town that nonetheless remained popular as a resort for elite southerners in the post-revolutionary era. Nancy opted for Newport on the advice of her sister Molly, who sometimes vacationed there herself. Molly described Newport as a "place of cheap living" and assured Nancy of "how friendly her acquaintances would be" toward her.[3] In addition, her kinsman Richard Kidder Randolph resided in Newport full time. All of these considerations led Nancy to a paradoxical choice: she would try to escape her past by moving to Newport, where she had some social connections and where her family was fairly well-known.

By November 1807, Nancy had arrived in Newport, where she stayed for nearly a year until money problems and gossip caused her to move on. Some of her Virginia acquaintances and others "who had resorted thither in quest of health" treated her kindly, at least initially, and she appears to have secured some sort of teaching position to earn some badly needed income. Soon, however, Nancy reported to St. George Tucker that her sister Molly "to the Natives accused me of every possible crime," whereupon they "defrauded me of the last cent . . . [and] said I had fled from justice in Virginia." Gossip isolated Nancy socially and presumably resulted in the loss of her job as well. Revealing his continuing faith in the probative power of the written word, the benevolent Tucker sprung to action, sending Nancy four copies of his "Address to the Public," the broadside he had published in 1793 in Richard's defense. By the time Tucker's papers arrived, however, Nancy had moved—first to New York City and then, by November 1808, to the town of Fairfield, Connecticut.[4]

In the interim, she had fortuitously encountered an old family friend, Gouverneur Morris of New York. Morris had met St. George Tucker in New York in 1785, and three years later, while attending the convention that debated Virginia's ratification of the Constitution, he became acquainted with Nancy's parents, whom he later visited at Tuckahoe. The New Yorker also knew one of Nancy's chief antagonists, David Meade Randolph, who shared his own Federalist political views. In August 1807, David and Molly's son, William Beverley Randolph, then a student at Princeton, solicited career advice from Morris. In language reminiscent of St. George Tucker's advice to his stepsons, Morris, who had made a fortune in law and land speculation, strongly urged young Randolph to study hard and eschew the planter's life. "If the learned Professions do not open splendid Prospects, and require much Labor in Youth," he observed, "they give Security for both Ease and Competence at a future date."[5]

When Morris met Nancy Randolph in 1808, he was fifty-six years old and had lived an eventful and productive life. He was born at Morrisania, a family estate located north of Manhattan Island in what was then part of Westchester County but is today the South Bronx. As a youth, Morris had attended the recently founded King's College (the future Columbia University) from which he graduated in 1768, after which he served a three-year legal apprenticeship. Receiving his license to practice law in 1771, Morris prospered as a young attorney and enjoyed a pleasurable social life. After 1774, he also became politically active as New Yorkers, like other colonists, became embroiled in the imperial crisis. A social conservative who feared that defying Britain would result in mob rule, Morris hoped to avoid revolution but, when forced to choose in 1776, he nonetheless supported American independence.[6]

While many of his relatives remained loyal to the Crown, Gouverneur made important contributions to the Revolution at both the state and continental levels. From 1775, he represented Westchester County in New York's Provincial Congress, precursor to the state legislature, and in 1777 he helped draft the state's first constitution. At New York's constitutional convention, Morris opposed expanding the suffrage and most other democratic reforms, but he spoke out strongly against slavery. For two years he represented New York in the Continental Congress and, in 1787, he played an important role at the convention that drafted the U.S. Constitution, where he spoke 173 times, more than any other delegate. While Morris's renewed denunciation of the "nefarious institution" of slavery had no effect on the proceedings, his ideas greatly influenced the convention's deliberations on the executive branch of the proposed government. While others had argued in favor of a weak executive—suggestions ranged from an executive committee to an individual who was appointed by and dependent on the legislature—Morris successfully advocated the creation of a strong president with substantial power. In addition, as the leading member of the Committee of Style, he composed the draft of the Constitution that the delegates accepted with few revisions on 17 September 1787. A superb literary stylist and a strong nationalist, Morris changed the beginning of Constitution's preamble from "We the people of the states" to "We the people."[7]

In 1789, Gouverneur Morris went to France on business, spending the next decade in Europe, where he served as U.S. minister to France, traveled extensively, and observed with disapproval the drama of the French Revolution. An ardent Federalist, he returned to the United States in late 1799, only to find his party rapidly declining in popularity. In the spring of 1800, one of New York's Federalist senators resigned his seat and the state legislature appointed Morris to complete his term in Washington. That fall, however, the opposition Republicans soundly defeated the Federalists, both in New York and nationally, and in 1802 the state legislature did not reappoint Morris as senator. Though retired from elective politics, Morris remained active in New York as an outspoken critic of the Republican administrations of Thomas Jefferson and James Madison. In 1804 he delivered the funeral oration of his friend and political associate, the arch-Federalist Alexander Hamilton, who was mortally wounded in a duel with Aaron Burr, vice president of the United States and a leading New York Republican.[8]

According to his most recent biographer, Morris "left a trail of lovers on two continents" and enjoyed a well-deserved reputation for conviviality among men and gallantry toward women. In 1780, when Morris's left leg was shattered in a carriage accident in Philadelphia, gossips rumored that the mishap resulted from a hasty attempt to escape his lover's irate husband. "Gouverneur's leg has been a tax on my heart," confided Morris's close friend John Jay, who added slyly, "I am almost tempted to wish he had lost *something else.*" In Paris, Morris had an intense six-year affair with Adèlaide de Flahut, the beautiful, witty, and intelligent wife of a French count, and enjoyed many other romantic liaisons in Europe after ending his relationship with her. A female friend from Morris's days in Paris remembered him as one who valued "all the conveniences, comforts, and pleasures of life, the advantages of fortune, the enjoyments of the arts, and the charms of society." The gregarious American, she observed, conceived "it to be following the order of Providence to enjoy all its gifts."[9]

In 1808, the tall, distinguished, and worldly Gouverneur Morris took an interest in Nancy Randolph. The circumstances of their meeting and subsequent courtship are murky, but what seems to have begun as an arrangement whereby he paid for her lodgings while she sought employment as a paid "attendant" accompanying "any Lady" to England evolved into a more personal relationship. The New Yorker admired Nancy's intelligence, industry, and good sense, and he believed she had "her share" of beauty, too. Some time in 1808, he visited Nancy at her lodgings and, in her words, "expressed a wish that some reduced gentlewoman would undertake to keep his house, as the lower class of house-keepers often provoked the servants to riot." Six months later, he returned and asked Nancy herself to become his housekeeper.[10]

Gouverneur knew of Nancy's past but was not deterred by it. On 3 March 1809, he acknowledged to her that he had once heard about the "Events which brought Distress" to her, and gently reassured her that "If ever we happen to be alone you shall tell your Tale of Sorrow when Tears from your Cheek may fall in my Bosom." He also counseled Nancy that "the Sufferings of Life are essential to its Enjoyments" and noted that true virtue, in his opinion, consisted of "a pure Heart, a chastened Spirit, Fortitude, Benevolence, [and] Charity." Six days later, Gouverneur professed his affection for her, insisting that Molly Randolph's gossip, though "calculated to alarm my fears," was to no avail. Twelve days later, in a letter dated 21 March 1809, Gouverneur Morris invited Nancy Randolph to live with him at Morrisania. In an uncharacteristic concession to social convention, he agreed that her residence in his house "must be founded on such obvious Reasons as may prevent the Laugh of Folly and the Sneer of Malice." Accordingly, he proposed to hire her as his housekeeper, and she accepted his offer. "I thought it much better to have employment than remain a burden on my friends," she explained years later to a friend in Virginia.[11]

Some time after 1 April 1809, Nancy arrived at Morrisania, the 1,400-acre estate that had been the Morris family seat since the 1670s. Gouverneur had purchased the property and its mansion from his Tory half-brother in 1786, and he rebuilt and refurbished the house, which had been plundered during the Revolution, on his return from France. The cosmopolitan Morris filled his expansive waterfront home with imported furniture, art, books, and other accoutrements of gentility. One visitor described Morrisania as a "large elegant house superbly furnished and delightfully situated near the [Long Island] Sound, and the junction of the Harlem and East rivers," where lively conversation and "viewing prospects, pictures, sculpture, tapestry, plate, china, etc., . . . make the time pass very swiftly." The house had "large and lofty" rooms and beautiful French parquet floors scarred by indentations from the wooden leg of its proprietor. A staff of thirteen domestic workers—white and black, free and slave—tended the Morris household.[12]

Despite his outspoken opposition to slavery and its overall decline in New York after the Revolution, Morris still had at least one slave among his staff at Morrisania in 1809. A decade earlier, the New York legislature had passed a gradual emancipation act providing that all black males and females born subsequently would be free at the age of twenty-eight and twenty-five, respectively. Although the law did not affect the status of enslaved people born before its passage, the cumulative effects of voluntary and statutory manumissions greatly reduced the presence of slavery in the Empire State while increasing the numbers of free African Americans. Nevertheless, some 15,000 New Yorkers remained enslaved when Nancy arrived in 1809; the population of Westchester County included about 900 slaves and a roughly equal number of free blacks. As housekeeper, Nancy was to oversee the work of one slave, four free African Americans, and seven white workers, besides the enslaved maid Phebe, who had accompanied her from Virginia.[13]

Figure 5.2 Morrisania. Gouverneur Morris's hospitable and lavishly furnished house must have reminded Nancy of her parents' home at Tuckahoe. First as housekeeper and then as mistress, Nancy presided over this gracious waterfront mansion, where she experienced some of the happiest years of her life. From Stephen Jenkins, *The Story of the Bronx, 1639–1912* (New York: G. P. Putnam's Sons, 1912).

Morris arranged his life at Morrisania to maximize his pleasure and delight. In 1809, he described his "establishment" there as "pleasant, and though expensive, not beyond the means which I ought to possess." Morris entertained extravagantly and often, but he also enjoyed the leisure of solitude. "I think of public affairs a little, read a little, play a little, and sleep a great deal," he informed a French friend. "With good air, a good cook, fine water and wine, I descend gradually towards the grave, full of gratitude to the Giver of all good."[14]

Nancy must have approached Morrisania with a combination of bittersweet nostalgia and cautious optimism. On the one hand, the scene may have reminded her of other genteel households—certainly Tuckahoe, perhaps Monticello—in which she had resided, leading her to hope for a return to the material comfort and sustaining sociability she enjoyed in those happier times. On the other hand, Nancy's position at Morrisania was ambiguous, and probably purposely so. Officially, she was the hired housekeeper, but the master of the house, who had already declared his affection for her, metaphorically suggested that he had other long-term plans. "When your shattered Bark shall have reached the Port [at Morrisania]," he wrote in April 1809, "we must endeavour to build up again what has been broken down and refit you for the next Voyage which Fate may announce."[15]

On 2 December 1809, Morris wrote to John Marshall, a fellow Federalist whose successful legal career, after serving as defense counsel in *Commonwealth v. Randolph,* culminated in 1801 with his appointment to the U.S. Supreme Court as its chief justice. Morris had at times corresponded with Marshall in the past, but on this occasion he wrote expressly to request his frank appraisal of "the Reputation Miss Randolph left in Virginia, and the Standing she held in Society." Morris claimed that his motives in making this inquiry were mainly political. If Nancy could be "depicted in black Colors, it may serve as a foundation for Calumny against me," he observed, which, by extension, might "serve a valuable Party Purpose" for Republicans seeking to stigmatize the entire Federalist party. The chief justice wrote back to inform Morris that "many believed the accusations brought against Miss Randolph [in 1792–93] to be true, while others attached no criminality to her conduct." Marshall counted himself among the latter group and reassured the New Yorker that "if . . . any [other] indiscretion was ascribed to that young Lady, the suspicion has never reached my ears." Morris received Marshall's letter on the evening of 23 December. The next morning, he prepared a prenuptial agreement, which he presented to Nancy. "This was the first Declaration made of my Wish," he reported, adding, "tho' I had perceived in her Manner that Good Will and amusing Conversation had produced that Effect on her Mind which ought not to be expected by People of my Age."[16]

On Christmas Day 1809, Nancy Randolph and Gouverneur Morris wed at Morrisania. The bride wore, she later recalled, "a gown patched at the elbows." The groom, who most regarded as a confirmed bachelor, rejoiced in finding a woman who, in his words, "with the qualities needful for my happiness, should also have the sentiments." That day, Gouverneur had invited his family (mostly siblings, nieces, and nephews) to dinner at Morrisania, and he took advantage of the opportunity to inform them of his marriage. The news, he reported in his diary, was "no small surprise to my guests." Although Nancy happily observed that all her husband's relatives treated her "with great affection," at least one of Gouverneur's nieces had the temerity to chide him for having "committed a folly in marrying" without prior consultation with his relatives and heirs. Morris, who was well aware that his young relatives expected to inherit his property, responded to such criticism with characteristic aplomb. "If I had married a rich Woman of seventy," he observed tartly, "the World might think it wiser than to take one of half that Age without a farthing . . . but . . . I thought I might, without offending others, endeavour to suit myself, and look rather into the head and heart than into the pocket."[17]

Figure 5.3 Gouverneur Morris in 1810. James Sharples produced this pastel drawing when he visited Morrisania. The artist captured the self-assured intelligence of his fifty-eight-year-old subject. National Portrait Gallery, Smithsonian Institution; gift of Mrs. Ethel Turnbull in memory of her brothers, John and Gouverneur Morris Wilkins Turnbull.

Marriage transformed Nancy Randolph into "Ann C. Morris," a new name that memorialized her beloved mother, announced her attachment to a famed and influential man, and nominally expunged her past identity as a Randolph, both at Tuckahoe and Bizarre. The day after the wedding, Nancy wrote an elated but hurried letter to her "beloved Father," St. George Tucker, announcing that "your long lost child became the wife of one who (like yourself) personifies every

Figure 5.4 Mrs. Gouverneur Morris in 1810. James Sharples's pastel is the only known surviving portrait of Nancy Randolph, who called herself "Ann C. Morris" after her marriage to Gouverneur. Nancy's expression suggests that she found profound satisfaction in her new life at Morrisania. Collection of Angus J. Mezies.

generous and truly noble quality." Tucker characteristically responded by asking Gouverneur's permission to "announce to the world through the medium of the public newspapers in Richmond, an event which may contribute to dispel the surmises, which . . . have been circulated in that place" since Nancy left

Virginia. In fact, Tucker did not wait for word from either of the newlyweds to act on his initial impulse. A brief announcement of their nuptials appeared in the *Richmond Enquirer* on 6 January 1810, just twelve days after the wedding and only one day after Tucker had penned his response to Nancy's news.[18]

Marriage to the worldly and convivial Gouverneur Morris afforded Nancy a wide range of new social opportunities. Following Gouverneur's established pattern, the newlyweds received guests nearly every day. Most visitors came from Morrisania's own "thickly settled Neighborhood" or sailed upriver from nearby New York City. But some, like Randolph Harrison and his son, came from Virginia to witness Nancy's good fortune, while other guests must have seemed interesting, even exotic, to the new mistress of the house. In 1810, James and Ellen Sharples, two English artists who spent years in the United States producing portraits of famous Americans, came with their daughter, Rolinda, to spend three days at Morrisania. While James executed pastel portraits of Nancy and Gouverneur, Ellen partook of "agreeable conversation" with her hosts. The well-traveled English guests found that "the time pass[ed] very swiftly" at Morrisania. "At dinner we had three courses every day on a magnificent service of silver, dessert on the most beautiful French china," Ellen reported. "Mr. M's extensive library, added to the other objects of interest . . . beauties both of nature and art, so excited my admiration and fixed my attention as entirely to take away all inclination to engage in any insignificant employment of which I was capable."[19]

Nancy also accompanied her husband as he pursued his civic activities in New York and elsewhere. In 1810, the state legislature chose Gouverneur to chair a seven-man commission charged with finding the best route for a canal to connect the Hudson River to the Great Lakes, thereby making New York City the chief entrepôt for agricultural produce from the Old Northwest. In June, Nancy accompanied Gouverneur on a trip "to inspect the country through which the new canal was to be built," which took them to Niagara Falls and to the sparsely settled westernmost reaches of the state. In December 1811, the Morrises traveled to Washington, where Gouverneur and fellow-commissioner DeWitt Clinton unsuccessfully sought federal funding for the project that eventually would come to fruition with the opening of the Erie Canal in 1825. In Washington, Nancy probably met Dolley Madison, and possibly the president, too, as she enjoyed the burgeoning social life of the nation's capital. The Morrises also had an apparently cordial meeting with Jack Randolph, whose oratory Nancy savored along with other well-heeled spectators who swelled the congressional galleries in the still-unfinished Capitol. "Here, my ever dear Sir, is your Friend—much delighted with all she hears and sees," an enraptured Nancy wrote to St. George Tucker from Washington. "Happiness such as mine now is," she mused, "makes me feel as if I had really entered another world."[20]

Closer to home, though Nancy accompanied her husband to functions at the New-York Historical Society and other public venues, she was not involved in any of the city's women's organizations or associations. A dynamic commercial center of more than 60,000 souls at the turn of the century, New York City's population soared to some 96,000 by 1810, making it by far the largest city in the United States. In New York, as in other American cities, elite women formed organizations to do benevolence work and to alleviate misery and disorder born of rapid urban growth. Gouverneur's niece, Isabella Ogden, was an active member of two of these groups, the Society for the Relief of Poor Widows with Small Children and New York's Orphan Asylum Society. Her aunt, Sarah Ogden Hoffman, Gouverneur's kinswoman by marriage, was one of the leaders of women's benevolence efforts in New York.[21]

Although many elite and middle-class women of the era found in organizational and benevolence work a sense of sisterhood or self-worth, Nancy remained aloof from such activities. Although Gouverneur's relations, who resented his marriage, may have actively excluded her from their organizations, which included women from the state's leading families, Nancy might have found membership in such groups unappealing on other grounds, too. While Nancy believed in God and probably attended religious services from time to time, unlike Judith and some of her other sisters in Virginia she never experienced the profound religious conversion so cherished by growing numbers of Protestant evangelicals. Nancy, whose religion was largely formulaic, may have distrusted the increasingly evangelical tone of the city's female activists.[22] In addition, given her troubled past, Nancy was less likely to find fulfillment and self-worth in the company of other women than at home with her husband. Because some men criticized women's public activities, moreover, Nancy may have worried that participation in benevolence work or any other public concern might compromise her attainment of the ideal of virtuous domesticity that she had struggled so hard to achieve and that she so highly valued.[23]

For whatever reason, Nancy devoted herself wholly to Gouverneur and, beginning in 1813, to their infant son. Nancy knew she was pregnant by June 1812, when she gave Gouverneur the "good news" and suffered "that sickness of the stomach" that is common in the first trimester. The arrival of Gouverneur Morris, Jr., on 9 February 1813, completed the wedded bliss of his thirty-nine-year-old mother and sixty-one-year-old father, who doted on him from birth. The happy parents received congratulations from St. George Tucker and Jack Randolph in Virginia, and Randolph Harrison visited Morrisania not long after the birth of their "lovely son." Gouverneur's relations, by contrast, were far from pleased by the birth of an infant who now superseded them as heir to Morris's vast estate. Martin Wilkins, one of Gouverneur's nephews, wryly suggested that the infant be named "Cutusoff"—ostensibly to honor General Mikhail Kutuzov, Napoleon's Russian adversary. The birth of Gouverneur Morris, Jr., the elder Gouverneur's nephews and nieces surmised, all but killed their own prospects for inheriting a substantial portion of their uncle's property.[24]

Despite the thinly veiled antipathy of her husband's relatives, Nancy's early years in New York were still much better than most in her often tumultuous and unhappy life. At Morrisania, she enjoyed material comfort and the affection of a husband she regarded as "goodness itself." She and Gouverneur, moreover, had been "blessed by Heaven with the most lovely boy . . . a darling Babe" whom Nancy proudly predicted would follow the example of his father by becoming "a Wise and Virtuous Man." Gouverneur Morris clearly shared his wife's happiness. In an 1816 letter to a friend, he extolled the joys of parenthood and his delight in marriage to "a kind companion, a tender female friend." Love, he explained, "is the only fountain of felicity, so it is in wedded love that the waters are most pure."[25]

Judith Randolph envied her sister's good fortune, though she was loath to show it. "I have heard before of Nancy's marriage, & join with you most fervently . . . in wishing her every earthly blessing," she wrote to St. George Tucker just three weeks after her sister's nuptials. Judith, however, implied that Nancy's worldly success had not been matched by moral progress. Although "those [blessings] which wealth can procure, (& surely they are not a few) are now completely within her reach," Judith observed, she nonetheless wondered, paraphrasing a devotional tract, whether Nancy's "prosperity may indeed be prosperous."[26]

Judith had good reason to be bitter. In the years following Nancy's departure from Bizarre, she suffered chronic financial problems and continuing poor health. In addition, she was increasingly estranged from her brother-in-law Jack. As her sons grew older, Judith's relations with them also became strained, especially as they became closer to their eccentric and erratic uncle. In despair, Judith Randolph turned to religion and to her siblings for support, especially after 1810, when Jack left Bizarre to live at Roanoke, the Charlotte County plantation that he had inherited from his father. A lonely Judith began to correspond with Nancy, apparently on the latter's initiative, around the time that Jack, who had been so instrumental in orchestrating Nancy's break with her sister, decided to leave Bizarre.[27]

Tensions between Jack and Judith over financial concerns, which arose initially shortly after Richard's death, became acute after Nancy's departure. In October 1807, the month Nancy left Virginia, Jack and Judith parted on bad terms when he went to Washington to resume his duties in Congress. Although the precise cause of their quarrel remains unclear, Judith's apologetic letter to her brother-in-law indicated that she had angered him, though she claimed to have "not complained of anything, nor asked any change" in their living arrangements at Bizarre. Judith apparently convinced Jack to come back to Bizarre, where he oversaw the final emancipation of Richard's slaves on Christmas 1809—the very same day that Nancy married Gouverneur Morris.[28] From then on, however, Judith and Jack quarreled often and by early 1810 the latter had permanently left Bizarre.

The heart of the problem appears to have been Judith's insistence on seeking advice from other men about financial matters and plantation management, which Jack interpreted as a challenge to his authority as the putative patriarch of Bizarre. Judith considered Jack's opinions during this period, but, aware that whatever decisions she made would have a profound impact on her sons, she also looked to others for counsel. In May 1809, Judith secretly wrote to Edward Dillon, a family friend, asking him to use his "influence" with Jack to persuade him to offer "more agreeable terms" to Mr. Hall, an employee she clearly valued. By August, she was pondering the possibility of leasing Bizarre to generate income for herself and her sons, though Beverley Tucker—St. George Tucker's son and Jack's half-brother—had advised her to sell the property. In November, she planned to ask St. George Tucker to assess her financial options. Unable to dissuade Judith from soliciting Tucker's opinion, Jack saved face by writing to his stepfather himself—a scenario that may have contributed to the final break between Jack and his stepfather, which became more or less complete around this time. Tucker suggested that Jack might lease Bizarre's plantation from Judith, who would continue to reside in the house there until she died, whereupon he would purchase the property for what Tucker believed to be "a fair price [of] £4,000." Jack rejected this proposal. Judith, who needed both a place to live and an income, continued to weigh her options.[29]

Finally, in early 1810, Judith unburdened herself to Creed Taylor, whom she described as "the friend in whom [Richard] had the highest confidence." While Judith carefully noted that she did not "doubt in the least [Jack's] right and honorable conduct," she worried that "in some respects he is less attentive even to his own interests, than I, as the Mother of a family, have a right to be." Then, however, Judith confided her misgivings about how Jack had divided Richard's slaves, taking some of them to his Charlotte County plantation to compensate for his payment of the balance due to Richard's creditors. "Such is my profound ignorance . . . that perhaps I write nonsense," she wrote, intimating that she nonetheless suspected that her own frugality and the sale of some slaves should have generated sufficient funds to satisfy Richard's debts. Judith informed Taylor that while she had lived in near-poverty for years, Jack "has made purchases of real Estate to the am[oun]t of upwards of £3,000 besides other large

expenditures"—a fact she professed to mention "only as proof of the great product of [Richard's father's] Estate, which for so many years I claimed no part of."[30]

Around the same time, Judith stated her grievances against Jack even more
bluntly to St. George Tucker. "Had the Estate been divided many years ago,
my situation would have been a different one; I would immediately have sold
my Roanoke land, & secured to myself enough to satisfy all my wants," she
explained in January 1810. "I will not conceal from you that I have incurred the
displeasure of my Brother [Jack] by the expression of some opinions," she wrote,
adding, "You cannot be ignorant that he cannot bear the least opposition, & I
am more certain that the interference with friends would irritate him more."[31]

As Judith's letters to Tucker and Taylor suggested, much more was at stake
here than money, land, and slaves. No matter how carefully she chose her words,
Judith was accusing her brother-in-law of either dishonesty or incompetence,
neither of which were qualities that fit the patriarchal ideal to which he so clearly
aspired. Judith was once again invoking maternal duty to justify her desire to
control the disposition of her husband's property, at least to the extent of seeking
counsel from men of her own choosing, and in so doing questioning the authority of her brother-in-law. To Jack, however, Judith's behavior signified ingratitude and a disrespect for his status as Richard's surrogate. In 1811, for example,
he informed Judith that her decision to cut down some old trees, which he
opposed, had made him feel like "but a guest" at Bizarre. Jack believed that
Judith, to whom he had devoted the "prime of my manhood," had "withdrawn
[her] confidence from me." His heart, he confided to a young kinsman, "was
wounded to the very core." In response, Jack Randolph left Bizarre and took up
residence at Roanoke in Charlotte County. There, he surrounded himself with
young male protégés and slave dependents and became "John Randolph of
Roanoke," widely known for his aristocratic demeanor and his hypersensitivity
to affronts to his honor.[32]

Although Jack and Judith remained on speaking terms, she asserted her independence in some important respects after he left Bizarre. After ceremoniously
emancipating Richard's seventy-two slaves when his debts were paid in full in
1809, Judith found it difficult to do without her "former servants." After some
unsatisfactory experiences with hired free black laborers, she gradually began to
reinstate slavery on a limited basis at Bizarre. In 1812, Judith paid taxes on six
bondpeople whom she probably rented from neighboring planters; her enslaved
labor force peaked at eight the following year.[33] And in what can be seen as
another striking deviation from Richard's most cherished wishes, Judith enrolled
her younger son, Tudor, in a nearby school run by the Reverend John Holt Rice,
her close friend and spiritual advisor. Unlike her deist husband, Judith always
had pious tendencies, and she experienced a profound religious conversion in

the summer or fall of 1810. She became increasingly devoted to Rice, an evangelical Presbyterian who sought to stimulate Tudor's religious conversion, apparently without success.[34] Finally, as her relationship with Jack deteriorated, Judith began to repair her ties to with her own estranged siblings, an effort she pursued more aggressively after he left Bizarre. Between 1808 and 1811, Judith re-established cordial relations with her sister Harriet Randolph Hackley, sister-in-law Martha Jefferson Randolph, and brother William. She and Nancy also began exchanging letters. Jack clearly resented the sisters' reconciliation. A decade later, he bitterly and inaccurately insisted that his devotion to Richard's family would have kept him at Bizarre "if the reunion of his widow with [Nancy] had not driven me to Roanoke."[35]

While Nancy was enjoying her new life as mistress of Morrisania, Judith struggled with money problems, chronic illness, and, above all, loneliness. After returning from England, her son St. George spent increasingly more time with his uncle, Jack, who characterized the unstable young man as "incurably alienated from his mother." After studying for three years with Rice in Cumberland, in 1812 Tudor left for Harvard, the college Jack deemed most suitable, despite Judith's express, but unexplained, "prejudice against *all* our American seminaries of learning." Stopping at Morrisania on his way to Cambridge, Tudor visited his aunt, on whom he came to rely for extra cash during his time at Harvard. Nancy welcomed the opportunity to become reacquainted with "Judy's sweet boy," who spent that Christmas with her and Gouverneur.[36]

Then, on Sunday 21 March 1813, Judith returned from church to find her house ablaze. A spark from the chimney set fire to the roof and "in a few moments," according to Jack, who witnessed the incident with his nephew St. George, Judith's "once comfortable & peaceful dwelling [was] a heap of ruins." Judith grieved for the loss of her home and the destruction of "all my hoard of pretty comforts and conveniences, which I had been accumulating by slow degrees," since coming to Cumberland as a young bride in 1790. "We saved three beds, a dining table & two or three small ones, some chairs, & a good number of books; but so many were lost, that the yard is still strewed with the burnt pages," she informed St. George Tucker two weeks after the conflagration. "All the rest of our furniture . . . together with twenty years labor in homespun; carpets, curtains, blankets, glass, china, a dozen new table spoons, & the same number of small ones, together with the cream pot which I kept as a relick . . . is lost."[37]

After the fire, Judith rented what she described as a "small & in every way uncomfortable house" in Farmville, the town built on land once owned by the Randolphs, situated directly across the Appomattox River from Bizarre. There, she learned some time in August 1814 that Tudor was ill at Morrisania. Though Nancy professed to "delight in attending" such an "amiable" and "interesting" guest, she became worried when her nephew's ailment lingered and worsened. In early October, Nancy, reporting "a tremendous discharge of blood from his lungs which almost suffocated him," summoned two physicians. Judith borrowed money from St. George Tucker to make the trip northward, getting to Morrisania on or around 12 October. Jack, who traveled separately from Richmond and was detained by "various accidents" en route, arrived there in time for dinner on Saturday 22 October. With his arrival, the principle surviving members of the Bizarre household were reunited for the first time since Nancy left Virginia.[38]

The visitors must have winced at the stark contrast between the splendor of Nancy's new home, which equaled and even exceeded that of her father's house, and the increasingly dire circumstances of her kin back in the Old Dominion. By 1814, at least eight of the ten children of Thomas Mann and Anne Cary Randolph of Tuckahoe were in grave financial trouble. Still, the Morrises and their guests appear to have gotten along well enough, at least initially. Whatever other feelings she harbored toward her sister, Judith must have been grateful to Nancy for caring for her beloved son. According to Nancy, her sister also "accepted presents from me with many thanks" when they visited New York City at Judith's behest. The reunion with Jack seemed equally amicable. When he arrived at Morrisania, Nancy later recalled, Jack "took me in his arms, . . . pressed me to [his] bosom, [and] impressed upon my lips a kiss which I received as a token of friendship from a near relation." During his stay, Nancy later claimed, Jack's "manner was kind, to me" and "most affectionate to Mr. M." Despite their deep political differences, both men abhorred President Madison's policies and vehemently opposed the war with Britain, which had begun in 1812. The next day, Jack embraced and kissed Nancy again on leaving Morrisania for New York, where he probably intended to spend the night before beginning his long journey back to Virginia. Judith and Tudor were to leave together a few days later. Nancy believed that she parted with all three of her guests on cordial terms.[39]

Though Judith and Tudor would leave for Virginia on 26 October, Jack remained in New York for more than a month. After leaving Morrisania, his carriage overturned, badly injuring one of his knees. "The patella is, in itself, unhurt," he explained to a young kinsman, "but the ligaments are very much wrenched, so that a tight bandage alone enables me to hobble . . . with the help of a stick." Unable to travel, Jack took up residence in a New York boarding house. During his stay, he had plenty of visitors—Judith, Tudor, the Morrises, his physician, and Harmanus Bleecker, a New York Federalist with whom he had become friendly during his last year or so in Congress. Perhaps with Bleecker's help, Jack also became acquainted with some of Gouverneur's disgruntled relatives.[40]

A combination of physical pain, the frustrations of enforced idleness, and the New Yorkers' influence probably led Jack to act on his hostility toward Nancy, which he had suppressed during his visit to Morrisania. Whereas in Virginia Nancy had been an appealing target in part because she lacked a male protector, in New York Jack found her no less odious for having acquired an indulgent husband who respected her and even may have regarded her as his equal. Though he maintained that men would "degenerate into brutes" without "female society," which he professed to enjoy, Jack clearly believed that in most respects women were inferior to men and should be subservient to them. Significantly, his own relationships with women were successful only when he played the role of benevolent mentor, pontificating endlessly to his nieces about marriage, manners, and books and favoring the wives of his friends with his opinions on *belles-lettres,* reading aloud from his favorite authors. Jack respected women who lived secluded lives and willingly took instruction from learned men, and he was censorious of those whom he believed were insufficiently dependent and deferential.[41] After his brief visit to Morrisania, Jack placed Nancy in the latter category, though, aside from her troubled past, she was in most respects an extremely conventional woman.

Within weeks, Nancy's New York in-laws had purposefully joined forces with Jack, spreading gossip about her in hopes of obtaining for themselves a share of the Morris estate. While Gouverneur's relatives had good reason to be circumspect in their criticism of Nancy, for fear of angering her aging husband, Jack operated under no such constraints. He was wealthy in his own right and under no personal obligation to the Morrises, save perhaps for their care of Tudor. He also had years of experience in using words to savage his foes—and to get what he wanted—in both public and private life.

On 31 October 1814, Jack Randolph wrote a letter that he hoped would destroy the Morrises' marriage, and thus Nancy's newfound happiness and respectability. Nancy retaliated with a letter of her own, targeting Jack's political career, which she rightly interpreted as being central to his aristocratic self-image and his sense personal and family honor. In this war of words, each combatant exposed real or imagined private, even intimate, sins to damage the public reputation of the other. In such an exchange, though the stakes were high for both women and men, gender determined the content of the accusations and the penalties that went with them. For a woman, chastity was the cardinal virtue, in part because it ensured the legitimacy of her offspring and thus prevented unlawful heirs from usurping the property of her husband. By accusing Nancy of being unchaste, therefore, Jack threatened not only her happiness and respectability but also the economic welfare of her and her young son. Nancy, in turn, characterized Jack as dishonest, irrational, and lacking in compassion. All of these qualities were politically damning at a time when Americans wanted leaders who were benevolent and reasonable and equated dishonesty with dishonor.[42]

Jack's opening salvo was a venomous eight-page letter written ostensibly to alert Gouverneur Morris to the great physical and financial dangers he faced as a result of his marriage to an unchaste and unrepentant woman. Although he opened the letter with the salutation "Dear Madam"—addressing it to Nancy herself—Jack sent the missive directly to Gouverneur, whom he appears to have regarded as a weak and deluded old man. Predictably, he began by dredging up the old charge of infanticide against Nancy and accusing her of having ruined his innocent brothers, noble Richard and weak Theo, by implicating them in her scandalous affair. But then Jack introduced four other major charges, all of which were carefully calculated to make marriage to Nancy seem perilous from the perspective of her husband. First, Jack asserted that Nancy had administered a lethal dose of poison to Richard to cause his sudden death in 1796, strongly implying that Gouverneur, too, should fear for his life. Second, Jack maintained that Nancy had married Gouverneur under false pretences, having manipulated him into writing to John Marshall, who was "misled with respect to the transactions at [Glentivar], and who knew no more of [her] general or subsequent life than the Archbishop of Canterbury." Third, Jack characterized Nancy as having been sexually promiscuous throughout her life in Virginia. He insisted that her "intimacy with one of the slaves" was the real cause of her banishment from Bizarre and asserted that she lived as a prostitute while lodging in Richmond. Fourth, and most tellingly, Jack contended that Nancy continued to indulge in "lewd amours" at Morrisania. This charge made the legitimacy of her son questionable, which, in turn, played into the hands of Morris's greedy relatives. Jack claimed that Tudor, too, described his aunt as an "unchaste woman," who regarded her young son primarily as an "instrument of power."[43]

The language of Jack's letter shows how he demonized the woman he still blamed so completely for the disgrace and demise of his family. In unusually graphic language, he described Nancy as "a vampire that, after sucking the best blood of my race, has flitted off to the North, and struck her harpy fangs into an infirm old man." Comparing Gouverneur to the ill-fated Richard who, Jack believed, by falling victim to her feminine manipulation and malice, had lost his "domestic peace, reputation, and life," Jack warned Nancy that Gouverneur, "if he be not both blind and deaf, . . . must sooner or later unmask you unless *he too die of cramps* in his *stomach.*" Jack concluded by sanctimoniously instructing Nancy to "Repent before it is too late." But vengeance, not repentance or reconciliation, was his true goal.[44]

Fixating on Nancy's role in the ruin of his beloved brother and the downfall of his family still helped Jack to make sense of his private world, while soothing the sting of his recent defeats in public life. When Jack visited Morrisania in 1814, he was no longer a member of the House of Representatives, having lost his bid for re-election from his district in the Virginia piedmont the preceding year. Jack suffered this first and only electoral defeat at the hands of Jefferson's son-in-law, John Wayles Eppes, who had moved into the district specifically to take on Jack in the 1813 campaign. While Jack had broken with the Republican party during Jefferson's presidency, Eppes remained an enthusiastic supporter of Jefferson and later Madison, as well as an avid proponent of war with Britain in 1812. Jack, who regarded Napoleon as a tyrant and was increasingly enamored of England's conservative constitutionalism, saw Britain and the United States as natural allies. For this reason and because he saw that war would strengthen the central government, Jack opposed the War of 1812, though doing so left him politically vulnerable. The resulting loss of his congressional seat to Eppes in 1813 compounded Jack's feelings of frustration and foreboding arising from his troubled private life.[45]

Gouverneur, who loved and esteemed Nancy and was well aware of the gossip about her past, dismissed Jack's diatribe and was reluctant to share the letter's contents with his wife. In December, however, Nancy received an "anonymous letter in a strange hand" that listed various charges against her, which a horrified St. George Tucker characterized as "the fabrication of some witch bent on destroying your happiness and that of your husband, and child." The Morrises attributed the letter first to Judith and then to Jack, though they never discovered the identity of its author. Gouverneur Morris informed Tucker that copies of the letter had been shown—by whom it is not clear—to four other people in New York. As the rumors spread about Nancy, he reported, New York's more respectable "Society" had been "driven away" from the Morrises. The women of Gouverneur's own family, moreover, stayed away from his Christmas dinner, which also commemorated the fifth anniversary of his and Nancy's nuptials. True to form, Tucker sent Morris yet another copy of his 1793 newspaper notice disavowing the Bizarre scandal. Morris, for his part, was content to wait until the gossip subsided. "Time," he predicted, "will I trust bring back as much of [society] as is worth having."[46]

Nancy was not so sanguine. While she could not doubt the sincerity of Gouverneur's trust, she believed that an unidentified illness had thrust her husband into "the jaws of death" at one point in 1814 and, given the difference in their ages, she could not help but worry that he would predecease her. While her husband lived, Nancy's position was secure, but when he died, who would protect her interests and those of their young son? If enough people concluded that Jack's accusations were true, she reasoned, young Gouverneur could be deemed illegitimate and thus lose his right to the Morris estate. Consequently,

Nancy believed it essential to respond to the letter that Jack had sent to Gouverneur. On 16 January, two and a half months after the letter arrived, she finally persuaded her husband to let her read it. With his consent, Nancy then spent the next few weeks penning a massive rebuttal—more than 7,000 words in all—of the old and new charges against her.[47]

Nancy addressed Jack's accusations at length, denying everything except the pregnancy that lay at the root of the Bizarre scandal. Tacitly admitting that she was with child in 1792, Nancy implied that a miscarriage, not an infanticide or an abortion, had occurred during the Randolphs' visit to Glentivar. Nancy asserted that Theo, whom she "considered as a husband in the presence of . . . God," was the child's father and that Richard "knew every circumstance" of their relationship. As "a man of honor," she claimed, Richard nobly kept her secret and insisted on standing trial himself to protect the memory of his brother. "This, Sir, passed in a remote county of Virginia more than twenty years ago," she wrote indignantly, asking why Jack "revived the slanderous tale in the most populous city in the United States?" Nancy maintained that Jack had pined for her unsuccessfully in his youth and now, resenting her good fortune, he was acting in league with Gouverneur's relatives to undermine her marriage and, by casting doubt on her virtue, call into question the legitimacy her son.[48]

In her response to Jack, Nancy combined outrage and reasoned argumentation to expose flaws in his thinking and his character. Nancy repeatedly, and usually correctly, emphasized that Jack had presented "not the shadow of evidence to support [his] slanders." Perhaps following the example of St. George Tucker's defense of Richard all those years ago, Nancy provided evidence to support her counter-arguments, attaching copies of letters—from Judith, her son St. George, from Jack himself—to show their gratitude and affection and also Jack's willingness to let both Judith and Tudor make an extended visit to the Morrises' home. If Jack truly believed her to be a murderer, why, Nancy asked pointedly, would he allow his beloved Tudor "to be fed from my bounty and nursed by my care during nearly three months" and then permit him to stay at Morrisania after the worst of his illness had passed? How could Judith, "a woman who moves in the sphere of a lady," be expected to live with a prostitute, who, according to Jack, had also been the "concubine of one of her slaves?" At the same time, Nancy took pleasure in rhetorically pricking the inflated ego of her eccentric kinsman. She ridiculed "the affectation of greatness" that led him to call himself "John Randolph of Roanoke"—a title whose pretension she mocked by enclosing it quotation marks whenever she wrote it.[49]

While Jack had portrayed Nancy as depraved and deviant in her lack of modesty, chastity, and other feminine virtues, Nancy presented herself as a flawed but sympathetic sentimental heroine who overcame daunting odds to lead a relatively conventional domestic life. Perhaps recalling that many Virginians, influenced by popular sentimental fiction, had offered her sympathy—while damning Richard—back in 1793, Nancy presented herself as a sentimental heroine when she responded to Jack's newest accusations. Nancy described herself as a virtual orphan, with no mother to guide her. Her father's attempt to force her to marry for money and against "the sentiment of my heart" left her at the mercy of the world and, like many a sentimental heroine, vulnerable to seduction by "the man she loved." Though Nancy succumbed to that temptation, she claimed to have lived a spotless life thereafter, thereby earning the happy ending so often denied to fictional victims of seduction. "I loved my husband before he made me his wife," she wrote. "I love him still more now that he has made me mother of one of the finest boys I ever saw; now that his kindness soothes the anguish which I cannot but feel from your unmanly attack." Nancy thus refashioned herself as a resilient sentimental heroine whose conventionally feminine domestic bliss stood in implicit but nonetheless marked contrast to the unmarried, childless, and "unmanly" state of her detractor.[50]

At the same time, Nancy portrayed "John Randolph of Roanoke" as passionate, selfish, and utterly dishonest—or, in other words, as lacking in those qualities that contemporaries associated with masculine gentility and honor. As a public man, and especially as a politician who claimed to derive his legitimacy as a leader from personal attributes rather than party influence, Jack was especially sensitive to such charges, and Nancy clearly recognized the political significance of his pretensions. In her letter, she ridiculed him as a trimmer who changed his political positions—on slavery, the French Revolution, and on Jefferson's presidency—opportunistically to suit his interests. She also threatened to inform Virginians of his ungentlemanly behavior toward her, going back to the 1790s. "It is well that your former constituents should know the creature in whom they put their trust," she asserted coolly, adding, "Virginians, in general, whatever may be their defects, have a high sense of honor."[51]

In truth, Nancy's letter to Jack was as much as political document as it was a personal one. Although she addressed her missive to Jack himself, she clearly intended it for a wider audience. What, after all, could she accomplish by presenting her arguments, evidence, and commentaries only to the very man who was most likely to ignore them? Instead, with her husband's blessing, but under her own name, Nancy sent copies of Jack's letter and her response to friends in Virginia and Washington, whom she urged to circulate the documents among their acquaintances. According to Martha Jefferson Randolph, at least twenty copies went to strategically placed Virginians, who might use the contents of the documents in their campaign against Jack in the upcoming congressional elections. By April 1815, Jack reported to his friend Harmanus Bleecker that

"Mr. G. M. & his *amiable* consort [have] distributed throughout this district for the purpose of influencing the election a number of libels of my character." Nancy was clearly trying to thwart Jack's attempt to recover his lost congressional seat and, in so doing, sought to diminish his public stature and influence by impugning his personal honor.[52]

Although Nancy relied mainly on family and friends to circulate copies of her exchange with Jack, she also sought the assistance of at least two political luminaries with whom she had at best only a slight acquaintance. The fact that Nancy wrote first to Dolley Madison and then to William Branch Giles, seeking to enlist them in her offensive against Jack, suggests that she herself saw her vendetta as both personal and political.

In 1815, Dolley Payne Todd Madison was the most politically influential woman in the United States and one of the most consequential people of either sex in the nation's capital. As the wife of President James Madison, she used balls, weekly drawing room receptions, casual visits, and other social events to forge political networks and alliances that helped her husband's administration to function effectively. In the process, she came to know nearly everyone in Washington. Around the same time she was preparing her response to Jack, Nancy sent Dolley Madison a letter written in her own hand but in the third person, describing Jack's vindictive and unwarranted offensive against her. The letter also included an account of Jack's hostility toward James Monroe—Madison's secretary of state, his likely successor as president, and benefactor to Jack's nephew, St. George Randolph, who in 1804 had traveled to England under the Monroes' care. Undoubtedly aware of Dolley Madison's extensive political influence and also of Jack's longstanding enmity toward the president, Nancy asked her correspondent to share the letter with any Virginians she encountered in Washington. The Virginians, in turn, could be expected to communicate the contents of Nancy's letter to their neighbors and constituents when they returned home.[53]

In early February 1815, Nancy also sought to enlist the support of William Branch Giles, a U.S. senator from Virginia and a leading figure in the state's Republican party. Nancy may have known that Giles had witnessed the court proceedings against Richard in 1793 and was satisfied with the justices' finding. She also may have met him a few years later at Monticello, where she was a frequent guest, when he unsuccessfully courted Thomas Jefferson's younger daughter, Maria. Now, years later, Nancy turned to Giles because of his political influence but also because, she confided, "at different times I heard of you defending me amid the fury of my enemies." Nancy first sent Giles a "certified copy" of Jack's letter and a copy of her own, informing him that she was "anxious that it should be seen in Richmond." She also wrote to Jack's opponent in the election, John Wayles Eppes, requesting that he call on Giles and read the documents she had sent. By mid-February, having received no acknowledgment from Giles, Nancy wrote to inquire if the documents had arrived, offering to send new copies if they had not. She wrote to Giles twice again in March.[54]

Neither William Branch Giles nor Dolley Madison appears to have acted openly on Nancy's proposal, though they probably spread her stories surreptitiously. The president's wife did not acknowledge Nancy's letter, while Giles, who eventually responded, offered Nancy his sympathy without explicitly endorsing her attempt to ambush Jack's congressional campaign. Only the last two pages of Giles's six-page letter have survived, but the tone of those pages suggests that he sought to soothe Nancy's feelings without encouraging her open or active involvement in electioneering in Virginia. The senator assured Nancy that he had perused Jack's letter and consulted with Chief Justice John Marshall about it. "In a conversation with the Chief Justice, after he had read the same letters," Giles informed her, "he assured me that his impressions were also unchanged." Marshall, furthermore, authorized Giles to tell Nancy that "he still entertained the same views of [the Bizarre scandal and her subsequent reputation] that he had formerly communicated to Mr. Morris."[55]

Notwithstanding the reluctance of such highly placed politicians to aid her openly, Nancy's efforts influenced the character of the campaign, and the stories her documents conveyed became part of the oral culture of central Virginia. Letters that circulated publicly became gossip, and gossip was an essential ingredient of the politics of the early republic. Jack himself worried that the supposed "libels" against him were "industriously circulated," forcing him to defend himself from such "hard imputations" among his constituents if he hoped to regain his seat in Congress. Accordingly, he assiduously sought to win back past supporters who were now wavering as a result of the documents' circulation. "I only beg you to suspend any opinion to my disadvantage," he wrote to one of his associates, "until you know *all.*" More belligerently, Jack nearly challenged Giles to a duel on hearing that he was sharing the letters "with others." The candidate angrily declared that he could not "consent that any one under the pretext that he is not the *author,* shall make himself the *vehicle* of calumny against me— neither will I suffer my family history to be raked up with the ashes of the peaceful to subserve the personal views of any man whatever."[56]

Nevertheless, if either Giles or John Wayles Eppes (or anyone else for that matter) made the documents available to Thomas Ritchie, editor of the strongly pro-Eppes *Richmond Enquirer,* Ritchie chose neither to publish them nor to mention Nancy's name in connection with the personal and political controversies of the Randolph campaign. Nancy's attempt to forge impersonal political relationships with these distant public figures seemingly failed to afford her access to the partisan press, which would have given her charges against Jack the widest possible circulation.

Why, in a time and place when the most private affairs of public figures were fair game for partisan editors, did such a juicy attack on the eccentric and controversial John Randolph of Roanoke fail to appear in Ritchie's *Enquirer*, the Republican organ that in April 1815 characterized him as living "in a world of his own creation," "crazed with care and disappointment," and bereft of "charity for others"?[57] One possibility is that Nancy's own well-known and checkered past undermined her value as a press informant. Though contemporaries generally deemed signed allegations more credible than those anonymously proffered, readers also evaluated the reliability of information by assessing the character of its author. Another even more plausible answer is that the *Enquirer*'s unflattering descriptions of Jack, which referred explicitly to his poor judgment, antiwar politics, and misrepresentations of his enemies, silently drew on Nancy's stories and her damning assessment of his character.[58]

While some male political leaders in Virginia were probably willing to use the dirt Nancy dished against Jack, they were understandably reluctant to acknowledge her as their source. As a woman who was married to a Federalist and residing in New York, Nancy was a political outsider in the eyes of Virginia Republicans. She was not part of the community of gossip she sought to address and, as a woman, she was doubly suspect. Women participated in the politics of the early republic by wearing partisan cockades or emblems, taking part in political toasts and conversations, and orchestrating and attending salons, balls, dinner parties, and other social occasions at which political business was conducted. They wrote and read political poems, essays, and plays, and even appeared in theatrical productions dealing with political themes in cities like Philadelphia. Women's enlistment in the partisan paper war of pamphlets, newspapers, and publicly disseminated personal letters was much less common, however, and typically couched in apolitical terms. The most politically influential women in the early republic typically denied their political interests even as they pursued them, adapting personal and social exchanges to political ends. Nancy got that formula backwards, mounting an overt political vendetta against John Randolph of Roanoke to settle their largely personal scores.[59]

Although Nancy had defended herself admirably in her exchange with Jack, it is unclear what effect, if any, her attempted paper war had on the outcome of the 1815 election. Randolph defeated the incumbent Eppes handily in 1815, due largely to the fact that the War of 1812 was over. Jack's return to Congress must have disappointed Nancy, who remained understandably bitter toward him as a result of his efforts to disrupt her happy domestic life. More than three years later, she was still pondering the "asperity of Mr Randolph's language" and considering taking legal action to refute his "Filthy tales."[60]

Nancy never again saw Jack or the other surviving members of the old Bizarre household. Tudor, who, after returning to Virginia from Morrisania, traveled at his uncle's behest to England for his health, died there in 1815, leaving both Jack and Judith overwhelmed by grief. Jack, who regarded the young man as a surrogate son and the sole hope for the survival of his family, marked Tudor's grave in England with a stone memorializing him as "the treasure of my heart." Judith sought solace in the home of the Reverend John Holt Rice and his wife in Richmond. "I am here in the midst of this busy city almost a prisoner, in a solitary chamber which I seldom quit, & where I see only those few friends who think it worth while to call on me," she informed St. George Tucker sadly, months after Tudor's death. In early 1816, Judith suffered a "severe attack of the influenza" and then "a violent pain in her side . . . accompanied with high fever." She died in Richmond in March, and by her "particular request" was buried near her mother's grave at Tuckahoe.[61]

Nancy, who held Judith at least partly responsible for Jack's savage attack on her, responded coolly to the news of her sister's death. While others noted Judith's long-suffering piety and reassured themselves that she would enjoy "everlasting Felicity" after death, Nancy expressed more concern for future of St. George Randolph, now the sole surviving member of Judith and Richard's unhappy family. Saint had never held a job. Deaf from infancy, he was now widely believed to be mentally unstable, too. Noting Judith's small bequests to her friend the Reverend Rice and to her sister Harriet Hackley, who had lived with her in Farmville, Nancy worried about Saint's future prospects. She wished that her nephew could be "protected in a life of comfort" and that "Dick's property had gone to his own Son undivided because I know what little Mercy a poor Orphan finds in the generality of Mankind."[62]

Not long after Judith died, Nancy decided to return to Virginia. Perhaps she anticipated a more pleasant reception without her sister's presence or maybe Judith's death made her homesick for family and friends in the Old Dominion. Or Nancy might have intended to prove that she had, indeed, attained respectability and happiness as a wife and mother, despite Jack's allegations against her. In September or early October, Nancy wrote a letter to Monticello, which she probably addressed to her sister-in-law Martha, informing the family of her intent to visit them in November or December. Thomas Jefferson responded with a cordial letter to Gouverneur Morris, professing himself "very happy indeed" to receive the Morrises and assuring the New Yorker of his "continued esteem," despite their past political differences.[63]

Nancy and Gouverneur, however, never made the trip southward. On 9 October, Gouverneur took to his bed in pain, suffering from a narrowing of the urinary tract, along with his customary gout. Within weeks, it became apparent that the patient was seriously ill and, indeed, might not recover. On 26 October, Gouverneur revised his will, naming Nancy and his attorney, Moss

Kent, as his co-executors. When his physicians' efforts produced no improvement in his condition, Gouverneur himself tried to clear the blockage with a whalebone, probably from one of Nancy's corsets. On 5 November 1816, his friend Rufus King reported that Morris's attempt at self-treatment produced only "lacerations and mortification." A day later, Gouverneur Morris died at Morrisania at the age of sixty-four. Nancy, who had nursed her husband through his final illness, now began to plan for the construction of his burial vault.[64]

Gouverneur's death ended the happiest, safest, and most conventional chapter of Nancy's adult life. Nine years earlier, she had left Virginia, seeking social acceptance and economic opportunity. In time, she found all that and more by virtue of her marriage to Gouverneur. Marriage and motherhood brought Nancy the love, material comfort, and respectability she craved; her years at Morrisania as a wife and mother were extraordinarily happy, despite persistent rumors about her past and present indiscretions. But Nancy's happiness, respectability, and material comfort were wholly contingent on her status as Gouverneur's wife and the mother of his son. In widowhood, she would sorely miss his love and protection, as the Bizarre scandal and other more recent allegations forced her to defend both her own reputation and the birthright of her only son.

6

NEW YORK AND VIRGINIA

Ann C. Morris survived her husband by nearly twenty-one years. After Gouverneur's death, she focused her efforts on three inter-related tasks. First, in concert with a succession of attorneys and advisors, Nancy settled her husband's affairs and managed his estate. Second, she defended her reputation in New York to thwart attempts by Gouverneur's relations to have her son declared illegitimate, which, in turn, would have resulted in the loss of his inheritance. Third, Nancy immersed herself in the joys and obligations of motherhood. She worked hard to raise and to educate Gouverneur Morris, Jr., who she considered her "richest treasure." Young Gouverneur was just three years old when his father died, and Nancy fretted that if she, too, died, the youth would be "really in Danger of Personal violence" at the hands of his New York cousins.[1]

As a widow, Nancy deployed an array of weapons—the law, the press, the advice of friends, and her own tenacity—to defend her husband's memory, her son's right to inherit his father's property, and her own identity as a conventionally virtuous woman. In widowhood, she also assiduously cultivated good relations with—and the good opinion of—her family and friends in Virginia, whose letters and visits she cherished as emblems of affection and honor.

In leaving the Old Dominion, Nancy rejected neither her family and friends there nor her Virginia heritage. In fact, her experiences in New York, especially after Gouverneur died, gradually led her to see herself as a Virginian and to identify more consciously with what she idealized as Virginia ways and values. Although Nancy's voluminous correspondence with her family and friends in the Old Dominion helped demonstrate to them and to herself that she had attained love, prosperity, and respectability at Morrisania, writing and receiving letters also led her to ponder the differences between New Yorkers and Virginians and to place herself decisively among the latter.

As she embarked on life without Gouverneur, Nancy took some comfort in the terms of her husband's last will and testament, which, in her view, revealed his "unbounded confidence" in her abilities and her character. In his will, Gouverneur confirmed a prenuptial agreement that gave Nancy $2,600 a year (about $32,500 in today's money) plus the use of Morrisania and all its stock, plate, and furnishings for life. Unlike many men who curtailed their widows' use of their property if they remarried, Gouverneur instead stipulated that, should Nancy take a second husband, she would receive an additional $600 "to defray the increased expenditure, which may attend that connexion." Gouverneur bequeathed nearly his entire estate to his young son, naming Nancy and Moss Kent, a Federalist lawyer, as his co-executors. Morris probably wanted Kent, who resided in Jefferson County in western New York, to manage his extensive western landholdings, which were far removed from Morrisania. Although he also expected Kent to advise Nancy on legal and financial matters, he nonetheless saw her as the final arbiter of decisions pertaining to the management of the Morris property.[2]

In his will, Gouverneur gave Nancy significant discretionary powers that attested to his confidence and trust in her. More impressive still, he stipulated that she should retain those powers even if the untimely death of Gouverneur Morris, Jr., meant that she was no longer guardian of the chief heir to his estate. The elder Morris gave Nancy sole authority to divide his estate among his male descendants as she saw fit if their son died before attaining his majority or without a will thereafter. He also ensured that his widow had some influence over the disposition of even that small part of his property that would not go either to her or to their son. Gouverneur set aside a sum of $25,000 for his grand-nephew and namesake Gouverneur Wilkins, but he stipulated that Wilkins would receive his inheritance at age thirty and then only if "his conduct shall be, in the opinion of my executor and executrix, such as becomes a good citizen."[3]

Gouverneur clearly intended each of these provisions to protect his wife and child from their enemies after he was gone. By empowering Nancy to pick and choose among potential legatees, for instance, he probably hoped to encourage at least some of his relatives to treat her well. By appointing Kent as his attorney and co-executor, Gouverneur chose an agent who, by virtue of his western residence, was less likely to be influenced by the New York City lawyers who were friendly with his disgruntled nephews, especially David Bayard Ogden, who was himself a prominent member of the city's legal fraternity. The fact that Moss Kent's older brother, James, presided over the state's court of chancery, which handled cases relating to wills and inheritance, also probably influenced Gouverneur's choice of co-executor.[4] Finally, by offering Nancy what amounted to a financial incentive to remarry, Gouverneur encouraged his widow to find another male protector—a loving and competent substitute for himself—to help her fight her battles.

Nancy never considered remarrying, but instead devoted herself to preserving both Gouverneur's estate and their son's right to inherit it. Her most dangerous and persistent foe was David Bayard Ogden, the son of Samuel Ogden and Gouverneur's sister Euphemia Morris. A successful New York City lawyer, Ogden was nonetheless deeply in debt, and he tried all sorts of ways to gain access to his uncle's money. While Gouverneur lived, Ogden asked for and sometimes received loans or outright gifts of cash. He also tried unsuccessfully to persuade his uncle to appoint him as executor of his estate. Ogden named his oldest son, born just months before his uncle married, Gouverneur Morris Ogden, probably in hopes of strengthening his family's claim to at least a portion of the Morris property. After 1813, he tried to convince his uncle that Nancy's son was not his child, making common cause with Jack Randolph in his ill-fated quest to destroy the Morrises' marriage.[5]

When Gouverneur died, Nancy discovered the full extent of Ogden's machinations. To her horror, she discovered that he had defrauded her husband, and, by extension, her son, of more than $100,000 (approximately $1.25 million in today's money). Ogden had given the elder Gouverneur's name as his security to obtain sizeable loans from both banks and individuals, making his uncle liable for his mounting debts. In one case, Gouverneur accepted a mortgage on some property in return for acting as his nephew's security, but Ogden then surreptitiously took out a second mortgage on the same property, for which his uncle would be liable if he himself could not repay the debt. In other instances, Ogden used his uncle's name without his knowledge to secure the funds he needed. Because Gouverneur Morris was highly regarded among New York's business elite, who, in turn, presumed his nephew to be a man of honor, Ogden got the loans he wanted. By 1817, however, Nancy surmised that Ogden was bankrupt, while she was left to deal with the consequences of his actions. She concluded that Gouverneur's estate had lost some $150,000 as a result of Ogden's "wicked swindling," between debts, interest, lawyers' fees, and the various unspecified "Bribes" she believed Ogden gave his supporters and co-conspirators.[6]

Nancy proved to be a tenacious and resourceful steward of her husband's property. Although she worked with a succession of legal advisors and agents, she was primarily responsible for putting the estate on a sound financial footing to safeguard her son's patrimony. In 1817, despite what she characterized as Moss Kent's "feeble-minded" advice that she delay taking action, Nancy decided to sell some western lands, mortgage all but fifty acres of Morrisania, and forgo the generous annual maintenance her husband had provided for her. By taking these steps, and by selling assorted livestock, furniture, and about $1,600 in silver plate, she expected to settle both Morris's legitimate debts and the claims of Ogden's creditors within roughly ten years. Dissatisfied with Kent, who quarreled with her agents and, she believed, mismanaged other matters, Nancy successfully sued to have him removed as co-executor in 1821.[7]

Thereafter, Nancy relied on a succession of other agents and advisors, with whom she was never reluctant to quarrel when, in her view, they did not act in the best interest of herself and her son. For example, Nancy refused to pay her lawyer, James A. Hamilton, fees that she considered unreasonable. Hamilton sued her, but after years of litigation Nancy negotiated an out-of-court settlement to pay him $4,000, which was about half of what he originally claimed she owed. Dudley Selden acted as Nancy's land agent for more than seven years before she dismissed him on the grounds that he, like Kent and Hamilton, "could not be expected to understand land agency." Beginning in 1822, Nancy relied primarily on her new attorneys, Peter Jay Munro and his son Henry, for legal and financial advice. Perhaps the Munros appreciated Nancy's tenacity and business acumen. She appears to have respected their abilities and regarded them as honest.[8]

In the end, however, it was clearly she alone who made the decisions and undertook the personal sacrifices necessary to preserve Morrisania for her son. Though Morrisania had a staff of thirteen domestic servants in Gouverneur's time, by 1818 Nancy had only one eleven-year-old servant girl to help her keep house. Hannah Simon, the daughter of an illiterate man who was probably a Morrisania tenant, had been indentured to the Morrises for ten years, beginning in 1814, so that she might be "well instructed in the . . . Business of a House Servant." Though Hannah probably had learned much in her first four years at Morrisania, Nancy nevertheless oversaw all of the housework and even did a great deal of it herself. She washed dishes, swept floors, cooked, and supervised the "Farmwork" on the estate. "I rise early and Toil constantly—each day is alike," she explained to St. George Tucker, adding, "Thank God my darling boy is every thing the fondest Mother can wish." Nancy confided to her attorney, "If I had not such a fine boy to protect I should prefer sewing for an honest & quiet life."[9]

While Nancy economized to save the estate from utter ruin, David Ogden schemed to have young Gouverneur disinherited. After his uncle died, Ogden intensified his efforts to convince New Yorkers that Nancy was a lewd woman and, most especially, that she had been an unchaste wife. Ogden's strategy was to prove that his uncle had no son. Because Morris's will dictated that his property be divided among his male descendants in the event of the death of Gouverneur Morris, Jr., it would have been logical for Ogden to assume that having the youngster declared illegitimate would yield the same result. Aside from his son, Morris's nearest male relations were his three surviving nephews: David Bayard Ogden, Lewis Morris Wilkins, and Isaac Wilkins. Nancy believed that Ogden was offering money to anyone who would believe his story and support his offensive. She also suspected that he was courting Rufus King, the prominent New York Federalist who had been Gouverneur's friend but who was also on good terms with both Ogden and Jack. Nancy became convinced that King was one of a growing number of prominent New Yorkers that Ogden had recruited to participate in his vendetta against her.[10]

Though Ogden's allegations against Nancy were the same as those Jack put forward in 1814, she correctly believed that the gossip circulating in New York was far more treacherous now that Gouverneur was dead. While Gouverneur lived, he alone had the right to govern his household and dispose of his property. His trust in Nancy therefore prevented gossip about her from having any material effect on her and her son. Once Gouverneur died, however, if Ogden persuaded enough people that Nancy was unchaste and that her son was illegitimate, he might ask the courts to decide the fate of both. Nancy could not have been optimistic about the outcome of such a suit, given Ogden's extensive connections in New York and her own status as a newcomer with a tainted past.

In January 1817, less than three months after Gouverneur's death, Nancy reported to St. George Tucker that David Ogden "boasts of having Jack [Randolph] as a Tool to swear unfounded calumnies" against her. Ogden was circulating what Nancy called his "swindling letters" throughout New York, and she was determined to fight back. Ogden and his supporters spread gossip about Nancy's alleged sexual promiscuity, her supposed responsibility for Richard's death, and her exploits as prostitute in Richmond. New Yorkers also were talking about how Nancy had seduced her nephews, St. George and Tudor, at Bizarre. While this particular story had not appeared on Jack's list of accusations, many New Yorkers nonetheless found it both appealingly salacious and plausible. Because of this story, Nancy informed Tucker sadly, "Boys 12 and 14 years old are warned against me." By mid-July, Nancy reported to St. George Tucker that Ogden's efforts had made her the subject of much "Street talk" among New Yorkers of all social ranks. "Everything low and mean—everything indecent," she explained, "has been put into the mouth of every Servant in New York."[11]

Clearly, Nancy felt like an outsider in New York after Gouverneur died. Although she sentimentally regarded Morrisania itself as a "beloved spot," she described New York generally as inhospitable and corrupt. Nancy attributed David Ogden's "swindling," along with the other problems of her early widowhood, to the depravity of New Yorkers, who she deemed incapable of true friendship. "Such is the state of New York society that [Ogden] is countenanced in all . . . except by those who have suffered in the same way by him," Nancy wrote to St. George Tucker in 1817. Only New Yorkers, she asserted, "would be bold enough to defend such a Tissue of crimes as David Ogden has committed."[12]

Nancy attributed the debasement of New Yorkers to the growing influence of democracy and "foreigners." Chancellor James Kent and his brother, Moss, she explained disparagingly, were "Yankees and Presbyterians"—in other words, people with New England roots that old-stock New Yorkers had long found suspect. In his 1760 will, New Yorker Lewis Morris had dictated that his son Gouverneur—Nancy's future husband—not attend college in Connecticut "lest he should imbibe . . . that low craft and cunning so incident to the people of that country." Nancy believed that New York also suffered the "general calamity of . . . [being] overrun by Unprincipled servants." New York's servant population was ethnically diverse, as was the state itself, but Nancy considered the Irish, who increasingly constituted the state's chief source of domestic workers, particularly vicious and untrustworthy. Most of New York's "Ladies and Gentlemen," she claimed, "have been Nursed and Suckled by corrupt Foreigners" whose unsavory influence gave rise to a "Society which does not dare to frown on Fraud, ingratitude, or Falsehood."[13]

Nancy's complaints about New Yorkers and about northern servants, in particular, drew on both her past experience as a member of Virginia's planter class and her present circumstances as a female member of New York's post-revolutionary elite. On the one hand, many New Yorkers shared Nancy's disparaging view of the Catholic Irish—who most American Protestants regarded as alien and not even white—and complaining about the servants was one of the marks of being a lady in this society where white domestic workers saw themselves not as a permanent servant class but rather as temporary hired "help." In early nineteenth-century New York, one historian has observed, "For ladies who were not entirely confident of their own class identity, asserting judgment over the immigrant poor affirmed their position and status."[14] Nancy, whose social status was vulnerable on both moral and material grounds, must have felt an especially strong impulse to act in ways that marked her as a member of the elite. On the other hand, the implicit contrast between New York and Virginia pervaded the letters Nancy sent to St. George Tucker and others in the Old Dominion. Her characterization of New York servants as lazy, dishonest, and unaccepting of their subservient status stood in marked contrast to the loyal, deferential, and supposedly childlike slave who was fast becoming a favored stereotype among apologists for slavery.[15]

So, too, did Nancy's portrayal of New York's elite as mercenary, deceitful, and corrupt stand as a mirror image of the southern ideal of masculine gentility and honor. Bravery, protectiveness toward family, and honesty—even transparency— in personal and business relationships were, as we have seen, hallmarks of an idealized southern manhood in the post-revolutionary era. Nancy's descriptions of David Ogden and his New York cronies, by contrast, paint them as dishonest and cowardly would-be usurpers of a fortune that rightfully belonged to a woman and child, the same dependent kin who merited a gentleman's protection and help. Moreover, the ideal southern gentleman, however much he pursued and enjoyed affluence, did not do so at the expense of his public reputation. Nancy condemned the New Yorkers as money-grubbing "swindlers" whose pursuit of wealth was single-minded and unconstrained by the niceties of morality or honor.[16]

In the years after Gouverneur's death, Nancy devoted much of her scarce leisure time to writing letters to friends and relatives in Virginia. While she occasionally solicited business or legal advice from St. George Tucker or Randolph Harrison, the purpose of most of her letters was more specifically social. Nancy wrote in part out of loneliness. While she had enjoyed a pleasant social life with Gouverneur, she had pursued no social activities on her own, and widowhood presented her with few opportunities for sociability. Lacking trustworthy adult companionship closer to home, she therefore sought to preserve or renew friendships and family relationships in the Old Dominion. At the same time, she looked on such relationships as evidence of her own virtue, interpreting the goodwill of her correspondents as tacit recognition of her own inherent goodness and value.

Throughout her troubled years in New York, Nancy took solace in reviewing the list of her Virginia correspondents, regarding each name on it as a sort of badge of honor. "I now owe letters to four of my Vir[gini]a friends—many of them are so kind in writing," she reported to St. George Tucker on New Year's Day in 1815, adding, "indeed, until the horrid return [Jack] made to my tender Friendship for and constant care of Tudor, I knew not how many persons in that State felt friendly emotions for me." Nancy resumed contact with all of her surviving siblings, except possibly Harriet, and she also exchanged letters with nieces and nephews in Virginia. Years later, reflecting on how much her Virginia friends and their letters meant to her over the years, she proudly listed some of her other correspondents for St. George Tucker's son-in-law, Joseph Carrington Cabell, whom she barely knew. "During many years the most steady correspondent I had, was my Sister Mrs. David [Molly] Randolph," she explained. "I now and then receive long affectionate letters from Mrs. R[andolph] Harrison and my Sister [Martha Jefferson Randolph]—also Lucy Randolph now of Alabama," besides her brother William. "A few others," she noted, also continued to keep her informed of news from Virginia. Nancy cited her correspondents as one would produce a list of personal references, giving Cabell evidence of her social respectability and good character.[17]

Although financial considerations compelled Nancy to remain in New York after Gouverneur's death, in widowhood she became deeply dependent on her Virginia connections for practical advice, emotional support, and ongoing validation of her self-image as a virtuous and industrious woman. Indeed, a combination of fatigue and homesickness must have inspired Nancy, in early 1818, to return to Virginia for the first time since her departure in disgrace in 1807. At the height of her troubles with David Ogden, she and young

Gouverneur fled New York, taking refuge among sympathetic kin and friends. The details of Nancy's trip are obscure, but she and Gouverneur appear to have visited the Harrisons at Clifton, the large white frame house near Glentivar where Randolph Harrison had grown up and where he, Mary, and their children took up residence some time around 1800. They also went to Monticello to see the Jefferson and Randolph families. Mother and son stopped in Richmond, where Nancy seems to have reconciled with her sister, Molly, who had vilified her in Newport. Nancy and Gouverneur had planned to go next to visit the Tuckers in Williamsburg, but business considerations cut short their trip. Besieged again by Ogden, Nancy returned regretfully to New York, where she would spend the ensuing years defending her son's inheritance.[18]

Although the specific circumstances that necessitated Nancy's return to New York are unknown, it seems reasonable to assume that David Ogden took advantage of her absence to step up his efforts to discredit her and secure the disinheritance of her now five-year-old son. Before leaving New York, Nancy had begun to defend herself by obtaining written statements from members of the Woodson family, who had been friends and neighbors of the Randolphs in Cumberland, attesting to her good character. She hoped to use the Woodsons' "certificates," which may have been sworn affidavits, to prove to the Ogdens and other New Yorkers that Jack had lied about her supposed misconduct at Bizarre. Nancy, however, soon concluded that evidence of any sort would not convince Ogden and his supporters, "who are outrageous at my husband's entire confidence in me." Consequently, in the summer of 1817, Nancy initiated libel proceedings against David Ogden. Although the suit never materialized, the mere threat of litigation, she believed, convinced many of her critics that the potentially damaging letters he had circulated with the intent of ruining Nancy and "swindling" the Morris estate had been forgeries.[19]

Nevertheless, the gossip continued, and its effects permeated even the more mundane aspects of Nancy's daily life. Nasty stories about her past made their way to Morrisania, where they became weapons in the hands of those who were disposed to challenge her authority as mistress or her overall credibility in business dealings. For example, when Nancy hired a tutor for young Gouverneur on a one-month trial basis, the man claimed that she had hired him for an entire year and that she had agreed to give him $400 and the use of a house at Morrisania in return for his services. The tutor sued and won, Nancy maintained, because the jurors believed the gossip about her past and therefore regarded her as generally untrustworthy. Similarly, in August 1818, gossip about Nancy emboldened a man and woman she discovered "stealing apples" from her property. After informing the couple that they were trespassing but nonetheless allowing them to keep the fruit they had, Nancy requested that they leave. The intruders complied, but not long afterward they sent her a "letter of abuse about [her] poisoning a Man and trying to seduce his sons." The implication of such episodes was clear. Anyone from David Bayard Ogden to nameless apple-pickers could exploit Nancy's reputation as an unchaste and treacherous woman to buttress their own claims, however spurious, against her.[20]

David Bayard Ogden, by contrast, had little to lose by his continual attack on Nancy's reputation. In the eyes of those who believed even a small fraction of the allegations against Nancy, Ogden was defending his family's property against a potential usurper and seeking to reassert patriarchal power. Others, even some who may have sympathized with Nancy, nonetheless also professed to understand how Ogden's financial predicament could have driven him, the father of eight, to be mercenary or even unethical in his dealings with his wealthy relatives. Randolph Harrison, for instance, took that position, which earned him Nancy's temporary enmity. Moreover, unlike Nancy, who had few friends and little influence in New York, Ogden had extensive connections in the city and its surrounding region. As a skilled attorney whose work Chief Justice John Marshall himself found praiseworthy, he was also a valued member of New York's business community. Indeed, between 1815 and 1818, at the height of his vendetta against Nancy, Ogden's legal practice flourished, due in part to a string of successful arguments he presented before the Marshall Court.[21]

Cultural conventions that valued men for their public accomplishments in business or in politics and women for their moral and sexual purity put Nancy at a distinct disadvantage in her dealings with David Ogden. Although she assailed him as a liar and a swindler, Ogden's thriving legal practice and prominent political contacts served as counter-evidence that enabled him to deflect her accusations, at least in the short term. Ogden, by contrast, condemned Nancy as an unchaste woman, a charge to which the Bizarre scandal made her plainly vulnerable. Small wonder, then, that Nancy, despite her continuing obsession with Ogden's malfeasance, came to focus her efforts on defending her own reputation and countering his specific charges against her.

As she assessed the situation in the troubled months after Gouverneur's death, Nancy had focused on the key questions that, in her view, made Ogden's allegations seem more plausible in the eyes of her detractors. Why, some might ask, did Gouverneur Morris do nothing to defend his wife against Jack Randolph's accusations? Why should they believe Nancy—who, after all, admitted to conceiving a child out-of-wedlock in 1792—when she denied Ogden's claim that she was unfaithful to her husband? Why should they believe that young Gouverneur, in other words, was her husband's legitimate son and heir? Nancy was convinced that her late husband's letters and papers could answer these questions to her critics' satisfaction by demonstrating both the happiness of their marriage and Gouverneur's "entire confidence" in her. Less than a year after his death, she had planned to find some "leisure" from her duties as executrix, mother, and housekeeper to locate and publish papers that she hoped would clear her name. She returned to that project with renewed vigor in the coming months.[22]

Unlike Nancy's earlier efforts to secure publication of her epistolary denunciation of Jack Randolph in Virginia, this second attempt to gain access to the public press was a qualified success. In 1815, Nancy had sought to savage the reputation of a political candidate by publicizing their violent disagreement about several exceedingly delicate personal matters. The tone of her letter was accusatory, argumentative, and rigorously rational. In effect, she tried to defend her feminine virtue by means that most of her contemporaries would have regarded as neither feminine nor virtuous. Now, however, Nancy wrote as a grieving, loyal, and vulnerable widow; most of the words she sought to publish were not even her own but rather those of her beloved husband. This time, her efforts were more successful because both the persona she adopted and the subject matter with which she dealt were more in keeping with contemporary ideals of virtuous womanhood.

Nancy pored over Gouverneur's writings, hoping to use them to vindicate their marriage and her status as a virtuous wife and mother. In 1818, she submitted one of her husband's letters and one of his poems to *The Columbian,* a newspaper for the Columbia College alumni who constituted a large portion of the cream of New York society. Because Gouverneur had been a well-known alumnus and benefactor of the college, the editors printed his letters, while they probably would not have published an essay penned by Nancy herself. (Nor would the editors have welcomed a hostile rebuttal from the pen of David Ogden, who had attended the University of Pennsylvania in Philadelphia.) Nancy sent *The Columbian* an 1812 letter in which Gouverneur acknowledged the "tender kindness" of his "dear wife," and opined that their life together at Morrisania was so content that "as to other folks, their civilities or want of them are of no consequence." The "other folks," of course, were Morris's own relations who had resented his marriage to Nancy from the start. Nancy also sent *The Columbian* a poem that Gouverneur had written for her in 1813 during an extended absence from Morrisania. His heartfelt verse amply attested to the happiness of their domestic life: "Kiss for me, my love, our charming boy/ I long to taste again the joy/ Of pressing to his father's breast/ The son and mother. Be they blest."[23]

Publication of these pieces, in effect, made the esteemed late Gouverneur Morris a character witness for his embattled wife. Nancy regarded the publication of Gouverneur's writings as a turning point in her widowhood, describing herself as "less persecuted" as a result of their appearance in print in September

1818. Even Rufus King, who previously had taken Ogden's side, she intimated, had "yielded to Evidence and pronounced [David Ogden] a Rascal."[24]

Whatever solace her 1818 publication brought, the following year Nancy again marshaled her husband's words in her defense. Perhaps her critics hypothesized that the Morrises' marriage may have soured in its later years, because this time "maternal duty" inspired Nancy to send the editors of *The Columbian* a letter Gouverneur addressed to a friend just four months before his death in 1816. "The woman to whom I am married has much genius, has been well educated, and possesses, with an affectionate temper, industry and a love of order," he stated after more than six years of marriage, adding that Nancy was also "a kind companion and a tender feminine friend." Nancy triumphantly sent a copy of the published piece to the sympathetic St. George Tucker. With a confidence in the power of the written word reminiscent of his own, she confided, "I must have quitted this place had I not given a check to the vile calumnies of disappointed avarice."[25]

Nancy's publications, along with her frugal management of her husband's estate and her maternal devotion, brought her some relief by the 1820s. So, too, did her son's increasingly "striking resemblance" to Gouverneur, which she believed helped convince many of his legitimacy. In 1824, Nancy reported to St. George Tucker that David Ogden now had few supporters in New York and that she had reconciled with other members of the extended Morris family. "Two great triumphs have been mine," she observed to Tucker, as she recovered from a serious, but unspecified illness. "I have paid my last bond for the swindling calumniator D B Ogden and had the satisfaction of finding the Morris kindred doing me justice." Two years later, though she complained of failing eyesight, weak teeth, and feeling "as if I were a thousand years old," a fifty-two-year-old Nancy nonetheless reflected with satisfaction on her own vindication and the fine prospects of her "good boy."[26]

Nancy adored her son and praised him profusely to Tucker and her other Virginia friends. Indeed, perhaps reflecting on the troubled lives of his Randolph stepsons, St. George Tucker strongly cautioned her against spoiling young Gouverneur and praising him too extravagantly. "Avoid this course, my beloved Nancy, for your *own* sake, and still more for your *Child's*," he counseled. "Let him not think himself born superior to those around him . . . and teach him to believe that [success] depends upon his own exertions, and on a steady moral course of conduct through life." Although Nancy never responded directly to Tucker's concerns, she must have taken his advice to heart. By all accounts, Gouverneur was a loving and respectful son to Nancy. Later in life, his less prosperous neighbors at Morrisania considered him to be "a good, charitable man and exceedingly democratic."[27]

As both she and Gouverneur advanced in years, Nancy thought often of returning to Virginia. In 1822, she considered moving to Albemarle County so that her son might attend the newly established University of Virginia, the brainchild of Thomas Jefferson, whom she still admired profusely. In 1826, spurred in part by "the fatality which has pursued my excellent Mother's offspring," Nancy pondered taking Gouverneur to Virginia "once more" before her own life, too, was over. Nevertheless, she continued to reside in New York for her son's benefit. Ever suspicious of David Ogden, Nancy stayed in New York to protect young Gouverneur's financial interests. At Morrisania, moreover, she could live more economically than she could in Virginia by virtue of the provision in her husband's will that gave her the use of his house and its furnishings as long as she lived. In addition, Nancy may have recognized the utility of her son's remaining in New York to make personal and business contacts that could be advantageous in his future life.[28]

Despite occasional encounters with thieving tenants, incompetent agents, and expensive lawyers, life at Morrisania became less frugal by the mid-1820s, and Nancy found herself able to increase the size of her household staff to spare herself from some of the drudgery she had endured since the death of Gouverneur. Nancy's dislike for white servants, coupled with her idealized past experience among slaveowning Virginians, may have led her to prefer African American workers, even if they were free. In the early 1820s she employed ten people, besides her indentured servant Hannah Simon, who would complete her ten-year term of service in 1824. Nancy chose five African American men—four free and one enslaved—one free black woman, and four white men to perform various domestic and agricultural tasks at Morrisania.[29]

In time, however, Nancy may have found even New York's free African American servants insufficiently dependent and deferential. In 1825, she wrote to her sisters, hoping to hire a "coloured woman" from Virginia, and she tried to hire some black domestics from Richmond a decade later. Unwilling or unable to retain the services of free black workers, by 1830 Nancy had an all-white workforce of six men and one woman at Morrisania. Nancy never articulated her feelings about slavery as either a labor system or social institution, and it is unlikely that she would have overtly favored a revival of slavery in New York, given the antislavery proclivities of her husband. Nevertheless, at least one of Nancy's Virginia correspondents interpreted her complaints about the servants in a proslavery and anti-northern light. "After all the Jeremiads of the people of the *Free States* against the evils of slavery," wrote an exasperated Carter Henry Harrison in 1835, "I think they would consider their blessings in comparison with dealing with the troubles of dealing with white servants, if they had tried both, as you have."[30]

As old age approached, Nancy remained in close contact with her Virginia kin and seemed to take a special care in cultivating relationships with members of the younger generation, among whom she acquired a reputation for generosity and compassion. She continually extended her hospitality to Virginians; youngsters, especially the Randolphs and Harrisons who journeyed northward to be educated, were among her frequent guests. Nieces and nephews requested (and often received) gifts of cash from Nancy; one niece even asked her to send Gouverneur's old cork leg to Virginia so a local artisan could copy it for a family friend who had recently had his own limb amputated. "I have always heard that a tale of distress would find ready access to your heart," wrote a daughter of Nancy's youngest sister, Virginia Randolph Cary, in 1828, "and that you were ever . . . rendering assistance when it was in your power."[31]

Nancy's contact with her Virginia family and friends helped her to appreciate the travails of her siblings and others who had inhabited the world of her youth. In the years since she and young Gouverneur had visited Virginia in 1818, Nancy's surviving brothers and sisters experienced deepening financial problems, and many of their children had left Virginia in search of economic opportunity. Thomas Mann Randolph was, like his brothers William and John, penniless by 1824; his wife, Martha, lived first with one married daughter in Boston and then with another in Washington following the sale of Monticello to pay off the debts of her father, who died in 1826. Molly, Nancy's eldest sister, who had run a boarding house in Richmond, also eventually moved to Washington, where she lived with her son and published a popular cookbook, *The Virginia House-Wife*, to earn some money. Jane watched over her family's dwindling finances, as her husband, Thomas Eston Randolph, sold Dungeness, his ancestral seat, and moved their large family to a small rented house in Lynchburg, where she started a school to generate income before the entire family left for Florida in the late 1820s. Harriet took in boarders and operated schools in Richmond, Norfolk, and Philadelphia. In widowhood, Virginia turned to teaching and writing for publication to earn money while she lived with a succession of relatives after the liquidation of the estate of her insolvent husband, Wilson Jefferson Cary.[32]

The good opinion of Virginians from her past remained important to Nancy, and she maintained particularly close contact with those who knew her best during her darkest days at Bizarre. St. George Tucker, for whom Nancy felt great "gratitude and affection," was her most valued correspondent, with whom she exchanged letters from the 1790s until his death in 1827 at the age of seventy-five. In addition, Nancy regularly exchanged letters with two people who had been present both at Glentivar and at the Cumberland County courthouse seven months later, Randolph and Mary Harrison. Most striking of all, however, was Nancy's effort to renew contact with Anna Dudley, Richard Randolph's cousin who, like her, had escaped a difficult family situation to find refuge at Bizarre in the 1790s. Nancy appears to have lost track of Dudley after she left Bizarre in 1796. Some time in the 1820s, however, Nancy discovered that Anna Dudley had moved to Franklin County, Tennessee, and she initiated a correspondence with her. Nancy felt a great sense of vindication on learning that Jack had mistreated Anna Dudley, too. As she triumphantly informed one of her correspondents in Virginia, Dudley sent her a letter "containing details of [Jack's] enormities toward her Son and Self."[33]

Despite her apparent vindication and social acceptance, Nancy still fretted about her troubled past and, perhaps emboldened by her modest success, never lost her faith in the power of her husband's words to secure her reputation as a virtuous wife and mother. As she read and reread Gouverneur's diary with its occasional comments on their "Dear, quiet, happy, home," she pondered its publication. In 1828, in what was clearly an attempt to create a written record of her child's acceptance as a member of the Morris family, she also considered compiling and publishing a history of his "relations on his father's side during three generations." In 1829, Nancy briefly negotiated with James A. Hamilton to "arrange and publish" Gouverneur's papers. Hamilton had been her attorney and business agent, and he was also the son of Gouverneur's good friend and Federalist political ally, Alexander Hamilton. The two never reached an agreement, however, perhaps because Hamilton, who later celebrated his father and other Federalist leaders in his own largely political reminiscences, was primarily interested in documenting Gouverneur's "illustrious" public life.[34]

In 1832, Jared Sparks published the first full-scale biography of Gouverneur Morris. Nancy, who had supplied Sparks with her husband's papers for the purpose of his research, hoped that the resulting book about her husband would prominently feature "an account of his domestic happiness." But Sparks, like Hamilton, sought to present Morris as a public man whose achievements could inspire patriotism in his readers. Well aware that Nancy sought personal vindication through publication, the historian nonetheless counseled that biographies of statesmen should focus on their public contributions, not their private affairs, and that they should especially stay clear of any controversial aspects of their subjects' private lives. From this perspective, Gouverneur's "retired habits of living" at Morrisania "afford[ed] but few materials for biography." Conversely, Sparks asserted that "slanders that are forgotten may be allowed to sleep." The family troubles that "embittered [Morris's] declining years," he counseled, "are the subjects of so personal and private a nature, and with which the public has so little concern that I am induced to believe that they should be touched upon lightly and briefly."[35]

Sparks's promise to include some letters in which Gouverneur expressed "in the clearest terms his happiness in his domestic relations" may have consoled

Nancy, who, of course, knew that the slanders and scandals were not "forgotten." Sparks kept his word, publishing excerpts from two of Gouverneur's letters toward the end of the first volume of his biography. Although he described Gouverneur's marriage to Nancy as "a source of continued satisfaction and happiness," Sparks devoted a grand total of only one paragraph of his two-volume work to the Morrises' domestic life.[36]

Flattering accounts of Nancy's life and character, like the scandal that shaped her life so profoundly, more likely circulated through oral or epistolary channels—private communications that could nonetheless have a wide influence among the public-at-large. At a time when the notion of motherhood as woman's special, even sacred, mission loomed large in American culture and consciousness, Nancy's devotion to her son offered her the possibility of rehabilitation.[37] Though most everyone still heard of her youthful indiscretions, at least some of her contemporaries eventually concluded that her purposeful and single-minded fulfillment of her maternal obligations had helped to redeem her in her later life.

Take, for instance, the case of Martha Jefferson Randolph, the sister-in-law who had fretted that the Bizarre scandal would reflect badly on her own family and who had testified in *Commonwealth v. Randolph* that she suspected Nancy of being pregnant at the time of her trip to Glentivar. Although Nancy later stayed with Martha's family at Monticello and Edgehill from time to time, she came to believe that her sister-in-law had turned against her by the time she left Virginia in 1807. Nevertheless, Martha had sympathized with Nancy in her battle with Jack in 1815. Three years later, Nancy and her son visited Monticello. Not long afterward, she and Martha began exchanging letters regularly. In middle age, Martha Jefferson Randolph became one of Nancy's main sources of information about her friends and relatives in Virginia.[38]

Martha's letters revealed a newfound respect for Nancy, who by then had proven her ability as a household manager and her selfless devotion as a mother. In sharing family news, domestic advice, and hopes and fears for her children's future, Martha showed that she regarded Nancy as her equal. In 1833, for example, Martha commiserated with Nancy about the rigors of housework at their advanced age and bemoaned the difficulty of finding good servants to assist them. She also addressed Nancy as a mother, praising Gouverneur and expressing pride in her own children, too, as well as gratitude for Nancy's kindness toward them. Martha urged Nancy to safeguard her health for the sake of her son. "You have laboured too hard and too long," she counseled, "spare yourself now dear sister, for his sake for whom all has been sacrificed, it is indeed time that you should enjoy with him the hard earned fruits of those labours."[39] That assessment, from the pen of a woman who embodied female rectitude and maternal sacrifice, must have brought an appreciative smile to the aging mistress of Morrisania.

Figure 6.1 Martha Jefferson Randolph, ca. 1823. This sister-in-law, who was the daughter of Thomas Jefferson, became Nancy's best source of information about friends and relatives in Virginia. Although relations between the two women were sometimes rocky in the years following the Bizarre scandal, Martha came to respect Nancy both for her ability to manage a household and her devotion to her son. Monticello/Thomas Jefferson Foundation, Inc.

In 1835, mother and son—the latter was now a man of twenty-two—again ventured southward, perhaps in hopes of finding a bride for Gouverneur among his Randolph cousins. Although Nancy's family and friends received her warmly, many of those she knew best had died or moved elsewhere since her last visit to central Virginia. Of her three brothers, only William was still alive. Sisters Molly,

Jane, and, of course, Judith, all were dead. Virginia, her youngest sister who, as a child had passed that fateful night with her at Glentivar, had recently moved from Norfolk to Fairfax County, near Washington. Harriet now lived in Philadelphia. But Martha Jefferson Randolph, rendered homeless by the debts and deaths of her father and husband, had returned to Albemarle after living in Boston and Washington and now resided at Edgehill with her eldest son.[40]

By 1835, most of the others who had firsthand knowledge of the Bizarre scandal also were dead or soon would be. St. George Tucker had died in 1827. Jack Randolph, who suffered from chronic physical illness and bouts of insanity in his later years, died in 1833 and was buried at his plantation at Roanoke. In his will, Jack freed his slaves in a final dramatic gesture of patriarchal mastery and noblesse oblige, an act that more sober and mercenary relatives would contest for many years to come.[41] The Harrisons were still living at Clifton when Nancy visited Virginia in early 1835, but Mary Harrison, who had discovered Nancy's bloody bedclothes at nearby Glentivar so many years before, died a few months later. Randolph Harrison died in 1839 at the age of seventy, leaving his ten surviving children property in land, slaves, stock, and sundry personal effects worth a total of nearly $90,000.[42]

As she, too, approached the end of life, Nancy was sometimes haunted by memories of Richard, Judith, "crazy Jack," and David Ogden, the "swindling calumniator." She also continued to worry about the fate of her nephew, St. George—the only other surviving member of the Bizarre household—who had surfaced in Baltimore, looking "wretchedly" in 1830.[43] But Nancy also looked on proudly as her son came of age and assumed responsibility for the estate she had worked so hard to preserve for him and his progeny. By 1836, Gouverneur had begun to follow in his father's footsteps, embarking on a career in business and real estate that would eventually make him a prominent figure in the American railroad industry.[44]

On 28 May 1837, Nancy died at Morrisania at the age of sixty-three. Although the precise cause of her death is not clear, she had been complaining for years of various unspecified age-related maladies. Two days after Nancy died, her funeral took place at Morrisania and her body was laid to rest in the vault she had constructed for Gouverneur two decades earlier. In 1841, however, Gouverneur Morris, Jr., had both his parents re-interred in a vault built beneath an Episcopal church he had erected at Morrisania at his own expense. Gouverneur insisted that the church be named St. Ann's, in Nancy's honor. Inside the church, a plaque memorializes Ann Cary Morris as "the wife and mother in memory of whom this church was created to the God she loved by filial veneration."[45] This inscription, which doubtless would have pleased Nancy, marked yet another effort to use the written word to eradicate the scandal that had so profoundly shaped her life.

Figure 6.2 St. Ann's Episcopal Church. Gouverneur Morris, Jr., had this church built in his mother's honor. Morris donated both the building and the land, which had been part of Morrisania, to the new Episcopal parish, which today ministers to the largely Latino and African American residents of the South Bronx. Photography—Richard King.

Figure 6.3 Grave of Ann Cary Morris. Both Nancy and Gouverneur are interred in a vault beneath the wooden floor of St. Ann's Church. A grating shields the engraved stone marker that memorializes Nancy as a "wife and mother." Photography—Richard King.

Although there is no evidence that Gouverneur Morris, Jr., ever regarded himself as anything other than a New Yorker, perhaps at his mother's urging he maintained his ties to friends and relatives in Virginia. Indeed, in 1842 Gouverneur married his first cousin, Patsy Jefferson Cary, the daughter of Nancy's youngest sister, Virginia, for whom Nancy had always professed a special fondness. While marriage between cousins was common among elites in both New York and Virginia as a means of conserving family wealth, Gouverneur's choice of a wife was nonetheless notable in light of the scandal that still tainted the reputation of his beloved mother.[46]

Gouverneur's prospective mother-in-law, Virginia Randolph Cary, was both the sole surviving witness to the incident at Glentivar and a personification of the feminine virtues that Nancy had found so elusive in her own life. Fifty years earlier, Virginia had shared Nancy's room at Glentivar. Since then, however, she had lived, in the words of an admiring cousin, a "secluded" and "virtuous" life as a wife, mother, and pious Christian. Just as Nancy's checkered past had been a barrier to employment in Virginia and social acceptance in New York, her sister's reputation as a model of feminine virtue helped her to succeed as an author and educator during her twenty-nine-year widowhood in Virginia. As the author of *Letters on Female Character* (1828) and other advice books, poems, and stories, Cary instructed young women in piety, modesty, and deference to male authority. When she died in 1852, according to her obituary, the public knew her as a "lady of superior intellect . . . [and] Christian benevolence and charity."[47]

Nancy never earned such public accolades, but neither did she suffer the fate of the fallen heroines of the sentimental novels.[48] Just as Virginia Cary's active widowhood as a teacher, author, and member of various benevolence associations belied her own advice that women remain secluded and submissive within the domestic sphere, Nancy's life after Glentivar and Bizarre shows that cultural prescription was not always reflected in social reality. When Gouverneur Morris, Jr., built St. Ann's Church, married a Virginian of impeccable virtue, and made his first daughter his mother's namesake, he commemorated her love and maternal devotion. Some, like Martha Jefferson Randolph, agreed that Nancy's long years of suffering and cultivating these conventional virtues amply compensated for the offenses of her youth, however horrid they had been. Others probably disagreed. Two things are certain. As a titillating tale or as a parable of malfunctioning patriarchy and fallen virtue, the Bizarre scandal cast a long shadow on the lives of its principals. It also offers observers, then and now, a revealing window onto the values and culture of Jefferson's America.

EPILOGUE

In 1857, St. George Randolph, the sole surviving son and heir of Richard and Judith Randolph, sold his landholdings in Cumberland County, thereby ending more than two centuries of his family's ownership of Bizarre. "Poor St. George," as his family commonly called him, had a difficult life. Completely deaf, he had nonetheless learned to read and write and even developed a fondness for Latin and French literature. He also became an expert hunter. By 1814, however, it had become clear that St. George was insane. For a while, he resided mostly at Roanoke with Jack, who relied on his slaves to restrain his nephew if he became violent or otherwise troublesome. But by December 1816, with Judith dead and Jack returning to Congress, the twenty-four-year-old St. George entered an insane asylum in Philadelphia; he later moved to a similar facility in Baltimore, where he remained until at least 1824. Then, probably some time after 1830, which is when one of Nancy's Morris in-laws saw him in Baltimore, St. George Randolph returned to Virginia.[1]

After Judith's house burned in 1813, no member of the Randolph family returned to Bizarre on a permanent basis, though someone—possibly St. George himself—began to rebuild on the foundation of the old house. After John Randolph of Roanoke died in 1833, St. George became involved, through a "committee" of representatives, in litigation that aimed to reverse Jack's decision to free his slaves and provide them with land in Ohio and instead divide his extensive property among nephews and nieces in Virginia. It is not clear whether St. George decided to contest his uncle's will on his own or whether the men who represented him pressed him to do so. Concern about the consequences of such a large-scale emancipation may have motivated St. George's representatives, who also would have received a fee for their services. Finally, in 1845, the estate was settled: the slaves got their freedom and some $30,000 to purchase land in Ohio, while St. George received property worth more than $50,000. St. George settled in Charlotte County, where he resided either in the home of one of his representatives, Wyatt Cardwell, or on the property he inherited from his uncle. In 1857, St. George Randolph liquidated his landholdings in Cumberland. He transferred "the whole of the Estate called Bizarr" to Patrick H. Jackson of Prince Edward County, who paid $14,065 for the property, and sold several smaller adjacent tracts to other buyers.[2]

Today, an asphalt version of the same road that carried the Randolphs from Bizarre to Glentivar in 1792 and then to the Cumberland County court the following April features a roadside historical marker not far from the site of the Randolphs' home. "Near here is the site of Bizarre, owned in 1742 by Richard Randolph of Curles," states the marker, which was erected by state government in 1929. The site's chief historical significance, its legend asserts, is that "In 1781 . . . John Randolph of Roanoke took refuge at Bizarre with his mother on account of [Benedict] Arnold's invasion [of Virginia]" and that "John Randolph lived here until 1810, when he removed to Roanoke in Charlotte County." Thus, the official history of the commonwealth cited Bizarre for its association with a famous post-revolutionary Virginian while ignoring the house's other residents and the scandal with which the name "Bizarre" was for many synonymous. A decade later, the state of New York erected a similar plaque in the Bronx, near St. Ann's Episcopal Church. Like the Bizarre marker, this one also emphasized the site's connection with famous public men without noting the church's origins as a monument to maternal devotion and domestic happiness.[3]

Although the Bizarre scandal did not become part of the official, largely political, written history of Virginia or even Cumberland County, the Randolphs' story nonetheless survived in the oral tradition of Virginia—and to a lesser extent that of New York, too—long after the deaths of its principals. The gossip of any era is difficult to recover, but one example should suffice to demonstrate the continuing interest in the Randolph family saga through the end of the nineteenth century.

In 1897, John Langbourne Williams, a Richmond banker who had married a granddaughter of Maria Ward, the one-time fiancée of John Randolph of Roanoke, wrote to his fellow Virginian Moncure Daniel Conway, hoping to find out what had happened among the Randolphs of Bizarre. Conway was a liberal reformer, religious freethinker, and prolific author, whose works included the edited writings of revolutionary radical Thomas Paine and a biography of Edmund Randolph, the first attorney general of the United States and grandfather of Williams's wife, Maria Ward Skelton. Conway had left Virginia in 1852, residing in Massachusetts, Washington, Ohio, London, and finally New York, but he remained both interested in and knowledgeable about the history of the Old Dominion. Moreover, he, like Williams, was especially curious about the role the "brilliant and pathetic" John Randolph of Roanoke played in the Bizarre saga and the causes of his eventual estrangement from both Nancy and Judith. "I would like to know the nature of the charges brought against [Nancy] by J.R., which drove her out of Virginia," he mused, "because it appears to me that Nancy may have indeed been a victim of calumny rather than error,—and if so this might be a fact of much interest to the Morris family of [New York] (some of whom I know)."[4]

Figure E.1 Bizarre roadside marker. This historical plaque commemorates Bizarre as the some time home of John Randolph of Roanoke. A similar marker in the South Bronx identifies "St. Ann's Shrine" as the site of the graves of Gouverneur Morris and his half-brother, Lewis, a signer of the Declaration of Independence. Photograph by the author.

As this exchange suggests, the Bizarre scandal (or certain aspects of it) was still widely known in both Virginia and New York more than a century after the Randolphs visited their friends at Glentivar. Yet, the story of the scandal, which had been interpreted variously by the Harrisons' slaves, the Tuckahoe Randolphs, St. George Tucker, Jack Randolph, and finally Nancy herself, was transformed yet again as later generations tried to understand and draw meaning from the Randolph family saga. In 1792–93, Richard had been the main character in a story that illustrated the perils of seduction and malfunctioning patriarchy. After Richard's death, under Jack's influence, Nancy became the story's chief villain, as the scandal itself became a cautionary tale about the corrosive influence of unchaste and immoral women. By the 1820s, however, in the minds of many the Bizarre story had transformed yet again into a tale of redemption, whose heroine overcame a grave but youthful moral lapse to become a virtuous wife and mother.

From the perspective of Conway and Williams in the 1890s, Nancy and especially Jack were the story's main characters. For them, the chief mystery was neither which Randolph brother, Richard or Theo, had fathered Nancy's child, nor whether she had, indeed, committed infanticide that night at Glentivar. Instead, their debate focused on the ensuing scandal itself and particularly Jack's role in reshaping and spreading the sordid rumors about what happened at Glentivar and Bizarre. Had the famous and controversial politician, John Randolph of Roanoke—variously damned and celebrated as an early advocate of states' rights and southern nationalism—slandered Nancy by claiming that she had committed infanticide and murder? Did he wrongly accuse her of having had sexual relations with an enslaved man at Bizarre and of having illicit affairs after her marriage to Gouverneur Morris? Jack's notoriety and erstwhile political influence heightened interest in his role in the scandal, just as his fame had made Bizarre plantation sufficiently noteworthy to merit a roadside historical marker.

But curiosity about Jack's vengeance or veracity also inevitably led people to scrutinize the evidence pertaining to Nancy's life and conduct. The best way, after all, to show that Jack had been a scoundrel was to prove Nancy's innocence. Conversely, if Nancy were guilty of the offenses imputed to her by Jack, he had been at worst a gossip or at best a would-be protector of Gouverneur Morris and his family. Perhaps continuing gossip and curiosity about Nancy inspired her granddaughter and namesake, Anne Cary Morris, to edit and publish a two-volume edition of her grandfather's writings in 1888.

Because Gouverneur Morris had written mainly about political and diplomatic topics even in his diary, such matters dominate this work, as they had the earlier biography by Jared Sparks. Nevertheless, Anne Cary Morris, in completing the pet project that Nancy herself had believed would discredit Jack and others who credited the various and vicious rumors about her past, also included a brief revisionist account of her grandmother's "sad" life. "Obliged by her father's ill-advised second marriage to leave her home," she wrote, Nancy "had struggled some time with but poor success to support herself." When Gouverneur Morris, "the old and trusted friend of her father and mother," heard of Nancy's "reduced pecuniary condition . . . [he] proposed, in the most delicate terms" that she become his hired housekeeper. Anne Cary Morris then quoted letters showing the opposition of Gouverneur's relatives to his marriage, along with his pungent response to their criticism. Elsewhere, she quoted a letter in which Gouverneur asserted his love for Nancy and their happiness at Morrisania, and noted the "dinner-party to celebrate the festival" of their son's second birthday in 1815.[5]

Anne Cary Morris's edition of her grandfather's papers neither mentioned the scandal nor alluded to it directly, thereby following the precedent set by earlier publications, including Nancy's own contributions to *The Columbian.* By 1888, four biographies—two of John Randolph and two of Patrick Henry—had pretty much ignored the Bizarre story, though one of the latter included a brief description of Henry's performance as counsel in *Commonwealth v. Randolph* as evidence of the "wonderful skill" that characterized his "brilliant career as an advocate" in the post-revolutionary era. In 1897, Moncure Conway, aware of the dearth of published work on the Bizarre scandal, informed his correspondent, John Langbourne Williams, that no historian would ever solve the Randolphs' mystery because "of course no historian would rake up in print the particulars of that old scandal and trial of [Nancy] and Richard R."[6]

Conway got it half right: what happened at Glentivar and Bizarre and even two decades later in New York is, indeed, still a mystery, but subsequent historians have probed the sordid details of the story of the Randolphs of Bizarre. While the cultural proclivities of nineteenth-century and early twentieth-century Americans may have made the Bizarre scandal unsuitable and even insignificant fare for serious historians or educational roadside markers, later historians have seen it as a revealing barometer of the power and perils of patriarchy in this watershed era. Some historians have viewed the scandal primarily through the lens of gender, interpreting Nancy's tribulations in Virginia as evidence of the oppression and suppression of white women in the Old South. Others, focusing on the offensive against Richard and the eventual disintegration of his family, have seen the scandal as emblematic of the plight of decayed gentry in post-revolutionary Virginia. One recent account, by contrast, emphasizes the adroit efforts of Richard's defenders to use the newspapers and the courts to influence "an ever-widening 'public' . . . to manipulate the public understanding of their behavior and their character."[7]

My account of the Bizarre scandal highlights all of these themes while using the Randolphs' story to gain insight into the complexity and contradictions of American society and culture in a crucial transitional era. In 1792, the initial gossip about Nancy's stay at Glentivar revealed the power of slaves' words, while the failure of the slaves' gossip to shame Randolph Harrison, who they deemed lacking in paternal benevolence, shows the susceptibility of black words to manipulation by whites whose agendas differed from their own. In *Commonwealth v. Randolph,* Richard's shrewd legal strategy and his stellar defense team were evidence of the persistence of gentry privilege in post-revolutionary America, but the fact that the authorities hauled him off to jail and into court suggested the limits of gentry authority. The gentry's attacks on Richard in 1792–93 signaled divisions in Virginia's once entrenched ruling elite and, like the subsequent conflict between Jack and Nancy, showed the persistent overlap of public and private, political and personal, in Jefferson's America. Nancy Randolph, who saw herself and was seen by others as a tragic victim of seduction, both internalized and overcame the bleak prescriptions of sentimental novelists who sadly consigned their fallen heroines to ignominious death. Her story, like those of her financially troubled sisters, suggests that while women could find male protection appealing, in the absence of such protection they willingly claimed independence and even power.

ABBREVIATIONS

APS	American Philosophical Society
JAH	*Journal of American History*
JER	*Journal of the Early Republic*
JSH	*Journal of Southern History*
LC	Library of Congress
LVa	Library of Virginia, Richmond
MCNY	Museum of the City of New York
Nc-U	Southern Historical Collection, University of North Carolina at Chapel Hill
Ny-CU	Butler Library, Columbia University
NYHS	New-York Historical Society
NYPL	New York Public Library
Vi-Hi	Virginia Historical Society
Vi-WM	Swem Library, College of William and Mary
Vi-U	Alderman Library, University of Virginia
VMHB	*Virginia Magazine of History and Biography*
WMQ	*William and Mary Quarterly*

NOTES

Prologue

1. Historians have reported the name of the Harrisons' home variously as "Glenlyvar" and "Glentivar." I have chosen the latter, which appears in both the Works Progress Administration (WPA) report on the property—which, in turn, was based on county records—as well as in the Harrison family history. See Marie K. Frazee, "Glentivar," WPA typescript, 1936, Cumberland County Circuit Court Office; Margaret Scott Harrison, "Sketch of the Family of Carter Henry Harrison (1736–1793) of 'Clifton' in Cumberland County, Virginia" (Hampton, Va., [typescript], 1959), 18. For details of the Randolphs' trip, see "Notes of Evidence," April 1793, in Charles T. Cullen and Herbert A. Johnson, et al., eds., *The Papers of John Marshall* (Chapel Hill: University of North Carolina Press, 1974–), 2: 170, 173. Richard Randolph owned a phaeton, a four-wheeled horse-drawn carriage with two seats (Cumberland County personal property tax lists, 1792, LVa).

2. Robert Dawidoff, *The Education of John Randolph* (New York: W. W. Norton, 1979), 25, 98–99.

3. Alice P. Kenney and Leslie J. Workman, "Ruins, Romance, and Reality: Medievalism in Anglo-American Imagination and Taste, 1750–1840," *Winterthur Portfolio*, 10 (1975): 131–39, 145, 148–49; Henry Glassie, *Folk Housing in Middle Virginia* (Knoxville: University of Tennessee Press, 1975), 65; Rhys Isaac, *The Transformation of Virginia, 1740–1790* (Chapel Hill: University of North Carolina Press, 1983), 32–42; Frazee, "Glentivar." On the Harrisons' house, which is no longer standing, see "Notes of Evidence," April 1793, in Cullen and Johnson, et al., eds., *Papers of John Marshall*, 2: 170.

4. Harrison, "Sketch of the Family of Carter Henry Harrison," 20, 37; Cumberland County personal property tax books, 1792, LVa; "Notes of Evidence," April 1793, in Cullen and Johnson, et al., eds., *Papers of John Marshall*, 2: 170. It is not clear where Virginia Randolph slept that night.

5. Testimony of Randolph Harrison and Mrs. Randolph [Mary] Harrison, in "Notes of Evidence," April 1793, in Cullen and Johnson, et al., eds., *Papers of John Marshall*, 2:170–72.

6. Ibid., 2: 170, 172. On colic, see Kay K. Moss, *Southern Folk Medicine, 1750–1820* (Columbia: University of South Carolina Press, 1999), 68.

7. "Notes of Evidence," April 1793, in Cullen and Johnson, eds., *Papers of John Marshall*, 2:171–72.

8. Ibid., 2: 171.

9. Ibid., 2: 171–73.

10. "Notes of Evidence," April 1793, in Cullen and Johnson, eds., *Papers of John Marshall,* 2: 171–73, 175.

11. Ibid., 2: 171–72.

12. Ibid., 2: 171.

13. On prescriptions for white women's sexual purity, see, for instance, Catherine Clinton, *The Plantation Mistress: Women's World in the Old South* (New York: Pantheon Books, 1982), 94, 103–22.

14. Ruth H. Bloch, "American Feminine Ideals in Transition: The Rise of the Moral Mother," *Feminist Studies,* 4 (1978): 101–26; Bloch, "The Gendered Meanings of Virtue in Revolutionary America," *Signs,* 13 (1987): 37–58.

15. Thomas Mann Randolph, Jr., to Thomas Mann Randolph, Sr., 17 Jan. 1793, Edgehill-Randolph Papers, Vi-U; William Cabell Bruce, *John Randolph of Roanoke, 1773–1833,* 2 vols. (New York: G. P. Putnam's Sons, 1922), 1: 118; Judith Randolph to Elizabeth Randolph Pleasants, 15 March 1793, in St. George Tucker, "To the Public," *Virginia Gazette, and General Advertiser,* 15 May 1793; St. George Tucker to John H. Randolph, 5 May 1793, in ibid.; Thomas Jefferson to Martha Jefferson Randolph, 28 April 1793, in Edward M. Betts and James Adam Bear, eds., *The Family Letters of Thomas Jefferson* (Columbia: University of Missouri Press, 1966), 115–16. For the law of incest in Virginia, see William Waller Hening, *The Statutes at Large . . . of Virginia,* 13 vols. (Richmond: Samuel Pleasants, Jr., 1819–23), 4: 245–46.

16. Alan Pell Crawford, *Unwise Passions: The True Story of a Remarkable Woman—and the First Great Scandal of Eighteenth-Century America* (New York: Simon & Schuster, 2000), is a popular history and the only book-length account of the episode. Other significant historical accounts are, in chronological order: William Wirt Henry, *Patrick Henry: Life, Correspondence and Speeches,* 3 vols. (1891; New York: Burt Franklin, 1969), 2: 491–92; Bruce, *John Randolph of Roanoke,* 1: 101–26, 2: 272–302; Clifford Raymond, "The Amazing Story of Nancy Randolph," *Liberty,* 27 March 1926, 7–11; 3 April 1926, 31–40; H. J. Eckenrode, *The Randolphs: The Story of a Virginia Family* (Indianapolis, Ind.: Bobbs-Merrill, 1946), 171–81; Howard Swiggett, *The Extraordinary Mr. Morris* (Garden City, N.Y.: Doubleday & Company, Inc., 1952), 270–75; Francis Biddle, "Scandal at Bizarre," *American Heritage,* 12 (Aug. 1961): 10–13, 79–82; Dumas Malone, *Thomas Jefferson and the Ordeal of Liberty* (Boston: Little, Brown, 1962), 173–74; Robert Douthat Meade, *Patrick Henry: Practical Revolutionary* (Philadelphia: J.B. Lippincott, 1969), 417–20; Jonathan Daniels, *The Randolphs of Virginia* (Garden City, N.Y.: Doubleday & Company, Inc., 1972), chap. 8; Leonard Baker, *John Marshall: A Life in Law* (New York: Macmillan, 1974), 139–45; Clinton, *Plantation Mistress,* 112–17; Elizabeth Langhorne, *Monticello: A Family Story* (Chapel Hill, N.C.: Algonquin Books, 1987), 64–71; Phillip Hamilton, *The Making and Unmaking of a Revolutionary Family: The Tuckers of Virginia, 1752–1830* (Charlottesville: University Press of Virginia, 2003), 101–6; Christopher L. Doyle, "The Randolph Scandal in Early National Virginia: New Voices in the 'Court of Honour,'" *JSH,* 69 (2003): 283–318. The novels are: Jay

and Audrey Walz, *The Bizarre Sisters* (New York: Duell, Sloan and Pearce, 1950); Barbara Bentley, *Mistress Nancy* (New York: McGraw-Hill, 1980); and Robert Bloom, *A Generation of Leaves* (New York: Ballantine Books, 1991). For the opera, Garrison Hull's "Nancy," see http://www.novaopera.org/spring_2004.html (accessed 10 March 2004).

17. On Nancy, see Raymond, "Amazing Story," 7; Clinton, *Plantation Mistress,* 117; Langhorne, *Monticello,* 65. Few accounts are critical of Richard. A notably perceptive exception is Doyle, "Randolph Scandal," 289–90.

18. Ann C. Morris to St. George Tucker, [1814?], Dec. 1814, 20 March 1815, Tucker-Coleman Papers, Vi-WM; Ann C. Morris to John Randolph, 16 Jan. 1815, in Bruce, *John Randolph of Roanoke,* 2: 282.

19. Two recent discussions of microhistory and its usefulness to early American historians are Jill Lepore, "Historians Who Love Too Much: Reflections on Microhistory and Biography," *JAH,* 88 (2001): 129–44; Richard D. Brown, "Microhistory and the Post-Modern Challenge," *JER,* 23 (2003): 1–20.

20. See generally, Cathy N. Davidson, *Revolution and the Word: The Rise of the Novel in America* (New York: Oxford University Press, 1986), and Jeffrey L. Passley, *"The Tyranny of Printers": Newspaper Politics in the Early American Republic* (Charlottesville: University Press of Virginia, 2001).

21. Brown, "Microhistory," 15.

22. For a general overview of this transformative period, see Gordon S. Wood, *The Radicalism of the American Revolution* (New York: Alfred A. Knopf, 1991).

Chapter 1

1. Marquis de Chastellux, *Travels in North America in the years 1780, 1781 and 1782,* ed. Howard C. Rice, Jr., 2 vols. (Chapel Hill: University of North Carolina Press, 1963), 2: 427.

2. Jonathan Daniels, *The Randolphs of Virginia* (Garden City, N.Y.: Doubleday & Company, Inc., 1972), 17–19, 23–24. On Bacon's Rebellion and its aftermath, see Edmund S. Morgan, *American Slavery, American Freedom: The Ordeal of Colonial Virginia* (New York: W. W. Norton, 1975), chaps. 13–14.

3. Daniels, *Randolphs of Virginia,* 27, 32, 41–43; Rhys Isaac, *The Transformation of Virginia, 1740–1790* (Chapel Hill: University of North Carolina Press, 1982), 130; Charles S. Sydnor, *Gentlemen Freeholders* (Chapel Hill: University of North Carolina Press, 1952), 15; Daniel Blake Smith, *Inside the Great House: Planter Life in Eighteenth-Century Chesapeake Society* (Ithaca, N.Y.: Cornell University Press, 1980), 61–62, 93–104; *The History of the College of William and Mary: From Its Foundation, 1660, to 1874* (Richmond: J. W. Randolph & English, 1874), 83. On the centrality of patronage in colonial business and politics, see Gordon S. Wood, *The Radicalism of the American Revolution* (New York: Alfred A. Knopf, 1991), 70–89.

4. Daphne S. Gentry and John S. Salmon, *Virginia Land Office Inventory,* 3rd ed. (Richmond: Virginia State Library Archives and Records, 1981), x–xiii; Smith,

Inside the Great House, 242–48; Allan Kulikoff, *Tobacco and Slaves: The Development of Southern Cultures in the Chesapeake, 1680–1800* (Chapel Hill: University of North Carolina Press, 1986), 265–66.

5. Daniels, *Randolphs of Virginia*, 32. On county formation, see Emily J. Salmon and Edward D. C. Campbell, *The Hornbook of Virginia History*, 4th ed. (Richmond: Library of Virginia, 1994), 159–77.

6. Land Patents, Book 9: 576; Book 11: 89, 91, 247, 302; Book 13: 157, 228, 398, 504; Book 15: 99, 149, 525; Book 16: 1; Book 17: 61, 63, 161, 472, 473, 475; Book 19: 701; Book 22: 607; Book 23: 607, 766, 1050, LVa; Daniels, *Randolphs of Virginia*, 42–43; Kulikoff, *Tobacco and Slaves*, 142–44; Warren Billings, John E. Selby, and Thad W. Tate, *Colonial Virginia: A History* (White Plain, N.Y.: KTO Press, 1986), 208–11. See also, Richard L. Morton, *Colonial Virginia*, vol. 2: *Westward Expansion and Prelude to Revolution, 1710–1763* (Chapel Hill: University of North Carolina Press, 1960).

7. William Cabell Bruce, *John Randolph of Roanoke*, 2 vols. (New York: G. P. Putnam's Sons, 1922), 1: 17–41; Phillip Hamilton, *The Making and Unmaking of a Revolutionary Family: The Tuckers of Virginia, 1752–1830* (Charlottesville: University Press of Virginia, 2003), 41–43, 55–59. Like other Powhatans, Pocahontas had two names. See Grace Steele Woodward, *Pocahontas* (Norman: University of Oklahoma Press, 1969), 40.

8. Cynthia Leonard Miller, comp., *The General Assembly of Virginia, July 30, 1619-January 11, 1978: A Bicentennial Register of Members* (Richmond: Virginia State Library, 1987), 82–107. On the local bases of gentry power, see Isaac, *Transformation of Virginia*, 30, 65, 90–94, 111–14; Sydnor, *Gentleman Freeholders*, chaps. 6–7; A. G. Roeber, "Authority, Law, and Custom: The Rituals of Court Day in Tidewater Virginia, 1720 to 1750," *WMQ*, 3rd ser., 37 (1980): 34, 37, 47–48; George Webb, *The Office and Authority of a Justice of the Peace . . .* (Williamsburg, Va.: William Parks, 1736), 201.

9. Jefferson Randolph Anderson, "Tuckahoe and the Tuckahoe Randolphs," *VMHB*, 45 (1937): 70–71; Daniels, *Randolphs of Virginia*, 58–59; Dumas Malone, *Jefferson: The Virginian* (Boston: Little, Brown, 1948), 19–22, 39–40.

10. Thomas Jefferson to Martha Jefferson Randolph, 17 July 1790, in Julian P. Boyd, et al., eds., *The Papers of Thomas Jefferson* (Princeton, N.J.: Princeton University Press, 1950-), 17: 215; Daniels, *Randolphs of Virginia*, 58–59; Anderson, "Tuckahoe and the Tuckahoe Randolphs," 70; Robert K. Brock, *Archibald Cary of Ampthill: Wheelhorse of the Revolution* (Richmond: Garrett and Massie, 1937), 6–20.

11. See generally, T. H. Breen, *Tobacco Culture: The Mentality of the Great Tidewater Planters on the Eve of Revolution* (Princeton, N.J.: Princeton University Press, 1985); W. A. Low, "Merchant and Planter Relations in Post-Revolutionary Virginia, 1783–1789," *VMHB*, 61 (1953): 308–18; Herbert E. Sloan, *Principle and Interest: Thomas Jefferson and the Problem of Debt* (New York: Oxford University Press, 1995), 26–32; Avery O. Craven, *Soil Exhaustion as a Factor in the Agricultural*

History of Virginia and Maryland, 1606–1860 (Urbana: University of Illinois Press, 1926), 72–81.

12. Jessie Thompson Krusen, "Tuckahoe," *Winterthur Portfolio,* 11 (1976): 103–22; Thomas Anburey, *Travels through the Interior Parts of America,* 2 vols. (Boston and New York: Houghton Mifflin Company, 1923), 2: 208; Evelyn M. Acomb, ed., "The Journal of Baron Von Closen," *WMQ,* 3rd ser., 10 (1953): 221–22.

13. Breen, *Tobacco Culture,* 84–85, 106–22, 125–28; John J. McCusker and Russell R. Menard, *The Economy of British America, 1607–1789* (Chapel Hill: University of North Carolina Press, 1985), 120–27; Low, "Merchant and Planter Relations," 309–10, 313–17; Bruce A. Ragsdale, *A Planters' Republic: The Search for Economic Independence in Revolutionary Virginia* (Madison, Wisc.: Madison House, 1996), 23–29, 252, 260–63; Daniels, *Randolphs of Virginia,* 118–19; Brock, *Archibald Cary,* 118–20, 135. Currency conversion is based on John J. McCusker, *How Much Is That in Real Money?* (Worcester, Mass.: American Antiquarian Society, 1992), Table A-3.

14. Netti Schreiner-Yantis and Florence Speakman Love, comps., *The 1787 Virginia Census,* 3 vols. (Springfield, Va.: Genealogical Books in Print, 1987), 1: 143, 2: 791, 797, 1077, 1086; Jackson T. Main, "The One Hundred," *WMQ,* 3rd ser. 11 (1954): 368–83; Low, "Planter and Merchant Relations," 317.

15. Sydnor, *Gentlemen Freeholders,* 27–29, 35–38; Isaac, *Transformation of Virginia,* 110–13; J. R. Pole, *Political Representation in England and the Origins of the American Republic* (New York: Oxford University Press, 1966), 281–86, 293; John E. Selby, *The Revolution in Virginia, 1775–1783* (Williamsburg, Va.: Colonial Williamsburg, 1988), 36–38.

16. Gordon S. Wood, *The Creation of the American Republic, 1776–1787* (Chapel Hill: University of North Carolina Press, 1969), 140; Selby, *Revolution in Virginia,* 116–18; Anthony F. Upton, "The Road to Power in Virginia in the Early Republic," *VMHB,* 62 (1954): 259–63; A. G. Roeber, *Faithful Magistrates and Republican Lawyers: Creators of Virginia's Legal Culture, 1680–1810* (Chapel Hill: University of North Carolina Press, 1981), 173–74, 183–84; Salmon and Campbell, *Hornbook of Virginia History,* 159–77. Both before and after 1776, each county sent two representatives to the lower house. See also, the Virginia constitution, June 1776, in Francis Newton Thorpe, comp., *The Federal and State Constitutions Colonial Charters . . .,* 7 vols. (Washington: U.S. Government Printing Office, 1909), 7: 3815–18.

17. Miller, comp., *General Assembly of Virginia,* 122–218; James LaVerne Anderson, "The Virginia Councillors and the American Revolution," *VMHB,* 82 (1974): 57, 68, 70–71; Main, "The One Hundred," 368–83; Jackson Turner Main, "Government by the People: The American Revolution and the Democratization of the Legislatures," *WMQ,* 3rd ser., 23 (1966): 396, 402. For the 18 burgesses, see Sydnor, *Gentlemen Freeholders,* 88–90.

18. Anburey, *Travels through the Interior Parts of America,* 2: 201, 215, 234.

19. Thomas Mann Randolph, Sr., to Thomas Mann Randolph, Jr., and William Randolph, 10 Oct. 1784, 29 Nov. 1785, Edgehill-Randolph Papers, Vi-U; William H. Gaines, Jr., *Thomas Mann Randolph: Jefferson's Son-in-Law* (Baton Rouge: Louisiana

State University Press, 1966), 13–21; Martha Jefferson Randolph to Ann Cary Randolph Morris, 10 April 1817, Smith Family Papers, APS. On the colonial ideal of a gentleman's education, Richard L. Bushman, *The Refinement of America: Persons, Houses, Cities* (New York: Alfred A. Knopf, 1992), esp. 79–99. On plantation tutors in colonial Virginia, see also Hunter Dickinson Farish, ed., *Journal and Letters of Philip Vickers Fithian, 1773–1774: A Plantation Tutor of the Old Dominion* (Williamsburg, Va.: Colonial Williamsburg, 1963).

20. Anburey, *Travels through the Interior Parts of America,* 2: 210; Thomas Mann Randolph, Sr. to Thomas Elder, 16 March 1786, Edgehill-Randolph Papers, Vi-U; John Leslie to Thomas Mann Randolph, Jr., 6 June 1789, Carr-Cary Papers, Vi-U; Thomas Mann Randolph to Anne Cary Randolph, 1 May 1788, Nicholas P. Trist Papers, Nc-U. On the education of young women generally during this period, see Linda K. Kerber, *Women of the Republic: Intellect and Ideology in Early America* (Chapel Hill: University of North Carolina Press, 1980), chaps. 7–8.

21. Judith Randolph to Martha Jefferson, 5 June 1784, 12 Feb. 1785, Nicholas P. Trist Papers, Nc-U; Ann Cary Randolph to St. George Tucker, Dec. 1801, 3 Feb. 1804, 28 Jan. 1805, 26 Dec. 1814, Tucker-Coleman Papers, Vi-WM; Cathy N. Davidson, *The Revolution and the Word: The Rise of the Novel in America* (New York: Oxford University Press, 1986), esp. chap. 6.

22. Peter S. Randolph to [?] Carr, 28 July 1787, in "Letters from Old Trunks: Randolph-Carr Letter," *VMHB,* 48 (1940): 240–41; John Leslie to Thomas Mann Randolph, Jr., 6 June 1789, Carr-Cary Papers, Vi-U; [John Leslie] to [Ann C. Morris], 25 Dec. 1822, Smith Family Papers, APS; Anne Cary Randolph to St. George Tucker, 23 Sept. 1788, Tucker-Coleman Papers, Vi-WM.

23. St. George Tucker to Richard Rush, 27 Oct. 1813, in "Randolph and Tucker Letters," *VMHB,* 42 (1934): 215; John Randolph to Tudor Randolph, 13 Dec. 1813, Grinnan Family Papers, Vi-Hi; Daniels, *Randolphs of Virginia,* 67; Hugh A. Garland, *The Life of John Randolph of Roanoke,* 2 vols. (1856; New York: Greenwood Press, 1969), 1: 60–61; Charles Campbell, ed., *The Bland Papers . . . ,* 2 vols. (Petersburg, Va., E. & J. Ruffin, 1840–43), 1: xiv–xvi; Phillip Hamilton, "Education in the St. George Tucker Household: Change and Continuity in Jeffersonian Virginia," *VMHB,* 102 (1994): 169, 175; Hamilton, *Making and Unmaking of a Revolutionary Family,* 41–44, 52.

24. Ruth L. Woodward and Wesley Frank Craven, *Princetonians, 1784–1790: A Biographical Dictionary* (Princeton, N.J.: Princeton University Press, 1991), 281–83; J. Jefferson Looney and Ruth Woodward, *Princetonians, 1791–1794: A Biographical Dictionary* (Princeton, N.J.: Princeton University Press, 1991), 89–92, 102–3; John Randolph to Tudor Randolph, 13 Dec. 1813, Grinnan Family Papers, Vi-Hi; Hamilton, *Making and Unmaking of a Revolutionary Family,* 54–55, 85–86.

25. Hamilton, *Making and Unmaking of a Revolutionary Family,* 88–91, 100; St. George Tucker to Theodorick Randolph, 29 Oct. 1788, 20 Feb. 1790, Bryan Family Papers, Vi-U; Theodorick Bland Randolph to St. George Tucker, 12 Nov. 1789; 18 Jan. 1790, Theodorick Bland Randolph Papers, Vi-Hi.

26. Hamilton, *Making and Unmaking of a Revolutionary Family,* 25–29, 73–79, and "Education," 169–80, 184–87, 190; St. George Tucker to Theodorick and John Randolph, 22 April 1787, Tucker-Coleman Papers, Vi-WM.

27. St. George Tucker to Frances Bland Randolph Tucker, 29 June 1786, Tucker-Coleman Papers, Vi-WM; William Maury to Theodorick Bland, 24 Aug. 1786, ibid.; William Maury to St. George Tucker, 24 Oct. 1786, ibid.; Richard Randolph to St. George Tucker, 12 April 1787, ibid.; St. George Tucker to Theodorick and John Randolph, 12 June 1787, ibid.; Richard Randolph to Frances Bland Randolph Tucker, 10 Sept. 1787, 28 Oct. 1787, ibid.; Woodward and Craven, *Princetonians, 1784–1790,* 281–83; Looney and Woodward, *Princetonians, 1791–1794,* 89–92, 102–5; Garland, *Life of John Randolph,* 1: 61–63. On sons' more general challenge to patriarchal authority, see Jay Fliegelman, *Prodigals and Pilgrims: The American Revolution against Patriarchal Authority* (Cambridge, U.K.: Cambridge University Press, 1982).

28. Richard Randolph to Frances Bland Randolph Tucker, 29 June 1786, Tucker-Coleman Papers, Vi-WM; Richard Randolph to "Citizen Creed Taylor," 28 Jan. 1795, 25 April 1795, 6 June 1795, Creed Taylor Papers, Vi-U; John Randolph to Tudor Randolph, 13 Dec. 1813, Grinnan Family Papers, Vi-Hi; Will of Richard Randolph, 18 Feb. 1796, Randolph Family Papers, Vi-Hi. See also F. N. Watkins, "The Randolph Emancipated Slaves," *DeBow's Review,* 24 (April 1858): 285–90.

On the attempts of post-revolutionary Virginians to address the slavery issue, see Douglas R. Egerton, *Gabriel's Rebellion: The Virginia Slave Conspiracies of 1800 and 1802* (Chapel Hill: University of North Carolina Press, 1993), 5–17, 45–48; Robert McColley, *Slavery and Jeffersonian Virginia* (Urbana: University of Illinois Press, 1964), 141–62; David Brion Davis, *The Problem of Slavery in the Age of Revolution, 1770–1823* (Ithaca, N.Y.: Cornell University Press, 1975), 169–84, 196–212; Frederika Teute Schmidt and Barbara Ripel Wilhelm, eds., "Early Proslavery Petitions in Virginia," *WMQ,* 3rd ser., 30 (1973): 133–46.

29. Ann C. Morris to St. George Tucker, 2 March 1815, 20 March 1815, Tucker-Coleman Papers, Vi-WM; Bruce, *John Randolph of Roanoke,* 1: 102, 135; Robert Dawidoff, *The Education of John Randolph* (New York: W. W. Norton, 1979), 98.

30. Smith, *Inside the Great House,* 130–40; Catherine Clinton, *The Plantation Mistress: Woman's World in the Old South* (New York: Pantheon Books, 1982), 60–65; John Randolph to Tudor Randolph, 13 Dec. 1813, Grinnan Family Papers, Vi-Hi; Daniels, *Randolphs of Virginia,* 121–24. On marriages between cousins among southern elites, see also Joan E. Cashin, "The Structure of Antebellum Planter Families: 'The Ties that Bound us Was Strong,' " *JSH,* 56 (1990): 65–67.

31. Anne Cary Randolph to St. George Tucker, 23 Sept. 1788, Tucker-Coleman Papers, Vi-WM; Anderson, "Tuckahoe and the Tuckahoe Randolphs," 71–72. White women in the Chesapeake appear to have married in their early twenties in the latter half of the eighteenth century and somewhat later after 1800. See Kulikoff, *Tobacco and Slaves,* 57–61; Smith, *Inside the Great House,* 128; Jane Turner Censer, *North Carolina Families and Their Children, 1800–1860* (Baton Rouge: Louisiana State University Press, 1984), 91–94; Clinton, *Plantation Mistress,* 60, 233.

32. Anne Cary Randolph to St. George Tucker, 23 Sept. 1788, Tucker-Coleman Papers, Vi-WM; Hamilton, *Making and Unmaking of a Revolutionary Family,* 100.

33. St. George Tucker to Thomas Mann Randolph, 15 Nov. 1789, Tucker-Coleman Papers, Vi-WM. The inscribed window is still legible.

34. Ann C. Morris to St. George Tucker, 20 March 1815, ibid.; Anderson, "Tuckahoe and the Tuckahoe Randolphs," 71–72; John Randolph to Tudor Randolph, 13 Dec. 1813, Grinnan Family Papers, Vi-Hi; Richard Godbeer, *Sexual Revolution in America* (Baltimore: Johns Hopkins University Press, 2002), esp. 265–67, 279, 293–97; Daniel Scott Smith and Michael S. Hindus, "Premarital Pregnancy in America, 1640–1971: An Overview and Interpretation," *Journal of Interdisciplinary History,* 4 (1974–75): 556–59. On the incidence of premarital conception among whites in a contemporary central Virginia county, see Brenda E. Stevenson, *Life in Black and White: Family and Community in the Slave South* (New York: Oxford University Press, 1996), 58–59.

35. Jane Carson, *Colonial Virginians at Play* (Williamsburg, Va.: Colonial Williamsburg, 1989), 5–9; Lee Ludwell Montague, ed., "Cornelia Lee's Wedding, As Reported in a Letter from Ann Calvert Stuart to Mrs. Elizabeth Lee, October 19, 1806," *VMHB,* 80 (1972): 457–60.

36. "The Cynic," 1 Jan. 1790, Tucker-Coleman Papers, Vi-WM. See also William S. Prince, ed., *The Poems of St. George Tucker of Williamsburg, Virginia, 1752–1827* (New York: Vantage Press, 1977), ix-xi, 139. Throughout his adult life Tucker wrote poetry, most of which was political or satirical. A "gammon" is a ham; "eryngo" is the candied root of the sea holly, which many believed to be an aphrodisiac.

37. Bruce, *John Randolph of Roanoke,* 1: 37–38; Suzanne Lebsock, *The Free Women of Petersburg: Status and Culture in a Southern Town, 1785–1860* (New York: W. W. Norton, 1985), 2–6.

38. Richard Randolph to Neill Buchanan, 24 Feb. 1790, 1 Sept. 1790, Tucker-Coleman Papers, Vi-WM; Richard Randolph to Duncan Rose, 27 April 1790, 30 April 1790, 6 May 1790, 11 May 1790, 15 May 1790, 20 May 1790, 23 May 1790, 25 May 1790, 9 June 1790, 12 June 1790, 15 June 1790, 16 June 1790, 17 June 1790, 20 June 1790, 22 June 1790, 25 June 1790, 29 June 1790, 4 July 1790, 22 July 1790, ibid.; John Woodson to St. George Tucker, 11 Jan. 1790, ibid.; James Brown to St. George Tucker, 14 March 1791, ibid.

39. Judith Randolph to Mary Randolph Harrison, 11 Nov. 1790, Harrison Family Papers, Vi-Hi; Hamilton, *Making and Unmaking of a Revolutionary Family,* 103; M. K. Vaughan, *Crucible and Cornerstone: A History of Cumberland County Virginia* (n.p., 1969), 36; *Oxford English Dictionary,* s.v., "bizarre."

40. Land Patents, Book 13, 1725–30: 398, 504; Book 15, 1732–35: 99, 525; Book 16, 1735: 1; Book 17, 1735–38: 61, 63, 161, 472, 473, 475; Book 23, 1743–45: 607, 1059; Book 25, 1745–47: 471; Book 29, 1749–51: 113, LVa; Cumberland County tithable lists, [1754], 1764, LVa; Main, "The One Hundred," 373; Ragsdale, *A Planters' Republic,* 14–18; Philip D. Morgan, *Slave Counterpoint: Black Culture in the Eighteenth-Century Chesapeake and Low Country* (Chapel

Hill: University of North Carolina Press, 1998), 40–42, 98; Philip D. Morgan and Michael L. Nicholls, "Slaves in Piedmont Virginia, 1720–1790," *WMQ,* 3rd ser., 46 (1989): 217, 238–39.

41. U.S. Census, 1790, available at: http://fisher.lib.virginia.edu/cgi-local/ censusbin/census/cen.pl (accessed 10 March 2004); Cumberland County personal property tax lists, 1790, 1791, 1792, LVa; Cumberland County land tax lists, 1790, LVa; Cumberland County tithable lists, 1759, 1768, LVa. The early distribution of tithables in the county was as follows:

	1759 % (N)	1768 % (N)
1-2 tithables	40.2 (220)	40.8 (302)
3-10 tithables	52.5 (287)	51.4 (381)
>10 tithables	7.3 (40)	7.8 (58)
>20 tithables	1.6 (9)	2.6 (19)

Because a typical household would have included only one or two tithables—a man and an adult son—the overwhelming majority of tithables in households claiming more than two would have been slaves. Philip D. Morgan and Michael L. Nicholls were "impressed by the general congruence between tithable and inventory data in Virginia" ("Slaves in Piedmont Virginia," 240n).

42. Marie Keller Frazee, "Bizarre," WPA typescript, 1936, Cumberland County Circuit Court Office; Edward C. Carter II and Angeline Polites, eds., *The Virginia Journals of Benjamin Henry Latrobe,* 2 vols. (New Haven, Conn.: Yale University Press, 1977), 1: 142; Bruce, *John Randolph of Roanoke,* 1: 42–48.

43. Carter and Polites, eds., *Virginia Journals of Benjamin Henry Latrobe,* 1: 142.

44. Ann C. Morris to St. George Tucker, [1814?], 2 March 1815, Tucker-Coleman Papers, Vi-WM; Martha Bland to St. George Tucker, 28 Sept. 1790, ibid.; John Randolph to Tudor Randolph, 13 Dec. 1813, Grinnan Family Papers, Vi-Hi.

45. Walker Maury to Theodorick Bland, 24 Aug. 1786, Tucker-Coleman Papers, Vi-WM; Walker Maury to St. George Tucker, 24 Oct. 1786, ibid.; Martha Bland to St. George Tucker, 28 Sept. 1790, ibid.; Eliza Tucker to St. George Tucker, 29 Aug. 1791, ibid.; John Holcombe to St. George Tucker, 9 Feb. 1792, ibid.; John Randolph to Tudor Randolph, 13 Dec. 1813, Grinnan Family Papers, Vi-Hi. See also Dawidoff, *Education of John Randolph,* 97.

46. Ann C. Morris, to St. George Tucker, [1814?], 2 March 1815, Tucker-Coleman Papers, Vi-WM.

47. Censer, *North Carolina Planters and Their Children,* 21; Thomas Jefferson to Martha Jefferson Randolph, 17 July 1790, in Boyd, et al., eds., *Papers of Thomas Jefferson,* 7: 215.

48. Krusen, "Tuckahoe," 112; Ann C. Morris to St. George Tucker, 2 March 1815, Tucker-Coleman Papers, Vi-WM.

49. Thomas Jefferson to Martha Jefferson Randolph, 17 July 1790, in Boyd, et al., eds., *Papers of Thomas Jefferson,* 7: 215; Mary Jefferson to Thomas Jefferson, 1 May [1791], ibid., 20: 335; Ann Cary Randolph to Mary Johnston, 21 Feb. 1805, Nancy Randolph Papers, Vi-WM; Sarah N. Randolph, *The Domestic Life of Thomas Jefferson* (New York: Harper & Brothers, 1871), 192–94.

50. Carter and Polites, eds., *Virginia Journals of Benjamin Henry Latrobe,* 1: 143; Powhatan Bouldin, *Home Reminiscences of John Randolph of Roanoke* (Danville and Richmond, Va.: Clemmitt & Jones, 1876), 4; Gouverneur Morris to Ann Cary Randolph, 3 March 1809, Gouverneur Morris Papers, LC.

51. "Notes of Evidence," April 1793, in Charles T. Cullen and Herbert A. Johnson, et al., eds., *The Papers of John Marshall* (Chapel Hill: University of North Carolina Press, 1974–), 2: 173–75.

52. For conventionally patriarchal views of family life in revolutionary times, see Mark E. Kann, *A Republic of Men: The American Founders, Gendered Language, and Patriarchal Politics* (New York: New York University Press, 1998), esp. chaps. 2–3.

53. Garland, *Life of John Randolph,* 1: 61–62; Bruce, *John Randolph of Roanoke,* 1: 102–3; St. George Tucker to Richard Rush, 27 Oct. 1813, in "Randolph and Tucker Letters," 215; Richard Randolph to St. George Tucker, 14 March 1793, Randolph Family Papers, Vi-Hi; St. George Tucker to ?, 7 May 1793, Bryan Family Papers, Vi-U.

54. Judith Randolph to St. George Tucker, 21 April 1793, printed in St. George Tucker, "To the Public," *Virginia Gazette, and General Advertiser,* 15 May 1793; Judith Randolph to St. George Tucker, 24 July 1796, 23 June 1797, 20 July 1812, 22 Feb. 1816, Tucker-Coleman Papers, Vi-WM; Judith Randolph to Mary Randolph Harrison, 16 Feb. 1798, 21 July 1797, Harrison Family Papers, Vi-Hi; Richard Randolph to Thomas Tudor Tucker, 15 Feb. 1790, Grinnan Family Papers, Vi-Hi. On naming customs among eighteenth-century Virginians, see Darrett B. And Anita H. Rutman, *A Place in Time: Explicatus* (New York: W. W. Norton, 1984), 89–93.

55. Ann Cary Randolph to St. George Tucker, 29 May 1798, [April 1806], Tucker-Coleman Papers, Vi-WM; Ann C. Morris to St. George Tucker, 26 Dec. 1809, Nov. 1814, Dec. 1814, [1817?], 26 Jan. 1817, 1 March 1817, 18 April 1817, 6 May 1817, 28 June 1817, 9 July 1817, 19 Oct. 1817, ibid.; St. George Tucker to Judith Randolph, 1 July 1814, ibid.; Judith Randolph to Mary Randolph Harrison, 15 Feb. 1796, Harrison Family Papers, Vi-Hi.

56. Mary Jefferson to Thomas Jefferson, 1 May 1791, in Boyd, et al., eds., *Papers of Thomas Jefferson,* 20: 335; Martha Jefferson Randolph to Thomas Jefferson, 20 Feb. 1792, 7 May 1792, ibid., 23: 126, 487; Thomas Mann Randolph, Jr., to Thomas Jefferson, 22 Oct. 1792, ibid., 24: 512; Judith Randolph to Mary Randolph Harrison, 11 Nov. 1790, Harrison Family Papers, Vi-Hi; "Notes of Evidence," April 1793, in Cullen and Johnson, eds., *Papers of John Marshall,* 2: 168–75; Ann C. Morris to St. George Tucker, 2 March 1815, 20 March 1815, Tucker-Coleman

Papers, Vi-WM. For an excellent analysis of changing patterns of visiting during this period, see Joan R. Gundersen, "Kith and Kin: Women's Networks in Colonial Virginia," in *The Devil's Lane: Sex and Race in the Early South,* ed. Catherine Clinton and Michele Gillespie (New York: Oxford University Press, 1997), 90–102.

57. Nannie H. Garrett, "A Sketch of the Life and Parentage of Randolph Harrison, Sr., of Clifton, Cumberland County, Va.," *VMHB,* 35 (1927): 303–6, 455; Margaret Scott Harrison, "Sketch of the Family of Carter Henry Harrison (1736–1793) of 'Clifton' in Cumberland County, Virginia" (Hampton, Va., [typescript], 1959), 37. For fertility rates, see Censer, *North Carolina Planters and Their Children,* 24–25; Sally G. McMillen, *Motherhood in the Old South* (Baton Rouge: Louisiana State University Press, 1990), 31–33, 107.

58. Harrison, "Sketch of the Family of Carter Henry Harrison," 5–12.

59. Ibid., 12–16, 36.

60. Ibid., 17–20; Main, "The One Hundred," 364, 376.

61. Harrison, "Sketch of the Family of Carter Henry Harrison," 19–20; Cumberland County personal property tax books, 1792, LVa.

Chapter 2

1. The quotations are from: Bertram Wyatt-Brown, *Southern Honor: Ethics and Behavior in the Old South* (New York: Oxford University Press, 1982), xv; Edward L. Ayers, *Vengeance and Justice: Crime and Punishment in the 19th-Century American South* (New York: Oxford University Press, 1984), 12. See also Kenneth S. Greenberg, *Honor and Slavery* (Princeton, N.J.: Princeton University Press, 1996), and Steven M. Stowe, *Intimacy and Power in the Old South: Ritual in the Lives of the Planters* (Baltimore: Johns Hopkins University Press, 1987), 6–8.

2. Wyatt-Brown, *Southern Honor,* 233–34; Ayers, *Vengeance and Justice,* 12–13; Greenberg, *Honor and Slavery,* 32–40; Catherine Clinton, *The Plantation Mistress: Women's World in the Old South* (New York: Pantheon Books, 1983), 108–12.

3. "Notes of Evidence," April 1793, in Charles T. Cullen and Herbert A. Johnson, et al., eds., *The Papers of John Marshall* (Chapel Hill: University of North Carolina Press, 1974-), 2: 171; John Randolph memorandum, [1796], Tucker-Coleman Papers, Vi-WM; William Cabell Bruce, *John Randolph of Roanoke, 1773–1833,* 2 vols. (New York: G. P. Putnam's Sons, 1922), 1: 118; John Wayles Eppes to Thomas Jefferson, 1 May 1793, in Julian P. Boyd, et al., eds., *The Papers of Thomas Jefferson* (Princeton, N.J.: Princeton University Press, 1950-), 25: 632–33; James Monroe to Thomas Jefferson, 9 May 1793, ibid., 25: 698.

4. Richard Randolph to St. George Tucker, 14 March 1793, Randolph Family Papers, Vi-Hi; Judith Randolph to Elizabeth Pleasants, 15 March 1793, in "To the Public" (broadside), 5 May 1793, Tucker-Coleman Papers, Vi-WM; Ann C. Morris to St. George Tucker, 2 March 1815, ibid.

5. Richard Randolph to St. George Tucker, 14 March 1793, Randolph Family Papers, Vi-Hi; Ann C. Morris to St. George Tucker, 9 Feb. 1815, Tucker-Coleman Papers, Vi-WM.

6. For a different reading, which sees the Tuckahoe Randolphs as more supportive of Richard, see Christopher L. Doyle, "The Randolph Scandal in Early National Virginia, 1792–1815: New Voices in the 'Court of Honor,'" *JSH*, 69 (2003): 285, 295.

7. Greenberg, *Honor and Slavery,* 33–35, 62–64; Wyatt-Brown, *Southern Honor,* 350, 362–63; Stowe, *Intimacy and Power in the Old South,* chap. 1; Joanne B. Freeman, *Affairs of Honor: National Politics in the New Republic* (New Haven, Conn.: Yale University Press, 2001), 167–71; Richard Randolph to the Public, 29 March 1793, in *Virginia Gazette, and General Advertiser,* 3 April 1793.

8. Greenberg, *Honor and Slavery,* xii, 58, 74; Freeman, *Affairs of Honor,* 171–80; Richard Randolph to St. George Tucker, 14 March 1793, Randolph Family Papers, Vi-Hi.

9. Wyatt-Brown, *Southern Honor,* 363, 384; Ayers, *Vengeance and Justice,* 31–32; Richard Randolph to St. George Tucker, 14 March 1793, Randolph Family Papers, Vi-Hi.

10. Richard Randolph to St. George Tucker, 14 March 1793, Randolph Family Papers, Vi-Hi; Richard Randolph to the Public, 29 March 1793, in *Virginia Gazette, and General Advertiser,* 3 April 1793; St. George Tucker, "To the Public," *Virginia Gazette, and General Advertiser,* 15 May 1793. On the emerging concept of "public opinion," see, for instance [James Madison], "Public Opinion," *National Gazette,* 19 Dec. 1791; Doyle, "Randolph Scandal," 295.

11. Richard Randolph to the Public, 29 March 1793, in *Virginia Gazette, and General Advertiser,* 3 April 1793.

12. Ibid.; Freeman, *Affairs of Honor,* chap. 3; Doyle, "Randolph Scandal," 287, 299.

13. Richard Randolph to the Public, 29 March 1793, in *Virginia Gazette, and General Advertiser,* 3 April 1793.

14. Judith Randolph to Mary Randolph Harrison, 7 April 1793, Harrison Family Papers, Vi-Hi.

15. Order of Joseph Michaux and Anderson Cocke, 18 April 1793, Cumberland County judgments, LVa; Order of N. Patteson, Benjamin Allen, and Anderson Cocke, 22 April 1793, ibid. I am grateful to Brent Tarter for informing me of the existence of these previously undiscovered documents.

16. Garland Evans Hopkins, "The Story of Cumberland County, Virginia," 1942 typescript, Vi-Hi, 14–15, 17, 30; *Cumberland County, Virginia, and its People* (Cumberland, Va.: Cumberland County Historical Society, 1983), 87–88; Cynthia Leonard Miller, comp., *The General Assembly of Virginia, July 30, 1619-January 11, 1978: A Bicentennial Register of Members* (Richmond: Virginia State Library, 1978); Will of George Carrington, 28 Feb. 1785, Cumberland County will book 2, 1769–92, 348. On political leadership in Virginia generally, and in the piedmont in particular, see Charles S. Sydnor, *Gentlemen Freeholders: Political Practices in Washington's Virginia* (Chapel Hill: University of North Carolina Press, 1952),

chaps. 5–6; and Albert H. Tillson, *Gentry and Common Folk: Political Culture on the Virginia Frontier, 1740–1789* (Lexington: University of Kentucky Press, 1991), 24–28.

17. Rhys Isaac, *The Transformation of Virginia, 1740–1790* (Chapel Hill: University of North Carolina Press, 1982), 88–94; Darrett B. and Anita H. Rutman, *A Place in Time: Middlesex County, Virginia, 1650–1750* (New York: W. W. Norton, 1984), 87–93, 120–27, 156–57; A. G. Roeber, *Faithful Magistrates and Republican Lawyers: Creators of Virginia Legal Culture, 1680–1810* (Chapel Hill: University of North Carolina Press, 1981), esp. chap. 2; Lorena S. Walsh, "Community Networks in the Early Chesapeake," in Lois Green Carr, Philip D. Morgan, and Jean B. Russo, eds., *Colonial Chesapeake Society* (Chapel Hill: University of North Carolina Press, 1988), 225–27, 233.

18. Roeber, *Faithful Magistrates and Republican Lawyers,* 86–89; Gwenda Morgan, "Law and Social Change in Colonial Virginia: The Role of the Grand Jury in Richmond County, 1692–1776," *VMHB,* 95 (1987): 453–80; Peter C. Hoffer, "Disorder and Deference: The Paradoxes of Criminal Justice in the Colonial Tidewater," in David J. Bodenhamer and James W. Ely, Jr., eds., *Ambivalent Legacy: A Legal History of the South* (Jackson: University of Mississippi Press, 1984), 191–98; David Thomas Konig, "Country Justice: The Rural Roots of Constitutionalism in Colonial Virginia," in Kermit D. Hall and James W. Ely Jr., eds., *An Uncertain Tradition: Constitutionalism and the History of the South* (Athens: University of Georgia Press, 1989), 72–73; Ayers, *Vengeance and Justice,* 9–19; Peter W. Bardaglio, *Reconstructing the Household: Families, Sex, and the Law in the Nineteenth-Century South* (Chapel Hill: University of North Carolina Press, 1995), 5–23.

19. Roeber, *Faithful Magistrates and Republican Lawyers,* 112–13, 171–78, 188–91, 203–7; St. George Tucker, *Blackstone's Commentaries: with Notes of Reference to the Constitution and Laws of the Federal Government of the United States and of the Commonwealth of Virginia,* 5 vols. (Philadelphia: William Young Birch & Abraham Small, 1803), appendix, 1: 135–37; William Waller Hening, *The Statutes at Large . . . of Virginia,* 13 vols. (Richmond: Samuel Pleasants, Jr., 1809–1823), 12: 754–58. On the changing outlook and growing intellectual sophistication of Virginia's lawyers, see E. Lee Shepard, "Lawyers Look at Themselves: Professional Consciousness and the Virginia Bar, 1770–1850," *American Journal of Legal History,* 25 (1981): 3–14.

20. John Wayles Eppes to Thomas Jefferson, 1 May 1793, in Boyd, et al., eds., *Papers of Thomas Jefferson,* 25: 633.

21. See, generally, Peter Charles Hoffer, "Introduction," in Hoffer and William B. Scott, eds., *Criminal Proceedings in Colonial Virginia: Records of Fines Examinations of Criminals, Trials of Slaves, etc., from March 1710 [1711] to 1754 [Richmond County, Virginia]* (Athens: University of Georgia Press, 1984), xvi–xvii; and Roeber, *Faithful Magistrates and Republican Lawyers,* 83–85. On violence, see also Ayers, *Vengeance and Justice,* 9–19; and Wyatt-Brown, *Southern Honor,* 552–61.

22. Cornelia Hughes Dayton, *Women Before the Bar: Gender, Law, and Society in Connecticut, 1639–1789* (Chapel Hill: University of North Carolina Press, 1995), chap. 6; Kathleen M. Brown, *Good Wives, Nasty Wenches, and Anxious Patriarchs: Gender, Race, and Power in Colonial Virginia* (Chapel Hill: University of North Carolina Press, 1996), 94–102, 145–49; Kirsten Fischer, " 'False, Feigned, and Scandalous Words': Sexual Slander and Racial Ideology Among Whites in Colonial North Carolina," in Catherine Clinton and Michele D. Gillespie, eds, *The Devil's Lane: Sex and Race in the Early South* (New York: Oxford University Press, 1997), 140–43; Fischer, *Suspect Relations: Sex, Race, and Resistance in Colonial North Carolina* (Ithaca, N.Y.: Cornell University Press, 2002), 140–45; Mary Beth Norton, "Slander and Defamation in Seventeenth-Century Maryland," *WMQ*, 3rd ser. (1987): 36–37; Andrew J. King, "Constructing Gender: Sexual Slander in Nineteenth-Century America," *Law and History Review,* 13 (1995): 71–72.

23. The district court heard three presumably related slander cases filed by John and Rebecca Montague (Prince Edward District Court order book, 1789–92, LVa). See also *Thomas and Elizabeth England v. Lucy Jones,* a trespass case involving the sexual reputation of Elizabeth England (Cumberland County order book, 1797, LVa). In several instances, plaintiffs filed suits for trespass in lieu of slander in cases involving sexual reputation. Two examples are *Sarah Gray v. John and Elizabeth Bates,* 1755, Cumberland County suit papers, box 2, LVa; and *Nathaniel Watkins v. Thomas Merriman,* 22 July 1793, Cumberland County order book, 1792–97, LVa. Although this practice cannot have been unique to Cumberland, I have found no discussion of it in the existing historiography. For the general decline of litigation for sexual slander during this period, see Dayton, *Women Before the Bar,* 304–7; Fischer, *Suspect Relations,* 142–43; and Helena M. Wall, *Fierce Communion: Family and Community in Early America* (Cambridge, Mass.: Harvard University Press, 1990), 127–37.

24. Arthur P. Scott, *Criminal Law in Virginia* (Chicago: University of Chicago Press, 1930), 279–81; Morgan, "Law and Social Change in Colonial Virginia," 469, 472; Hoffer, "Introduction," in Hoffer and Scott, eds., *Criminal Proceedings in Colonial Virginia,* xxvi. On interracial sex, see Joshua D. Rothman, *Notorious in the Neighborhood: Sex and Families across the Color Line in Virginia, 1787–1861* (Chapel Hill: University of North Carolina Press, 2003).

25. Cumberland County order books, 27 April 1772, 28 Aug. 1786, 23 March 1789, LVa.

26. Roeber, *Faithful Magistrates and Republican Lawyers,* 89–90n; Morgan, "Law and Social Change in Colonial Virginia," 469, 472; Scott, *Criminal Law in Colonial Virginia,* 280–82; Robert V. Wells, "Illegitimacy and Bridal Pregnancy in Colonial America," in Peter Laslett, Karla Oosterveen, and Richard M. Smith, eds., *Bastardy and its Comparative History* (London: E. Arnold, 1980), 354–56. Similarly, Donna J. Spindel's survey of North Carolina county court records found "the unlikely total of forty-six bastardy prosecutions for the entire colonial period" *(Crime and Society in North Carolina. 1663–1776* [Baton Rouge: Louisiana State University Press,

1989], 62–63). See also Brown, *Good Wives, Nasty Wenches, and Anxious Patriarchs,* 191–92; and Fischer, *Suspect Relations,* 102–4. The numbers of bastardy cases the Cumberland County court considered are as follows:

1749–1760	0
1761–1770	5
1771–1780	2
1781–1790	10
1791–1800	7

The notable increase during the 1780s and 1790s probably reflected the social and economic dislocation of the postwar years.

27. *Elizabeth Bandy v. William Moss,* 1755–56, Cumberland County suit papers, box 1, LVa; *Elizabeth Bandy v. Anne Moss,* 1759, ibid., box 2; *Richard Bandy v. Jarrett Breeky,* 1761, ibid., box 2; *Churchwardens of Southam Parish v. Elizabeth Bandy,* 1754, ibid., box 5; Cumberland County order books, 25 Aug. 1789, 27 Feb. 1792, LVa; Katherine B. Elliott, *Marriage Records, 1749–1840, Cumberland County, Virginia* (South Hill, Va.: n.p., 1969), 31, 46.

28. Cumberland County order books, 24 April 1787, 23 July 1787, LVa.

29. Linda K. Kerber, *Women of the Republic: Intellect and Ideology in Revolutionary America* (Chapel Hill: University of North Carolina Press, 1980), chap. 9; Jan Lewis, "The Republican Wife: Virtue and Seduction in the Early Republic," *WMQ,* 3rd ser., 44 (1987): 689–712; Ruth H. Bloch, "American Feminine Ideals in Transition: The Rise of the Moral Mother," *Feminist Studies,* 4 (1978): 101–26; Bloch, "The Gendered Meanings of Virtue in Revolutionary America," *Signs,* 13 (1987): 37–58.

30. Catherine Kerrison, "By the Book: Eliza Ambler Brent Carrington and Conduct Literature in Late Eighteenth-Century Virginia," *VMHB,* 105 (1997): 27–52; Clinton, *Plantation Mistress,* 113–14.

31. Hening, comp., *Statutes at Large,* 3: 516–17; Peter C. Hoffer and N. E. H. Hull, *Murdering Mothers: Infanticide in England and New England, 1558–1803* (New York: New York University Press, 1981), esp. chap. 1; Allyson N. May, " 'She at first denied it': Infanticide Trials at the Old Baily," in Valerie Frith, ed., *Women and History: Voices from Early Modern England* (Toronto: Coach House Books, 1995), 19; Brown, *Good Wives, Nasty Wenches, and Anxious Patriarchs,* 204.

32. Cumberland County order book, 30 July 1785, LVa; Cumberland County tithable list, 1758, LVa; *Heads of Families at the First Census of the United States Taken in the Year 1790; Records of the State Enumerations, 1782–1785: Virginia* (Baltimore: Genealogical Publishing Co., 1976), 15; Netti Schreiner-Yantis and Florence Speakman Love, *The 1787 Census of Virginia,* 3 vols. (Springfield, Va.: Genealogical Books in Print, 1987), 1: 335. On the preponderance of marginal women among infanticide defendants, see Hoffer and Null, *Murdering Mothers,* chap. 4; Dayton, *Women Before the Bar,* 211–12; and May, " 'She at first denied it,' " 22–23.

The *Virginia Gazette* reported all convictions in capital cases in 1736–39, 1766–69, and 1771–74; during these years the court tendered a total of twelve guilty verdicts—and twelve death sentences—for infanticide. See Scott, *Criminal Law in Colonial Virginia*, 314; and Hugh Rankin, *Criminal Trial Proceedings in the General Court of Colonial Virginia* (Williamsburg, Va.: Colonial Williamsburg, 1965), 136, 205–6.

33. There were also two cases of "maiming" and one of "attempting to deflower" a young unmarried woman (Cumberland County order books, 4 Nov. 1762, 6 Aug. 1764, 26 Nov. 1764, 22 Dec. 1766, LVa; *King v. Archibald Hatcher*, 1762, Cumberland County suit papers, box 9 LVa; *King v. James Theoohilus Dillon*, 1764, ibid., box 11; *King v. Stephen Darby*, 1767, ibid., box 22). The court dismissed one rape case and fined the defendant a nominal one shilling in the other. On the infrequency of rape prosecutions in Virginia generally, see Rankin, *Criminal Trial Proceedings*, 219–22; and Brown, *Good Wives, Nasty Wenches, and Anxious Patriarchs*, 207–11.

    The Cumberland County order books list the following prosecutions of slaves between 1749 and 1800:

Arson	1
Burglary	2
Poisoning	9
Murder	12
Theft	1
Unspecified felony	2

    The court acquitted seven of the above slave defendants—of whom six had been charged with murder and one with poisoning—and convicted the others.

34. Philip J. Schwarz, *Twice Condemned: Slaves and the Criminal Laws of Virginia, 1705–1865* (Baton Rouge: Louisiana State University Press, 1988), 16–17; Rankin, *Criminal Trial Proceedings*, 78–79; Roeber, *Faithful Magistrates and Republican Lawyers*, 42–43.

35. Cumberland County order books, 15 June 1761, 28 July 1761, 30 April 1763, 9 June 1766, 7 July 1771, 28 Sept. 1772, 30 July 1785, 22 Dec. 1788, LVa.

36. On the Chiswell case, see Carl Bridenbaugh, "Violence and Virtue in Virginia, 1766: or, The Importance of the Trivial," *Massachusetts Historical Society Proceedings*, 76 (1964): 3–29; and Woody Holton, *Forced Founders: Indians, Debtors, Slaves, and the Making of the American Revolution in Virginia* (Chapel Hill: University of North Carolina Press, 1999), 39–43.

37. Cumberland County order book, 29 April 1793, LVa. An excellent brief analysis of the courts' proceedings and of Richard's defense appears in Doyle, "Randolph Scandal," 293–98.

38. Bruce, *John Randolph of Roanoke*, 1: 20–21; Hopkins, "Story of Cumberland County," 46; *Cumberland County, Virginia, and its People: First Supplement* (Cumberland, Va.: Cumberland County Historical Society, 1987), 5; Cumberland

County land tax lists, 1793, LVa; Cumberland County personal property tax lists, 1793, LVa.

39. Order of Joseph Michaux and Anderson Cocke, 19 April 1793, Cumberland County judgments, LVa; Summons [2], 24 April 1793, ibid.; John Wayles Eppes to Thomas Jefferson, 1 May 1793, in Boyd, ed., *Papers of Thomas Jefferson*, 25: 633.

40. Richard Randolph to the Public, 29 March 1793, in *Virginia Gazette, and General Advertiser*, 3 April 1793.

41. Roeber, *Faithful Magistrates and Republican Lawyers*, 203–4, 214–15; Charles T. Cullen, *St. George Tucker and Law in Virginia, 1772–1804* (New York: Garland Publishing, 1987), 40–41; Rankin, *Criminal Trial Proceedings*, 78–79, 89–90.

42. For Tucker's views on untrained judges and juries, see Tucker, *Blackstone's Commentaries*, app., 1: 135–37; 4: 64–67.

43. Albert J. Beveridge, *The Life of John Marshall*, vol. 2: *Politician, Diplomatist, and Statesman, 1789–1801* (Boston and New York: Houghton Mifflin Company, 1919), 181, 185–86; Cullen and Johnson, eds., *Papers of John Marshall*, 2: 140–45, 3: 31n; Will of Richard Randolph, 18 Feb. 1796, Randolph Family Papers, Vi-Hi; Bruce, *John Randolph of Roanoke*, 1: 112.

44. Richard R. Beeman, *Patrick Henry: A Biography* (New York: McGraw-Hill, 1974), 13–24; Clement Eaton, "The Mirror of the Southern Colonial Lawyer: The Fee Books of Patrick Henry, Thomas Jefferson, and Waightsill Avery," *WMQ*, 3rd ser., 8 (1951): 524, 533; St. George Tucker to William Wirt, c.1800 [extract], Henry Family Papers, Vi-Hi; Henry St. George Tucker, "Patrick Henry and St. George Tucker," undated unpublished essay, ibid.

45. William Wirt Henry, *Patrick Henry: Life, Correspondence and Speeches*, 3 vols. (1891; New York: Burt Franklin, 1969), 2: 490–91.

46. Beveridge, *Life of John Marshall*, 2: 186–88; Beeman, *Patrick Henry*, 177–80; Thomas E. Buckley, S.J., *The Great Catastrophe of My Life: Divorce in the Old Dominion* (Chapel Hill: University of North Carolina Press, 2002), 19.

47. Beveridge, *Life of John Marshall*, 2: 192–94; Jay Fliegelman, *Declaring Independence: Jefferson, Natural Law, and the Culture of Performance* (Stanford, Calif.: Stanford University Press, 1993), 95–96; Unsigned account of Patrick Henry as orator, c.1800, Henry Family Papers, Vi-Hi.

48. Sandra M. Gustafson, *Eloquence Is Power: Oratory and Performance in Early America* (Chapel Hill: University of North Carolina Press, 2000), 141–42, 162–65; Fliegelman, *Declaring Independence*, 94–95; St. George Tucker to William Wirt, c.1800, Henry Family Papers, Vi-Hi.

49. Beeman, *Patrick Henry*, 1, 42–43; Spencer Roane to William Wirt, c. 1800, Henry Family Papers, Vi-Hi; Diary of Richard N. Venable, 5 April 1791, 3 Sept. 1791, Vi-Hi.

50. Daniel Blake Smith, *Inside the Great House: Planter Family Life in Eighteenth-Century Chesapeake Society* (Ithaca, N.Y.: Cornell University Press, 1980), esp. chap. 1; Jan Lewis, *The Pursuit of Happiness: Family and Values in Jefferson's Virginia* (Cambridge, U.K.: Cambridge University Press, 1983); Lewis, " 'The Blessings of

Domestic Society': Thomas Jefferson's Family and the Transformation of American Politics," in Peter Onuf, ed., *Jeffersonian Legacies* (Charlottesville: University Press of Virginia, 1993), 109–46; Andrew Burstein, *Sentimental Democracy: The Evolution of America's Romantic Self-Image* (New York: Hill and Wang, 1999), esp. 10–21. See also Janet Todd, *Sensibility: An Introduction* (New York: Methuen, 1986), esp. 2–18; and G. J. Barker-Benfield, "The Origins of Anglo-American Sensibility," in Lawrence J. Friedman and Mark D. Garvie, eds., *Charity, Philanthropy, and Civility in American History* (Cambridge, U.K.: Cambridge University Press, 2003), 71–90.

51. "Notes of Evidence," April 1793, in Cullen and Johnson, eds., *Papers of John Marshall,* 2: 173–74; Kay K. Moss, *Southern Folk Medicine, 1750–1820* (Columbia: University of South Carolina Press, 1999), 135–37.

52. "Notes of Evidence," April 1793, in Cullen and Johnson, eds., *Papers of John Marshall,* 2: 168–70, 172–73, 175.

53. Ibid., 2: 170–71; Clinton, *Plantation Mistress,* 143–46; Marli F. Wiener, *Mistresses and Slaves: Plantation Women in South Carolina, 1830–80* (Urbana: University of Illinois Press, 1998), 44–46; Sally G. McMillen, *Motherhood in the Old South: Pregnancy, Childbirth, and Infant Rearing* (Baton Rouge: Louisiana State University Press, 1990), chap. 6. On the healing work of enslaved women and on the exchange of herbal remedies between slaveholders and the enslaved, see Sharla M. Fett, *Working Cures: Healing, Health, and Power on Southern Plantations* (Chapel Hill: University of North Carolina Press, 2002), 62–67, 113–25.

54. "Notes of Evidence," April 1793, in Cullen and Johnson, eds., *Papers of John Marshall,* 2: 168–69; Robert S. Munger, "Guaiacum: The Holy Wood from the New World," *Journal of the History of Medicine and Allied Sciences,* 4 (1949): 218; Moss, *Southern Folk Medicine,* 82, 84, 186; Benjamin Barton Smith, *Professor Cullen's Treatise of the Materia Medica* (Philadelphia: Edward Parker, 1812), 2: 139–42; William Cook, M.D., *The Physiomedical Dispensary* (Cincinnati: William H. Cook, 1869), available at: http://medherb.com/cook/html/GUAIACUM_OFFICINALE.htm#_VPID_175 (accessed 10 March 2004); *PDR for Herbal Medicines,* 1st ed. (Montvale, N.J.: Medical Economics Company, 1998), 884.

55. Smith, *Professor Cullen's Treatise of the Materia Medica,* 2: 142; John M. Riddle, *Eve's Herbs: A History of Abortion and Contraception in the West* (Cambridge, Mass.: Harvard University Press, 1997), 193–96, 202; Cook, *Physiomedical Dispensary.* The fact that modern authorities on medicinal herbs do not classify gum guaiacum as an abortifacient suggests that it was less effective than some other herbs. See, for instance, *PDR for Herbal Medicines,* 884, and "The Medicinal Herb MedFAQ: Herbal Abortives and Birth Control," available at: http://www.ibiblio.org /herbmed/faqs/medi-3–7-abortives.html (accessed 10 March 2004).

56. Ibid., 2: 173, 175.

57. Ibid., 2: 169; Henry, *Patrick Henry,* 2: 491–92; On the employment of women as expert witnesses in infanticide and related criminal cases, see Laurel Thatcher Ulrich, *A Midwife's Tale: The Life of Martha Ballard Based on Her Diary, 1785–1812*

(New York: Alfred A. Knopf, 1990), 115–26; Brown, *Good Wives, Nasty Wenches, and Anxious Patriarchs,* 99–100, 285–86, 306–12; Mary Beth Norton, *Founding Mothers and Fathers: Gendered Power and the Forming of American Society* (New York: Alfred A. Knopf, 1996), 253, 261.

58. "Notes of Evidence," April 1793, in Cullen and Johnson, eds., *Papers of John Marshall,* 2: 175–78.

59. John Wayles Eppes to Thomas Jefferson, 1 May 1793, in Boyd., ed., *Papers of Thomas Jefferson,* 25: 632–33; James Monroe to Thomas Jefferson, 9 May 1793, ibid., 25: 698; Martha Jefferson Randolph to Thomas Jefferson, 16 May 1793, ibid., 26: 53.

60. St. George Tucker to [?], 7 May 1793, Bryan Family Papers, Vi-Hi.

Chapter 3

1. St. George Tucker, "To the Public" (broadside), 5 May 1793, Tucker-Coleman Papers, Vi-WM.

2. On newspapers, see Jeffrey L. Passley, *"The Tyranny of Printers": Newspaper Politics in the Early American Republic* (Charlottesville: University Press of Virginia, 2001), esp. 11–13. On the mails, see Richard R. John, *Spreading the News: The American Postal System from Franklin to Morse* (Cambridge, Mass.: Harvard University Press, 1995), esp. 42–44, 156–61.

3. William Maxwell, *A Memoir of the Rev. John H. Rice, D.D., the First Professor of Christian Theology in Union Theological Seminary, Virginia* (Philadelphia: J. Whetham; Richmond: R.I. Smith, 1835), 59–60n.

4. F. G. Bailey, "Gifts and Poison," in *Gifts and Poison: The Politics of Reputation,* ed. F. G. Bailey (New York: Schocken Books, 1981), 2, 19–20; Jörg R. Bergmann, *Discreet Indiscretions: The Social Organization of Gossip,* trans. John Bednarz, Jr., and Eva Kafka Barron (New York: Aldine de Gruyter, 1993), chap. 5; Sally Engle Merry, "Rethinking Gossip and Scandal," in Donald Black, ed., *Toward a General Theory of Social Control,* vol. 1: *Fundamentals* (Orlando, Fla., and New York: Academic Press, 1984), 272–77.

5. Sylvia R. Frey, *Water From the Rock: Black Resistance in a Revolutionary Age* (Princeton, N.J.: Princeton University Press, 1991), esp. chaps. 7–8; Richard S. Dunn, "Black Society in the Chesapeake, 1776–1810," in Ira Berlin and Ronald Hoffman, eds., *Slavery and Freedom in the Age of the American Revolution* (Urbana: University of Illinois Press, 1983), 49–82; Douglas R. Egerton, *Gabriel's Rebellion: The Virginia Slave Conspiracies of 1801 and 1802* (Chapel Hill: University of North Carolina Press, 1993), 6–13.

6. Dunn, "Black Society in the Chesapeake," 74–80; Lorena S. Walsh, "Work and Resistance in the New Republic: The Case of the Chesapeake, 1770–1820," in Mary Turner, ed., *From Chattel Slaves to Wage Slaves: The Dynamics of Labor Bargaining in the Americas* (Kingston, Jamaica: Ian Randle Publishers, 1995), 97–122; Philip D. Morgan, *Slave Counterpoint : Black Culture in the Eighteenth-Century Chesapeake and Lowcountry* (Chapel Hill: University of North Carolina Press, 1998), 490. See

http://fisher.lib.virginia.edu/census/ for census data. Note that because the 1790 U.S. Census for Virginia is not extant, the state census of 1782–83 is typically substituted.

7. Dunn, "Black Society in the Chesapeake," 58–59; Allan Kulikoff, "Uprooted Peoples: Black Migrants in the Age of the American Revolution 1790–1820," in Berlin and Hoffman, eds., *Slavery and Freedom in the Age of the American Revolution,* 143–171.

8. James Sidbury, *Ploughshares into Swords: Race, Rebellion, and Identity in Gabriel's Virginia* (Cambridge, U.K.: Cambridge University Press, 1997), 27–39; Brenda E. Stevenson, *Life in Black and White: Family and Community in the Slave South* (New York: Oxford University Press, 1996), 171–75; Egerton, *Gabriel's Rebellion,* 16–17; Morgan, *Slave Counterpoint,* 511. The total population of Cumberland County increased by seventeen percent between 1783 and 1800; slave population grew twenty-two percent during this period.

9. Stevenson, *Life in Black and White,* 164–65, 204–24; Ira Berlin, *Many Thousands Gone: The First Two Centuries of Slavery in North America* (Cambridge, Mass.: Harvard University Press, 1998), 268–69.

10. Cumberland County personal property tax lists, 1790–93, LVa.

11. Cumberland County personal property tax lists, 1809–39, LVa; Cumberland County land tax lists, 1796–1804, LVa; Will of Carter Henry Harrison, 8 Oct. 1793, Cumberland County will books, 3: 20–221, LVa; Will of Randolph Harrison, 13 July 1839, ibid., 10: 164; Margaret Scott Harrison, "Sketch of the Family of Carter Henry Harrison (1736–1793) of 'Clifton' in Cumberland County, Virginia" (Hampton, Va., [typescript], 1959), 12, 14–20.

12. Randolph Harrison to Mary Randolph Harrison, 9 Dec. 1826, 18 Jan. 1828, 18 Jan. 1829, Harrison Family Papers, Vi-Hi; Affidavit of Robert Lewis, 23 July 1824, ibid.; Affidavit of Charles A. Merryman, 18 Aug. 1828, ibid.; Harrison, "Sketch of the Family of Carter Henry Harrison," 20.

13. Will of Ryland Randolph, 7 Dec. 1784, Henrico County will books, 1: 179–80. On Tucker, who in 1796 became the only Virginia statesman to propose a practical plan for the abolition of slavery in the state, see Robert McColley, *Slavery and Jeffersonian Virginia* (Urbana: University of Illinois Press, 1964), 115; Phillip Hamilton, *The Making and Unmaking of a Revolutionary Family: The Tuckers of Virginia, 1752–1830* (Charlottesville: University Press of Virginia, 2003), 80–83; St. George Tucker, *A Dissertation on Slavery: With a Proposal for the Gradual Abolition of it in the State of Virginia* (Philadelphia: Mathew Carey, 1796).

14. On Richard, see Hugh A. Garland, *The Life of John Randolph of Roanoke,* 2 vols. (1856; New York: Greenwood Press, 1969), 1: 63.

15. On slave resistance in general, see, for example, Eugene D. Genovese, *Roll, Jordan, Roll: The World the Slaves Made* (New York: Pantheon Books, 1974), 587–621, 648–57; Berlin, *Many Thousands Gone,* 277–82.

16. James C. Scott, *Weapons of the Weak: Everyday Forms of Peasant Resistance* (New Haven, Conn.: Yale University Press, 1985); Kenneth S. Greenberg, *Honor and Slavery* (Baltimore: Johns Hopkins University Press, 1996), 34, 39–42.

17. Christopher L. Doyle, "The Randolph Scandal in Early National Virginia, 1792–1815: New Voices in the 'Court of Honor,'" *JSH*, 69 (2003): 295–97.

18. Scott, *Weapons of the Weak,* 282. On the growing expectation for planter benevolence or paternalism in late eighteenth-century Virginia, see Philip D. Morgan, "Three Planters and Their Slaves: Perspectives on Slavery in Virginia, South Carolina, and Jamaica," in Winthrop D. Jordan and Sheila L. Skemp, eds., *Race and Slavery in the Colonial South* (Jackson: University Press of Mississippi, 1987), 39–41, 50–54, 79.

19. Morgan, *Slave Counterpoint,* chaps. 6–7; Timothy James Lockley, *Lines in the Sand: Race and Class in Lowcountry Georgia, 1750–1860* (Athens: University of Georgia Press, 2001), chaps. 2–3; Betty Wood, *Women's Work, Men's Work: The Informal Slave Economies of Lowcountry Georgia* (Athens: University of Georgia Press, 1995), 12–14, 49–52, 71; Marli F. Weiner, *Mistresses and Slaves: Plantation Women in South Carolina, 1830–80* (Urbana: University of Illinois Press, 1997), 120–21; Joshua D. Rothman, *Notorious in the Neighborhood: Sex and Families across the Color Line in Virginia, 1787–1861* (Chapel Hill: University of North Carolina Press, 2003), 13.

20. Jack P. Greene, ed., *The Diary of Landon Carter of Sabine Hall, 1752–1778,* 2 vols. (Charlottesville: University Press of Virginia, 1965), passim. On Carter's reading, see ibid., 1: 530, 2: 882, 2: 914, 2: 954, 2: 958, 2: 960, 2: 1011. On the sources of his political and military news, see also ibid., 1: 529, 2: 860, 2: 953, 2: 967–68, 2: 972, 2: 988, 2: 999, 2: 1007, 2: 1056–57, 2: 1071, 2: 1074, 2: 1091, 2: 1097, 2: 1131–33. On gossip as a "woman's weapon," see Mary Beth Norton, *Founding Mothers and Fathers: Gendered Power and the Forming of American Society* (New York: Alfred A. Knopf, 1996), 253; Kathleen M. Brown, *Good Wives, Nasty Wenches, and Anxious Patriarchs: Gender, Race, and Power in Colonial Virginia* (Chapel Hill: University of North Carolina Press, 1996), 99–100, 285–86.

21. Greene, ed., *Diary of Landon Carter,* passim. See also Hunter Dickinson Farish, ed., *The Journal and Letters of Philip Vickers Fithian: A Plantation Tutor of the Old Dominion, 1773–1774* (Williamsburg, Va.: Colonial Williamsburg, 1957), esp. 86–88, 110, 187, 203; Richard D. Brown, *Knowledge is Power: The Diffusion of Information in Early America, 1700–1865* (New York: Oxford University Press, 1989), 254–56.

22. Greene, ed., *Diary of Landon Carter,* 2: 732–33.

23. Ibid., esp. 1: 401, 1: 473–74, 1: 483–84, 2: 806–7; T. H. Breen, *Tobacco Culture: The Mentality of the Great Tidewater Planters on the Eve of Revolution* (Princeton, N.J.: Princeton University Press, 1985), 60–72, 85–91, 175–86. On Carter's diary as both a source and reflection of his changing self-definition, see Rhys Isaac, "Stories and Constructions of Identity: Folk Tellings and Diary Inscriptions on Revolutionary Virginia," in Ronald Hoffman, Mechal Sobel, and Fredrika J. Teute, eds., *Through a Glass Darkly: Reflections on Personal Identity in Early America* (Chapel Hill: University of North Carolina Press, 1997), 218–25. For men's gossip about sexual escapades, see,

for instance, Farish, ed., *Journal and Letters of Philip Vickers Fithian,* 85–86; James Gordon, "Diary of Colonel James Gordon . . . ," *WMQ,* 1st ser., 12 (1903): 1–2.

24. See, generally, Rhys Isaac, *The Transformation of Virginia, 1740–1790* (Chapel Hill: University of North Carolina Press, 1982), chap. 13; Wood, *The Radicalism of the American Revolution* (New York: Alfred A. Knopf, 1992), 30–33, 115–17, 177–79; Jan Lewis, *The Pursuit of Happiness: Family and Values in Jefferson's Virginia* (Cambridge, U.K.: Cambridge University Press, 1983), chaps. 1 and 4; Daniel Blake Smith, *Inside the Great House: Planter Family Life in Eighteenth-Century Chesapeake Society* (Ithaca, N.Y.: Cornell University Press, 1980), chap. 1.

25. See Jan Ellen Lewis, "The White Jeffersons," in Jan Ellen Lewis and Peter S. Onuf, eds., *Sally Hemings and Thomas Jefferson: History, Memory, and Civic Culture* (Charlottesville: University Press of Virginia, 1999), 144–45.

26. F. G. Bailey, "Gifts and Poison," 19–20; Wood, *Radicalism of the American Revolution,* 271–85.

27. Martha Jefferson Randolph to Thomas Jefferson, 16 May 1793, in Julian P. Boyd, ed., *The Papers of Thomas Jefferson* (Princeton, N.J.: Princeton University Press, 1950-), 26: 53.

28. Garland, *Life of John Randolph,* 1:63; Will of Richard Randolph, 18 Feb. 1796, Randolph Family Papers, Vi-Hi; McColley, *Slavery in Jeffersonian Virginia,* 141–62; Frederika Teute Schmidt and Barbara Ripel Wilhelm, eds., "Early Proslavery Petitions in Virginia," *WMQ,* 3rd ser., 30 (1973): 133–46. A balanced assessment of Jefferson's words and actions (or lack thereof) pertaining to slavery can be found in William Cohen, "Thomas Jefferson and the Problem of Slavery," *JAH,* 56 (1969): 503–526.

29. St. George Tucker to [?], 7 May 1793, Bryan Family Papers, Vi-U.

30. Richard D. Brown, *The Strength of A People: The Idea of an Informed Citizenry in America, 1650–1870* (Chapel Hill: University of North Carolina Press, 1996), esp. 11–15, and Brown, *Knowledge is Power,* 12–13; John, *Spreading the News,* 30–36; Wood, *Radicalism of the American Revolution,* 347–56; Christopher Grasso, *A Speaking Aristocracy: Transforming Public Discourse in Eighteenth-Century Connecticut* (Chapel Hill: University of North Carolina Press, 1999), 406–31; David Waldstreicher, *In the Midst of Perpetual Fetes: The Making of American Nationalism, 1776–1820* (Chapel Hill: University of North Carolina Press, 1997), 10–11; Passley, *"The Tyranny of Printers."*

    By 1793, Virginia had fourteen newspapers that were scattered throughout the state, compared to only two, both of which were published in Williamsburg, in the last decade of the colonial era. Between 1736 and 1766, the weekly *Virginia Gazette* of Williamsburg was the province's only newspaper. See Clarence S. Brigham, *History and Bibliography of American Newspapers, 1690–1820,* 2 vols. (Worcester, Mass.: American Antiquarian Society, 1947), 2: 1103–68.

31. Wood, *Radicalism of the American Revolution,* 70–81, 174–80; Grasso, *Speaking Aristocracy,* 281–84, 302–26; Michael Warner, *Letters of the Republic: Publication and the Public Sphere in Eighteenth-Century America* (Cambridge, Mass.: Harvard

University Press, 1990), 42–43, 67–72; Robert M. Weir, "The Role of the Newspaper Press in the Southern Colonies on the Eve of the Revolution: An Interpretation," in Bernard Bailyn and John B. Hench, eds., *The Press and the American Revolution* (Worcester, Mass.: American Antiquarian Society, 1980), 144–46; Passley, *The "Tyranny of Printers"*, 11–13, 48–50, 153–75.

32. Joanne B. Freeman, *Affairs of Honor: National Politics in the New Republic* (New Haven, Conn.: Yale University Press, 2001); Freeman, "Slander, Poison, Whispers, and Fame: Jefferson's 'Anas' and Political Gossip in the Early Republic," *JER*, 15 (1995): 28–29, 32, 51–52; Robert H. Wiebe, *The Opening of American Society: From the Adoption of the Constitution to the Eve of Disunion* (New York: Alfred A. Knopf, 1984), 99–102; Joshua D. Rothman, "James Callendar and Social Knowledge of Interracial Sex in Antebellum Virginia," in Lewis and Onuf, eds., *Sally Hemings and Thomas Jefferson*, 88–99, 106; Michael Drury, *"With the Hammer of Truth": James Thomson Callendar and America's Early National Heroes* (Charlottesville: University Press of Virginia, 1990), 93–94, 148–52, 160; Charles A. Jellison, "That Scoundrel Callender," *VMHB*, 67 (1959): 295–306; Jacob Katz Cogan, "The Reynolds Affair and the Politics of Character," *JER*, 16 (1996): 389–417.

33. Bertram Wyatt-Brown, *Southern Honor: Ethics and Behavior in the Old South* (New York: Oxford University Press, 1982), 295–97, 305–24; Peter Bardaglio, " 'An Outrage upon Nature': Incest and the Law in the Nineteenth-Century South," in Carol Bleser, ed., *In Joy and in Sorrow: Women, Family, and Marriage in the Victorian South, 1830–1900* (New York: Oxford University Press, 1991), 32–51; Catherine Clinton, *The Plantation Mistress: Woman's World in the Old South* (New York: Pantheon, 1982), esp. chap. 11. See generally, Rothman, *Notorious in the Neighborhood*, for the impressive variety of interracial sexual relationships that post-revolutionary Virginians at least tacitly accepted.

34. "Lee, Henry," in *American National Biography* (New York: Oxford University Press, 1999), 13: 374–75; Paul C. Nagel, *The Lees of Virginia: Seven Generations of an American Family* (New York: Oxford University Press, 1990), 206–12.

35. Nagel, *Lees of Virginia*, 206–12; Annette Gordon-Reed, *Thomas Jefferson and Sally Hemings: An American Controversy* (Charlottesville: University Press of Virginia, 1997), 23, 160–61. Liaisons between brothers- and sisters-in-law, which resulted in four appellate-level court cases between 1800 and 1900, accounted for eight percent of all incest cases that came before southern high courts during this period (Bardaglio, " 'An Outrage upon Nature,' " 39–40).

36. Woody Holton, *Forced Founders: Indians, Debtors, Slaves, and the Making of the American Revolution in Virginia* (Chapel Hill: University of North Carolina Press, 1999), 216–18.

37. Rothman, "James Callendar and Social Knowledge of Interracial Sex," 89–90, 98–99, 106; Gordon-Reed, *Thomas Jefferson and Sally Hemings*, 63, 65–66; Nagel, *Lees of Virginia*, 212–13, 219.

38. [Washington] *National Intelligencer*, 11 March 1830; *Richmond Enquirer*, 16 March 1830; Henry Lee to William Berkeley Lewis, 26 July 1833, Lee Family Papers,

Vi-Hi. See also Douglas Southall Freeman, *R. E. Lee: A Biography,* 4 vols. (New York: Charles Scribner's Sons, 1934), 1: 97–98.

39. Thomas E. Buckley, S.J., *The Great Catastrophe of My Life: Divorce in the Old Dominion* (Chapel Hill: University of North Carolina Press, 2002), 25–26, 192, 215; Suzanne Lebsock, *The Free Women of Petersburg: Status and Culture in a Southern Town, 1784–1860* (New York: W. W. Norton, 1984), 69; *Virginia Argus,* 11 July 1811.

40. St. George Tucker, "To the Public" (broadside), 5 May 1793, Tucker-Coleman Papers, Vi-WM.

41. Ibid.

42. Judith Randolph to Elizabeth Randolph Pleasants, 15 March 1793, in ibid.

43. Judith Randolph to St. George Tucker, 21 April 1793, in ibid.

44. Ibid.

45. John Page to St. George Tucker, 17 Aug. 1793, Tucker-Coleman Papers, Vi-WM; Ann Cary Randolph to St. George Tucker, 8 Nov. 1808, 17 Dec. 1808, ibid.

46. Cathy N. Davidson, *Revolution and the Word: The Rise of the Novel in America* (New York: Oxford University Press, 1986), esp. 110–35; Sarah Emily Newton, "Wise and Foolish Virgins: 'Usable Fiction' and the Early American Conduct Tradition," *Early American Literature,* 25 (1990): 139–67; Richard Godbeer, *Sexual Revolution in Early America* (Baltimore: Johns Hopkins University Press, 2002), 288–93; Catherine Kerrison, "The Novel as Teacher: Learning To Be Female in the Early American South," *JSH,* 69 (2003): 513–48.

47. Susanna Haswell Rowson, *Charlotte Temple,* ed. Cathy N. Davidson (New York: Oxford University Press, 1986), 5; Hannah Webster Foster, *The Coquette,* ed. Cathy N. Davidson (New York: Oxford University Press, 1986), 168.

48. Anne Dalke, "Original Vice: The Political Implications of Incest in the Early American Novel," *Early American Literature,* 23 (1988): 188–201; William Hill Brown, *The Power of Sympathy,* ed. Carla Mulford (New York: Penguin, 1996), xxxvi–xli.

49. Brown, *Power of Sympathy,* 37–40. See also the discussion in Catherine Kerrison, "By the Book: Eliza Ambler Brent Carrington and Conduct Literature in Late Eighteenth-Century Virginia," *VMHB,* 105 (1997): 27–52, for another case in which a real-life seduction story was told and retold according to the conventions of the sentimental novel.

50. Ibid., 37–39, 42–43.

51. Thomas Jefferson to Martha Jefferson Randolph, 28 April 1793, Boyd, et al., eds., *Papers of Thomas Jefferson,* 25: 621; Martha Jefferson Randolph to Thomas Jefferson, 16 May 1793, ibid., 26: 53.

52. John Page to St. George Tucker, 17 Aug. 1793, Tucker-Coleman Papers, Vi-WM; Lines by Mrs. Page addressed to Mrs. Tucker on seeing a copy of the proceeding sent to Mr. Page, 17 Aug. 1793, ibid.

53. John Randolph memorandum, [1796], ibid.

54. Judith Randolph to Mary Randolph Harrison, 12 May 1793, 23 May 1794, Harrison Family Papers, Vi-Hi [first emphasis added].

55. Richard Randolph to St. George Tucker, 14 March 1793, Randolph Family Papers, Vi-Hi; Ann C. Morris to St. George Tucker, [1814?], Dec. 1814, 2 March 1815, 20 March 1815, Tucker-Coleman Papers, Vi-WM; Ann C. Morris to John Randolph, 16 Jan. 1815, in William Cabell Bruce, *John Randolph of Roanoke*, 2 vols. (New York: G. P. Putnam's Sons, 1922), 2: 282.

56. Jonathan Daniels, *The Randolphs of Virginia* (Garden City, N.Y.: Doubleday & Company, 1972), 169; Lewis, *Pursuit of Happiness*, chap. 2; Judith Randolph to Mary Randolph Harrison, 21 Dec. 1793, Harrison Family Papers, Vi-Hi.

57. Ann Cary Randolph to St. George Tucker, 8 Feb. 1799, 23 March 1804, Tucker-Coleman Papers, Vi-WM; Ann C. Morris to St. George Tucker, Dec. 1814, 17 Dec. 1822, ibid.; Martha Jefferson Randolph to Thomas Jefferson, 16 May 1793, Boyd, et al., eds., *Papers of Thomas Jefferson*, 26: 53; Buckley, *Great Catastrophe of My Life*, 6–8, 270.

58. Cumberland County order book, 28 July 1794, LVa; Judith Randolph to Mary Randolph Harrison, 23 May 1794, Harrison Family Papers, Vi-Hi; Judith Randolph to John Randolph, [c.1806], Bryan Family Papers, Vi-U; Richard Randolph to Creed Taylor, 28 Jan. 1795, 25 April 1795, 6 June 1795, Creed Taylor Papers, Vi-U; Ann Cary Randolph to Sarah Taylor, [c.1793], 24 Oct. 1800, ibid.; Bruce, *John Randolph of Roanoke*, 1: 120–23.

59. Cumberland County order book, 28 July 1794, LVa; Judith Randolph to Mary Randolph Harrison, 23 May 1794, Harrison Family Papers, Vi-Hi; Judith Randolph to John Randolph, [c.1806], Bryan Family Papers, Vi-U; On Anna Dudley, see "Historical and Genealogical Notes," *Tyler's Quarterly Historical and Genealogical Magazine*, 6 (1925): 213–14; Anna Bland Eaton Dudley to St. George Tucker, 27 March 1786, Tucker-Coleman Papers, Vi-WM; Ann Cary Randolph to St. George Tucker, 2 Aug. 1800, ibid.; Bruce, *John Randolph of Roanoke*, 2: 471; Garland, *Life of John Randolph of Roanoke*, 1: 11, 61–63; Herbert Clarence Bradshaw, *History of Prince Edward County, Virginia: From its Earliest Settlements through its Establishment in 1754 to its Bicentennial Year* (Richmond: Dietz Press, 1955), 223.

60. Edward C. Carter II and Angeline Polites, eds., *The Virginia Journals of Benjamin Henry Latrobe*, 2 vols. (New Haven, Conn.: Yale University Press, 1977), 1: 143–44.

61. Ibid.; Ann Cary Randolph to St. George Tucker, [June 1796], Tucker-Coleman Papers, Vi-WM.

62. Lewis, *Pursuit of Happiness*, 77–98, 188–204, 188–204; Anya Jabour, *Marriage in the Early Republic: Elizabeth and William Wirt and the Companionate Ideal* (Baltimore: Johns Hopkins University Press, 1998), 1–7; Ann Cary Randolph to St. George Tucker, 14 July 1796, 16 Dec. 1808, Tucker-Coleman Papers, Vi-WM; Ann C. Morris to St. George Tucker, 26 Dec. 1814, 9 Feb. 1815, 2 March 1815, ibid.; Judith Randolph to St. George Tucker, 24 July 1796, 5 Nov. 1797, ibid.; Judith Randolph to Mary Randolph Harrison, 21 June 1797, 29 April 1799, Harrison Family Papers, Vi-Hi.

63. Robert Dawidoff, *The Education of John Randolph* (New York: W. W. Norton, 1979), 98–101; Bruce, *John Randolph of Roanoke,* 2: 319–24; Garland, *Life of John Randolph of Roanoke,* 2: 36–37; [Nathaniel Beverley Tucker], "Garland's Life of Randolph," *Southern Quarterly Review,* new series, 4 (July 1851): 45–46.

Chapter 4

1. Judith Randolph to Mary Randolph Harrison, 18 June 1801, Harrison Family Papers, Vi-Hi.
2. Ann Cary Randolph to St. George Tucker, 10 Feb. 1807, Tucker-Coleman Papers, Vi-WM.
3. Robert Dawidoff, *The Education of John Randolph of Roanoke* (New York: W. W. Norton, 1979), 25, 99; Powhatan Bouldin, *Home Reminiscences of John Randolph of Roanoke* (Danville and Richmond, Va.: Clemmitt & Jones, 1878), 10–13, 28, 35–36.
4. Dawidoff, *Education of John Randolph,* 26–27.
5. T. H. Breen, *Tobacco Culture: The Mentality of the Great Tidewater Planters on the Eve of Revolution* (Princeton, N.J.: Princeton University Press, 1985), esp. 91–95, 186–210; Jan Lewis, *The Pursuit of Happiness: Family and Values in Jefferson's Virginia* (Cambridge, U.K.: Cambridge University Press, 1983), 109–10. For an instructive parallel, see Toby L. Ditz, "Shipwrecked; or, Masculinity Imperiled: Mercantile Representation of Failure and the Gendered Self in Eighteenth-Century Philadelphia," *JAH,* 81 (1994): 58, 72–73.
6. John Page, Jr., to John Norton, 10 April 1769, 27 May 1769, 31 July 1771, 21 July 1773, in Frances Norton Mason, ed., *John Norton & Sons, Merchants of London and Virginia: Being the Papers from their Counting House for the Years 1750 to 1795* (Richmond: Dietz Press, 1937), 91, 94, 172, 338–39.
7. John Page, Jr., to John Norton, 6 April 1792, in Mason, ed., *John Norton & Sons,* 502–3.
8. Thomas Mann Randolph, Jr., to Judith Randolph, 22 Feb. 1794, Tucker-Coleman Papers; Thomas Mann Randolph, Jr., to St. George Tucker, 4 April 1794, ibid.
9. Dawidoff, *Education of John Randolph,* 78–82, 91–93.
10. Bouldin, *Home Reminiscences of John Randolph of Roanoke,* 20–23, 35–36, 69–70; William Cabell Bruce, *John Randolph of Roanoke,* 2 vols. (New York: G. P. Putnam's Sons, 1922), 2: 49–60, 670–79; Hugh A. Garland, *The Life of John Randolph of Roanoke,* 2 vols. (1856; New York: Greenwood Press, 1969), 2: 272–75; John Randolph to Tudor Randolph, 13 Dec. 1813, Grinnan Family Papers, Vi-Hi; Martha Jefferson Randolph to Ann C. Morris, 17 Aug. 1836, Smith Family Papers, APS. See also, T. H. Breen, "Horses and Gentlemen: The Cultural Significance of Gambling Among the Gentry of Virginia," *WMQ,* 3rd ser. 34 (1977): 239–57.
11. Bouldin, *Home Remininscences of John Randolph of Roanoke,* 35–37, 94; Dawidoff, *Education of John Randolph,* 88–92, 204–12; Garland, *Life of John Randolph of*

Roanoke, 1: 19; John Randolph to Harmanus Bleecker, 23 Sept. 1814, John Randolph-Harmanus Bleecker Correspondence, Vi-U. On the reform of Virginia inheritance law, see Merrill D. Peterson, *Thomas Jefferson and the New Nation: A Biography* (New York: Oxford University Press, 1970), 113–16; and Holly Brewer, "Entailing Aristocracy in Colonial Virginia: 'Ancient Feudal Restraints' and Revolutionary Reform," *WMQ,* 3rd ser., 54 (1997): 307–46.

12. Garland, *Life of John Randolph of Roanoke,* 1: 182–84; Bruce, *John Randolph of Roanoke,* 2: 325–28, 588; Robert Douhat Meade, "John Randolph of Roanoke: Some New Information," *WMQ,* 2nd ser., 13 (1933): 256–64; Judith Randolph to St. George Tucker, 22 April 1799, Tucker-Coleman Papers, Vi-WM; Frances Bland Tucker Coalter to St. George Tucker, 9 May 1805, ibid.

13. Bruce, *John Randolph of Roanoke,* 2: 49–60, 456–506, 509–12, 524–42, 690–702; Garland, *Life of John Randolph of Roanoke,* 2: 85; Dawidoff, *Education of John Randolph,* 50–54, 211; John Randolph to Theodore Bland Dudley, Sept. 1813, 7 March 1814, 24 Dec. 1814, Aug. 1818, in *Letters of John Randolph to a Young Relative . . .* (Philadelphia: Carey, Lea & Blanchard, 1834), 142–43, 154, 168, 203–4. On Randolph and slavery, see also Russell Kirk, *Randolph of Roanoke: A Study in Conservative Thought* (Chicago: University of Chicago Press, 1951), 107–28.

14. Thomas Jefferson to John Adams, 28 Oct. 1813, in Merrill D. Peterson, ed., *The Portable Thomas Jefferson* (New York: Penguin, 1975), 536.

15. The complete data on the legislative service for members of the three families Jefferson mentioned is as follows:

	1750–1775		1775–1800		1801–1825	
	Men	Terms	Men	Terms	Men	Terms
Randolph	18	78	7	27	6	15
Carter	11	45	15	40	8	16
Burwell	10	29	3	8	5	12

See Cynthia Leonard Miller, comp., *The General Assembly of Virginia, July 30, 1619-January 11, 1978: A Bicentennial Register of Members* (Richmond: Virginia State Library, 1978), 82–107, 122–327.

16. On Thomas Mann Randolph, Jr., see William H. Gaines, Jr., *Thomas Mann Randolph: Jefferson's Son-in-Law* (Baton Rouge: Louisiana State University Press, 1966), 50–67, 139; H. J. Eckenrode, *The Randolphs: The Story of a Virginia Family* (Indianapolis, Ind.: Bobbs-Merrill Co., 1946), 234; and Daniel P. Jordan, *Political Leadership in Jefferson's Virginia* (Charlottesville: University Press of Virginia, 1983), 99, 157–70. Under the constitution of 1776, the state legislature elected the governor (Francis Newton Thorpe, comp., *The Federal and State Constitutions Colonial Charters . . . ,* 7 vols. [Washington: U.S. Government Printing Office, 1909], 7: 3815–18). On Cary, see Jonathan Daniels, *The Randolphs of Virginia,* (Garden

City, N.Y.: Doubleday & Company, 1972), 214–15; and [Fairfax Harrison], *The Virginia Carys, An Essay in Genealogy* (New York: DeVinne Press, 1919), 112.

17. Dawidoff, *Education of John Randolph,* 169–90, 218–22; Kirk, *Randolph of Roanoke,* 12–19, 26, 46, 84–86; Bruce, *John Randolph of Roanoke,* 1: 141–43.

18. Bruce, *John Randolph of Roanoke,* 1: 142–54; William Maxwell, *A Memoir of the Rev. John H. Rice, D.D.* (Philadelphia and Richmond: J. Whetham, 1835), 20–21. For "bug-eater," see Mitford M. Mathews, *A Dictionary of Americanisms on Historical Principles* (Chicago: University of Chicago Press, 1956), 210.

19. Bruce, *John Randolph of Roanoke,* 2: 98–217; Dawidoff, *Education of John Randolph,* 189–94; Bouldin, *Home Reminiscences of John Randolph of Roanoke,* 43, 119–24.

20. Garland, *Life of John Randolph of Roanoke,* 1: 19; Thomas Jefferson to John Adams, 28 Oct. 1813, in Peterson, ed., *Portable Thomas Jefferson,* 537. Recent scholarship suggests that Randolph correctly perceived the role of colonial inheritance law in maintaining social hierarchy (Brewer, "Entailing Aristocracy in Colonial Virginia"). On Randolph's eventual break with Jefferson, see Norman K. Risjord, *The Old Republicans: Southern Conservatism in the Age of Jefferson* (New York: Columbia University Press, 1965), chaps. 2–3.

21. Bruce, *John Randolph,* 1: 76–78, 2: 267–72; Garland, *Life of John Randolph of Roanoke,* 2: 3–39; Phillip Hamilton, *The Making and Unmaking of a Revolutionary Family: The Tuckers of Virginia, 1752–1830* (Charlottesville: University Press of Virginia, 2003), 178–80.

22. Will of Richard Randolph, 18 Feb. 1796, Randolph Family Papers, Vi-Hi; Judith Randolph to John Randolph, 25 Sept. 1796, Bryan Family Papers, Vi-U. See also Kirsten E. Wood, "Fictive Mastery: Slaveholding Widows in the American Southeast, 1790–1860" (Ph.D. diss., University of Pennsylvania, 1998), esp. 1–10, and Wood, "Broken Reeds and Competent Farmers: Slaveholding Widows in the Southeastern United States, 1790–1860," *Journal of Women's History,* 13 (2001): 34–57.

23. Garland, *Life of John Randolph,* 1: 166–75; Ann Cary Randolph to St. George Tucker, April 1800, Tucker-Coleman Papers, Vi-WM; John Randolph to Theodore Dudley, 29 Oct. 1810, in *Letters of John Randolph to a Young Relative,* 73; Henry St. George Tucker to John Coalter, 12 Feb. 1816, Grinnan Family Papers, Vi-Hi.

24. Cara Anzilloti, *In the Affairs of the World: Women, Patriarchy, and Power in Colonial South Carolina* (Westport, Conn.: Greenwood Press, 2002), 136–44; Wood, "Broken Reeds and Competent Farmers," 37–41.

25. Judith Randolph to St. George Tucker, 24 July 1796, Tucker-Coleman Papers, Vi-WM.

26. Judith Randolph to St. George Tucker, 2 Aug. 1796, 23 June 1797, 19 Sept. 1797, ibid.; Ann Cary Randolph to St. George Tucker, 19 Sept. 1797, ibid.; Henry Tucker to St. George Tucker, 7 Sept. 1796, 26 Sept. 1796, 9 Oct. 1796, ibid. See also Judith Randolph to Mary Randolph Harrison, 21 June 1797, 21 July 1797, Harrison Family Papers, Vi-Hi.

27. Judith Randolph to Mary Randolph Harrison, 16 Feb. 1798, Harrison Family Papers, Vi-Hi; Judith Randolph to Creed Taylor, 29 Feb. 1798, Creed Taylor Papers, Vi-U; Mary Randolph Harrison to Virginia Randolph Cary, 7 April 1816, Carr-Cary Family Papers, Vi-U.

28. Judith Randolph to Mary Randolph Harrison, 26 May 1798, 4 June 1798, 8 July 1798, Harrison Family Papers, Vi-Hi.

29. Ann Cary Randolph to St. George Tucker, 29 May 1798, 23 July 1798, Tucker-Coleman Papers, Vi-WM.

30. Ann Cary Randolph to St. George Tucker, 29 May 1798, ibid.

31. Ann Cary Randolph to St. George Tucker, 8 March 1799, 15 June 1799, 13 Aug. 1799, ibid.; Judith Randolph to St. George Tucker, 8 March 1799, 8 Dec. 1799, ibid.

32. Henry St. George Tucker to St. George Tucker, 24 Aug. 1800, ibid.; Judith Randolph to St. George Tucker, 23 June 1797, 7 Feb. 1806, 8 Sept. 1811, ibid.; Judith Randolph to Mary Randolph Harrison, 21 July 1797, Harrison Family Papers, Vi-Hi; Frances Tucker to St. George Tucker, 17 Aug. 1801, 16 Oct. 1801, Tucker Family Papers, Vi-Hi; Frances Tucker Coalter to John St. George Randolph, 11 Dec. 1809, Ann Frances Bland Tucker Coalter Letter, Vi-Hi; Judith Randolph to John Randolph, 13 June 1813, Bryan Family Papers, Vi-U.

33. Ann Cary Randolph to St. George Tucker, 30 Jan. 1803, Tucker-Coleman Papers, Vi-WM. On plantation mistresses' work generally, see Catherine Clinton, *The Plantation Mistress: Women's World in the Old South* (New York: Pantheon, 1982), esp. 16–36; Marli F. Wiener, *Mistresses and Slaves: Plantation Women in South Carolina, 1830–80* (Urbana, Ill., 1998), chap. 2.

34. Judith Randolph to Mary Randolph Harrison, 26 May 1798, 29 April 1799, Harrison Family Papers, Vi-Hi.

35. On the Virginia springs, see Charlene Boyer Lewis, *Ladies and Gentlemen on Display: Planter Society at the Virginia Springs, 1790–1860* (Charlottesville: University Press of Virginia, 2001).

36. Ann C. Morris to John Randolph, 31 Oct. 1814, in Bruce, *John Randolph of Roanoke*, 2: 285–86; Judith Randolph to Mary Randolph Harrison, 1 Oct. 1802, Harrison Family Papers, Vi-Hi.

37. Ann Frances Bland Tucker to St. George Tucker, 11 Aug. 1799, Tucker-Coleman Papers, Vi-WM; Judith Randolph to Mary Randolph Harrison, 18 June 1801, 7 Aug. 1801, 1 Oct. 1802, Harrison Family Papers, Vi-Hi.

38. Lewis, *Ladies and Gentlemen on Display*, chap. 2; Clinton, *Plantation Mistress*, 148–50. See also Carroll Smith-Rosenberg, "The Female World of Love and Ritual: Relations Between Women in Nineteenth-Century America," *Signs*, 1 (1975): 1–30.

39. Judith Randolph to St. George Tucker, 13 Dec. 1800, 8 March 1801, 25 Dec. 1802, 21 Aug. 1803, 25 Dec. 1803, 14 Jan. 1804, 23 Nov. 1806, Tucker-Coleman Papers, Vi-WM; Frances Bland Tucker Coalter to St. George Tucker, 27 Jan. 1804, ibid.

40. Judith Randolph to Mary Randolph Harrison, 26 May 1798, 22 March 1799, 7 Dec. 1800, Harrison Family Papers, Vi-Hi. On women's visiting, see also Joan R. Gundersen, "Kith and Kin: Women's Networks in Colonial Virginia," in *The Devil's Lane: Sex and Race in the Early South,* ed. Catherine Clinton and Michele Gillespie (New York: Oxford University Press, 1997), 90–102; and Joan E. Cashin, "The Structure of Antebellum Planter Families: 'The Ties that Bound us Was Strong,' " *JSH,* 56 (1990): 56–60.

41. On Judith's relationship with Maria Ward, see Ann Cary Randolph to St. George Tucker, April 1800, 30 Jan. 1803, 9 Aug. 1804, 25 Nov. 1804, 5 May 1805, Tucker-Coleman Papers, Vi-WM; Judith Randolph to St. George Tucker, 4 June 1803, 25 Dec. 1803, 15 Jan. 1804, 1 June 1805, ibid.; Frances Bland Tucker Coalter to St. George Tucker, 27 Jan. 1804, ibid.

42. Judith Randolph to St. George Tucker, 10 March 1805, 1 June 1805, ibid.; Henry St. George Tucker to St. George Tucker, 25 July 1805, ibid.; John St. George Tucker Randolph to St. George Tucker, 16 Jan. 1804, ibid.; Judith Randolph to John Randolph, April 1803, Bryan Family Papers, Vi-U; Judith Randolph to Mary Randolph Harrison, 18 June 1801, 24 Nov. 1805, Harrison Family Papers, Vi-Hi.

43. Judith Randolph to Mary Randolph Harrison, 24 Nov. 1805, Harrison Family Papers, Vi-Hi; Judith Randolph to St. George Tucker, 14 March 1806, 26 July 1806, 31 Aug. 1806, Tucker-Coleman Papers, Vi-WM; Jonathan Daniels, *Randolphs of Virginia,* 206–7, 232–33.

44. Ann Cary Randolph to St. George Tucker, 25 Dec. 1803, 28 May 1804, 9 Aug. 1804, 28 Jan. 1805, 5 May 1805, Tucker-Coleman Papers, Vi-WM.

45. Ann Cary Randolph to St. George Tucker, 23 March 1804, 28 May 1804, ibid.

46. Ann Cary Randolph to St. George Tucker, 23 March 1804, ibid.

47. Ibid.; Ann Cary Randolph to St. George Tucker, 9 June 1805, ibid. On women and taverns, see, for instance, Jessica Kross, "Mansions, Men, Women, and the Creation of Multiple Publics in Eighteenth-Century America," *Social History,* 33 (1999): 385–86, 390; Kross, " 'If you will not drink with me, you must fight with me': The Sociology of Drinking in the Middle Colonies," *Pennsylvania History,* 64 (1997): 38–40; Peter Clark, *The English Alehouse: A Social History, 1200–1800* (London: Longman, 1983), 131–32, 148–49; Judith M. Bennett, *Ale, Beer, and Brewster in England: Women's Work in a Changing World, 1300–1600* (New York: Oxford University Press, 1996), 139–41; and Kym S. Rice, *Early American Taverns: For the Entertainment of Friends and Strangers* (New York: Fraunces Tavern Museum, 1983), 108–10. On early Virginia specifically, see Harold B. Gill, Jr., "Williamsburg and the Demimonde: Disorderly Houses, the Blue Bell, and Certain Hints of Harlotry," *Colonial Williamsburg,* 23 (Autumn 2001), available at: http://www.history.org/foundation/journal/Autumn01/ Demimonde.cfm (accessed 10 March 2004).

48. Ann Cary Randolph to St. George Tucker, 22 Aug. 1804, Tucker-Coleman Papers, Vi-WM.

49. Ann Cary Randolph to Edward Dillon, 28 Jan. 1805, Dillon-Polk Family Papers, Nc-U; Ann Cary Randolph to St. George Tucker, 28 Jan. 1805, 7 April 1805, 5 May 1805, 29 June 1805, 20 Aug. 1805 [April 1806], Tucker-Coleman Papers, Vi-WM; Judith Randolph to St. George Tucker, 10 March 1805, 1 June 1805, 7 Feb. 1806, 14 March 1806, ibid.

50. Ann Cary Randolph to St. George Tucker, 28 May 1804, 9 Aug. 1804, 20 Sept. 1804, Oct. 1804, Tucker-Coleman Papers, Vi-WM. On Edgehill, which Tom purchased from his father for $2,000, see Gaines, *Thomas Mann Randolph*, 32–34.

51. Ann Cary Randolph to St. George Tucker, 6 Nov. 1806, ibid.

52. Thomas Mann Randolph to Ann C. Morris, 10 April 1817, Smith Family Papers, APS; Ronald Vern Jackson and G. R. Teeples, comps., *Virginia 1810 Census,* 2 vols. (Bountiful, Utah: Accelerated Indexing Systems, 1974), 2: 1055; Martha Jefferson Randolph to Thomas Jefferson, 2 Jan. 1808, in Edward M. Betts and James Adam Bears, eds., *The Family Letters of Thomas Jefferson* (Columbia: University of Missouri Press, 1966), 318; Gaines, *Thomas Mann Randolph,* 40–42, 76–78, 83–84, 101–4, 148, 155–63.

53. Cynthia A. Kierner, " 'The dark and dense cloud perpetually lowering over us': Gender and the Decline of the Gentry in Postrevolutionary Virginia," *JER,* 22 (2000): 192–93; Jane Randolph to Mary Randolph Harrison, 25 Nov. 1815, Harrison Family Papers, Vi-Hi.

54. Ann Cary Randolph to St. George Tucker, [April 1806], 6 June 1806, 2 Nov. 1806, Tucker-Coleman Papers, Vi-WM.

55. Ann Cary Randolph to St. George Tucker, 2 Nov. 1806, 23 Jan. 1807, 10 Feb. 1807, ibid.

56. Virginius Dabney, *Richmond: The Story of a City* (Charlottesville: University Press of Virginia, 1990), 20, 46, 59–64.

57. Suzanne D. Lebsock, *The Free Women of Petersburg: Status and Culture in a Southern Town, 1784–1860* (New York: W. W. Norton, 1985), 169–83; Linda K. Kerber, *Women of the Republic: Ideology and Intellect in Revolutionary America* (Chapel Hill: University of North Carolina Press, 1980), chaps. 7, 9; Cynthia A. Kierner, *Beyond the Household: Women's Place in the Early South, 1700–1835* (Ithaca, N.Y.: Cornell University Press, 1998), 147–53, 155–61; Margaret Meagher, *Education in Richmond* (Richmond: n.p., 1939), 36–45.

58. On Lucy Randolph, a Virginia-born London milliner who traded primarily with Virginia kin, see Gerald Steffens Cowden, "Spared by Lightning: The Story of Lucy (Harrison) Randolph Necks," *VMHB,* 89 (1981): 294–307. On Mary Randolph's Richmond career, see Sterling P. Anderson, Jr., " 'Queen Molly' and *The Virginia Housewife,*" *Virginia Cavalcade,* 20 (Spring 1971): 29–35; Margaret Husted, "Mary Randolph's *The Virginia Housewife:* America's First Regional Cookbook," ibid., 30 (Autumn 1980): 76–78; Daniels, *Randolphs of Virginia,* 198, 221–22; and Edward T. James, Janet Wilson James, and Paul S. Boyer, eds., *Notable American Women, 1607–1950: A Biographical Dictionary,* 3 vols. (Cambridge, Mass.: Harvard University Press, 1971), 3: 117–18.

59. Meagher, *Education in Richmond,* 43; Kierner, *Beyond the Household,* 155–61.

60. Ann Cary Randolph to St. George Tucker, 23 Jan. 1807, 10 Feb. 1807, 26 Feb. 1807, 8 March 1807, 16 Dec. 1807, 26 Dec. 1814, Tucker-Coleman Papers, Vi-WM; Ann C. Morris to John Randolph, 16 Jan. 1816, in Bruce, *John Randolph of Roanoke,* 2: 289.

61. Samuel Mordecai, *Virginia, especially Richmond, in By-Gone Days; with a Glance at the Present* (Richmond: West & Johnston, 1860), 219–20; Dabney, *Richmond,* 85; Thomas E. Buckley, S.J., *The Great Catastrophe of My Life: Divorce in the Old Dominion* (Chapel Hill: University of North Carolina Press, 2002), 189; Ann Cary Randolph Morris to John Randolph, 16 Jan. 1816, in Bruce, *John Randolph of Roanoke,* 2: 288.

62. Buckley, *Great Catastrophe,* 188–95, 220–21; Petition of John Pryor, 1 Dec. 1811, Legislative Petitions, Richmond City, LVa.

63. Ann Cary Randolph to St. George Tucker, 26 Feb. 1807, Tucker-Coleman Papers, Vi-WM; Ann C. Morris to John Randolph, 16 Jan. 1815, in Bruce, *John Randolph of Roanoke,* 2: 289.

64. Ann Cary Randolph to St. George Tucker, 26 Feb. 1807, 8 March 1807, Tucker-Coleman Papers, Vi-WM.

65. Ann Cary Randolph to St. George Tucker, [1806], [1807?], ibid.; Kenneth Shorey, ed., *Collected Letters of John Randolph of Roanoke to Dr. John Brockenbrough, 1812–1833* (New Brunswick, N.J.: Transaction Books, 1988), xxi-xxii. On the Burr conspiracy and trial, see Milton Lomask, *Aaron Burr: The Conspiracy and Exile Years, 1805–1836* (New York: Farrar, Straus, & Giroux, 1982).

66. Ann Cary Randolph to St. George Tucker, 23 Jan. 1807, 10 Feb. 1807, 26 Feb. 1807, 8 March 1807, 16 Dec. 1807, 26 Dec. 1814, Tucker-Coleman Papers, Vi-WM; Ann C. Morris to John Randolph, 16 Jan. 1815, in Bruce, *John Randolph of Roanoke,* 2: 288; Ann C. Morris to William Randolph, [Jan. 1815], Dillon and Polk Family Papers, Nc-U.

67. Risjord, *Old Republicans,* 29–33, 40–62, 66, 71; Dawidoff, *Education of John Randolph,* 185–97.

68. Risjord, *Old Republicans,* 33–34, 38–39, 53, 86–88; Gaines, *Thomas Mann Randolph,* 61–63.

69. Bruce, *John Randolph,* 1: 76–78, 2: 267–72; Garland, *Life of John Randolph of Roanoke,* 2: 3–39. See also John Randolph to St. George Tucker, 14 April 1814, Tucker-Coleman Papers, Vi-WM; John Randolph to St. George Tucker, 28 Feb. 1817, John Randolph of Roanoke Papers, Vi-U.

70. Ann Cary Randolph to Mary Johnston, 21 Feb. 1805 [undated], Nancy Randolph Papers, Vi-WM.

71. Daniels, *Randolphs of Virginia,* 196–202, 221–24; Raymond E. Fitch, ed., *Breaking with Burr: Harman Blennerhassett's Journal, 1807* (Athens: Ohio University Press, 1988), 134–35.

72. Ann Cary Randolph to St. George Tucker, [1807], Tucker-Coleman Papers, Vi-WM.

73. Judith Randolph to St. George Tucker, 3 Oct. 1807, 19 Oct. 1807, ibid.

Chapter 5

1. John Gregory, *A Father's Legacy to His Daughters* (London: W. Strahan, 1774), 115; Judith Randolph to Mary Randolph Harrison, 24 Nov. 1805, Harrison Family Papers, Vi-Hi; Virginia Randolph Cary, *Letters on Female Character* (Richmond: A. Works, 1828).

2. Ann Cary Randolph to St. George Tucker, 17 Dec. 1808, Tucker-Coleman Papers, Vi-WM.

3. Ann Cary Randolph to St. George Tucker, 17 Dec. 1808, 26 Dec. 1814, ibid. On Newport, see Jon Sterngass, *First Resorts: Pursuing Pleasure at Saratoga Springs, Newport & Coney Island* (Baltimore: Johns Hopkins University Press, 2001), 40–44.

4. Ann Cary Randolph to John Randolph, 11 Nov. 1807, Tucker-Coleman Papers, Vi-WM; Ann Cary Randolph to St. George Tucker, 8 Nov. 1808, 17 Dec. 1808, ibid.; [Ann Cary Randolph] to [Gouverneur Morris], 16 June 1808, Smith Family Papers, APS; Ann C. Morris to Joseph C. Cabell, 30 May 1828, Cabell Family Papers, Vi-U; Anne Cary Morris, ed., *The Diary and Letters of Gouverneur Morris,* 2 vols. (New York: C. Scribner's Sons, 1888), 2: 515–16.

5. Gouverneur Morris to St. George Tucker, 15 March 1785, Tucker-Coleman Papers, Vi-WM; Ann Cary Randolph to St. George Tucker, 16 Dec. 1808, ibid.; [Ann Cary Randolph] to [Gouverneur Morris], 16 June 1808, Smith Family Papers, APS; Gouverneur Morris to Alexander Hamilton, 13 June 1788, in Harold C. Syrett and Jacob E. Cooke, eds., *The Papers of Alexander Hamilton,* 27 vols. (New York: Columbia University Press, 1961–87), 5: 7–8; Gouverneur Morris to William Beverley Randolph, 12 Aug. 1807, Gouverneur Morris Papers, LC.

6. The best source on Morris's early life is Max M. Mintz, *Gouverneur Morris and the American Revolution* (Norman: University of Oklahoma Press, 1970), chaps. 1–3.

7. Ibid., 68–87, 176–81, 188, 192–95, 198–202; Richard Brookhiser, *Gentleman Revolutionary: Gouverneur Morris—The Rake Who Wrote the Constitution* (New York: Free Press, 2003), 31–34, 78–93.

8. Mintz, *Gouverneur Morris,* chaps. 10–11; Brookhiser, *Gentleman Revolutionary,* 162–69; Jared Sparks, *The Life of Gouverneur Morris,* 2 vols. (Boston: Gray & Bowen, 1832), 1: 486–87. On the politics of the Burr/Hamilton duel, see Joanne B. Freeman, *Affairs of Honor: National Politics in the New Republic* (New Haven, Conn.: Yale University Press, 2001), chap. 4.

9. Brookhiser, *Gentleman Revolutionary,* 11, 59–63, 111–13, 144–49; Howard Swiggett, *The Extraordinary Mr. Morris* (Garden City, N.Y.: Doubleday & Company, Inc., 1952), 79–81, 157–238 passim; Mintz, *Gouvernuer Morris,* 138–43, 207–8; Sparks, *Life of Gouverneur Morris,* 1: 511.

10. Ann C. Morris to Joseph C. Cabell, 14 Oct. 1831, Cabell Family Papers, Vi-U.

11. Ibid.; Gouverneur Morris to Ann Cary Randolph, 3 March 1809, 9 March 1809, Gouverneur Morris Papers, LC; Ann Cary Randolph to St. George Tucker, 16 Dec. 1808 [1809?], Tucker-Coleman Papers, Vi-WM; [Gouverneur Morris] to [Ann Cary Randolph], 21 March 1809, 1 April 1809, [1809?], Smith Family Papers, APS; Gouverneur Morris to John Marshall, 28 Dec. 1809, in Charles T. Cullen and

Herbert A. Johnson, et al., eds., *The Papers of John Marshall* (Chapel Hill: University of North Carolina Press, 1974–), 7: 222; Gouverneur Morris to John Parish, 6 July 1816, in Morris, ed., *Diary and Letters of Gouverneur Morris,* 2: 600–1.

12. Mintz, *Gouverneur Morris,* 171–75, 228; Swiggett, *Extraordinary Mr. Morris,* 338–39; Edwin G. Burrows and Mike Wallace, *Gotham: A History of New York to 1898* (New York: Oxford University Press, 1999), 245, 255; Stephen Jenkins, *The Story of the Bronx, 1639–1912* (New York: G. P. Putnam's Sons, 1912), 364; Katharine McCook Knox, *The Sharples: Their Portraits of George Washington and His Contemporaries . . .* (New Haven, Conn.: Yale University Press, 1930), 38; [Gouverneur Morris] to [Ann Cary Randolph], 1 April 1809, Smith Family Papers, APS.

13. U.S. Census, Westchester County, New York, 1810, 253. On the gradual curtailment of slavery in New York, see Graham Russell Hodges, *Root and Branch: African Americans in New York and New Jersey, 1613–1863* (Chapel Hill: University of North Carolina Press, 1999), 163–76, 220–21; Ira Berlin, *Many Thousands Gone: The First Two Centuries of Slavery in North America* (Cambridge, Mass.: Belknap Press of Harvard University Press, 1998), chap. 9. By 1830, there were only seventy-five slaves in the entire state and none in Westchester County. By contrast, Westchester's free black population had soared to 2,115 by 1830 (U.S. Census Data, 1810, 1820, 1830, available at: http://fisher.lib.virginia.edu/cgi-local/ censusbin/census/cen.pl [accessed 10 March 2004]).

14. Sparks, *Life of Gouverneur Morris* 1: 493–94.

15. [Gouverneur Morris] to [Ann Cary Randolph], 1 April 1809, Smith Family Papers, APS.

16. Gouverneur Morris to John Marshall, 2 Dec. 1809, 28 Dec. 1809, in Cullen and Johnson, et al., eds., *Papers of John Marshall,* 7: 219–20, 222; John Marshall to Gouverneur Morris, 12 Dec. 1809, ibid., 7: 220–21.

17. Morris, ed., *Diary and Letters of Gouverneur Morris,* 2: 515–16; Ann C. Morris to Joseph C. Cabell, 30 May 1828, Cabell Family Papers, Vi-U; Ann C. Morris to St. George Tucker, 14 June 1810, Tucker-Coleman Papers, Vi-WM; Gouverneur Morris to Gertrude Meredith, 10 Jan. 1810, Gouverneur Morris Papers, LC.

18. Ann C. Morris to St. George Tucker, 26 Dec. 1809, Tucker-Coleman Papers, Vi-WM; St. George Tucker to Gouverneur Morris, 5 Jan. 1810, ibid.; *Richmond Enquirer,* 6 Jan. 1810.

19. Ann C. Morris to St. George Tucker, 9 Sept. 1812, Tucker-Coleman Papers, Vi-WM; Ann C. Morris to St. George Tucker, 12 Nov. 1813, ibid.; [C. H. Harrison] to Ann C. Morris, 20 Oct. 1835, Smith Family Papers, APS; Knox, *The Sharples,* 38.

20. Robert E. Shaw, *Erie Water West: A History of the Erie Canal, 1792–1854* (Lexington: University of Kentucky Press, 1966), 45–47; Brookhiser, *Gentleman Revolutionary,* 188–91; Ann C. Morris to St. George Tucker, 24 Dec. 1811, 13 Feb. 1812, 13 Sept. 1816, Tucker-Coleman Papers, Vi-WM. On Dolley Madison, see Catherine Allgor, *Parlor Politics: In Which the Ladies of Washington Help Build a City and a Government* (Charlottesville: University Press of Virginia, 2000), chap. 2;

David B. Mattern and Holly C. Shulman, eds., *The Selected Letters of Dolley Payne Madison* (Charlottesville: University Press of Virginia, 2003), 6, 92–97.

21. Anne M. Boylan, *The Origins of Women's Activism: New York and Boston, 1797–1840* (Chapel Hill: University of North Carolina Press, 2002), esp. chap. 1; Christine Stansell, *City of Women: Sex and Class in New York, 1789–1860* (Urbana: University of Illinois Press, 1987), chaps. 1–2; Marilyn Hillery Pettit, "Women, Sunday Schools, and Politics: Early National New York City, 1797–1827" (Ph.D. diss., New York University, 1991), esp. 51, 53, 95–96; Samuel Latham Mitchill, *The Picture of New York* (New York: I. Riley and Co., 1807), iii, 33–38, 102–28.

22. Boylan, *Origins of Women's Activism,* 25–32; Stansell, *City of Women,* chap. 4. On religion among the Randolph sisters, see Cynthia A. Kierner, " 'The dark and dense cloud perpetually lowering over us': Gender and the Decline of the Gentry in Post-revolutionary Virginia," *JER,* 22 (2000): 196–99.

23. Contemporary critics of women's organizations included Jack Randolph, who, in 1828, chastised women who "to the neglect of their domestic duties and . . . to the injury of their reputations, are . . . forming themselves into clubs of one sort or another" (John Randolph to Elizabeth Coalter, 25 Dec. 1828, John Randolph of Roanoke Papers, Vi-U).

24. [Gouverneur Morris] to [Ann C. Morris], 12 June 1812, Smith Family Papers, APS; [Ann C. Morris] to [Gouverneur Morris], 15 June 1812, ibid.; John Randolph to Gouverneur Morris, 14 Feb. 1812, Tucker-Coleman Papers, Vi-WM; Ann C. Morris to St. George Tucker, 12 Nov. 1813, ibid.; Randolph Harrison to Gouverneur Morris, 11 Oct. 1813, Gouverneur Morris Papers, Ny-CU; Gouverneur Morris to John Parish, 6 July 1816, in Morris, ed., *Diary and Letters of Gouverneur Morris,* 2: 600–1; Mintz, *Gouverneur Morris,* 235.

25. Ann C. Morris to St. George Tucker, 29 Jan. 1814, Nov. 1814, Tucker-Coleman Papers, Vi-WM; Gouverneur Morris to John Parish, 6 July 1816, in Morris, ed., *Diary and Letters of Gouverneur Morris,* 2: 600–1.

26. Judith Randolph to St. George Tucker, 15 Jan. 1810, Tucker-Coleman Papers, Vi-WM.

27. Judith Randolph to St. George Tucker, 12 Aug. 1810, 4 Feb. 1811, 30 Nov. 1812, ibid.; Ann C. Morris to St. George Tucker, Feb. 1811, 8 March 1811, 9 Sept. 1812, 28 Oct. 1812, 21 Dec. 1813, ibid.

28. Judith Randolph to John Randolph, 19 Oct. 1807, ibid.; Judith Randolph to St. George Tucker, 28 July 1809, 15 Jan. 1810, ibid.

29. Judith Randolph to St. George Tucker, 3 Nov. 1809 [2], ibid.; St. George Tucker, "Sketch of the material parts of a Letter to John Randolph," 7 Nov. 1809, Lucas Family Papers, Vi-Hi; Judith Randolph to Edward Dillon, May 1809, Dillon and Polk Family Papers, NC-U; Judith Randolph to John Randolph, 22 Aug. 1809, Bryan Family Papers, Vi-U; Robert Dawidoff, *The Education of John Randolph* (New York: W. W. Norton, 1979), 204.

30. Judith Randolph to Creed Taylor, 1810, Creed Taylor Papers, Vi-U.

31. Judith Randolph to St. George Tucker, 27 Jan. 1810, Tucker-Coleman Papers, Vi-WM.

32. John Randolph to Theodore Bland Dudley, 15 Nov. 18[10], in *Letters of John Randolph to a Young Relative* . . . (Philadelphia: Carey, Lea & Blanchard, 1834), 76; John Randolph to Judith Randolph, 17 Nov. 1811, John Randolph of Roanoke Papers, Vi-U; Dawidoff, *Education of John Randolph.*

33. Cumberland County personal property tax lists, 1810–16, LVa; Judith Randolph to Edward Dillon, 6 March 1810, Dillon and Polk Family Papers, Nc-U; Judith Randolph to St. George Tucker, 4 Feb. 1811, Tucker-Coleman Papers, Vi-WM. See also F. N. Watkins, "The Randolph Emancipated Slaves," *DeBow's Review,* 24 (April 1854): 285–90. Judith owned no slaves when she died in 1816 (Will of Judith Randolph, 9 March 1816, Tucker-Coleman Papers, Vi-WM).

34. William Maxwell, *A Memoir of the Rev. John H. Rice, D.D., the First Professor of Christian Theology in Union Theological Seminary, Virginia* (Philadelphia and Richmond: J. Whetham, 1835), 59n; John Holt Rice to Archibald Alexander, 17 Oct. 1810, in ibid., 54–55; John Holt Rice to Tudor Randolph, 23 Sept. 1812, ibid., 85–86. On Rice, see also Arthur Dicken Thomas, "Reasonable Revivalism: Presbyterian Evangelization of Educated Virginians," *Journal of Presbyterian History,* 61 (1983): 316–34.

35. Judith Randolph to St. George Tucker, 14 Jan. 1808, 29 Sept. 1808, 12 Aug. 1810, 12 May 1811, 27 March 1814, 17 May 1815, Tucker-Coleman Papers, Vi-WM; St. George Randolph to John Randolph, 8 Nov. 1812, 19 April 1814, ibid.; John Randolph to John Brockenbrough, 24 July 1824, in Hugh A. Garland, *The Life of John Randolph of Roanoke,* 2 vols. (1856; New York: Greenwood Press, 1969), 2: 224. In his letter to Brockenbrough, Jack referred to Nancy as "the———of [Judith's] husband."

36. Ann C. Morris to St. George Tucker, 9 Sept. 1812, 28 Oct. 1812, Nov. 1814, Tucker-Coleman Papers, Vi-WM. On St. George Randolph, see Jonathan Daniels, *The Randolphs of Virginia* (Garden City, N.Y.: Doubleday & Company, 1972), 233–34; William Cabell Bruce, *John Randolph of Roanoke,* 2 vols. (New York: G. P. Putnam's Sons, 1922), 2: 497–98. On Tudor Randolph, see Judith Randolph to St. George Tucker, 12 Aug. 1810, 4 Feb. 1811, 20 July 1812, Tucker-Coleman Papers, Vi-WM.

37. Judith Randolph to St. George Tucker, 4 April 1813, Tucker-Coleman Papers, Vi-WM; John Randolph to Harmanus Bleecker, 25 March 1813, John Randolph-Harmanus Bleecker Correspondence, Vi-U. Surviving letters contain no evidence of Nancy's reaction to the fire.

38. Ann C. Morris to St. George Tucker, 17 Aug. 1814, 8 Oct. 1814, Nov. 1814, Tucker-Coleman Papers, Vi-WM; John Randolph to Gouverneur Morris (transcripts), 1814, Aug. 1814, ibid.; John Randolph to Theodore Bland Dudley, 23 Oct. 1814, in *Letters of John Randolph to a Young Relative,* 163; H. Clarence Bradshaw, *History of Farmville, Virginia, 1798–1948* (Farmville, Va.: The Farmville Herald, 1948), 3.

39. Ann C. Morris to St. George Tucker, Nov. 1814, Dec. 1814, 26 Dec. 1814, Tucker-Coleman Papers, Vi-WM; Ann C. Morris to John Randolph, 16 March 1816, in Bruce, *John Randolph of Roanoke,* 2: 281.

40. John Randolph to Theodore Bland Dudley, 23 Oct. 1814, 17 Nov. 1814, 4 Dec. 1814, in *Letters of John Randolph to a Young Relative,* 163–65; John Randolph to Harmanus Bleecker, Dec. 1814, John Randolph-Harmanus Bleecker Correspondence, Vi-U; Ann C. Morris to John Randolph, 16 Jan 1815, in Bruce, *John Randolph of Roanoke,* 2: 279; Ann C. Morris to Joseph Carrington Cabell, 7 June 1830, Cabell Family Papers, Vi-U. On Bleecker, see Norman K. Risjord, *The Old Republicans: Southern Conservatism in the Age of Jefferson* (New York: Columbia University Press, 1965), 147.

41. Bruce, *John Randolph,* 2: 363, 388–404; Dawidoff, *Education of John Randolph,* 99; Powhatan Bouldin, *Home Reminscences of John Randolph of Roanoke* (Danville and Richmond, Va.: Clemmitt & Jones, 1876), 76–77; Kenneth Shorey, ed., *Collected Letters of John Randolph of Roanoke to Dr. John Brockenbrough, 1812–1833* (New Brunswick, N.J.: Transaction Books, 1988), xxii; John Randolph to Frances Lelia Coalter, 26 Sept. 1814, Grinnan Family Papers, Vi-Hi; John Randolph to Elizabeth Tucker Coalter, 19 Jan. 1822, 27 Jan. 1822, 12 March 1824, 18 Aug. 1828, 15 Dec. 1828, in John Stewart Bryan, comp., "Materials concerning John Randolph of Roanoke, 1787–1903," typescript, Vi-Hi, 244, 260, 262, 269–70, 297, 301.

42. For an excellent analysis of the exchange between John Randolph and Nancy Morris, which is essentially compatible with my own, see Christopher L. Doyle, "The Randolph Scandal in Early National Virginia, 1792–1815," *JSH,* 69 (2003): 301–17.

43. John Randolph to Ann C. Morris, 31 Oct. 1814, in Bruce, *John Randolph of Roanoke,* 2: 274–78.

44. Ibid., 2: 278.

45. Dawidoff, *Education of John Randolph,* 221–23; Risjord, *Old Republicans,* 129–43; Bruce, *John Randolph of Roanoke,* 1: 386–87.

46. [St. George Tucker] to [Ann C. Morris], 16 Dec. 1814, Smith Family Papers, APS; Ann C. Morris to St. George Tucker, Dec. 1814, Tucker-Coleman Papers, Vi-WM; Gouverneur Morris to St. George Tucker, 26 Dec. 1814, ibid.; Gouverneur Morris to Randolph Harrison, 26 Sept. 1818 (copy), ibid.; Ann C. Morris to Dolley Madison, [Jan. 1815], in Mattern and Shulman, eds., *Selected Letters of Dolley Payne Madison,* 195–97.

47. Ann C. Morris to John Randolph, 16 Jan. 1815, in Bruce, *John Randolph of Roanoke,* 2: 278–95; Ann C. Morris to St. George Tucker, 8 Oct. 1814, 16 Jan. 1815, 9 Feb. 1815, Tucker-Coleman Papers, Vi-WM;

48. Ann C. Morris to John Randolph, 16 Jan. 1815, in Bruce, *John Randolph of Roanoke,* 2: 279, 282–84.

49. Ibid., 2: 280–81, 285, 294–95.

50. Ibid., 282–83, 290, 293.

51. Ibid., 2: 286–87.

52. Ann C. Morris to Edward Dillon, 20 Jan. 1815, Dillon and Polk Family Papers, Nc-U.; Ann C. Morris to St. George Tucker, 9 Feb. 1815, Tucker-Coleman Papers, Vi-WM; Martha Jefferson Randolph to Elizabeth House Trist, 31 May 1815, Elizabeth House Trist Papers, Vi-Hi; John Randolph to Harmanus Bleecker, 18 April 1815, John Randolph-Harmanus Bleecker Correspondence, Vi-U.

53. Ann C. Morris to Dolley Madison [Jan. 1815], in Mattern and Shulman, eds., *Selected Letters of Dolley Payne Madison,* 195–97. On Dolley Madison's use of social occasions to foster political influence, see Allgor, *Parlor Politics,* 70–89. On the use of "public-minded personal letters" to address select political audiences in the early republic, see Freeman, *Affairs of Honor,* 36, 114–16.

54. Ann C. Morris to William Branch Giles, 7 Feb. 1815, 17 Feb. 1815, 22 March 1815, William Branch Giles Papers, Vi-Hi; Statement of Ann C. Morris, 14 March 1815, ibid.; William Branch Giles to Ann C. Morris, [1815]. Gouverneur Morris Papers, Ny-CU; Lucia Stanton, *Free Some Day: The African-American Families of Monticello* (Charlottesville: University Press of Virginia, 2000), 48. On Giles, see also Dice Robins Anderson, *William Branch Giles: A Study in the Politics of Virginia and the Nation from 1790 to 1830* (Menasha, Wisc.: George Banta Pub. Co., 1914).

55. William Branch Giles to Ann C. Morris, [1815], Gouverneur Morris Papers, Ny-CU.

56. John Randolph to Harmanus Bleecker, 18 April 1815, John Randolph-Harmanus Bleecker Correspondence, Vi-U; Martha Jefferson Randolph to Elizabeth House Trist, 31 May 1815, Elizabeth House Trist Papers, Vi-Hi; John Randolph to Henry Heth, 29 March 1815, John Randolph of Roanoke Papers, Vi-U; John Randolph to William Branch Giles, 12 March 1815, Miscellaneous Papers, NYPL. See also Freeman, *Affairs of Honor,* 79–85.

57. *Richmond Enquirer,* 1 April 1815. On 25 March 1815, the *Enquirer* described Randolph as "insane" in his attempt to justify the British destruction of Washington.

58. Freeman, *Affairs of Honor,* 127–28. Christopher L. Doyle makes a strong case for the latter view ("Randolph Scandal," 311).

59. Rosemarie Zagarri, "Gender and the First Party System," in Doron Ben-Atar and Barbara B. Oberg, eds., *The Federalists Reconsidered* (Charlottesville: University Press of Virginia, 1998), 118–34; Allgor, *Parlor Politics,* chaps. 2, 3; Susan Branson, *These Fiery Frenchified Dames: Women and Political Culture in Early National Philadelphia* (Philadelphia: University of Pennsylvania Press, 2001). On communities of political gossip in the early republic, see Freeman, *Affairs of Honor,* 74–77. The gossip community of the Republican leader, Thomas Jefferson, purposefully excluded women.

60. Ann C. Morris to St. George Tucker, 26 Sept. 1818, Tucker-Coleman Papers, Vi-WM.

61. Judith Randolph to St. George Tucker, 8 April 1815, 14 Oct. 1815, 22 Feb. 1816, Tucker-Coleman Papers, Vi-WM; St. George Tucker to John Coalter, 15 March 1816, Grinnan Family Papers, Vi-U; Mary Randolph Harrison to Virginia

Randolph Cary, 17 April 1816, Carr-Cary Family Papers, Vi-U; Dawidoff, *Education of John Randolph,* 211–12; Daniels, *Randolphs of Virginia,* 240.

62. Ann C. Morris to St. George Tucker, 20 March 1816, 10 April 1816, Tucker-Coleman Papers, Vi-WM; Eliza Tucker Coalter to St. George Tucker, 28 April 1824, ibid.; Daniels, *Randolphs of Bizarre,* 233–34.

63. Thomas Jefferson to Gouverneur Morris, 20 Oct. 1816, Gouverneur Morris Papers, Ny-CU.

64. Mintz, *Gouverneur Morris,* 240; Swiggett, *Extraordinary Mr. Morris,* 438–42; Brookhiser, *Gentleman Revolutionary,* 215; Rufus King to Christopher Gore, 5 Nov. 1816, in Charles R. King, ed., *The Life and Correspondence of Rufus King,* 6 vols. (New York: G. P. Putnam's Sons, 1894–99), 6: 35; Ann C. Morris to St. George Tucker, 2 Dec. 1816, Tucker-Coleman Papers, Vi-WM.

Chapter 6

1. Ann C. Morris to St. George Tucker, 27 July 1818, Tucker-Coleman Papers, Vi-WM; Ann C. Morris to Joseph C. Cabell, 30 May 1828, Cabell Family Papers, Vi-U.

2. Will of Gouvernuer Morris, 26 Oct. 1816, in Jared Sparks, *The Life of Gouverneur Morris,* 2 vols. (Boston: Gray & Bowen, 1832), 1: 504–5; Richard Brookhiser, *Gentleman Revolutionary: Gouverneur Morris—The Rake Who Wrote the Constitution* (New York: Free Press, 2003), 215. On Kent, see Alan Taylor, *William Cooper's Town: Power and Persuasion on the Frontier of the Early American Republic* (New York: Alfred A. Knopf, 1995), 235–41, 347–48, 515n.

3. Will of Gouverneur Morris, 26 Oct. 1816, in Sparks, *Life of Gouverneur Morris,* 1: 504.

4. Ann C. Morris to Peter Jay Munro, 10 May 1822, Morris Papers, MCNY.

5. Ann C. Morris to St. George Tucker, 26 Jan. 1817, Tucker-Coleman Papers, Vi-WM. See also Howard Swiggett, *The Extraordinary Mr. Morris* (Garden City, N.Y.: Doubleday & Company, Inc., 1952), 340, 377, 393–94, 424–25.

6. Ann C. Morris to St. George Tucker, 2 Dec. 1816, 10 Oct. 1817, Tucker-Coleman Papers, Vi-WM; Swiggett, *Extraordinary Mr. Morris,* 443–45.

7. Ann C. Morris to St. George Tucker, 1 March 1817, 18 April 1817, 28 June 1817, 10 Oct. 1817, 10 June 1819, 16 Feb. 1820, 3 May 1821, Tucker-Coleman Papers, Vi-WM; Ann C. Morris to Peter Jay Munro, 10 May 1822, Morris Papers, MCNY.

8. Moss Kent to Ann C. Morris, 20 May 1818, Morris Papers, MCNY; Ann C. Morris to Peter Jay Munro, 10 May 1822, ibid.; Ann C. Morris to Henry Munro, 7 April 1828, 10 April 1828, ibid.; Financial memo of Ann C. Morris, 1816–27, Gouverneur Morris Papers, LC; Ann C. Morris to Joseph C. Cabell, 14 Oct. 1831, Cabell Family Papers, Vi-U.

9. Ann C. Morris to St. George Tucker, 13 July 1818, 8 Oct. 1822, Tucker-Coleman Papers, Vi-WM; Ann C. Morris to Peter Jay Munro, 10 May 1822, Morris Papers, MCNY. See also Agreement between Gouverneur Morris and Andrew Simon, 9 Oct. 1814, Gouverneur Morris Papers, Ny-CU; Agreement between

Ann C. Morris and Andrew Simon, 6 Oct. 1824, ibid. Andrew Simon received $50 for "Wearing Apparel" for Hannah on her completion of the ten-year indenture. Andrew Simon was not listed in the New York census for either 1810 or 1820.

10. Ann C. Morris to St. George Tucker, 1817, 25 July 1817, 27 July 1817, Tucker-Coleman Papers, Vi-WM; Ann C. Morris to Rufus King, 6 Jan. 1817, Rufus King Papers, NYHS.

11. Ann C. Morris to St. George Tucker, 26 Jan. 1817, 25 July 1817, 27 July 1818, 16 Aug. 1818, Tucker-Coleman Papers, Vi-WM.

12. Ann C. Morris to St. George Tucker, 6 May 1817, 9 July 1817, 10 Oct. 1817, 16 Aug. 1818, 1 Dec. 1824, ibid.

13. Ann C. Morris to St. George Tucker, 2 Nov. 1813, 6 May 1817, 9 July 1817, 10 Oct. 1817, 16 Aug. 1818, ibid.; Taylor, *William Cooper's Town,* 89–95; Dixon Ryan Fox, *Yankees and Yorkers* (New York: New York University Press, 1940). On domestic servants, see Christine Stansell, *City of Women: Sex and Class in New York, 1789–1860* (New York: Alfred A. Knopf, 1982), 156–57. See also Noel Ignatiev, *How the Irish Became White* (New York: Routledge, 1995), esp. chap. 2.

14. Stansell, *City of Women,* 161; Faye Dudden, *Serving Women: Household Service in Nineteenth-Century America* (Middletown, Conn.: Wesleyan University Press, 1983), 60–73; David R. Roediger, *The Wages of Whiteness: Race and the Making of the American Working Class* (New York: Verso Books, 1991), 47–50.

15. Jeffrey Robert Young, *Domesticating Slavery: The Master Class in Georgia and South Carolina, 1670–1837* (Chapel Hill: University of North Carolina Press, 1999), 121–24, 128–33, 140–43; Larry E. Tise, *Proslavery: A History of the Defense of Slavery in America, 1701–1840* (Athens: University of Georgia Press, 1987), 65–67; Philip D. Morgan, "Three Planters and Their Slaves: Perspectives on Slavery in Virginia, South Carolina, and Jamaica" in Winthrop D. Jordan and Sheila L. Skemp, eds., *Race and Slavery in the Colonial South* (Jackson: University Press of Mississippi, 1987), 39–41.

16. See, generally, Bertram Wyatt-Brown, *Southern Honor: Ethics and Behavior in the Old South* (New York: Oxford University Press, 1982), 34–36, 71–72; Eugene D. Genovese, *Roll, Jordan, Roll: The World the Slaves Made* (New York: Random House, 1972), 297–99.

17. Ann C. Morris to Joseph Carrington Cabell, 7 Sept. 1831, 14 Oct. 1831, Cabell Family Papers, Vi-U; Ann C. Morris to St. George Tucker, 1 Jan. 1816, 27 Jan. 1826, Tucker-Coleman Papers, Vi-WM.

18. Ellen W. Randolph to Jane Hollins Randolph, 15 Dec. 1817, Nicholas P. Trist Papers, Nc-U; Ann C. Morris to St. George Tucker, 30 Jan. 1818, Feb. 1818, Tucker-Coleman Papers, Vi-WM; Martha Jefferson Randolph to Ann C. Morris, 4 Dec. 1820, Smith Family Papers, APS; Margaret Scott Harrison, "Sketch of the Family of Carter Henry Harrison (1736–1793) of 'Clifton' in Cumberland County, Virginia" (Hampton, Va. [typescript], 1959), 18.

19. Ann C. Morris to St. George Tucker, 25 July 1817, Tucker-Coleman Papers, Vi-WM.

20. Ann C. Morris to St. George Tucker, [1817], 27 Aug. 1818, ibid. On the ability of accusations of immorality to undermine women's perceived trustworthiness in general, see, for instance, Cornelia Hughes Dayton, *Women Before the Bar: Gender, Law, and Society in Connecticut, 1639–1789* (Chapel Hill: University of North Carolina Press, 1995), 308–14, 325–27.

21. *Dictionary of American Biography*, s.v. "Ogden, David Bayard." See also Ann C. Morris to Peter Jay Munro, 10 May 1822, Morris Papers, MCNY.

22. Ann C. Morris to St. George Tucker, 26 Sept. 1817, 27 July 1818, Tucker-Coleman Papers, Vi-WM.

23. Ann C. Morris to St. George Tucker, 26 Sept. 1818, ibid.; *Dictionary of American Biography*, s.v. "Ogden, David Bayard."

24. Ann C. Morris to St. George Tucker, 26 Sept. 1818, Tucker-Coleman Papers, Vi-WM; Swiggett, *Extraordinary Mr. Morris,* 414, 418.

25. Ann C. Morris to St. George Tucker, 10 June 1819, Tucker-Coleman Papers, Vi-WM; *The Columbian* 1819, fragment, ibid.; Swiggett, *Extraordinary Mr. Morris,* 446.

26. Ann C. Morris to St. George Tucker, 1 Dec. 1824, 19 March 1819, Tucker-Coleman Papers, Vi-WM.

27. St. George Tucker to Ann C. Morris, 16 July 1821, ibid.; Ann C. Morris to St. George Tucker, 8 Oct. 1822, 27 Jan. 1826, ibid.; Stephen Jenkins, *The Story of the Bronx, 1639–1912* (New York: G. P. Putnam's Sons, 1912).

28. Ann Cary Randolph Bankhead to Ann C. Morris, 24 Dec. 1822, Smith Family Papers, APS; C. H. Harrison to Ann C. Morris, 20 Oct. 1835, ibid.; Ann C. Morris to St. George Tucker, 19 March 1826, Tucker-Coleman Papers, Vi-WM.

29. U.S. Census, Westchester County, New York, 1820, 142.

30. U.S. Census, Westchester County, New York, 1830, 127; Martha Jefferson Randolph to Ann C. Morris, 8 Aug. 1825, Smith Family Papers, APS; Lucia C. Page to Ann C. Morris, 3 Aug. 1835, ibid.; Carter Henry Harrison to Ann C. Morris, 20 Oct. 1835, ibid. At least one scholar has characterized the spread of proslavery sentiment in the northern states as part of a more general conservative reaction to the rise of democracy in the wake of the American and French revolutions (Tise, *Proslavery,* chaps. 8, 9).

31. Jane Cary Randolph to Mary Randolph Harrison, 31 Dec. 1815, 4 Feb. 1816, Harrison Family Papers, Vi-Hi; Ann C. Morris to St. George Tucker, 2 July 1821, Tucker-Coleman Papers, Vi-WM; Martha Jefferson Randolph to Ann C. Morris, 8 Aug. 1825, 1 May 1826, Smith Family Papers, APS; J. A. Randolph to Ann C. Morris, 24 Jan. 1827, ibid.; Susan Randolph to Ann C. Morris, 2 Oct. 1827, ibid.; Mary R. Cary to Ann C. Morris, 18 Feb. 1828, ibid.; Thomas M. Randolph to Ann C. Morris, 6 May 1828, ibid.

32. Cynthia A. Kierner, " 'The dark and dense cloud perpetually lowering over us': Gender and the Decline of the Gentry in Postrevolutionary Virginia," *JER* 20 (2000): 208–17.

33. Ann C. Morris to Joseph Carrington Cabell, 30 May 1828, 7 Sept. 1831, Cabell Family Papers, Vi-U.

34. Ann C. Morris to St. George Tucker, 27 May 1819, Tucker-Coleman Papers, Vi-WM; Ann C. Morris to Henry Munro, 1828, Morris Papers, MCNY; James A. Hamilton to Ann C. Morris, 10 March 1829, 25 March 1829, Smith Family Papers, APS. See also James A. Hamilton, *Reminiscences of James A. Hamilton; or, Men and Events, at Home and Abroad, during Three Quarters of a Century* (New York: Charles Scribner & Co., 1869).

35. Ann C. Morris to Joseph C. Cabell, 14 Oct. 1831, Cabell Family Papers, Vi-U; Herbert B. Adams, *The Life and Writings of Jared Sparks,* 2 vols. (1893; Freeport, N.Y.: Books for Libraries Press, 1970), 2: 163, 168–69; Sparks, *Life of Gouverneur Morris,* 1: 485; Scott E. Casper, *Constructing American Lives: Biography and Culture in Nineteenth-Century America* (Chapel Hill: University of North Carolina Press, 1999), 135–42.

36. Sparks, *Life of Gouverneur Morris,* 1: 494–95.

37. On motherhood, see, for example, Nancy F. Cott, *The Bonds of Womanhood: "Woman's Sphere" in New England, 1780–1835* (New Haven: Yale University Press, 1977), 84–92; Carl N. Degler, *At Odds: Women and the Family in America from the Revolution to the Present* (New York: Oxford University Press, 1980), 73–85; Sally G. McMillen, *Motherhood in the Old South: Pregnancy, Childbirth, and Infant Rearing* (Baton Rouge: Louisiana State University Press, 1990), esp. 3, 170; Marli F. Wiener, *Mistresses and Slaves: Plantation Women in South Carolina, 1830–80* (Urbana, Ill., 1998), 64–67.

38. "Notes of Evidence," April 1793, in Charles T. Cullen and Herbert A. Johnson, et al., eds., *The Papers of John Marshall* (Chapel Hill: University of North Carolina Press, 1974–), 2: 169; Thomas Jefferson to Martha Jefferson Randolph, 28 April 1793, Julian P. Boyd, et al., eds., *The Papers of Thomas Jefferson* (Princeton, N.J.: Princeton University Press, 1950–), 25: 621; Ann Cary Randolph to St. George Tucker, 6 Nov. 1806, Tucker-Coleman Papers, Vi-WM; Martha Jefferson Randolph to Elizabeth House Trist, 31 May 1815, Elizabeth House Trist Papers, Vi-Hi; Martha Jefferson Randolph to Ann C. Morris, 4 Dec. 1820, Smith Family Papers, APS.

39. Martha Jefferson Randolph to Ann C. Morris, 8 Feb. 1833, 3 Nov. 1833, Smith Family Papers, APS.

40. Jefferson Randolph Anderson, "Tuckahoe and the Tuckahoe Randolphs," *VMHB,* 45 (1937): 71–72; Harriet Randolph Hackley to Andrew Talcott and Harriet Hackley Talcott, 30 May 1835, 15 June 1835, 25 Aug. 1837, Talcott Family Papers, VI-Hi; Martha Jefferson Randolph to Ann C. Morris, 22 March 1835, Smith Family Papers, APS; C. J. Randolph to Ann C. Morris, 10 May 1835, ibid.; Randolph Harrison to Ann C. Morris, 2 May 1835, ibid.; Mary Randolph Harrison to Ann C. Morris, 4 May 1835, ibid.; Carter Henry Harrison to Ann C. Morris, 27 July 1835, ibid.

41. William Cabell, Bruce, *John Randolph of Roanoke,* 2 vols. (New York: G. P. Putnam's Sons, 1922), 2: 49–60, 331–79, 690–702; Robert Dawidoff, *The Education of John Randolph* (New York: W. W. Norton, 1979), 46–51, 269–89;

Kenneth S. Greenberg, *Honor and Slavery* (Princeton, N.J.: Princeton University Press, 1996), 66–67.

42. Inventory of the estate of Randolph Harrison, 20 Aug. 1841, Cumberland County will books, 10: 310–14.

43. Ann C. Morris to Joseph C. Cabell, 30 May 1828, 7 June 1830, 6 Sept. 1831, 7 Sept. 1831, 14 Oct. 1831, Cabell Family Papers, Vi-U; Nathaniel Beverly Tucker to Ann C. Morris, 1 March 1837, Smith Family Papers, APS.

44. C. H. Harrison to Ann C. Morris, 28 September 1836, Smith Family Papers, APS. On Gouverneur Morris, Jr., see also Jenkins, *The Story of the Bronx,* 366–67.

45. Rev. Harold G. Willis, et al., *St. Ann's Church of Morrisania: A Shrine to American Patriotism* (New York: Press of John C. Rankin Co., 1919), 12, 15, 17; *New-York Commercial Advertiser,* 29 May 1837.

46. Jonathan Daniels, *The Randolphs of Virginia* (Garden City, N.Y.: Doubleday & Company, 1972), 149, 285–86; Joan E. Cashin, "The Structure of Antebellum Planter Families: 'The Ties that Bound us Was Strong,'" *JSH,* 56 (Feb. 1990), 65–67; Cynthia A. Kierner, *Traders and Gentlefolk: The Livingstons of New York, 1675–1790* (Ithaca, N.Y.: Cornell University Press, 1992), 244.

47. Mary Jane [?] to Virginia Randolph Cary, 12 Dec. 1818, Nicholas P. Trist Papers, Nc-U; Martha Jefferson Randolph to Ann C. Morris, 4 Dec. 1826, 24 Jan. 1828, 8 Feb. 1833, Smith Family Papers, APS; *Alexandria Gazette,* 8 May 1852; Washington *National Intelligencer,* 8 May 1852.

48. Death notices for Ann C. Morris appeared in *New-York Commercial Advertiser,* 29 May 1837, and *New-York American,* 31 May 1837. Because New York City was already so large by the 1830s, in almost every case newspapers carried perfunctory notices of deaths rather than full obituaries.

Epilogue

1. Cumberland County Circuit Court Office; Cumberland County deed book, 1857, 28: 436, 602, 622, 644; 29: 119–20; William Cabell Bruce, *John Randolph of Roanoke,* 2 vols. (New York: G. P. Putnam's Sons, 1922), 2: 495–501; Jonathan Daniels, *The Randolphs of Virginia* (Garden City, N.Y.: Doubleday & Company, 1972), 286–87. For references to St. George in family correspondence, see, for instance, Ann C. Morris to St. George Tucker, 10 April 1816, Tucker-Coleman Papers, Vi-WM; Eliza Tucker Coalter to St. George Tucker, 28 April 1824, ibid.; St. George Tucker to John Coalter, 6 March 1816, Grinnan Family Papers, Vi-U; Mary Randolph Harrison to Virginia Randolph Cary, 7 April 1816, Carr-Cary Papers, Vi-U; Ann C. Morris to Joseph Carrington Cabell, 7 June 1830, Cabell Family Papers, Vi-U; St. George Tucker to Ann C. Morris, 17 June 1816, Smith Family Papers, APS; Nathaniel Beverley Tucker to Ann C. Morris, 1 March 1837, ibid.

2. Marie Keller Frazee, "Bizarre," WPA typescript, 1936, Cumberland County Circuit Court Office; Cumberland County deed book, 1857, 28: 436, 602, 622, 644;

29: 119–20; Bruce, *John Randolph of Roanoke,* 2: 49–57, 500. See also, Frank F. Mathias, "John Randolph's Freedman: The Thwarting of a Will," *JSH,* 39 (1973): 263–72.

3. For the Bizarre scandal in contemporary historical memory, see Alan Pell Crawford, "A House Called Bizarre," *Washington Post,* 26 Nov. 2000, available at: http://www.washingtonpost.com/ac2/wp-dyn/A56720–2000Nov25?language= printer (accessed 10 March 2004). For the St. Ann's marker, see http://www.forgot-ten-ny.com/STREET%20SCENES/motthaven/mott.html (accessed 10 March 2004).

4. Moncure Daniel Conway to J. L. Williams, 11 Sept. 1897, Moncure Daniel Conway Letter, Vi-Hi. On Conway and Williams, see also "Conway, Moncure Daniel," in *American National Biography* (New York: Oxford University Press, 1999), 5: 362–63; Paul Brandon Barringer, et al., *The University of Virginia,* 2 vols. (New York: Lewis, 1904), 2: 174–75.

5. Anne Cary Morris, ed., *The Diary and Letters of Gouverneur Morris,* 2 vols. (New York: Charles Scribner's Sons, 1888), 2: 515–17, 582, 600–1.

6. Moncure Daniel Conway to J. L. Williams, 11 Sept. 1897, Moncure Daniel Conway Letter, Vi-Hi. The four biographies were William Wirt, *Sketches of the Life and Character of Patrick Henry* (Philadelphia: James Webster, 1817), 3–11; Hugh A. Garland, *The Life of John Randolph of Roanoke,* 2 vols. (1856; New York: Greenwood Press, 1969), 1: 61; Powhatan Bouldin, *Home Reminiscences of John Randolph of Roanoke* (Danville and Richmond, Va.: Clemmitt & Jones, 1878), 4; William Wirt Henry, *Patrick Henry: Life, Correspondence and Speeches,* 3 vols. (1891; New York: Burt Franklin, 1969), 2: 491–92.

7. On gender, see Clifford Raymond, "The Amazing Story of Nancy Randolph," *Liberty,* 27 March 1926, 7–11; 3 April 1926, 31–40; and Catherine Clinton, *The Plantation Mistress: Woman's World in the Old South* (New York: Pantheon Books, 1982), 110–17. On the Bizarre scandal as emblematic of gentry malaise, see H. J. Eckenrode, *The Randolphs: The Story of a Family* (Indianapolis, Ind.: Bobbs Merrill, 1946), 13–15, 171–87; Daniels, *Randolphs of Virginia,* esp. 7–9, 214; and Elizabeth Langhorn, *Monticello: A Family Story* (Chapel Hill, N.C.: Algonquin Books, 1987), 54, 61, 64, 71. See also Christopher L. Doyle, "The Randolph Scandal in Early National Virginia: New Voices in the 'Court of Honour,' " *JSH,* 69 (2003): 287.

Bibliography

Unpublished Primary Sources

American Philosophical Society, Philadelphia
    Smith Family Papers
College of William and Mary, Swem Library
    Nancy Randolph Papers
    Tucker-Coleman Papers
Columbia University, Butler Library
    Gouverneur Morris Papers
Cumberland County Circuit Court Office, Cumberland, Virginia
    Deed Books
    WPA Typescripts
Library of Congress, Washington
    Gouverneur Morris Papers
Library of Virginia, Richmond
    Cumberland County Court Order Books
    Cumberland County Court Judgments
    Cumberland County Court Suit Papers
    Cumberland County Land Tax Lists
    Cumberland County Personal Property Tax Lists
    Cumberland County Tithable Lists
    Land Patent Books
    Legislative Petitions
    Prince Edward District Court Order Books
    Will Books: Cumberland County; Henrico County
Museum of the City of New York
    Gouverneur Morris Papers
National Archives, Washington
    U.S. Census, Westchester County, New York (microfilm)
New-York Historical Society
    Rufus King Papers
New York Public Library
    Miscellaneous Papers
University of North Carolina at Chapel Hill, Southern Historical Collection
    Dillon-Polk Family Papers
    Nicholas P. Trist Papers

University of Virginia, Alderman Library
   Bryan Family Papers
   Cabell Family Papers
   Carr-Cary Papers
   Creed Taylor Papers
   Edgehill-Randolph Papers
   John Randolph-Harmanus Bleecker Correspondence
   John Randolph of Roanoke Papers
Virginia Historical Society, Richmond
   Ann Frances Bland Tucker Coalter Letter
   Elizabeth House Trist Papers
   Grinnan Family Papers
   Harrison Family Papers
   Henry Family Papers
   Lucas Family Papers
   Moncure Daniel Conway Letter
   Randolph Family Papers
   Richard Venable Diary
   Talcott Family Papers
   Theodorick Bland Randolph Papers
   Tucker Family Papers
   William Branch Giles Papers

Newspapers

The Columbian (New York)
National Intelligencer (Washington)
Richmond Enquirer
Virginia Argus (Richmond)
Virginia Gazette (Williamsburg)
Virginia Gazette, and General Advertiser (Richmond)

Published Primary Sources

Acomb, Evelyn M., ed. "The Journal of Baron Von Closen." *William and Mary Quarterly*, 3rd ser., 10 (1953): 196–236.

Anburey, Thomas. *Travels through the Interior Parts of America*, 2 vols. Boston and New York: Houghton Mifflin Company, 1923.

Betts, Edward Morris, and James Adam Bear, eds. *The Family Letters of Thomas Jefferson.* Columbia: University of Missouri Press, 1966.

Bouldin, Powhatan. *Home Reminiscences of John Randolph of Roanoke.* Danville and Richmond Va.: Clemmitt & Jones, 1876.

Boyd, Julian P., et al., eds. *The Papers of Thomas Jefferson.* Princeton, N.J.: Princeton University Press, 1950–.

Brown, William Hill. *The Power of Sympathy.* Edited by Carla Mulford. New York: Penguin, 1996.

Bryan, John Stewart, comp. "Materials concerning John Randolph of Roanoke, 1787–1903." Virginia Historical Society: typescript, n.d.

Campbell, Charles, ed. *The Bland Papers. . . ,* 2 vols. Petersburg, Va., E. & J. Ruffin, 1840–43.

Carter, Edward C., II, and Angeline Polites, eds. *The Virginia Journals of Benjamin Henry Latrobe,* 2 vols. New Haven, Conn.: Yale University Press, 1977.

Cary, Virginia Randolph. *Letters on Female Character.* Richmond, Va.: A. Works, 1828.

Chastellux, Marquis de. *Travels in North America in the years 1780, 1781 and 1782,* 2 vols. Edited by Howard C. Rice, Jr. Chapel Hill: University of North Carolina Press, 1963.

Cook, William. *The Physiomedical Dispensary.* Cincinnati: William H. Cook, 1869.

Cullen, Charles T., and Herbert A. Johnson et al., eds., *The Papers of John Marshall* (Chapel Hill: University of North Carolina Press, 1974 –).

Farish, Hunter Dickinson, ed. *Journal and Letters of Philip Vickers Fithian, 1773–1774: A Plantation Tutor of the Old Dominion.* Williamsburg, Va.: Colonial Williamsburg, 1963.

Fitch, Raymond E., ed. *Breaking with Burr: Harman Blennerhassett's Journal, 1807.* Athens: Ohio University Press, 1988.

Foster, Hannah Webster. *The Coquette.* Edited by Cathy N. Davidson. New York: Oxford University Press, 1986.

Gordon, James. "Diary of Colonel James Gordon. . . . " *William and Mary Quarterly,* 1st ser., 11 (1902): 98–112, 195–205, 217–36; 12 (1903): 1–12.

Greene, Jack P., ed. *The Diary of Landon Carter of Sabine Hall, 1752–1778,* 2 vols. Charlottesville: University Press of Virginia, 1965.

Gregory, John. *A Father's Legacy to His Daughters.* London: W. Strahan, 1774.

Hamilton, James A. *Reminiscences of James A. Hamilton; or, Men and Events, at Home and Abroad, during Three Quarters of a Century.* New York: Charles Scribner & Co., 1869.

Heads of Families at the First Census of the United States Taken in the Year 1790; Records of the State Enumerations, 1782–1785: Virginia. Baltimore: Genealogical Publishing Co., 1976.

Hening, William Waller. *The Statutes at Large . . . of Virginia,* 13 vols. Richmond: Samuel Pleasants, Jr., 1819–23.

Henry, William Wirt. *Patrick Henry: Life, Correspondence and Speeches,* 3 vols. 1891; New York: Burt Franklin, 1969.

Jackson, Ronald Vern, and G. R. Teeples, comps. *Virginia 1810 Census,* 2 vols. Bountiful, Utah: Accelerated Indexing Systems, 1974.

King, Charles R., ed. *The Life and Correspondence of Rufus King,* 6 vols. New York: G. P. Putnam's Sons, 1894–99.

"Letters from Old Trunks: Randolph-Carr Letter." *Virginia Magazine of History and Biography,* 48 (1940): 238–42.

Letters of John Randolph to a Young Relative. . . . Philadelphia: Carey, Lea & Blanchard, 1834.

Mason, Frances Norton, ed. *John Norton & Sons, Merchants of London and Virginia: Being the Papers from their Counting House for the Years 1750 to 1795.* Richmond: Dietz Press, 1937.

Mattern, David B., and Holly C. Shulman, eds. *The Selected Letters of Dolley Payne Madison.* Charlottesville: University Press of Virginia, 2003.

Maxwell, William. *A Memoir of the Rev. John H. Rice, D.D., the First Professor of Christian Theology in Union Theological Seminary, Virginia.* Philadelphia: J. Whetham; Richmond, Va.: R.I. Smith, 1835.

Mitchill, Samuel Latham. *The Picture of New York.* New York: I Riley and Co., 1807.

Montague, Lee Ludwell, ed. "Cornelia Lee's Wedding, As Reported in a Letter from Ann Calvert Stuart to Mrs. Elizabeth Lee, October 19, 1806." *Virginia Magazine of History and Biography,* 80 (1972): 453–60.

Morris, Anne Cary, ed. *The Diary and Letters of Gouverneur Morris,* 2 vols. New York: C. Scribner's Sons, 1888.

Peterson, Merrill D., ed. *The Portable Thomas Jefferson.* New York: Penguin, 1975.

Prince, William S., ed. *The Poems of St. George Tucker of Williamsburg, Virginia, 1752–1827.* New York: Vantage Press, 1977.

Randolph, Mary. *The Virginia House-Wife.* Edited by Karen Hess. Columbia: University of South Carolina Press, 1984.

Randolph, Sarah N. *The Domestic Life of Thomas Jefferson.* New York: Harper Brothers, 1871.

"Randolph and Tucker Letters." *Virginia Magazine of History and Biography,* 42 (1934): 47–52, 129–31, 211–23, 317–24.

Rowson, Susanna Haswell. *Charlotte Temple.* Edited by Cathy N. Davidson. New York: Oxford University Press, 1986.

Schmidt, Frederika Teute, and Barbara Ripel Wilhelm, eds. "Early Proslavery Petitions in Virginia." *William and Mary Quarterly,* 3rd ser., 30 (1973): 133–46.

Schreiner-Yantis, Netti, and Florence Speakman Love, comps. *The 1787 Virginia Census,* 3 vols. Springfield, Va.: Genealogical Books in Print, 1987.

Shorey, Kenneth, ed. *Collected Letters of John Randolph of Roanoke to Dr. John Brockenbrough, 1812–1833.* New Brunswick, N.J.: Transaction Books, 1988.

Smith, Benjamin Barton. *Professor Cullen's Treatise of the Materia Medica,* 2 vols. Philadelphia: Edward Parker, 1812.

Syrett, Harold C., and Jacob E. Cooke, eds. *The Papers of Alexander Hamilton,* 27 vols. New York: Columbia University Press, 1961–87.

Thorpe, Francis Newton, comp. *The Federal and State Constitutions Colonial Charters* . . . , 7 vols. Washington: U.S. Government Printing Office, 1909.

Tucker, St. George. *Blackstone's Commentaries: with Notes of Reference to the Constitution and Laws of the Federal Government of the United States and of the Commonwealth of Virginia,* 5 vols. Philadelphia: William Young Birch & Abraham Small, 1803.

———. *A Dissertation on Slavery: With a Proposal for the Gradual Abolition of it in the State of Virginia.* Philadelphia: Mathew Carey, 1796.

[Tucker, Nathaniel Beverley]. "Garland's Life of Randolph." *Southern Quarterly Review*, new series, 4 (July 1851): 45–46.

U.S. Census Data. Available at: http://fisher.lib.virginia.edu/cgi-local/censusbin/census/cen.pl (accessed 10 Mar. 2004).

Watkins, F. N. "The Randolph Emancipated Slaves." *DeBow's Review*, 24 (April 1858): 285–90.

Webb, George. *The Office and Authority of a Justice of the Peace.* . . . Williamsburg, Va.: William Parks, 1736.

Secondary Sources

Adams, Herbert B. *The Life and Writings of Jared Sparks*, 2 vols. 1893; Freeport, N.Y.: Books for Libraries Press, 1970.

Allgor, Catherine. *Parlor Politics: In Which the Ladies of Washington Help Build a City and a Government.* Charlottesville: University Press of Virginia, 2000.

Anderson, Dice Robins. *William Branch Giles: A Study in the Politics of Virginia and the Nation from 1790 to 1830.* Menasha, Wisc.: George Banta Pub. Co., 1914.

Anderson, James LaVerne. "The Virginia Councillors and the American Revolution." *Virginia Magazine of History and Biography*, 82 (1974): 56–74.

Anderson, Jefferson Randolph. "Tuckahoe and the Tuckahoe Randolphs." *Virginia Magazine of History and Biography*, 45 (1937): 55–86, 392–405.

Anderson, Sterling P., Jr., "'Queen Molly' and *The Virginia Housewife*." *Virginia Cavalcade*, 20 (Spring 1971): 29–35.

Anzilloti, Cara. *In the Affairs of the World: Women, Patriarchy, and Power in Colonial South Carolina.* Westport, Conn.: Greenwood Press, 2002.

Ayers, Edward L. *Vengeance and Justice: Crime and Punishment in the 19th-Century American South.* New York: Oxford University Press, 1984.

Bailey, F. G., ed. *Gifts and Poison: The Politics of Reputation.* New York: Schocken Books, 1981.

Bailyn, Bernard, and John B. Hench, eds. *The Press and the American Revolution.* Worcester, Mass.: American Antiquarian Society, 1980.

Baker, Leonard Baker. *John Marshall: A Life in Law.* New York: Macmillan, 1974.

Bardaglio, Peter W. *Reconstructing the Household: Families, Sex, and the Law in the Nineteenth-Century South.* Chapel Hill: University of North Carolina Press, 1995.

Barringer, Paul Brandon, James Mercer Garnett, and Roswell Page. *The University of Virginia*, 2 vols. New York: Lewis, 1904.

Basch, Norma. "Manners, Morals, and Politics in the Election of 1828." *Journal of American History*, 80 (1993): 890–918.

Beeman, Richard R. *Patrick Henry: A Biography.* New York: McGraw-Hill, 1974.

Ben-Atar, Doron, and Barbara B. Oberg, eds. *The Federalists Reconsidered.* Charlottesville: University Press of Virginia, 1998.

Bennett, Judith M. *Ale, Beer, and Brewster in England: Women's Work in a Changing World, 1300–1600.* New York: Oxford University Press, 1996.

Bentley, Barbara. *Mistress Nancy.* New York: McGraw-Hill, 1980.

Bergmann, Jörg R. *Discreet Indiscretions: The Social Organization of Gossip.* Trans. by John Bednarz, Jr., and Eva Kafka Barron. New York: Aldine de Gruyter, 1993.

Berlin, Ira. *Many Thousands Gone: The First Two Centuries of Slavery in North America.* Cambridge, Mass.: Harvard University Press, 1998.

——, and Ronald Hoffman, eds. *Slavery and Freedom in the Age of the American Revolution.* Urbana: University of Illinois Press, 1983.

Beveridge, Albert J. *The Life of John Marshall,* vol. 2: *Politician, Diplomatist, and Statesman, 1789–1801.* Boston and New York: Houghton Mifflin Company, 1919.

Biddle, Francis. "Scandal at Bizarre." *American Heritage,* 12 (Aug. 1961): 10–13, 79–82.

Billings, Warren, John E. Selby, and Thad W. Tate. *Colonial Virginia: A History.* White Plains, N.Y.: KTO Press, 1986.

Black, Donald, ed. *Toward a General Theory of Social Control,* vol. 1: *Fundamentals.* Orlando, Fla., and New York: Academic Press, 1984.

Bleser, Carol, ed. *In Joy and in Sorrow: Women, Family, and Marriage in the Victorian South, 1830–1900.* New York: Oxford University Press, 1991.

Bloch, Ruth H. "American Feminine Ideals in Transition: The Rise of the Moral Mother." *Feminist Studies,* 4 (1978): 101–26.

——. "The Gendered Meanings of Virtue in Revolutionary America." *Signs,* 13 (1987): 37–58.

Bloom, Robert. *A Generation of Leaves.* New York: Ballantine Books, 1991.

Bodenhamer, David J., and James W. Ely, Jr., eds. *Ambivalent Legacy: A Legal History of the South.* Jackson: University of Mississippi Press, 1984.

Bowler, Clara Ann. "Carted Whores and White Shrouded Apologies: Slander in the County Courts of Seventeenth-Century Virginia." *Virginia Magazine of History and Biography,* 85 (1977): 411–26.

Boylan, Anne M. *The Origins of Women's Activism: New York and Boston, 1797–1840.* Chapel Hill: University of North Carolina Press, 2002.

Bradshaw, Clarence. *History of Prince Edward County, Virginia: From its Earliest Settlements through its Establishment in 1754 to its Bicentennial Year.* Richmond: Dietz Press, 1955.

Bradshaw, H. Clarence. *History of Farmville, Virginia, 1798–1948.* Farmville, Va.: The Farmville Herald, 1948.

Branson, Susan. *These Fiery Frenchified Dames: Women and Political Culture in Early National Philadelphia.* Philadelphia: University of Pennsylvania Press, 2001.

Breen, T. H. " 'Baubles of Britain': The American and Consumer Revolutions of the Eighteenth Century." *Past and Present,* 119 (1988): 73–104.

——. "Horses and Gentlemen: The Cultural Significance of Gambling among the Gentry of Virginia." *William and Mary Quarterly,* 3rd ser., 34 (1977): 239–57.

——. *Tobacco Culture: The Mentality of the Great Tidewater Planters on the Eve of Revolution.* Princeton, N.J.: Princeton University Press, 1985.

Brewer, Holly. "Entailing Aristocracy in Colonial Virginia: 'Ancient Feudal Restraints' and Revolutionary Reform." *William and Mary Quarterly,* 3rd ser., 54 (1997): 307–46.

Bridenbaugh, Carl. "Violence and Virtue in Virginia, 1766: Or, The Importance of the Trivial." Massachusetts Historical Society *Proceedings,* 76 (1964): 3–29.

Brigham, Clarence S. *History and Bibliography of American Newspapers, 1690–1820,* 2 vols. Worcester, Mass.: American Antiquarian Society, 1947.

Brock, Robert K. *Archibald Cary of Ampthill: Wheelhorse of the Revolution.* Richmond: Garrett and Massie, 1937.

Brookhiser, Richard. *Gentleman Revolutionary: Gouverneur Morris—The Rake Who Wrote the Constitution.* New York: Free Press, 2003.

Brown, Kathleen M. *Good Wives, Nasty Wenches, and Anxious Patriarchs: Gender, Race, and Power in Colonial Virginia.* Chapel Hill: University of North Carolina Press, 1996.

Brown, Richard D. *Knowledge Is Power: The Diffusion of Information in Early America, 1700–1865.* New York: Oxford University Press, 1989.

——. "Microhistory and the Post-Modern Challenge." *Journal of the Early Republic,* 23 (2003): 1–20.

——. *The Strength of a People: The Idea of an Informed Citizenry in America, 1650–1870.* Chapel Hill: University of North Carolina Press, 1996.

Bruce, William Cabell. *John Randolph of Roanoke, 1773–1833,* 2 vols. New York: G. P. Putnam's Sons, 1922.

Buckley, Thomas E., S.J. *The Great Catastrophe of My Life: Divorce in the Old Dominion.* Chapel Hill: University of North Carolina Press, 2002.

Burrows, Edwin G., and Mike Wallace. *Gotham: A History of New York to 1898.* New York: Oxford University Press, 1999.

Burstein, Andrew. *Sentimental Democracy: The Evolution of America's Romantic Self-Image.* New York: Hill and Wang, 1999.

Bushman, Richard L. *The Refinement of America: Persons, Houses, Cities.* New York: Alfred A. Knopf, 1992.

Carr, Lois Green, Philip D. Morgan, and Jean B. Russo, eds. *Colonial Chesapeake Society.* Chapel Hill: University of North Carolina Press, 1988.

Carson, Jane. *Colonial Virginians at Play.* Williamsburg, Va.: Colonial Williamsburg, 1989.

Cashin, Joan E. "The Structure of Antebellum Planter Families: 'The Ties that Bound us Was Strong.' " *Journal of Southern History,* 56 (1990): 55–70.

Casper, Scott E. *Constructing American Lives: Biography and Culture in Nineteenth-Century America.* Chapel Hill: University of North Carolina Press, 1999.

Censer, Jane Turner. *North Carolina Families and Their Children, 1800–1860.* Baton Rouge: Louisiana State University Press, 1984.

Clark, Anna. *Scandal: The Sexual Politics of the British Constitution.* Princeton: Princeton University Press, 2004.

Clark, Peter. *The English Alehouse: A Social History, 1200–1800.* London: Longman, 1983.

Clinton, Catherine. *The Plantation Mistress: Women's World in the Old South*. New York: Pantheon Books, 1982.

——, and Michele Gillespie, eds. *The Devil's Lane: Sex and Race in the Early South*. New York: Oxford University Press, 1997.

Cogan, Jacob Katz. "The Reynolds Affair and the Politics of Character." *Journal of the Early Republic*, 16 (1996): 389–417.

Cohen, William. "Thomas Jefferson and the Problem of Slavery." *Journal of American History*, 56 (1969): 503–526.

Cott, Nancy F. *The Bonds of Womanhood: "Woman's Sphere" in New England, 1780–1835*. New Haven: Yale University Press, 1977.

Cowden, Gerald Steffens. "Spared by Lightning: The Story of Lucy (Harrison) Randolph Necks." *Virginia Magazine of History and Biography*, 89 (1981): 294–307.

Craven, Avery O. *Soil Exhaustion as a Factor in the Agricultural History of Virginia and Maryland, 1606–1860*. Urbana: University of Illinois Press, 1926.

Crawford, Alan Pell. *Unwise Passions: The True Story of a Remarkable Woman—and the First Great Scandal of Eighteenth-Century America*. New York: Simon & Schuster, 2000.

Cullen, Charles T. *St. George Tucker and Law in Virginia, 1772–1804*. New York: Garland Publishing, 1987.

Cumberland County, Virginia, and its People. Cumberland, Va.: Cumberland County Historical Society, 1983.

Cumberland County, Virginia, and its People: First Supplement. Cumberland, Va.: Cumberland County Historical Society, 1987.

Dabney, Virginius. *Richmond: The Story of a City*. Charlottesville: University Press of Virginia, 1990.

Dalke, Anne. "Original Vice: The Political Implications of Incest in the Early American Novel." *Early American Literature*, 23 (1988): 188–201.

Daniels, Jonathan. *The Randolphs of Virginia*. Garden City, N.Y.: Doubleday & Company, Inc., 1972.

Davidson, Cathy N. *Revolution and the Word: The Rise of the Novel in America*. New York: Oxford University Press, 1986.

Davis, David Brion. *The Problem of Slavery in the Age of Revolution, 1770–1823*. Ithaca, N.Y.: Cornell University Press, 1975.

Dawidoff, Robert. *The Education of John Randolph*. New York: W. W. Norton, 1979.

Dayton, Cornelia Hughes. *Women Before the Bar: Gender, Law, and Society in Connecticut, 1639–1789*. Chapel Hill: University of North Carolina Press, 1995.

Degler, Carl N. *At Odds: Women and the Family in America from the Revolution to the Present*. New York: Oxford University Press, 1980.

Ditz, Toby L. "Shipwrecked; or, Masculinity Imperiled: Mercantile Representation of Failure and the Gendered Self in Eighteenth-Century Philadelphia." *Journal of American History*, 81 (1994): 51–80.

Doyle, Christopher L. "The Randolph Scandal in Early National Virginia: New Voices in the 'Court of Honour.' " *Journal of Southern History*, 69 (2003): 283–18.

Drury, Michael. *"With the Hammer of Truth": James Thomson Callendar and America's Early National Heroes.* Charlottesville: University Press of Virginia, 1990.

Dudden, Faye. *Serving Women: Household Service in Nineteenth-Century America.* Middletown, Conn.: Wesleyan University Press, 1983.

Eaton, Clement. "The Mirror of the Southern Colonial Lawyer: The Fee Books of Patrick Henry, Thomas Jefferson, and Waightsill Avery." *William and Mary Quarterly,* 3rd ser., 8 (1951): 520–34.

Eckenrode, H. J. *The Randolphs: The Story of a Virginia Family.* Indianapolis, Ind.: Bobbs-Merrill, 1946.

Egerton, Douglas R. *Gabriel's Rebellion: The Virginia Slave Conspiracies of 1800 and 1802.* Chapel Hill: University of North Carolina Press, 1993.

Ellis, Joseph J. *American Sphinx: The Character of Thomas Jefferson.* New York: Alfred A. Knopf, 1997.

Elliott, Katherine B. *Marriage Records, 1749–1840, Cumberland County, Virginia.* South Hill, Va., n.p., 1969.

Fett, Sharla M. *Working Cures: Healing, Health, and Power on Southern Plantations.* Chapel Hill: University of North Carolina Press, 2002.

Fischer, Kirsten. *Suspect Relations: Sex, Race, and Resistance in Colonial North Carolina.* Ithaca, N.Y.: Cornell University Press, 2002.

Fliegelman, Jay. *Declaring Independence: Jefferson, Natural Law, and the Culture of Performance.* Stanford, Calif.: Stanford University Press, 1993.

——. *Prodigals and Pilgrims: The American Revolution against Patriarchal Authority.* Cambridge, U.K.: Cambridge University Press, 1982.

Fox, Dixon Ryan. *Yankees and Yorkers.* New York: New York University Press, 1940.

Fox-Genovese, Elizabeth. *Within the Plantation Household: Black and White Women of the Old South.* Chapel Hill: University of North Carolina Press, 1988.

Freeman, Douglas Southall. *R. E. Lee: A Biography,* 4 vols. New York: Charles Scribner's Sons, 1934–35.

Freeman, Joanne B. *Affairs of Honor: National Politics in the New Republic.* New Haven, Conn.: Yale University Press, 2001.

——. "Slander, Poison, Whispers, and Fame: Jefferson's 'Anas' and Political Gossip in the Early Republic." *Journal of the Early Republic,* 15 (1995): 25–57.

Frey, Sylvia R. *Water From the Rock: Black Resistance in a Revolutionary Age.* Princeton, N.J.: Princeton University Press, 1991.

Friedman, Lawrence J., and Mark D. Garvie, eds. *Charity, Philanthropy, and Civility in American History.* Cambridge, U.K.: Cambridge University Press, 2003.

Frith, Valerie, ed. *Women and History: Voices from Early Modern England.* Toronto: Coach House Books, 1995.

Gaines, William H., Jr. *Thomas Mann Randolph: Jefferson's Son-in-Law.* Baton Rouge: Louisiana State University Press, 1966.

Garland, Hugh A. *The Life of John Randolph of Roanoke,* 2 vols. 1856; New York: Greenwood Press, 1969.

Garrett, Nannie H. "A Sketch of the Life and Parentage of Randolph Harrison, Sr., of Clifton, Cumberland County, Va." *Virginia Magazine of History and Biography*, 35 (1927): 209–11, 302–9, 451–54.

Genovese, Eugene D. *Roll, Jordan, Roll: The World the Slaves Made*. New York: Pantheon Books, 1974.

Gentry, Daphne S., and John S. Salmon. *Virginia Land Office Inventory*, 3rd ed. Richmond: Virginia State Library Archives and Records, 1981.

Glassie, Henry. *Folk Housing in Middle Virginia*. Knoxville: University of Tennessee Press, 1975.

Godbeer, Richard. *Sexual Revolution in America*. Baltimore: Johns Hopkins University Press, 2002.

Gordon-Reed, Annette. *Thomas Jefferson and Sally Hemings: An American Controversy*. Charlottesville: University Press of Virginia, 1997.

Grasso, Christopher. *A Speaking Aristocracy: Transforming Public Discourse in Eighteenth-Century Connecticut*. Chapel Hill: University of North Carolina Press, 1999.

Greenberg, Kenneth S. *Honor and Slavery*. Princeton, N.J.: Princeton University Press, 1996.

Grossberg, Michael. *Governing the Hearth: Law and the Family in Nineteenth-Century America*. Chapel Hill: University of North Carolina Press, 1985.

Gundersen, Joan R., and Gwen Victor Gampel. "Married Women's Legal Status in Eighteenth-Century New York and Virginia." *William and Mary Quarterly*, 3rd ser., 39 (1982): 114–34.

Gustafson, Sandra M. *Eloquence Is Power: Oratory and Performance in Early America*. Chapel Hill: University of North Carolina Press, 2000.

Hall, Kermit D., and James W. Ely Jr., eds. *An Uncertain Tradition: Constitutionalism and the History of the South*. Athens: University of Georgia Press, 1989.

Hamilton, Phillip. "Education in the St. George Tucker Household: Change and Continuity in Jeffersonian Virginia." *Virginia Magazine of History and Biography*, 102 (1994): 167–92.

———. *The Making and Unmaking of a Revolutionary Family: The Tuckers of Virginia, 1752–1830*. Charlottesville: University Press of Virginia, 2003.

———. "Revolutionary Principles and Family Loyalties: Slavery's Transformation in the St. George Tucker Household of Early National Virginia." *William and Mary Quarterly*, 3rd ser., 54 (1998): 531–56.

[Harrison, Fairfax]. *The Virginia Carys, An Essay in Genealogy*. New York: DeVinne Press, 1919.

Harrison, Margaret Scott. "Sketch of the Family of Carter Henry Harrison (1736–1793) of 'Clifton' in Cumberland County, Virginia." Hampton, Va., [typescript], 1959.

Hindus, Michael Stephen. *Prison and Plantation: Crime, Justice, and Authority in Massachusetts and South Carolina, 1767–1878*. Chapel Hill: University of North Carolina Press, 1980.

The History of the College of William and Mary: From Its Foundation, 1660, to 1874. Richmond: J.W. Randolph & English, 1874.

Hodges, Graham Russell. *Root and Branch: African Americans in New York and New Jersey, 1613–1863*. Chapel Hill: University of North Carolina Press, 1999.

Hoffer, Peter C., and N. E. H. Hull. *Murdering Mothers: Infanticide in England and New England, 1558–1803*. New York: New York University Press, 1981.

Hoffer, Peter Charles, and William B. Scott, eds. *Criminal Proceedings in Colonial Virginia: Records of Fines Examinations of Criminals: Trials of Slaves, etc., . . . from March 1710 [1711] to 1754 [Richmond County, Virginia]*. Athens: University of Georgia Press, 1984.

Hoffman, Ronald, Mechal Sobel, and Fredrika J. Teute, eds. *Through a Glass Darkly: Reflections on Personal Identity in Early America*. Chapel Hill: University of North Carolina Press, 1997.

Holton, Woody. *Forced Founders: Indians. Debtors, Slaves, and the Making of the American Revolution in Virginia*. Chapel Hill: University of North Carolina Press, 1999.

Husted, Margaret. "Mary Randolph's *The Virginia Housewife:* America's First Regional Cookbook." *Virginia Cavalcade,* 30 (Autumn 1980): 76–78.

Ignatiev, Noel. *How the Irish Became White*. New York: Routledge, 1995.

Isaac, Rhys. *The Transformation of Virginia, 1740–1790*. Chapel Hill: University of North Carolina Press, 1983.

Jabour, Anya. *Marriage in the Early Republic: Elizabeth and William Wirt and the Companionate Ideal*. Baltimore: Johns Hopkins University Press, 1998.

Jellison, Charles A. "That Scoundrel Callender." *Virginia Magazine of History and Biography,* 67 (1959): 295–306.

Jenkins, Stephen. *The Story of the Bronx, 1639–1912*. New York: G. P. Putnam's Sons, 1912.

John, Richard R. *Spreading the News: The American Postal System from Franklin to Morse*. Cambridge, Mass.: Harvard University Press, 1995.

Jordan, Daniel P. *Political Leadership in Jefferson's Virginia*. Charlottesville: University Press of Virginia, 1983.

Jordan, Winthrop D., and Sheila L. Skemp, eds. *Race and Slavery in the Colonial South*. Jackson: University Press of Mississippi, 1987.

Kamensky, Jane. *Governing the Tongue: The Politics of Speech in Early New England*. New York: Oxford University Press, 1997.

Kann, Mark E. *A Republic of Men: The American Founders, Gendered Language, and Patriarchal Politics*. New York: New York University Press, 1998.

Kenney, Alice P., and Leslie J. Workman, "Ruins, Romance, and Reality: Medievalism in Anglo-American Imagination and Taste, 1750–1840." *Winterthur Portfolio,* 10 (1975): 131–63.

Kerber, Linda K. *Women of the Republic: Intellect and Ideology in Early America*. Chapel Hill: University of North Carolina Press, 1980.

Kerrison, Catherine. "By the Book: Eliza Ambler Brent Carrington and Conduct Literature in Late Eighteenth-Century Virginia." *Virginia Magazine of History and Biography,* 105 (1997): 27–52.

Kerrison, Catherine. "The Novel as Teacher: Learning to be Female in the Early American South." *Journal of Southern History,* 69 (2003): 513–48.

Kierner, Cynthia A. *Beyond the Household: Women's Place in the Early South, 1700–1835.* Ithaca, N.Y.: Cornell University Press, 1998.

———. " 'The dark and dense cloud perpetually lowering over us': Gender and the Decline of the Gentry in Postrevolutionary Virginia." *Journal of the Early Republic,* 22 (2000): 185–217.

———. *Traders and Gentlefolk: The Livingstons of New York, 1675–1790.* Ithaca, N.Y.: Cornell University Press, 1992.

King, Andrew J. "Constructing Gender: Sexual Slander in Nineteenth-Century America." *Law and History Review,* 13 (1995): 63–110.

Kirk, Russell. *Randolph of Roanoke: A Study in Conservative Thought.* Chicago: University of Chicago Press, 1951.

Knox, Katharine McCook. *The Sharples: Their Portraits of George Washington and His Contemporaries.* . . . New Haven, Conn.: Yale University Press, 1930.

Kozol, Jonathan. *Amazing Grace: The Lives of Children and the Conscience of a Nation.* New York: Crown, 1995.

Kross, Jessica. " 'If you will not drink with me, you must fight with me': The Sociology of Drinking in the Middle Colonies." *Pennsylvania History,* 64 (1997): 28–55.

———. "Mansions, Men, Women, and the Creation of Multiple Publics in Eighteenth-Century British North America." *Journal of Social History,* 33 (1999): 385–408.

Krusen, Jessie Thompson. "Tuckahoe." *Winterthur Portfolio,* 11 (1976): 103–22.

Kulikoff, Allan. *Tobacco and Slaves: The Development of Southern Cultures in the Chesapeake, 1680–1800.* Chapel Hill: University of North Carolina Press, 1986.

Langhorne, Elizabeth. *Monticello: A Family Story.* Chapel Hill, N.C.: Algonquin Books, 1987.

Laslet, Peter, Karla Oosterveen, and Richard M. Smith, eds. *Bastardy and its Comparative History.* London: E. Arnold, 1980.

Lebsock, Suzanne. *The Free Women of Petersburg: Status and Culture in a Southern Town, 1785–1860.* New York: W. W. Norton, 1985.

———. *"A Share of Honour": Virginia Women, 1600–1945.* Richmond: Virginia Women's Cultural History Project, 1984.

Lepore, Jill. "Historians Who Love too Much: Reflections on Microhistory and Biography." *Journal of American History,* 88 (2001): 129–44.

Lewis, Charlene Boyer. *Ladies and Gentlemen on Display: Planter Society at the Virginia Springs, 1790–1860.* Charlottesville: University Press of Virginia, 2001.

Lewis, Jan. *The Pursuit of Happiness: Family and Values in Jefferson's Virginia.* Cambridge, U.K.: Cambridge University Press, 1983.

———. "The Republican Wife: Virtue and Seduction in the Early Republic." *William and Mary Quarterly,* 3rd ser., 44 (1987): 689–712.

———, and Peter S. Onuf, eds. *Sally Hemings and Thomas Jefferson: History, Memory, and Civic Culture.* Charlottesville: University Press of Virginia, 1999.

Lockley, Timothy James. *Lines in the Sand: Race and Class in Lowcountry Georgia, 1750–1860.* Athens: University of Georgia Press, 2001.

Lomask, Milton. *Aaron Burr: The Conspiracy and Exile Years, 1805–1836* (New York: Farrar, Straus, & Giroux, 1982.

Looney, J. Jefferson, and Ruth Woodward. *Princetonians, 1791–1794: A Biographical Dictionary.* Princeton, N.J.: Princeton University Press, 1991.

Low, W. A. "Merchant and Planter Relations in Post-Revolutionary Virginia, 1783–1789." *Virginia Magazine of History and Biography,* 61 (1953): 308–18.

Main, Jackson Turner. "Government by the People: The American Revolution and the Democratization of the Legislatures." *William and Mary Quarterly,* 3rd ser., 23 (1966): 391–407.

———. "The One Hundred." *William and Mary Quarterly,* 3rd ser. 11 (1954): 354–84.

Malone, Dumas. *Thomas Jefferson and the Ordeal of Liberty.* Boston: Little, Brown, 1962.

———. *Jefferson: The Virginian.* Boston: Little, Brown, 1948.

Mathias, Frank F. "John Randolph's Freedmen: The Thwarting of a Will." *Journal of Southern History,* 39 (1973): 263–72.

McColley, Robert. *Slavery and Jeffersonian Virginia.* Urbana: University of Illinois Press, 1964.

McCurry, Stephanie. *Masters of Small Worlds: Yeoman Households, Gender Relations, and the Political Culture of the Antebellum South Carolina Low Country.* New York: Oxford University Press, 1995.

McCusker, John J. *How Much Is That in Real Money?* Worcester, Mass.: American Antiquarian Society, 1992.

———, and Russell R. Menard. *The Economy of British America, 1607–1789.* Chapel Hill: University of North Carolina Press, 1985.

McMillen, Sally G. *Motherhood in the Old South.* Baton Rouge: Louisiana State University Press, 1990.

Meade, Robert Douthat. "John Randolph of Roanoke: Some New Information." *William and Mary Quarterly,* 2nd ser., 13 (1933): 256–64.

———. *Patrick Henry: Practical Revolutionary.* Philadelphia: J.B. Lippincott, 1969.

Meagher, Margaret. *Education in Richmond.* Richmond: n.p., 1939.

Miller, Cynthia Leonard, comp., *The General Assembly of Virginia, July 30, 1619-January 11, 1978: A Bicentennial Register of Members.* Richmond: Virginia State Library, 1987.

Mintz, Max M. *Gouverneur Morris and the American Revolution.* Norman: University of Oklahoma Press, 1970.

Mordecai, Samuel. *Virginia, especially Richmond, in By-Gone Days; with a Glance at the Present.* Richmond: West & Johnston, 1860.

Morgan, Edmund S. *American Slavery, American Freedom: The Ordeal of Colonial Virginia.* New York: W. W. Norton, 1975.

Morgan, Gwenda. "Law and Social Change in Colonial Virginia: The Role of the Grand Jury in Richmond County, 1692–1776." *Virginia Magazine of History and Biography,* 95 (1987): 453–80.

Morgan, Philip D. *Slave Counterpoint: Black Culture in the Eighteenth-Century Chesapeake and Low Country.* Chapel Hill: University of North Carolina Press, 1998.

——, and Michael L. Nicholls. "Slaves in Piedmont Virginia, 1720–1790." *William and Mary Quarterly,* 3rd ser., 46 (1989): 211–51.

Morton, Richard L. *Colonial Virginia,* Vol. 2: *Westward Expansion and Prelude to Revolution, 1710–1763.* Chapel Hill: University of North Carolina Press, 1960.

Moss, Kay K. *Southern Folk Medicine, 1750–1820.* Columbia: University of South Carolina Press, 1999.

Munger, Robert S. "Guaiacum: The Holy Wood from the New World." *Journal of the History of Medicine and Allied Sciences,* 4 (1949): 196–229.

Nagel, Paul C. *The Lees of Virginia: Seven Generations of an American Family.* New York: Oxford University Press, 1990.

Newton, Sarah Emily. "Wise and Foolish Virgins: 'Usable Fiction' and the Early American Conduct Tradition." *Early American Literature,* 25 (1990): 139–67.

Norton, Mary Beth. *Founding Mothers and Fathers: Gendered Power and the Forming of American Society.* New York: Alfred A. Knopf, 1996.

——. *Liberty's Daughters: The Revolutionary Experience of American Women, 1750–1800.* Boston: Little, Brown, 1980.

——. "Slander and Defamation in Seventeenth-Century Maryland." *William and Mary Quarterly,* 3rd ser. (1987): 3–39.

Onuf, Peter, ed. *Jeffersonian Legacies.* Charlottesville: University Press of Virginia, 1993.

Passley, Jeffrey L. *"The Tyranny of Printers": Newspaper Politics in the Early American Republic.* Charlottesville: University Press of Virginia, 2001.

PDR for Herbal Medicines, 1st ed. Montvale, N.J.: Medical Economics Company, 1998.

Peterson, Merrill D. *Thomas Jefferson and the New Nation: A Biography.* New York: Oxford University Press, 1970.

Pettit, Marilyn Hillery. "Women, Sunday Schools, and Politics: Early National New York City, 1797–1827." Ph.D. diss., New York University, 1991.

Pole, J. R. *Political Representation in England and the Origins of the American Republic.* New York: Oxford University Press, 1966.

Ragsdale, Bruce A. *A Planters' Republic: The Search for Economic Independence in Revolutionary Virginia.* Madison, Wisc.: Madison House, 1996.

Rankin, Hugh. *Criminal Trial Proceedings in the General Court of Colonial Virginia.* Williamsburg, Va.: Colonial Williamsburg, 1965.

Raymond, Clifford. "The Amazing Story of Nancy Randolph" *Liberty,* 27 March 1926, 7–11; 3 April 1926, 31–40.

Rice, Kym S. *Early American Taverns: For the Entertainment of Friends and Strangers.* New York: Fraunces Tavern Museum, 1983.

Riddle, John M. *Eve's Herbs: A History of Abortion and Contraception in the West.* Cambridge, Mass.: Harvard University Press, 1997.

Risjord, Norman K. *The Old Republicans: Southern Conservatism in the Age of Jefferson.* New York: Columbia University Press, 1965.

Roeber, A. G. "Authority, Law, and Custom: The Rituals of Court Day in Tidewater Virginia, 1720 to 1750." *William and Mary Quarterly,* 3rd ser., 37 (1980): 29–52.

——. *Faithful Magistrates and Republican Lawyers: Creators of Virginia's Legal Culture, 1680–1810.* Chapel Hill: University of North Carolina Press, 1981.

Roediger, David R. *The Wages of Whiteness: Race and the Making of the American Working Class.* New York: Verso Books, 1991.

Rothman, Joshua D. *Notorious in the Neighborhood: Sex and Families Across the Color Line in Virginia, 1787–1861.* Chapel Hill: University of North Carolina Press, 2003.

Rutman, Darrett B., and Anita H. Rutman. *A Place in Time: Middlesex County, Virginia, 1650–1750.* New York: W. W. Norton, 1984.

——. *A Place in Time: Explicatus.* New York: W. W. Norton, 1984.

Salmon, Emily J., and Edward D. C. Campbell. *The Hornbook of Virginia History,* 4th ed. Richmond: Library of Virginia, 1994.

Salmon, Marylynn. *Women and the Law of Property in Early America.* Chapel Hill: University of North Carolina Press, 1986.

Schwarz, Philip J. *Twice Condemned: Slaves and the Criminal Laws of Virginia, 1705–1865.* Baton Rouge: Louisiana State University Press, 1988.

Scott, Arthur P. *Criminal Law in Virginia.* Chicago: University of Chicago Press, 1930.

Scott, James C. *Weapons of the Weak: Everyday Forms of Peasant Resistance.* New Haven, Conn.: Yale University Press, 1985.

Selby, John E. *The Revolution in Virginia, 1775–1783.* Williamsburg, Va.: Colonial Williamsburg, 1988.

Shade, William G. *Democratizing the Old Dominion: Virginia and the Second Party System, 1824–1861.* Charlottesville: University Press of Virginia, 1996.

Shaw, Robert E. *Erie Water West: A History of the Erie Canal, 1792–1854.* Lexington: University of Kentucky Press, 1966.

Shepard, E. Lee. "Lawyers Look at Themselves: Professional Consciousness and the Virginia Bar, 1770–1850." *American Journal of Legal History,* 25 (1981): 1–23.

Sidbury, James. *Ploughshares into Swords: Race, Rebellion, and Identity in Gabriel's Virginia.* Cambridge, U.K.: Cambridge University Press, 1997.

Sloan, Herbert E. *Principle and Interest: Thomas Jefferson and the Problem of Debt.* New York: Oxford University Press, 1995.

Smith, Daniel Blake. *Inside the Great House: Planter Life in Eighteenth-Century Chesapeake Society.* Ithaca, N.Y.: Cornell University Press, 1980.

Smith, Daniel Scott, and Michael S. Hindus. "Premarital Pregnancy in America, 1640–1971: An Overview and Interpretation." *Journal of Interdisciplinary History,* 4 (1974–75): 537–70.

Smith-Rosenberg, Carroll. "The Female World of Love and Ritual: Relations Between Women in Nineteenth-Century America." *Signs,* 1 (1975): 1–30.

Snyder, Terri L. *Brabbling Women: Disorderly Speech and the Law in Early Virginia.* Ithaca, N.Y.: Cornell University Press, 2003.

Spacks, Patricia Meyer. *Gossip.* New York: Alfred A. Knopf, 1985.

Sparks, Jared. *The Life of Gouverneur Morris,* 2 vols. Boston: Gray & Bowen, 1832.

Spindel, Donna J. *Crime and Society in North Carolina. 1663–1776.* Baton Rouge: Louisiana State University Press, 1989.

Spruill, Julia Cherry. *Women's Life and Work in the Southern Colonies.* Chapel Hill: University of North Carolina Press, 1938.

Stansell, Christine. *City of Women: Sex and Class in New York, 1789–1860.* Urbana: University of Illinois Press, 1987.

Stanton, Lucia. *Free Some Day: The African-American Families of Monticello.* Charlottesville: University Press of Virginia, 2000.

Sterngass, Jon. *First Resorts: Pursuing Pleasure at Saratoga Springs, Newport & Coney Island.* Baltimore: Johns Hopkins University Press, 2001.

Stevenson, Brenda E. *Life in Black and White: Family and Community in the Slave South.* New York: Oxford University Press, 1996.

Stowe, Steven M. *Intimacy and Power in the Old South: Ritual in the Lives of the Planters.* Baltimore: Johns Hopkins University Press, 1987.

Sturtz, Linda L. *Within Her Power: Propertied Women in Colonial Virginia.* New York: Routledge, 2002.

Sutton, Robert. "Nostalgia, Pessimism, and Malaise: The Doomed Aristocrat in Late-Jeffersonian Virginia." *Virginia Magazine of History and Biography,* 76 (1968): 41–55.

Swiggett, Howard. *The Extraordinary Mr. Morris.* Garden City, N.Y.: Doubleday & Company, Inc., 1952.

Sydnor, Charles S. *Gentlemen Freeholders.* Chapel Hill: University of North Carolina Press, 1952.

Taylor, Alan. *William Cooper's Town: Power and Persuasion on the Frontier of the Early American Republic.* New York: Alfred A. Knopf, 1995.

Terry, Gail S. "Sustaining the Bonds of Kinship in a Trans-Appalachian Migration, 1790–1811. *Virginia Magazine of History and Biography,* 102 (1994): 455–76.

Thomas, Arthur Dicken. "Reasonable Revivalism: Presbyterian Evangelization of Educated Virginians." *Journal of Presbyterian History,* 61 (1983): 316–34.

Tillson, Albert H. *Gentry and Common Folk: Political Culture on the Virginia Frontier, 1740–1789.* Lexington: University of Kentucky Press, 1991.

Tise, Larry E. *Proslavery: A History of the Defense of Slavery in America, 1701–1840.* Athens: University of Georgia Press, 1987.

Todd, Janet. *Sensibility: An Introduction.* New York: Methuen, 1986.

Tomlins, Christopher, and Bruce H. Mann, eds. *The Many Legalities of Early America.* Chapel Hill: University of North Carolina Press, 2001.

Turner, Mary Turner, ed. *From Chattel Slaves to Wage Slaves: The Dynamics of Labor Bargaining in the Americas.* Kingston, Jamaica: Ian Randle Publishers, 1995.

Tyler-McGraw, Marie. *At the Falls: Richmond, Virginia, and its People.* Chapel Hill: University of North Carolina Press, 1994.

Ulrich, Laurel Thatcher. *A Midwife's Tale: The Life of Martha Ballard Based on Her Diary, 1785–1812.* New York: Alfred A. Knopf, 1990.

Upton, Anthony F. "The Road to Power in Virginia in the Early Republic." *Virginia Magazine of History and Biography,* 62 (1954): 259–80.

Varon, Elizabeth. *We Mean to be Counted: White Women and Politics in Antebellum Virginia.* Chapel Hill: University of North Carolina Press, 1998.

Vaughan, M. K. *Crucible and Cornerstone: A History of Cumberland County Virginia.* N.p., 1969.

Waldstreicher, David. *In the Midst of Perpetual Fetes: The Making of American Nationalism, 1776–1820.* Chapel Hill: University of North Carolina Press, 1997.

Wall, Helena M. *Fierce Communion: Family and Community in Early America.* Cambridge, Mass.: Harvard University Press, 1990.

Walz, Jay, and Audrey Walz. *The Bizarre Sisters.* New York: Duell, Sloan and Pearce, 1950.

Warner, Michael. *Letters of the Republic: Publication and the Public Sphere in Eighteenth-Century America.* Cambridge, Mass.: Harvard University Press, 1990.

Wiebe, Robert H. *The Opening of American Society: From the Adoption of the Constitution to the Eve of Disunion.* New York: Alfred A. Knopf, 1984.

Wiener, Marli F. *Mistresses and Slaves: Plantation Women in South Carolina, 1830–80.* Urbana: University of Illinois Press, 1998.

Willis, Rev. Harold G., et al. *St. Ann's Church of Morrisania: A Shrine to American Patriotism.* New York: Press of John C. Rankin Co., 1919.

Wood, Betty. *Women's Work, Men's Work: The Informal Slave Economies of Lowcountry Georgia.* Athens: University of Georgia Press, 1995.

Wood, Gordon S. *The Creation of the American Republic, 1776–1787.* Chapel Hill: University of North Carolina Press, 1969.

———. *The Radicalism of the American Revolution.* New York: Alfred A. Knopf, 1991.

Wood, Kirsten E. "Broken Reeds and Competent Farmers: Slaveholding Widows in the Southeastern United States, 1790–1860." *Journal of Women's History,* 13 (2001): 34–57.

———. "Fictive Mastery: Slaveholding Widows in the American Southeast, 1790–1860." Ph.D. diss., University of Pennsylvania, 1998.

Woodward, Grace Steele. *Pocahontas.* Norman: University of Oklahoma Press, 1969.

Woodward, Ruth L., and Wesley Frank Craven. *Princetonians, 1784–1790: A Biographical Dictionary.* Princeton, N.J.: Princeton University Press, 1991.

Wyatt-Brown, Bertram. *Southern Honor: Ethics and Behavior in the Old South.* New York: Oxford University Press, 1982.

Young, Jeffrey Robert. *Domesticating Slavery: The Master Class in Georgia and South Carolina, 1670–1837.* Chapel Hill: University of North Carolina Press, 1999.

Zagarri, Rosemarie. "Morals, Manners, and the Republican Mother." *American Quarterly,* 44 (1992): 192–215.

INDEX

References to maps, illustrations, and tables appear in bold type.